THE BIG BOOK OF
TRANSPORT

Octopus Books

Road Transport
Written by Pavel Augusta
Illustrated by Spytimír Bursík

Rail Transport
Written by Jaroslav Pacovský
Illustrated by Jiří Bouda

Water Transport
Written by Vladimír Hulpach
Illustrated by Miroslav Rada

Air Transport
Written by Václav Houžvička
Illustrated by Jaroslav Velc

Municipal Transport
Written by Ludvík Losos
Illustrated by Jiří Bouda

Special Forms of Transport
Written by Pavel Augusta
Illustrated by Jiří Bouda

Translated by Stephen Finn
Graphic design by František Fabík

This edition first published in 1987 by
Octopus Books Limited
59 Grosvenor Street, London W1
© Artia 1987, Prague
ISBN 0 7064 2656 8
Printed in Czechoslovakia by
TSNP Martin
1/19/05/51-01

CONTENTS

Road TRANSPORT

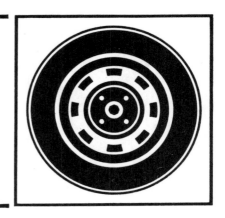

The prehistoric hunter carried all his belongings on his back, as well as small children and anything he caught while hunting.

A Babylonian relief depicting a sledge drawn by a bull.

From the very dawn of history men have been obliged to travel long distances. Whether they lived by gathering the edible parts of plants, or by hunting, they had to cover many kilometres every day. Prehistoric hunters would sometimes spend weeks on end trekking in search of game. The first, and for a thousand years the only means of transport which served to ease the traveller's burden was the skid, consisting of a pair of poles tied together. Initially, people pulled these themselves, but later they harnessed animals such as dogs and horses to them.

By a process of gradual improvement, the skid developed into the sledge, which is still used for crossing snow. Long after the invention of the wheel, sledges were retained alongside carts, especially for transporting heavy loads.

Domesticated animals were a great help to man on his travels. They carried both riders and baggage. It is estimated that domesticated animals are capable of carrying loads up to forty times greater than those their wild counterparts could bear. Man's first mount, later to be used as a draught animal, was not, as we might suppose, the

The North American prairie Indians were still using skids in the 19th century.

horse, but the ox, whose domestication began in Asia Minor in the 8th millennium B.C. Oxen not only carried men on their backs and transported their goods for them, but also provided milk, meat and leather. Since they were capable of covering long distances they helped trade to develop, and allowed armies to undertake prolonged marches. Obsidian from Anatolia (modern Turkey), for instance, was taken to places over a thousand kilometres away.

The wheel probably had its origin in the short, round tree trunks which were laid beneath heavy loads to make them easier to move.

In time men used other animals, too, for purposes of transport. They included dogs, and possibly even goats, judging by evidence dating from the second millennium B.C. In the far north the reindeer is still used both as a draught animal and a mount. In deserts the camel has become indispensable to man. It requires a minimum of food and water, and can carry up to 300 kg (660 lb). In both ancient and medieval times camels were the chief means of transport in the inhospitable regions of Asia and northern Africa.

Without a doubt the mightiest of the riding animals is the elephant. The ancient Sumerians called it 'the wild bull with a finger', at a time when elephants still lived in the Near East. Because of its great size and strength, the elephant was also used as a fighting animal. Hannibal, the warrior of Carthage, used elephants in his successful invasion of Italy in the third century B.C., terrorizing the Roman legions. In

On the slopes of the Andes, in South America, lives a close relative of the camel, the llama. The Indians kept llamas as pack animals long before the white man's coming. Llamas have neither the endurance nor the strength of the camel, however, being able to carry a maximum of 50 kg (110 lb) for some 20 km (12 miles) daily.

By far the most important animals bred for transport are the horse and its relatives the donkey and the wild ass, or onager. Some 3000 years B.C. the Sumerians harnessed onagers to their chariots. The donkey

thousands of years a pedigree horse was among the greatest treasures a man might own.

Hybrids between horses and donkeys were also very common and popular beasts of burden. A cross between a he-ass and a mare is called a mule, which is more like a horse in appearance, but closer to a donkey in behaviour. The opposite combination yields a hinny, which looks and behaves more like a donkey.

The invention of the wheel and the cart revolutionized transport. The first carts, which appeared in

recent times, practically to this day, elephants have been used for heavy work, mainly in India and south-east Asia.

The inhabitants of the Tibetan mountains ride on yaks, and use them as pack and draught animals. The yak, which is a high-mountain ox, may be up to 190 cm tall and weighs around 900 kg (1985 lb). Its long, thick hair protects it from the cold. Yaks can climb steep slopes and are sure-footed on the steepest of paths.

was the chief means of transport in ancient Egypt, but it was the horse which was to become the most revered animal of all. For almost 4000 years it was a symbol of the warrior's pride. In Europe and Asia whole nations built their lives around the horse, in both war and peace. There is an Arabian proverb that says 'This land's fortune rests upon a horse's back', and Richard III of England is said to have offered his kingdom for a horse after losing the Battle of Bosworth Field. For

Sumer over 5000 years ago, had solid wheels attached firmly to their axle. Surviving pictures and clay models show that the technology improved fairly rapidly. Thus 2600 years ago King Assurbanipal of Assyria already had lightweight wheels fitted to his hunting chariot. The original two-wheeled carts later gave rise to four-wheeled ones, but in many areas two-wheeled carts were retained until modern times, being much more manoeuvrable. Turning a four-wheeler, particularly

An Egyptian relief depicting a light war, or hunting, chariot.

in the days before pivoted front axles were invented, must have taken some doing.

From the very start, wheeled vehicles were used not only for transport, but also in war. In the ancient civilizations of the Middle East the charioteers were among the élite units of the army. They played a role similar to that of the medieval knights-in-armour or a modern tank division.

Although there were plenty of wheeled vehicles, the litter was the favoured means of transport among the richer Romans.

About 2500 years B.C., the Sumerians were using two different types of war chariot, a heavier one with four wheels and a lighter, single-axle model. Both were pulled by asses. It was not until the time of Hammurabi that horses were first harnessed in the Near East. There has even survived a letter to the king from one of his courtiers in which he is advised: 'My Lord, drive not with horses, but in a chariot drawn by asses.' It had soon become a matter of courtesy to ask first after the health of one's family, and then about the welfare of one's stable.

Carts, however, were not always drawn by animals. The two-wheeled cart enabled a man of only average strength to move even very heavy loads. The ancient Chinese exploited this type of vehicle to the full. The important thing was for the goods or passengers to be loaded in such a way that the weight was evenly distributed. The Chinese took advantage of favourable winds, using sails to help their carts along.

Greek chariots were of outstanding lightness and elegance. They

often had artistic forms of decoration. For the most part the frame was of fir, the shafts of ash and the wheels of oak. Greek chariots were drawn either by horses or by oxen, though we are told how those exemplary sons Cleobis and Biton drew their mother's chariot themselves when the team of oxen did not return from the fields in time to take her to the temple.

The Romans, like the Greeks, did not use war chariots in classical times. The core of the Roman army was the highly-trained infantry legion, but two and four-wheeled vehicles were widely used for transporting goods and people and for religious purposes, and were drawn by horses, oxen, hinnies and donkeys. In those days there was no such thing as a collar, draught animals being attached either by means of a yoke or in simple forms of harness.

Carts were extremely important to the Romans and protected by special laws. So, for instance, it was forbidden to take a farmer's grain cart in settlement of a debt. This was to be retained in French law, and was confirmed in the 18th century by Louis XIV.

The high standard of Roman roads meant that vehicles could be exploited to the full, and the Romans had nearly thirty types of wheeled conveyance, from heavy

A relief showing an Etruscan car, for centuries a typical means of transport in the Mediterranean region.

A Roman tile showing a quadriga at full gallop.

The heavy Assyrian war chariots, as seen depicted in this bronze relief, were driven only by the élite warriors of the Assyrian army.

agricultural carts with large wheels to exquisitely decorated ceremonial carriages.

The Romans continued the tradition of the ancient war chariots in their racing chariots. These were light two-wheelers drawn by teams of two, three or four horses — the *biga, triga* and *quadriga* respectively. Chariot racing was a highly popular sport in ancient Rome, and the Emperor Caligula even had a marble stable erected for his racehorse Incitatus, with an ivory trough inside. He also presented his horse with a house and servants so that its guests could be entertained!

Chariot races were not, however, a Roman invention. The epic Greek poem the Iliad tells how Achilles held races outside Troy in honour of his fallen comrade Patrocles. We even know the name of the winner of what was probably the first race ever recorded in literature. It was the hero Diomedes, followed by Achilles' best friend Antiloches, with the Spartan king, Menelaus, third.

A Greek double herm.

While people were still obliged to travel on their own two feet, they could more or less choose their own route. In forests and thickets they made use of trails trodden by animals, but after the invention of the wheel and wheeled vehicles some sort of roads were required, however primitive.

As long ago as 4000 B.C., the Chinese were constructing relatively broad and firm roads. The Egyptians and Babylonians even paved their main roads. In his description of the building of the Pyramid of Cheops, the Greek historian Herodotus notes that the Egyptians made wide, stone-paved roads along which the huge building blocks were transported to the construction site. Modern research suggests that the Egyptians probably used sledges, scattering sand in front of the runners when necessary to assist progress.

In the 5th century B.C., the Persians built an extensive road network. The main road, called the 'Royal Way', led from Susa, the capital, through Asia Minor to Sardis, a distance of 2,500 km (1,550 miles). It seems to have been fairly well-constructed, since royal messengers were able to complete the journey in some seventy hours, thus maintaining an average speed of about 35 km/h (22 mph).

The Greeks learned the art of road-building from the Phoenicians. The early roads consisted of a pair of grooves 140 to 150 cm (55 to 59 in) apart for the wheels of carts. Later, paved ways were constructed, and drainage was provided for the foundations. Instead of signposts there were heaps of stones, or herms — busts (originally of Hermes) on a marble or bronze base, which marked sacred or otherwise important spots.

The Romans proved to have a real talent for building roads. It was no accident that all roads were said to lead to Rome. Roman roads stretched out across Europe like arteries joining the empire's heart to its farthest parts. Their total length is estimated at some 160,000 km (99,350 miles). Sixteen of the nineteen biggest roads did indeed lead to Rome. The most famous of them to this day is the Via Appia, from Rome to Brindisi. It was built at the end of the 4th century B.C., is paved throughout its length, and in places is eight metres (26 ft) wide. Many stretches are still usable.

The Romans took the business of road-making very seriously. Their first roads were about four metres wide, but they later increased the width to between six and eight metres. A layer of gravel was placed on stone foundations, and on this the paving stones were laid in a bed of mortar. The Romans distinguished between roadway and pavement, and ditches were dug alongside.

At intervals along Roman roads stones were placed to help riders mount their horses. Milestones indicated the distance from the starting-point of the road and to the next town. In the case of roads leading from Rome, distances were calculated from a golden marker set in the Forum by the Emperor Augustus. Milestones also gave other information, such as the name of the road, who built it, and when.

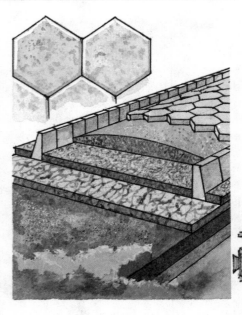

The sophistication of Roman road-building is best shown by this cross-section.

The famous Roman legions marched along their equally famous roads.

A system of staging posts was set up along the Roman roads, with fresh horses available at all times. Every 30 km (18 miles), or about the distance a marching legion could be expected to cover in a day, there were dormitories, taverns, smithies and the like.

There was so much traffic that the Romans had to establish a sort of highway code, imposing certain limitations. So, for instance, at one time loaded carts were not allowed to enter Rome for the first ten hours after dawn.

After the fall of the Roman Empire, road-building slipped into a long period of neglect. Good roads were actually considered dangerous, in that they permitted enemies to advance more rapidly. Though trade continued, it was mostly conducted by way of narrow and poorly negotiable tracks.

Something which was almost of equal importance to the roads themselves was the quality of harnesses for draught animals. The first, primitive forms of harness made poor use of the animals' strength, often consisting of a rope placed around the horns. The yoke was an improvement on this, but in the 2nd century B.C. the Chinese made an important advance by using the animal's strength at the chest rather than the neck. They introduced shafts to replace the yoke. From the 3rd century A.D. the Chinese used a collar to harness horses. It was found to be up to five times as efficient as the yoke, but did not reach Europe until between the 9th and 12th centuries. It was at about this time that horses were first shod. The improvement in harness was even more important in agriculture than in transport.

A 16th-century wagon.

With the demise of the Roman road, lightweight vehicles also entered a decline. Only heavy carts and wagons were able to withstand the rigours of medieval tracks. Often, under extreme conditions such as those of mountain passes, pack animals were used instead. These were usually donkeys or horses.

Wheeled vehicles were not widely used for carrying passengers. It was considered a sign of weakness to travel that way, and even the nobility preferred to ride on horseback rather than endure the discomfort of an unsprung cart on an unpaved road. Either that, or they continued to use litters. Even ladies rode horses. During the 14th century a 'lady's' saddle made its appearance, allowing women to ride sidesaddle instead of sitting astride the horse. This style of riding is said to have been introduced into England by the Bohemian princess Anne, wife of Richard II. The lady's saddle had probably reached Bohemia from France.

Medieval roads ran through broad or narrow gullies, as the lie of the land dictated, or followed the route the drivers took to avoid muddy places or heavily rutted sections. In the Middle Ages the roads had neither a firm foundation nor ditches to drain them. The only reinforcement used was wattle bound together with flexible branches: this was laid in marshy spots, but was renewed only sporadically.

In wooded countryside there was a further danger — robbers. Though there were gallows at most of the important crossroads which were often festooned with the bodies of captured highwaymen, and though the ground was cleared for up to thirty metres on either side of the road for security reasons, the only sure way to avoid robbery was to form a caravan protected by armed guards. Even the Emperor Sigismund was five days late for a conference at Regensburg in the 15th century because he had been ambushed by a marauding knight and was released only on payment of a ransom.

Another unpleasant feature of travelling in those days was the necessity of paying frequent tolls, i.e. taxes for the use of bridges, roads, etc. Some of the landowners whose estates the roads crossed had very strange rights indeed, such as the right to confiscate a wagon and its load if the axle touched the ground. This was common enough whenever a wheel broke, and scarcely an encouragement to keep the roads in good repair.

In the Middle Ages the cart made a comeback as a weapon of war. This time it was not a means of attack, as had been the case with ancient chariots, but took the form of a heavy wagon used for defence. Numerous such wagons were drawn up in lines to act as a rampart behind which the defenders could fight off a larger or better-armed enemy. They were employed with great success by Jan Žižka of Trocnov in the Hussite Wars of Bohemia in the early 15th century. In Italy special wagons called 'caroccio' were used as the symbol of the nation at arms. Ceremonially decked carts with banners and trumpeters were wheeled into bat-

From the Middle Ages to the 18th century carter's wagons were 'kings of the road'.

tle as a sign of strength. They were surrounded by the cream of the troops, and their loss meant total defeat.

For many centuries the extremely poor quality of roads made improvements in the design of vehicles impossible. Nevertheless, in the 15th century a major change came about. The pivoted front axle was introduced, which greatly enhanced manoeuvrability and paved the way for substantial progress in four-wheeled transport.

In the 16th and 17th centuries travelling became much more com-

A barricade of Hussite war wagons. Not even knights in armour were able to break through.

fortable. Vehicle bodies were hung from the frame by strong straps, which went some way towards making the ride smoother. Later, the seats themselves were similarly suspended inside the body, to reduce the danger of overturning caused by the body swinging during travel at high speed on rough roads.

Large, heavy coaches were difficult to control, especially in the narrow streets of medieval towns. This fact proved fateful for Henri IV of France when his coach was brought to a halt by a traffic jam on May 16, 1610. The religious fanatic François Ravaillac seized the opportunity to leap forward and stab the king with a long knife. He went down in history as the first assassin to attack a head of state in his own coach.

Nor was the coachman's lot always a happy one. A certain Madrid coachman was said to have eavesdropped on his VIP passengers and betrayed state secrets. As a result, a royal decree was issued forbidding coachmen to ride on the box and requiring them to sit in the saddle of one of the team of horses.

Robbers and bad roads were hazards that travellers in the Middle Ages had to accept.

This law remained in force in Spain until the 19th century.

Up to the middle of the 18th century goods were mainly transported in slow, heavy, carter's wagons drawn by one or two pairs of powerful horses. In order to get up hills the carter would often use the services of an auxiliary team. A telling reminder of those days is provided by the numerous wayside inns still found at many crossroads.

After a long period of stagnation transport and travel were revitalized in the 16th century. Gold and fine carvings began to decorate noble carriages, whose chief function was to proclaim the wealth and status of their owners. Today the carriages of the rulers and aristocrats of that bygone age are exhibited as works of art. A fine example is the coach of the Duke of Eggenberg, ambassador to the court of Pope Urban VIII. It took leading Roman artists and craftsmen a whole year to build. All wooden parts, including the shafts and wheels, were gilded, and

A 17th-century Baroque carriage.

engineer Thomas Telford. His were mostly paved, and thus very expensive. John McAdam, a fellow Scot, used a much cheaper method. He did not dig deep foundations, just draining and reinforcing the ground along the proposed route. The road itself was then made of broken stones known as 'metal', rolled to form a smooth, water-resistant surface. The brilliance of McAdam's invention was that the roads, rather than being damaged by constant traffic, were actually made stronger. They fulfilled their purpose admirably until the advent of the inflatable tyre. The rapidly rotating and flexible rubber did not tamp down the road surface as the heavy solid wheels had done; on the contrary, rubber tyres tended to fling the metal out of place and damage the road. Once these 'macadamized' roads lost their water-resistance through such damage, they quickly deteriorated. Rain, frost and traffic took a heavy toll, and it was only a matter of months before the road was useless. The spread of the inflatable tyre therefore required roads to have a protective layer of tar or asphalt. The first asphalt roads, however, had been made by the French engineer, A. Merian, around 1850.

Good roads speeded up travel enormously. The first post-chaises appeared, and were able to cover up to 50 km (30 miles) a day. The 650 km (400 miles) from London to

the iron components were silver plated. The trappings included sixty velvet curtains embroidered with gold and set with pearls. The irony of it is that when the owner of this exquisite and extremely expensive vehicle set off for the papal palace on November 16, 1638, he rode in front of the empty coach on horseback. Such vehicles were rather slow and clumsy, and quite unsuitable for long-distance travel. In fact, the original coaches (named after the small town of Kocs in Hungary) were altogether lighter and faster conveyances.

It became more and more apparent that no matter how much the construction of vehicles was improved, road travel would never be satisfactory without proper roads. So in 1720 the French army formed its Corps des Ingénieurs des Ponts et Chaussées, and shortly afterwards established a school of bridge and road building. The inspiration for both institutions came from Pierre Tresaguet, whose method of road construction was based on two important principles − a firm foundation and a good surface which was resistant to water. Tresaguet built roads from stones and gravel, laying drainage ditches along each side. He preferred somewhat tortuous routes, avoiding fertile fields and steep hills and conforming as closely as possible to the lie of the land. He placed great emphasis on constant and careful repair.

In England and Scotland in the early 19th century modern roads were being built by the Scottish

A britzka.

A small closed brougham.

Edinburgh took the fastest post-chaise twelve days. The post-chaises ran dead on time — you could set your watch by them, as many people did. Travelling was a good deal more comfortable, too. Passenger vehicles were now fitted with leaf springs, and the occupants were saved the worst of the bumps. An important step forward was the invention of the kingpin method of steering, attributed to Georg Längensperger of Munich in 1816.

Coach and carriage design developed greatly. All manner of specialized types of vehicles appeared. The main conveyance used for long distances was a heavy coach with a folding roof divided down the middle. This vehicle was called a landau and took its name from the Bavarian town of Landau where the first such carriage was made in the 18th century. The light four-wheeled carriage with a tall, suspended body called a berlin was popular for fast trips. Berlins had their body suspended on S-shaped springs, which made for perfect springing. For driving in town or for hunting there were many sorts of two-wheeled carriage, usually drawn by a single horse.

A very popular vehicle in England was the small closed carriage called a brougham, given both its form and its name by Lord Brougham in 1840. The original version was a two-seater drawn by a single horse, after which the 'double'

A simple carriage with one axle.

brougham, drawn by two horses and seating four passengers and a driver, became popular.

The typical American conveyance was the light trap, or buggy, with either two or four wheels and a body on a frame, often with a folding roof. It was generally for two passengers, who drove themselves.

The coachmen in charge of these vehicles often had a difficult job. Most of them lacked the good fortune of the King of Spain's coachman, whose master allowed him to wear a hat in heavy rain — thus raising him at once to the ranks of the nobility, since only the Spanish grandees had the privilege of remaining hatted in the king's presence.

In Paris, by contrast, it is said that at the time of Louis XV a man

especially knowledgeable about coachmanship would stop those he considered to be inept drivers and hand them a sealed envelope for their masters. The message read: 'Sir, this is to inform you that your coachman does not know how to handle either your team or your coach.'

In the 19th century the development of the horse-drawn vehicle reached its peak, with a wide variety of types suited to all manner of purposes. These vehicles were elegantly designed and constructed with consummate craftsmanship — and they had reasonably good roads to drive on. Yet the peak was at the same time the beginning of the end: slowly but surely the motorcar was starting to take over. A new era was dawning.

The stage-coaches were so punctual that you could set your watch by them.

Like their modern counterparts, the tracks and paths of bygone days included a variety of obstacles along the route. Among the most frequent and least easily overcome were watercourses. For centuries the usual way of crossing rivers and streams was either by fording them or by using some sort of ferry. Bridges were few and far between. The art of bridge-building required very special skills.

The very first bridges seem to have consisted of the trunks of trees felled in such a way as to join the

the Bosphorus, and his son, King Xerxex, the Hellespont, now the Dardanelles, in 480 B.C. Both were leading armies against Greece. The bridge used by Xerxes and his troops was almost 1,400 m (4,550 ft) long, and is said to have had 674 pontoons.

In the year 412 A.D. the Buddhist monk Fa-sien described strange rope bridges he had seen on his journey through India. One he crossed was 92 m (300 ft) long. These hanging bridges were widely used in Central and South America,

Three types of bridge.

The drawbridge of a medieval castle — an important defensive element.

A covered wooden bridge.

A stone valley bridge.

two banks of rivers. The oldest bridge of which records exist was that spanning the River Euphrates in ancient Babylon. It consisted of cedar and cypress beams laid a-cross masonry pillars, with a floor of rough-hewn palm trunks. These last are said to have been removed every evening to prevent anyone crossing the bridge during the night.

In ancient times broad rivers and sea straits were crossed by means of pontoon-bridges. That was how the Persian king Darius I crossed

south-east Asia, China and India. In the tropical rainforest the materials used were lianas and bamboo. Such bridges were not uncommon along the mountain tracks of Peru even in the last century.

The Etruscans were masters of bridge-building, and the Romans carried the art a stage further. As long ago as 612 B.C. there was a bridge across the Tiber in Rome that stretched for 150 m, was made of wood and rested on wooden piers. One of the most famous Roman bridges was that built by Julius

Caesar to enable his army to cross the Rhine in 50 B.C. It took only ten days from start to finish. No less remarkable was Trajan's thousand-metre bridge across the Danube, close to Iron Gate. It rested on sixteen stone piers more than 40 m (130 ft) apart.

After the fall of the Roman Empire, Europe was dotted with arched bridges constructed of massive stones and left behind by the master builders of Rome. For many centuries no one could equal their skills and the art of bridge-building fell

34 ft). One of them was made of wood, and could be opened up to let ships pass through. It is a feature which has survived in London to this day. There were houses and shops along the length of the bridge, with traffic passing beneath them.

The building of medieval bridges was often surrounded by legends. When the famous stone bridge of Prague was built, the mortar was strengthened by the addition of egg-white. The emperor, Charles IV, ordered eggs to be sent from all

individual spans could be much wider.

By that time wood and stone had ceased to be the only bridge-building materials used. In 1779 the first iron bridge was built, across the River Severn in England. In the course of the 19th century steel bridges became the symbol of the modern age. Not only are most of them in service to this day, but many, like the daring constructions of the French engineer Alexandre Gustave Eiffel, have become a part of the cultural heritage of their time.

The 14th-century Charles Bridge in Prague — one of the most beautiful bridges in the world.

into decline. It was only much later that renewed interest in constructing bridges began to appear, chiefly due to the efforts of the Church. Thus the stone bridge at Avignon was built in 1177, spanning the Rhône with its twenty-one arches, each up to thirty-five metres wide.

The first stone bridge over the Thames was also the work of ecclesiastical architects. The monk Peter of Colechurch spent thirty years building it, finishing it in 1209. It had twenty arches of various spans, from 4.5 to 10.5 m (14½ to

over Bohemia. According to legend, the inhabitants of one town were anxious to ensure that their eggs did not get broken on the journey, so they sent them hard-boiled.

The history of modern bridge-building starts with Jean Rudolphe Perronet, chief engineer of the Corps des Ingénieurs des Ponts et Chaussées. His chief contribution was to substitute a bold elliptical shape for the traditional semicircular arch, as can be seen in the Pont de la Concorde in Paris, completed in 1791. The new arch meant that

Basic types of modern bridge: girder or beam (1, 2), arch (3), suspension (4).

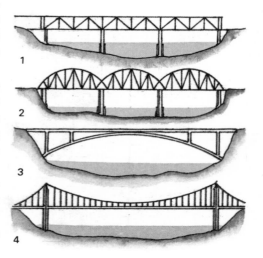

One of A. Dürer's triumphal carriages.

The desire to have a vehicle at least apparently moving of its own accord seems to be a very ancient one. There is a record of a priest at a temple in Athens using, around the year 1000 B.C., a conveyance powered by its occupants by means of levers attached to the wheels. The Roman Emperor Commodus, assassinated in 192 A.D., also left behind carriages which ran without horses. They are said to have been propelled by slaves through a system of toothed gears. Commodus seems to have had a nice line in customized vehicles. Among the 'extras' fitted to his carriages were revolving seats which enabled the passengers to keep their backs to the wind, and even some sort of primitive milometer, which dropped a pebble into a container for every Roman mile driven.

Neither in classical, nor medieval, nor even in modern times have mechanical vehicles powered by men been particularly useful. They were probably never intended to be, but were rather meant to serve as a spectacle on ceremonial occasions, or to further military ends. Drawings dating from 1526 depict nine remarkable designs of triumphal carriages for the Emperor Maximilian; the method of propulsion relies on springs, recirculating worms and cogwheels, and the designer was Albrecht Dürer or one of his pupils. Though these vehicles were never constructed, the designs are a tribute to the technical ingenuity of their time.

One of the most renowned of self-propelling vehicles was that constructed in 1649 by the Nuremberg clockmaker Johann Hautsch. The inventor claimed that it was driven by a strong clock spring, but in fact several young lads concealed inside cranked it along. Hautsch's 'artistic coach of Nuremberg' moved very slowly, but it was magnificently decorated. On either side, statues of angels raised trumpets to their lips, sounding them when

J. Hautsch's mechanical carriage which was bought by the Swedish Crown Prince. Another was built for the Danish King.

necessary. If the vehicle had any trouble getting through the crowd, a dragon's head at the front would spray water on the pedestrians blocking the way. If contemporary accounts are to be believed, the spouting dragon rolled its eyes menacingly.

The fame of Hautsch's vehicle soon spread beyond the frontiers of Germany. In the end the Swedish crown prince, Gustav Adolf, bought it. Hautsch is then said to have produced an even more magnificent version for the King of Denmark.

Another Nuremberg clockmaker, Stephan Farffler, came up with something far more useful in 1655. He was paralysed from the waist down, and his tricycle driven by cranks, connected with cogs to the front wheel, became the forerunner of the modern invalid carriage.

Yet another pedal car had an indirect connection with medicine, this time in the person of its owner. For several years from about 1690, French doctor Elie Richard rode around Paris in a vehicle which he steered himself but which was propelled by a servant standing at the back, using a system of pedal levers.

Though the wonderfully varied means of transmitting power to the driving wheels were sometimes ingenious, they still only amounted to replacing draught animals by human effort. A much more attractive proposition involved making use of wind power, already a tried and tested method of powering boats. Sail-driven vehicles had been used in China in ancient times, but the idea did not reach Europe until the beginning of the 17th century. The inventor was the Dutch mathematician Simon Stevin. He built sailing

Doctor Elie Richard on his way to a medical gathering.

vehicles capable of carrying up to twenty-eight people. They were usually two-masters, steered by means of a rudder which turned the rear axle. He built several such vehicles for the army of the Prince Regent, William of Orange, during a war with France. There is also an original design for a wind-powered vehicle in a manuscript of Roberto Valturius, dating back to 1472. It is in fact a mobile windmill, the power from the rotating vanes being transmitted to the road-wheels by means of cogwheels. It is not known whether any such vehicle was ever built, let alone whether it actually went anywhere.

Land yachts spread quite widely in the flat seaboard regions of Holland, France and England in the 17th and 18th centuries, for there was no lack of wind. An Englishman by the name of Poccock even flew a couple of kites in addition to his sails, provided the wind was favourable, thus increasing his speed even more. He used to travel between Bristol and London, and could cover more than 30 km (18 miles) in an hour, a speed with which no man-powered conveyance could dream of competing. His 'engine' was silent, powerful and cheap, but rather unreliable. Poccock, however, thought of everything: he is reported to have carried a stand-by pony in case the wind dropped.

The sailed carriage of S. Stevin, which carried up to 30 passengers.

R. Trevithick's steam carriage,
built in 1802.

Though England was the cradle of the steam engine, the first steam-powered vehicle appeared on the other side of the Channel. The engineer Nicolas Joseph Cugnot experimented with a vehicle driven by an atmospheric steam engine in Paris in the seventeen-sixties. Initially he encountered the sort of good fortune enjoyed by very few inventors. The French army needed a means of propulsion for heavy field-guns, and Cugnot received generous assistance. He designed a vehicle which carried four persons and travelled at about 3 km/h (2 mph), but the boiler was too small and could scarcely manage to supply power for a quarter of an hour at a time. Late in 1770 Cugnot completed an improved version which was capable of carrying almost five tonnes. It was difficult to steer, and even knocked down a wall during trials, but it worked, none the less. Its demise was due not to technical failings but to politics: the French Revolution came along, and no one was interested in half-baked inventions, no matter how promising.

At about the same time that Cugnot died in obscurity, Richard Trevithick carried out successful experiments with a steam-powered vehicle in England. He and his cousin drove around London for about eight months in the machine, enjoying great acclaim. After one trip the famous physicist Sir Humphry Davy nicknamed the vehicle 'Captain Trevithick's Dragon', and the name stuck. In the end the poor state of the roads led Trevithick to conclude that the future of steam lay in rail transport, and in 1804 he built the first steam locomotive.

It was no accident that Trevithick started working on steam propulsion. He was led to do so by William Murdock, an inspector at the mine where Trevithick's father was paymaster. Murdock had been a colleague of James Watt, who had patented his steam engine in 1769, and was one of the first to dream of a steam-powered vehicle. He even constructed a working model, which he drove around the house. One day he decided to try it out in the street. He carried it outside and lit the fire under its boiler, but as soon as he opened the steam inlet, the model shot off at speed and quickly disappeared from the startled inventor's view. The bumpy cobblestones soon caused it to overturn, however — right at the feet of the local vicar. The astonished cleric could only suppose that this fiery apparition was none other than

The first self-propelled carriage —
N. Cugnot's steam vehicle of 1770.

the devil himself. He had a heart attack and dropped down dead, probably the first ever fatality in an automobile accident. The ensuing court case, and Watt's opposition to the use of steam for road transport, put an end to Murdock's experiments.

Where Murdock failed, other pioneers soon stepped forward. Julius Griffith built a whole series of steam vehicles, including a three-tonne monster carrying twelve passengers. David Gordon's design was truly remarkable. His tricycle was moved along by something like artificial horse's legs. The steam vehicle was steered by means of the front wheel and driven, not by the back wheels, but by six hollow iron legs with steel feet. The legs could be lengthened or shortened according to road conditions, but they themselves were less than kind to the surface.

Another pioneer of steam automobiles was Walter Hancock. He was the first man to run a bus service. In 1836 his steam vehicles covered almost 7,000 km (4,350 miles) along the London-Paddington route without serious accident.

Hancock also gave his omnibuses a new look, getting away from the traditional coach shape. One of his vehicles, the 'Drag', saw service as far afield as Vienna.

Without a doubt one of the most beautiful steam vehicles of its age was that designed by Dr. William Church of Birmingham. Church's cars were not only technically of a very high standard for their time, but good-looking as well. He used special wheels to alleviate some of the roughness of the roads. Instead of the usual fellies they had leaf springs, which (according to the inventor at least) prevented shocks from being transmitted to the hub, and thus to the vehicle itself.

For the pioneers of steam the path to progress was often a thorny one. One of those who would surely agree was Robert Gurney, a highly regarded London surgeon. His vehi-

W. Hancock's coupé *Autopsy,* **which travelled between Finsburg Square and Pentonville in 1834. It could carry six passengers.**

cle was 6 m (20 ft) long and 3 m (10 ft) wide, but when he finally managed to get it to the stage when it was capable of making the London-Bath run on a regular basis without major problems, he discovered that to carry four passengers he required an equal number of men to operate the steam engine. As if that were not enough, another twelve men with a horse and cart had to go along to keep the automobile supplied with fuel and water. In spite of this venerable escort

The steam vehicles of Dr. W. Church were described as 'a combination of perfect work, science and beauty'.

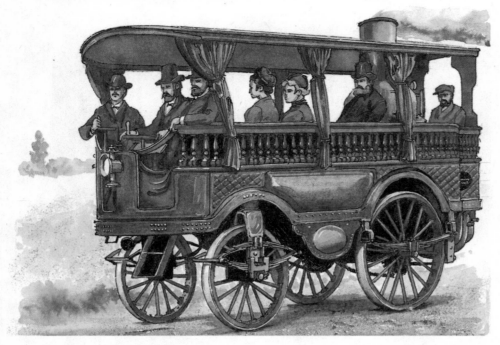

A. Bollée's steam vehicle was one
of the finest ever made. *L'Obéissante*, shown here, carried 12 passengers
at a speed of 15 km/h (9.3 mph).

it was frequently greeted with insults and missiles in the towns and villages it passed through.

Another English enthusiast employed cunning to ensure a smooth passage for his five-tonne colossus. He and his companions donned firemen's uniforms, which saved them from prosecution for speeding. The same gentleman is said to have been extremely proud of a speeding ticket he received for travelling 48 km/h (30 mph). It was indeed a remarkable speed at the time.

In spite of technical and commercial successes, however, storm clouds were gathering over steam travel in England. Public hostility, fanned by traditional carriers in an attempt to ward off competition, led to ever greater restrictions being imposed, and frequently to acts of violence. The last nail in the coffin of steam was the famous Locomotive Acts of 1861 and 1865. The second of these (known as the 'Red Flag Act') decreed that steam vehicles must be attended by at least three persons, one of whom must precede the vehicle by fifty yards, carrying a red flag to warn riders and coach drivers of its approach. This virtually tolled the death knell of steam road vehicles in Britain.

On the continent, especially in France, the situation was quite different. There were no legal restrictions to hamper the inventor, and remarkable vehicles were made. Among the most popular builders of steam engines were the unlikely pair of Count Albert de Dion, a Parisian aristocrat, and a suburban locksmith named Georges Bouton. The count's family was quite distraught over his 'childish fancy', but de Dion persisted. He produced lightweight tricycles and four-wheelers which achieved speeds of up to 40 km/h (25 mph).

Among the outstanding steam-powered creations were those designed by Amédée Bollée with the names 'L'Obéissante' (obedient) and 'La Mancelle'. True to her name, *L'Obéissante* ran quietly and fast. Her coal consumption was no more than 2,5 kg per km (8.8 lb per mile), and her water supply lasted 25 km (16 miles). The smaller *La Mancelle*, christened in honour of Bollée's home town of Le Mans, took part in the 1878 Paris exhibition. The inventor had no commercial success with his vehicles, attracting only a single customer. The name of this purchaser was Benjamin Peugeot, and his descendants were to take more than a passing interest in cars.

Across the Atlantic, Oliver Evans of Philadelphia became one of the pioneers of steam vehicles, almost by accident. He was commissioned to build a huge steam shovel for the local port. There were two obvious courses open to him: either to con-

L. Serpollet's 'eggs' reached speeds
of up to 130 km/h (80 mph).

Thompson's traction engine.

struct the machine in his downtown workshops and transport it to the harbour in pieces, or to build it on site and in the open air. Evans, however, chose a third way – to assemble the machine in his workshops and then drive it down to the docks under its own power. He added four wheels to the design, and the mechanical shovel slowly but surely made its way to the docks under its own steam, thus becoming the first automobile in the United States.

At the end of the 19th century steam cars were still able to hold their own against the internal combustion engine, and in many respects they were actually superior

to the new type of car. The peak of steam design was attained by Léon Serpollet, whose vehicles were light, quiet and manoeuvrable. He built his first steam tricycle when he was not quite eighteen, using wood as the main material. He strove to create a 'lightning' boiler, which would get up sufficient steam within five minutes. He was successful, and even obtained permission for his vehicles to drive through 'all the streets of Paris equally', which was in effect the very first licence for a motor vehicle. In the year 1900 Serpollet's factory produced 200 steam vehicles, and he sold them all. His clients included such eminent people as the Shah of Persia

and the Prince of Wales, later King Edward VII.

The French inventor was concerned not only with elegance but also with performance. He used paraffin to heat his boilers instead of wood or coal, which meant not only greater power, but also less pollution. In 1900 one of Serpollet's steam cars became the first vehicle to break the 100 km/h (62 mph) barrier. A steam car was eventually to travel over 200 km/h (124 mph), in the United States, where the Stanley brothers and others continued to develop steam automobiles into the nineteen-thirties. In Europe, however, the demise of the steam roadster was imminent.

William Henry James's 1829 steam vehicle.

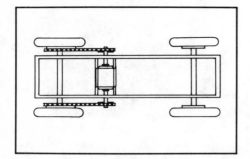

A diagram of the mounting of the engine in Bersey's electric vehicle.

W. Bersey's phaeton for the Prince of Wales.

The first person to use an electric motor to drive a vehicle was probably Prof. Moritz Hermann Jacobi of St. Petersburg University. In 1834 he travelled along the River Neva in an electric boat driven by 320 galvanic cells. Only a year later Dutchman Sibrandus Stratingh fitted an electric motor to a car and thus became the inventor of the electric automobile.

The electric motor offers a number of advantages as a means of powering vehicles. It is flexible, easy to start, runs quietly and without exhaust fumes, and is very simple to construct. In fact, the only disadvantage is the energy source itself. Heavy batteries increase the dead weight of the vehicle beyond reasonable limits and only a relatively modest range can be achieved. Designers have been trying to crack this particular nut for a century and a half, but the beginnings were promising enough.

In the eighties and nineties of the last century, H. Krieger introduced electric hansom-cabs in Paris with great success. They had two electric motors over the front axle, and each drove one of the front wheels. In case one broke down, the other was capable of propelling the vehicle on its own. During the same period great rivalry developed between Count Gaston de Chasseloup-Laubat, driving electric cars designed by Jeantaud, and racing driver Camille Jenatzy. They broke one speed record after another. In the end it was Jenatzy who took the winner's laurels, attaining a speed of 105,8 km/h (65,7 mph) in a car with the proud name *Jamais Contente* (Never Satisfied). For the year 1899 it was a very respectable speed.

Electric cars were not only able to notch up good speeds – they occasionally travelled a long way, too. Once again it was Krieger who took up the challenge. In September, 1905 he covered the 307 km (190 miles) from Paris to Trouville with-

One of H. Krieger's electric cabs which criss-crossed Paris from 1887.

out changing or recharging his vehicle's batteries. It must be said, however, that all available space in his car was crammed with batteries.

There were electric cars on the continent, in England and, first and foremost, in the United States. In the year 1900 electric cars still occupied a third of the space at the exhibition of the Automobile Club of America. They were best suited to situations where they did not have to travel far afield, i.e. in town traffic. To this day there are electric delivery vans, post office vans, refuse collection vehicles and beer lorries, and they are now becoming popular. In Britain alone the number of electric vehicles, mainly delivery vans, is estimated at 100,000.

One of the first English electric vehicles served quite a different purpose. Walter Bersey began with an electric omnibus and followed this up by building a lorry for the Post Office. In this lorry, three months before the repeal of the 'flag' law, he exceeded the 3 km/h (2 mph) speed limit and was prosecuted. In 1894 he built a luxurious phaeton, in which Edward, Prince of Wales, took his first drive in an automobile. Two years later Bersey also owned an elegant covered car, which was one of twenty automobiles that took part in the first motorized wedding in the world.

Around the turn of the century there appeared the first electric cars to be equipped with a dynamo driven by a petrol engine. This combination of electricity and the internal combustion engine is still used on the railways, but has remained a curiosity on the roads.

In spite of isolated successes, however, the electric car was unable to compete in the long run with the ever-improving internal combustion engine. The relative primitiveness of the battery remained an insurmountable obstacle. In 1881 a reporter wrote in the French newspaper *L'Officiel:* 'G. Trouvé has just put into operation an electric velocipede. One of his friends tried it out

Jamais Contente **(Never Satisfied).**

in the asphalted streets of Valois. He rode up and down several times at a fair speed. These trial runs lasted an hour and a half. This is clearly only the beginning, but it is a promising one. As soon as it is possible to accumulate a relatively large supply of energy in a relatively small mass, electricity will be exploitable on a large scale.'

This is a rare example of a field of technology where, after more than a century, we can more or less say exactly the same.

An American electric car of Rauch and Lang.

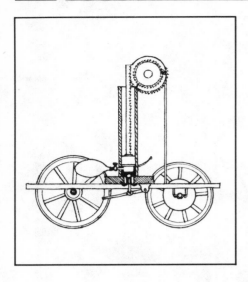

A diagram of I. de Rivaz's automobile.

The steam engine was a very practical invention, but even its inventors knew that it was extremely inefficient, as only a fraction of the heat produced to fire the boiler was actually transformed into useful energy. It was only a small step from realizing this fact to adopting the new idea of burning the fuel inside the piston chamber.

In fact the very first experiments with the internal combustion engine took place before the invention of the steam engine. The ignition of gunpowder inside the cylinder of an engine was suggested by the Dutch physicist Christiaan Huygens in 1681. The suggestion was taken up by his assistant Denis Papin, but he eventually gave up and turned his attention to steam, though others carried on experimenting.

The French engineer Philippe Lebon patented in 1786 a method of producing coal gas from wood, and along with it an engine driven by coal gas. Lebon's engine was a dual-action one, the gas-air mixture being ignited alternately on either side of the piston. It never ran properly, but it showed the way to others.

The first internal combustion engines were gas-powered, with only a few exceptions. One of the most remarkable of these was the small engine developed by the Nicéphor brothers which ran on a very strange fuel indeed — moss spores. They called their invention 'pyroleophor', and it seems to have worked, since we know what its fuel consumption was — 125 grains a minute. The brothers used it to propel a boat.

In perfecting the gas engine significant advances were made independently by two different inventors. They were Jean Lenoir, a Belgian living in France, and the German businessman Nikolaus Otto. Their efforts produced a small, light engine that could be used almost anywhere and was economical on fuel. It could scarcely be used in transport, however, since it relied upon the gas main to supply it. Yet Lenoir looked forward to the day when gas would be 'replaced by hydrogen vapour mixed with air, paraffin and other fuels'.

In 1863 Lenoir built a vehicle propelled by such an engine and drove from Paris to Joinville-le-Pont and back again in it. The car was heavy and the 1.1 kW (1.6 hp) engine only got up to 100 rpm, but the automobile with an internal combustion engine had become a reality.

The Otto-Langen engine of 1866.

A diagram of J. Lenoir's gas engine of 1860 and its improved version four years later.

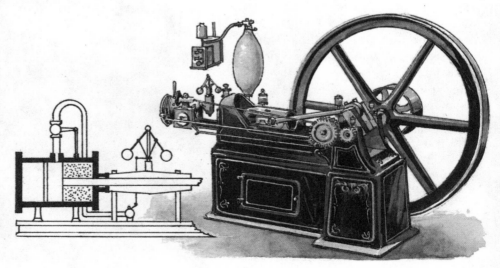

In spite of his undoubted contribution, Lenoir is not regarded as the father of the modern car. That title is given to a man who realized the hopes of generations almost half a century before Lenoir. Isaac de Rivaz, a retired French army major, lived in what is now Switzerland. In 1807 he built (and patented) the first 'automobile' driven by an internal combustion engine. Rivaz used the expansion of burning gas (a mixture of hydrogen and air) to drive a piston linked to the driving wheel of a vehicle.

Rivaz was led to this idea by memories of the training he received in an officers' school. There the future French officers had been shown a gas pistol fired by means of a spark, demonstrated by none other than the famous scientist Alessandro Volta. The idea seems to have been at the back of Rivaz's mind for years that if, instead of a bullet, such a gas pistol were to drive a piston, that piston might do useful work. So it was that in a remote mountain pass a symbol of the modern age was born.

Rivaz's vehicle was extremely primitive. It did not even have any steering, so it was no wonder that his practical trials were disastrous — on one occasion his shed was demolished — and he was unable to make any progress.

Another almost forgotten pioneer of motoring is (to quote his epitaph) the 'inventor, engineer and mechanic' Siegfried Marcus. His first petrol-driven car drove around a military training-ground in Vienna in 1864, but his second car, built in 1875, was especially interesting. It had a number of features which anticipated later developments, such as worm-gear steering, a carburettor, differential-like transmission and, most significant of all, electromagnetic ignition. Even the outward appearance of Marcus's vehicle was more like a modern car than his predecessors' coach-like contraptions. Marcus was a brilliant inventor, but he lacked the patience and perseverance to see his ideas through to the end. His car was therefore destined to become no more than a prized exhibit at the Vienna technical museum.

The history of the modern car proper did not start until Karl Friedrich Benz and Gottlieb Daimler came along. Though they both were Germans, they were not actually acquainted, in spite of having a great deal in common. Both had previously worked on gas engines, but with the express intention of developing an engine suitable for transport. In the end it was Benz who first achieved this. His motor tricycle took to the road on July 3, 1886, while Daimler's cycle did not have its first run until November 10 of that year.

At first Benz's experiments failed to attract any major public interest. His wife, Berta, decided to set this to rights by secretly undertaking a longer and more demanding trip in order to publicize her husband's invention. The result was surprising. Berta and her two sons, fifteen-year-old Eugen and fourteen-year-old Richard, surreptitiously borrowed father's car and set off from Mannheim to Pforzheim to visit grandmother. They completed the round trip of 113 km (70 miles) without any major breakdowns. Berta 'tanked up' at various chemist's shops along the route, and repaired minor faults with great ingenuity, replacing a burnt piece of insulation with her garter and using a hairpin to clear a blocked inlet-pipe. Given the condition of contemporary roads and the considerable skill required of the driver, the feat was truly amazing.

It is not known how Benz reacted to the secret outing, but its success encouraged him to intensify his research and he turned to four-wheeled vehicles. He managed to build one to his satisfaction in 1893, christening it Victoria, to mark his victory over the complex problem of steering. His car was also a commercial success, so that even before the turn of the century his Mannheim factory was turning out almost 600 cars a year.

Daimler too, after experimenting with a motorized two-wheeler, the forerunner of the motorcycle, started to fit his engine to four-

The first Daimler car, which appeared on the streets as early as 1866.

wheeled vehicles. Throughout he received valuable assistance from a friend, the talented designer

K. F. Benz's famous three-wheeler.

Victoria – **1893.**

Wilhelm Maybach. It was this team that solved the main problem of internal combustion engines at that time – the fact that the explosions in the cylinder succeeded each other at too great an interval, thus severely limiting performance. The chief obstacle to higher revolutions was the imperfect manner of ignition. Daimler proposed a new system based on a glow tube, which protruded from the cylinder head and was heated by a small flame. On compression of the mixture the heat of the tube was sufficient to ignite it, and by this means Daimler was able to achieve up to 900 rpm instead of the 200 or so then current.

Like Benz in the early days, Daimler too remained virtually unrecognized in his own country, but his engines were a great success in France, where renowned makers such as Peugeot and Panhard-Levassor fitted them to their vehicles. At the dawn of the age of motoring it was the petrol vehicles of René Panhard and Emile Levassor that triumphed in competitive runs, though Armand Peugeot, a former velocipede manufacturer and steam-car designer, was a keen rival.

The first official contest between automobiles was the 1894 Paris-Rouen race. Entries were accepted from vehicles propelled by any mechanical means, from petrol and steam-driven cars to those with compressed-air engines. There was even one entry whose engine was 'the weight of its passengers'. The first to complete the 126-km (78-mile) course was a de Dion-Bouton steam tractor pulling a carriage. Its time was 5 hours 40 minutes, representing an average speed of over 20 km/h (12 mph). It was disqualified after the race, however, on the grounds that the tractor-trailer combination did not fully accord with the race rules, but it demonstrated that steam was still able at that stage to defeat its rivals.

The following year, 1895, was important because of the Paris-Bordeaux-Paris race. This formidable test was easily won by the petrol-driven vehicle of Emile Levassor, fitted with a Daimler engine. The next three places went to Peugeot-engined vehicles. The winner's lead at the conclusion of the 1,200-km (745-mile) course was six hours. In the end, however, this car won second prize, since the rules stated that the first prize could be awarded only to a four-seater, and Levassor's vehicle had only two seats. But the point had been made – the internal combustion engine obviously had a great future.

Among the French pioneers were the vehicles of R. Panhard – E. Levassor.

At a time when the thick smoke of puffing steamers swirled across the waters of rivers and seas, when steel rails hummed beneath the speeding weight of giant locomotives and the internal combustion engine was being developed in Europe, there were still some parts of the world where technology was able to make an impact only slowly and with difficulty. On the mysterious and frequently perilous fringes of the modern age man was still using transport that was centuries old. In the endless prairies, the vast northern ice fields and the high-mountain passes, the horse, the dog-team or the ox were often much more than a mere way of getting from place to place — they might be a man's only lifeline.

The story of how the American West was won is important in the history of the modern world, yet the great migration of 'prairie schooners', heavy wagons covered with canvas and drawn by several pairs of oxen, did not take place until half way through the 19th century. Tens of thousands of settlers trekked westwards in search of land, gold, work, or just simply adventure. For them the wagons were their only home for months on end, and often their only protection against danger.

Around the year 1840 there were two main trails westward. The Oregon route led across the plains of the Missouri, the sandy region of the River Platte, and the merciless Rocky Mountains. The famous Santa Fé route set out from the town of Independence and near Cimmaron split in two, one branch leading through Colorado, the other through New Mexico, until they rejoined in Santa Fé. Teams of pack animals had used this route since 1804, between 80 and 200 mules chalking up an average of 25 km (10 miles) a day.

The era of the covered wagons began in 1826 with Captain Beckwell's expedition. Initially wagon-trains left for Santa Fé once a year,

Caravans of heavy wagons drove westwards continually.

but by 1860 they were setting off once a week. A fully-laden wagon, drawn by at least two pairs of oxen, weighed three and a half tonnes and covered an average of about 27 km (17 miles) a day. At the height of the westward migration, around the year 1870, one railroad station in Nebraska was the starting point for over 800 wagons a day, drawn by thousands of oxen.

The Pony Express required a strong and courageous team of men.

On April 3, 1860 United States postal history was made when the Overland Pony Express Company came into being, providing a postal service from Mississippi, through Kansas, Nebraska, Wyoming, Utah and Nevada, to California. Throughout a route nearly 3,000 km (1,870 miles) long, crossing wild country roamed by hostile Indians and white bandits, the Pony Express riders galloped back and forth for just twenty-five dollars a week. The company was never short of riders, though recruitment posters were

nothing if not realistic: 'We are looking for brave men of slim figure, good riders, above 18, ready to risk their life every day. Orphans are welcome.'

The list of riders who worked for Pony Express includes many famous names, including those of Buffalo Bill Cody and Wild Bill Hickock. The standard equipment of a Pony Express rider was a knife and a pair of pistols. The mail was carried in two saddlebags, so that when changing horses it was enough to sling them across the fresh mount

and leap into the saddle. These changes of horse took an average of one minute ten seconds. It was only by riding flat out that the riders were able to travel the huge distance in first ten, later a mere eight days. The safety of the mail came first, and the company regulations expressly prohibited acts of bravado.

None the less, a good many of the riders became famous for their feats of courage. Bill Haslam, for example, was obliged to ride 600 km (370 miles) with only ten hours' rest, and a rider named Moor once rode

280 km (175 miles) in 31 hours, non-stop.

Pony Express was unable to carry either passengers or any but the smallest packages. This was the task of the stage-coaches, and they did the job until the start of the 20th century. The 'stages' of the Wild West were heavyweights whose bodies were suspended on deerskin straps. There was no glass in the windows, since it would not have survived the first kilometre of the lurching ride. Thick linen curtains offered passengers a modicum of

The Deadwood stage is still a legend.

protection from dust and rain. Drawn by a foursome, the stages could put up to 170 km (105 miles) a day behind them, covering the Pony Express route in 18 days.

In addition to the privations imposed by natural obstacles, the stage-coaches had to run the gauntlet of Indian attacks and ambushes by white outlaws. Though a guard would 'ride shotgun' beside the driver, his sawn-off shotgun a lethal weapon at anything up to fifteen or twenty metres, the fate of a stage-coach and its passengers frequently depended on the speed of its horses and a good helping of luck.

Perhaps the best-known vehicle in all America at that time was the Deadwood stage. It was built in the town of Concord, New Hampshire, and arrived in California by sea via Cape Horn. During the gold rush days it ran from San Francisco to the prospecting area, along the valley of the Sacramento and the untamed tracks of Utah to the town of Deadwood in Dakota, where rich gold deposits were found in 1875. Riddled with bullet-holes and marked by countless arrows, it ended up at the bottom of a gorge after being ambushed. Years later it was recovered by William Cody, who drove it all the way back across the continent to Concord, where he had it repaired by the firm that had built it. The rejuvenated stage-coach became one of the attractions of Buffalo Bill's Wild West Show.

Let us now leave the Wild West and the New World and consider quite a different continent. For centuries caravans of Bactrian camels had been setting out from Peking across the Gobi Desert with tea for the markets of Siberia, from where it was carried on carts or sledges to Europe. Before the Trans-Siberian Railway was built it took six months to get the tea into the pots of European connoisseurs.

In the desert lands of northern Africa, Arabia and the Near East, caravans were still the usual, sometimes the only means of transport well into the 20th century. They were made up of dromedaries, or one-humped camels. These animals do not walk very fast — at about the same speed as man, though with much greater stamina — but specially bred racing camels were able to outstrip horses over a sufficiently long distance, and the camel's modest requirements are well known. Because it can store them in its body, a camel can survive for several days without food and water. This is the only way it is able to cover long stretches of arid country between oases.

The main caravan routes across the Sahara led from the Mediterranean ports, southwards to Lake Chad and Timbuctoo. The round trip of about 5,000 km (3,000 miles) took a whole year. It was not until modern roads were built and the aeroplane was invented that the journey across the world's largest desert could be shortened to a matter of days, even hours.

In some corners of the globe anyone who wished to travel, whether in the cause of science or in the interests of trade, had to get by without any assistance whatever apart from simple human effort. In the jungles of equatorial Africa, for instance, where there were no paths at all save a few narrow trails trodden out on foot, and where no domesticated animal could survive the difficult climate, the only means of transport was a team of porters. None of the great African explorers of the last century or the beginning of the present one was able to manage without native porters. In fact it was they, with their willingness and ability to conquer the dangers and difficulties of these trips, who to a great extent determined the success of the expedition and the safety of those who took part.

Civilization continues, of course, to penetrate even the most desolate and hostile areas of the world. The desert sands have long since covered the tracks of the camel trains, but there are still some regions that resist man's attempts to conquer them. Mountain porters are still indispensable to anyone seeking to conquer the giant peaks of the Himalayas. The tonnes of material

The 'ships of the desert'.

Black porters could withstand

the fearful climate and the rigours of travel in places where even animals collapsed from exhaustion.

that are needed to set up camps from which to assault these mountain peaks have to be carried to heights where the air is too thin even for helicopters to operate. The only means of getting loads up precipitous mountain paths or along glaciers is on a man's back. The Sherpas of the Himalayas are famous as porters and climbers, and one of them, Tenzing Norgay, shared the honour of being the first man to reach the summit of Mount Everest with Edmund Hillary in 1953.

Men have crossed deserts, climbed mountains, and hacked their way through jungles in considerable numbers, and the only large areas of the world which remain inaccessible for most people are the white wastes of the far north and south. Here, more than anywhere, the dog is man's best friend. During the Alaskan gold rush of the late 19th century a good dog team was literally worth its weight in gold. In winter they drew sleds, and in summer they carried their load on backpacks. It was fairly easy to put a dog in a canoe, and when his master paddled the long water-trails of Canada and Alaska he could be not only a helper, but a companion, too.

The renowned Antarctic explorer, Captain Robert Falcon Scott, was to learn to his cost the great value of dogs in areas of perpetual snow and ice. It was in 1911 that the dramatic race to be the first man to reach the South Pole began in earnest. Captain Scott and the experienced Norwegian polar explorer Roald Amundsen set off almost at the same time. Scott was beset with misfortune from the start. He took with him two motorized sleds, seventeen ponies and thirty dogs. He had little faith in the dogs, and there was no one in his party who knew how to handle them properly. The foul weather conditions took their toll of one pony after another, the motor sleds were soon no more than crippled hulks, and the dog pack became undisciplined and utterly useless. In the end the members of Scott's expedition had to rely on human strength alone.

Meanwhile, Amundsen, who had learnt from the Eskimoes the art of handling huskies, had used his dog teams to set up one cache of supplies after another on his route to the Pole. On October 19 he set off with four sleds and fifty-two dogs, and without major hitches raised the Norwegian flag at 90° southern latitude on December 15.

The exhausted British party reached the Pole on January 17, 1912. There was not a single pony left alive, and the dogs had been sent back to base because of a shortage of food. This cruel disappointment transformed the return journey into a bitter struggle for Scott and his companions. Eventually a blizzard kept them confined to their tent and without food just 18 km (11 miles) short of a supply dump. It was a journey they were never to complete.

The Arctic mail.

The immediate ancestor of the bicycle is considered to have been the dandy-horse, though the method of propulsion was more that of a child's scooter. It first saw the light of day in 1813, and the invention is credited to the forester Karl von Drais. This is not quite accurate, however, as the principle of the dandy-horse had been known and used before that. In fact, Chinese chroniclers state that in the era before Christ the riding of similar contraptions became so popular that people neglected their work. Eventually the emperor had to issue a decree threatening these early cyclists with severe punishment. What was truly original in Drais's invention was the steerable front wheel, which was an immense improvement. He called his brainchild the Laufmaschine, and made a publicity run from Mannheim to Karlsruhe, cutting the usual sixteen hours walking time down to a mere four. He failed to make any great impression on the public, however.

In 1860 the French locksmith and wheelwright Pierre Michaux came to the rescue of all those who were wearing out their footwear on dandy-horses, by inventing pedal cranks for the front wheel. He named his device the 'vélocipède', and it laid the foundations for the most widespread means of transport in human history. Like the dandy-horse, the velocipede was made of wood. The ride was a rather uncomfortable one – in England the machine was rechristened 'the boneshaker' – but it far outstripped the dandy-horse when it came to speed.

The new invention achieved its greatest popularity in England. Before long all-metal velocipedes were being produced. At the same time the designers realized that the bigger the front wheel was, the greater the distance travelled for one turn of the pedals. This led to an absurd increase in the size of the front wheel, so that riders of small stature were sometimes unable to reach the pedals from the saddle. In the middle of the 1870s the diameter of this front wheel was sometimes as much as 2.2 m (7 ft). On such a machine it was possible to travel at speeds of 30 km/h (18 mph). A man called Stevens from San Francisco rode round the

This bicycle was made mainly of wood.

world on one. It took him two and a half years. The 'penny-farthing', as it came to be called, was fast, but unsteady and dangerous, quite unsuitable for non-sporting types or for women and children. As girls, too, wanted to take to wheels, various types of tricycle became popular. One of the added attractions of tricycles, for the young at least, was that they were for the most part 'made for two'.

From the technical point of view tricycles were a step backwards, and they could never match the speed and mobility of the velocipede. The real transition to a fast but safe bicycle began with the 'kangaroo', which had a much more reasonably-sized front wheel and chain-drives on either side of the fork, and was completed by the 'rover' type of bicycle with a low profile. Rovers, which were practically speaking modern bicycles, were immensely successful. They opened cycling up to a broad section of the public, since it really was possible for anyone to ride them. Not only that, but they were able to beat their taller rivals on the race track.

When the Paris magazine Le Petit Journal held its non-stop Paris-Brest-Paris race in 1891, all 206 starters rode rovers. They were

The dandy-horse was an object of ridicule.

A penny-farthing.

The Kangaroo.

The world-famous Rover.

racing models — by the standards of their day, that is. So, for instance, the cycle that won the race weighed all of 22 kg (48 lb). The race turned into a duel between the two great rivals Charles Terront and Jiel-Laval. It is nowadays hard to imagine the difficulties faced by the competitors in negotiating a route 1,200 km (745 miles) long over dusty and rock-strewn roads.

As the race progressed, punctures alternated with broken chains, but Terront battled on, and by the time he reached one of the final checkpoints he had built up a considerable lead. It was two o'clock in the morning, however, and the umpires were asleep, so that by the time they were roused precious minutes had been lost. Nevertheless, at half past six in the morning Terront broke the finishing tape in Paris after seventy-one hours of gruelling effort. Jiel-Laval did not reach Paris until two o'clock in the afternoon, and the third cyclist to finish arrived the next day. During the event Terront had smoked his favourite strong cigars along the way!

Together with the rover, there were three other inventions which made the advent of mass cycling possible. The most important was the pneumatic tyre, which helped transform the pastime from an ordeal into a pleasure. The second was the brake, whether the back-pedal type, or the shoe type invented by Sir Harold Bowden. Lastly, there was a system of changing gears, which made riding easier in hilly country.

The bicycle, simplest and most widespread of all the world's transport, entered the 20th century in very much the same form as we know it today.

The tricycle was ideal for lovers......

or for the delicate.

The motorcycle was born on November 10, 1886, when Gottlieb Daimler straddled his wooden two-wheeler and rode it a few dozen metres. Actually, Daimler wasn't interested in motorcycles at all — he just needed something to try his new engine out on. He probably couldn't even ride a bicycle, since he attached to his motorcycle a couple of side-wheels to improve stability, and even then drove at 'walking speed'. Nor did the inventor ever turn his attention to motorcycles again: once he had satisfied himself as to the performance of his engine, he devoted all his efforts to four-wheeled vehicles. In order to set the record straight, it must be said that a different sort of motorized two-wheeler had already taken to the road five years earlier — Gustave Trouvé's electrocycle. There were even steam motorcycles, three-wheelers for the most part, though some were velocipedes fitted with steam engines. Yet despite all this, the true forerunner of today's motorcycle was undoubtedly Daimler's machine.

In spite of Daimler's lack of interest, the motorcycle soon found itself in other capable hands. In 1893, designers Heinrich Hildebrand and Alois Wolfmüller built a two-wheeler with a two-cylinder engine. The method of power transmission

The main original feature of Millet's motorcycle was the position of the engine.

they chose was to connect the piston-rods directly to the rear wheel, which also served as the flywheel. Though this system did not entirely give a smooth ride, the motorcycle was surprisingly popular, particularly in France, where it was manufactured under licence as 'La

This Daimler two-wheeler was the first motorcycle.

Pétrolette'. A Frenchman, Millet, designed a curious motorcycle with a five-cylinder radial engine built into the wheel.

The first machine to receive widespread use was that invented by the Werner brothers, who were Russian journalists living in Paris. They named it 'La Motocyclette', which soon became the general name for such vehicles. Its construction was very simple, based on an ordinary bicycle. The small engine was mounted over the front wheel, which it drove by means of a belt. Though it was more a motorized bicycle than a true motorcycle, and was not very powerful, the Werners' machine, perhaps by virtue of its simplicity, enjoyed great popularity.

Another very popular vehicle of that era was the de Dion-Bouton motor tricycle, which shared many features with the true motorcycle. It is noteworthy as having been the first such vehicle to drive in combination, though not as yet with a sidecar — the passenger rode in a two-wheeled trailer. It is said to have taken considerable skill on the part of the driver not to lose both.

A major advance in motorcycle design came with the Swiss-manufactured 'La Motosacoche'. It

Elegant sidecars became the hallmark of the motorcycle.

Fashion is fashion!

The US Indian
is an unforgettable marque.

had a relatively powerful and reliable engine mounted in a triangular frame on what was still, in effect, a bicycle, but a completely enclosed in metal covers.

The early days of the motorcycle, like those of the car, would not have been the same without races. In 1904 the Motocycle Club de France first held a prestigious race called La Coupe Internationale des Motocyclettes on a road circuit near Dourdan. In 1905 the race was won by the Czech rider Václav Vondřich on a machine made by the company Laurin and Klement. According to the rules of the race, the next competition was to be held in the winner's homeland, but in 1906 the French riders failed to regain the trophy, which went to another Czech, this time on a machine from the Austrian Puch works. The French organizers were so disgusted that they abolished the event altogether.

The motorcycle was slower to develop in the United States than in Europe. The car became the vehicle for everyday use, and two-wheelers were considered merely a hobby. In spite of this, two marques deserve a mention at least – Indian and Harley-Davidson, which acquired fame both at home and abroad. The main way in which they differed from most of their European counterparts was in their massive construction and large engine capacity, giving them a correspondingly superior performance.

In the pioneer days, both cars and bicycles were more a form of sport indulged in by hardy enthusiasts than a means of general transport. This was in no small measure due to the fact that their tyres were made of hard rubber, which served to protect the wheel rims, but contributed little to the comfort of the ride. The invention of the pneumatic tyre revolutionized road transport.

It may be surprising, but one of the first people you meet along the road leading to the modern tyre is none other than Christopher Columbus. During his voyages of discovery in the late 15th century, either he himself or one of his successors noted that the American Indians fashioned themselves rubber balls from the dried juice of the tree *Hevea brasiliensis.* Not until the 18th century, however, did the first samples of raw india-rubber reach Europe. They were brought back by the members of an expedi-

tion sent out to South America by the French academy of sciences to measure the meridian, with a view to establishing a new unit of length, the metre.

In 1839 Charles Goodyear invented the process of vulcanization of rubber using sulphur and heat, and thus obtained a product that could be used in industry. Goodyear was an inventor in the classical mould – he left behind more than sixty patents (none of them relating to rubber) and debts amounting to $200,000. The first inflatable tyre was patented six years later by the Englishman Robert Thomson, but his invention passed almost unnoticed.

Then, one day in 1887, Scottish-born vet John Boyd Dunlop bought his son a bicycle. Either the Dunlop boy was somewhat spoilt, or his father was more devoted than most, for while thousands of other cyclists just had to put up with a bumpy ride,

Dunlop decided that his son would cycle in comfort. He made a couple of rubber tubes, inflated them using a football pump, and laboriously attached them to the wheel rims. In spite of the crudeness of the system, it proved surprisingly successful. The boy rode merrily up and down

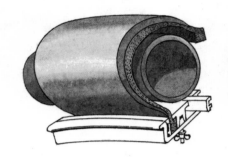

Cross-section of a Michelin tyre, disc and inner tube.

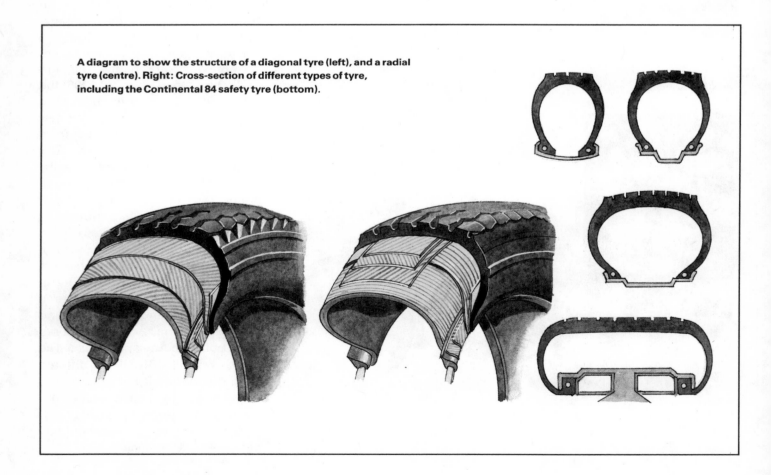

A diagram to show the structure of a diagonal tyre (left), and a radial tyre (centre). Right: Cross-section of different types of tyre, including the Continental 84 safety tyre (bottom).

the bumpy cobblestones of Belfast, attracting the attention of other cyclists, and, what was more important, of the bicycle dealers. The inflatable tyre had been born. In 1890 it took the form of an inner tube fitted with a valve and an outer casing with reinforced edges and a wire insert for fitting to the wheel rim. The modern tyre was well on the way.

The credit for introducing pneumatic tyres on cars goes to the Michelin brothers, André and Edouard. Automobile design had

The first car with pneumatic tyres was called *Eclair*. The Michelin brothers provided its 'footwear' in 1895.

J. B. Dunlop's son was the first cyclist to have a comfortable ride. The inventor himself could not ride a bicycle.

found itself in a vicious circle. The constant shocks transmitted by solid tyres meant that cars had to be ever stronger and more heavily built. The increased weight not only stretched the low-performance engines to the limit, but in itself contributed to the battering the solid tyres took. The Michelins saw that the only way out lay in the pneumatic tyre. After numerous trials, Edouard entered the Paris-Bordeaux-Paris race of 1895 in a car with inflated tyres. The race was a gruelling one for Edouard, since none of the tyres lasted more than 150 km (90 miles), and repairs were tedious, for each tyre was attached to the rim by twenty screws! But he finally arrived in Paris, and the next year de Dion, Delahay and other manufacturers adopted pneumatic tyres, too.

The development of tyres went hand-in-hand with that of the motor-car. Ever-increasing speeds called for better and better tyres. What had started out as a simple rubber tube became a sophisticated industrial product. The 'ride', shape and load-bearing capacity of a tyre are mainly determined by the quality of the carcase. The carcase of a modern tyre is made up of several strands of artificial fibres which are extremely strong. A milestone in tyre design was reached in 1948, when Michelin produced the first radial tyre. The carcase based on radially arranged material is the most significant development of modern times in the construction of tyres for both cars and lorries. Improved adhesion and an increase in the area of contact with the road surface reduce both braking distances and fuel consumption, thus bringing greater safety and economy.

Around the turn of the century, with its pioneer days behind it, it was clear that if the motor-car was to find favour it must cease to be a toy for the enthusiast or the wealthy and become a much more general means of transport. Out of dozens of manufacturers, many of whom ceased to exist long before they could make a name for themselves, there began to emerge the firms that form the backbone of today's automobile industry. Peugeot and Citroën became established in France, Rolls-Royce and Bentley in England, and Fiat in Italy. In 1900 Daimler's son Paul brought the Mercedes into the world; it is still one of the most famous German cars, enjoying a high reputation everywhere.

Ruthlessly, the motor-car set out to conquer the world, taking its toll of innocent victims right from the start. The first recorded accident involving a car with an internal combustion engine dates from 17 August, 1896. The unfortunate pedestrian was a Mrs. Driscolls of London, who was knocked down on her way to the theatre. Though the car was travelling at only 6 km/h (4 mph) when it hit her, the accident was a fatal one. The inquest found that Mrs. Driscolls had, through her own negligence, been killed by an automobile on a public thoroughfare.

The advent of a truly reliable car, capable of being run by a layman, was still a long way off. It was not until the first decade of this century that the early single-cylinder and two-cylinder engines started to give way to multi-cylinder designs. Automobile engineers also began to tackle the question of ignition. Heated tubes were liable to be put out of action by the wind, and not until 1902 did high-voltage systems employing a magnet achieve some practical success. The early evaporation carburettors were also troublesome. It was Wilhelm Maybach, a brilliant designer working for Daimler, who invented the

The de Dion-Bouton Voiturette
was particularly popular because of its reliability and economy.

float chamber carburettor, the principle of which is used to this day. There was, too, a continuing dispute as to the relative advantages of air and water cooling. In the end water-cooled engines became the norm, thanks mainly to Mercedes and Fiat, which early this century introduced

fairly efficient honeycomb radiators. Fiat also developed a plate clutch in an oil bath, giving a much gentler takeup, which made gear-changing easier and made moving off a smoother business.

Gearbox and steering design were equally challenging. The use

The 1900 four-cylinder Mercedes
was named after the beautiful daughter of the Austrian Consul in Nice,
who was an expert on Daimler vehicles.

A Renault of 1901.

of a pair of reins to steer the vehicle was a somewhat extreme solution, although some vehicles for American farmers were indeed so equipped, but it was not until 1898 that the first steering-wheel appeared. Even then it was some time before paired kingpins were introduced, and to begin with the whole front axle was turned, which did little to improve the stability of the vehicle.

Between 1893 and 1897 the German engineer Rudolf Diesel developed an entirely new type of engine employing compression-ignition, which came to be named after its inventor. The diesel engine ran on much less refined fuels, particularly fuel oil. Though its inventor mysteriously disappeared from the deck of a ship on a stormy night in the English Channel, the engines became indispensable, especially in heavy vehicles, in marine applications, on the railways and in electricity generators. Due mainly to their economical operation, they are at

One of the first versions of the Model T Ford. The car had a top speed of up to 70 km/h (43 mph).

present enjoying unprecedented popularity as power units for cars.

Let us leave Europe, the cradle of motoring, and turn our attention once more to the United States, home of the man who was to make the motor-car the very symbol of our century. Henry Ford was born in 1863 on a small farm in Michigan. His interest in motoring was aroused at the age of twelve by a steam-car. In the early days he, too, experimented with steam-propelled vehicles, but by 1893 he was already building his first internal-combustion car. It also happened to be the first, and for a long time the only, automobile in Detroit, which was destined to emerge as the largest centre of motor manufacturing in the world.

In those days the only effective advertisement for a vehicle was racing success. For this reason Ford constructed two racing-cars, the '999' and the 'Arrow'. To drive these, which was no mean task, equipped as they were with a sort of rudder rather than a steering-wheel, Ford engaged the services of a well-known racing cyclist called

Barney Oldfield. Though Oldfield had never sat in a motor-car before, after only a week's training he managed to win his very first race.

Still, commercial success was elusive, until Ford had a stroke of genius. In 1909 he began production of a 'universal vehicle' — the legendary Model T, or 'Tin Lizzie'. The Model T was the car for everyman. Through streamlined efficiency, specialization in specific tasks and production-line assembly, Ford was able to turn out cars in unprecedented numbers. He used his profits not only to extend his premises, but also to raise his workers' wages, and above all to cut the price of the product. Business boomed. The Model T did not offer outstanding comfort or performance, but it was reliable, and it was cheap. It became the car of the masses. It was produced, with only minor modifications, for eighteen years, by which time a total of 15,176,888 had been made. This record remained unchallenged for many years, until the immensely popular Volkswagen 'Beetle' came along in the late nineteen-forties.

In November, 1896, the committee of the French Automobile Club displayed great foresight in announcing a contest for freight vehicles with a payload of at least one tonne. Its members seem to have appreciated the importance of this new type of vehicle.

There were eight entries, all of them steam-powered. In fact, steam was to play a major role in freight transport for quite some time. Slow-moving steam 'monsters' could frequently be seen on the roads into the nineteen-twenties, and steam lorries of advanced design such as those made by Sentinel or Foden were found in many parts of Europe in the fifties.

In 1892, the well-known firm of Panhard-Levassor produced a petrol-driven tractor-trailer combination designed for the transport of either goods or passengers. A year later they introduced a lorry with an engine at the front and a large freight platform behind.

The first goods vehicles powered by an internal-combustion engine were in effect motorized carts with iron or solid rubber tyres. In 1896 Daimler constructed a five-tonne lorry with a 7 kW (10 hp) engine, which attracted considerable attention.

Two years later the first lorry was built in Kopřivnice (Nesselsdorf), in what was then the Austro-Hungarian Empire. The factory mainly produced rolling-stock, which was apparent in the design of this first road vehicle. It was propelled by a pair of Benz engines placed side by side, with a total capacity of 5,430 cc and an output of 8.8 kW (12hp). Starting was effected by hand-cranking one engine, the other being set in motion when the lorry moved off. The vehicle had a payload of 2.5 t and a maximum speed of 20 km/h (12 mph). The nominal consumption was stated in somewhat quaint units — 4 kg of petrol per hour! The vehicle had a number of original features, such as a condenser extending over the whole roof, which

K. Benz's first lorry, 1901.

returned water to the cooling system. The lorry was steered by means of a rudder operated with one hand, since the driver required his other hand for the performance of numerous tasks such as regulating the timing of both engines, opening and closing the throttle, and changing gear.

An important inventor of buses was Dr. Büssing. The illustration shows a 1904 model.
▼

▲
A Laurin and Klement post-office vehicle (1911).

Firemen in a 1913
Laurin and Klement vehicle.

Karl Benz got round to lorries somewhat later. He built his first in 1901, and that was only a one-tonner. Though the first Daimler and Benz lorries reached speeds of only 3 to 12 km/h (2 to 7 mph) and their petrol consumption was high, the demand for them was consider-

A 1911 Panhard-Levassor. ▲

A 1920 steam Foden demonstrates
that steam propulsion
was not short-lived.
▼

able, especially in England. Lorries were exported to the United States only after they had been improved by the use of pneumatic tyres. The first to use them for delivering goods is said to have been the famous piano manufacturer Wilhelm Steinway. Daimler enjoyed greatest success in the transatlantic market, mainly because of an after-sale service which was well ahead of its time.

In the early twenties more specialized lorries came on sale, the most common of these being fire-engines with pumps or ladders, and searchlight carriers designed mainly for military use. An interesting product was the Jaguar 4R traction unit for heavy trailers, produced by the Kopřivnice (Nesselsdorf) works in 1908. Its 13,619 cc petrol engine developed 58.8 kW (80 hp), with the drive on all four wheels.

The history of buses also begins with steam, this time in England, where Walter Hancock started the first public transport service in 1832. The first petrol-powered omnibus was made in Benz's factory. From 1895 it was to provide a service between the town of Siegen and its environs; it had seats for eight passengers, and solid rubber tyres. Three years later Benz's rival Daimler also built an omnibus, this time for twelve passengers. Another outstanding German omnibus manufacturer was Dr. Henrich Büssing. Among his innovations was entry by a side-door, previous buses having followed the tradition of the old horse-trams in having the door at the back. While earlier models had been powered by two or four-cylinder engines producing 5—10 kW (7—14 hp), Büssing applied six-cylinder power units developing up to 60 kW (80 hp). Then chain-drives were replaced by propeller-shafts with universal joints. Bus manufacture in Germany reached such a high standard that at one stage even the legendary London double-deckers were imported from German factories.

The new forms of transport — bicycle, motorcycle and automobile — naturally aroused the keen interest of the army. At the turn of the century the glory of the picturesque dragoons and hussars was fading for ever in Europe, and the generals were looking for a way of getting about more in keeping with the age.

It was the bicycle that seemed most suitable. Almost every military exercise had its contingent of 'cavalry' with folding bicycles. Machine-guns were usually transported on tricycles, because of their greater stability, but the First World War showed bicycles to be quite unsuitable in combat.

The motorcycle was a different matter. By 1914 there were powerful machines suitable for military use. Automobiles also found a place in the equipment of both sides. At the start of hostilities there were not many purpose-built armoured cars available, so as the war progressed civil vehicles were frequently adapted to service in the field.

Some of the military vehicles represented the best of contemporary technology. The pride of the Austrian army, for instance, was a diesel-electric tractor for heavy field guns. It bore the designation Austro-Daimler, and it was propelled by electric motors mounted in the wheel hubs. The automobile left its mark in the history of the First World

A Rolls-Royce, converted for field service.

War at two great battles in particular, but as a means of transport rather than as a fighting machine.

On September 7, 1914, the dour struggle which was to become known as the Battle of the Marne was at its height. France was a hair's breadth away from defeat. The reserve troops, artillery and supplies of food and ammunition which might tip the balance in favour of the French were still in Paris, 70 km (40 miles) away from the battlefield. The rail links with the front line were congested, so that 7,000 troops ready for battle were still drawn up in front of the station. Then General Galliéni had a bright idea. He com-

The 'Holy Way' — lifeline to Verdun.

mandeered nearly 600 taxis and municipal buses, drivers and all, and the first great motorized troop movement in history was soon under way. It was the day the automobile came to France's rescue.

The second occasion on which this relatively new means of transport played a major role in the First World War was at the Battle of Verdun. The greatest problem in defending this system of fortifications was the lack of supply lines. Apart from a small railway line, Verdun was only accessible by a single rough road seven metres wide and unbanked. From February 26 to March 6, 1916, 190,000 men

and 5,500 tonnes of munitions and other supplies were transported by lorry along this 'Holy Way', as it came to be called. Up to 3,500 vehicles shuttled non-stop along a single 75 km (47 mile) stretch. There was no stopping — if a lorry broke down it was simply shoved into the ditch — and most of the drivers worked without a break in shifts of eighteen to twenty hours. To them is due some of the credit for holding off the German offensive at Verdun.

The stalemate of trench warfare fuelled the desire for a weapon capable of winning the war once and for all. Various types of armoured car were tried, but failed, mainly because of the difficult terrain. Then Major Ernest Swinton came up with the idea of using caterpillar tracks. The first tank saw the light of day. The name was no accident, for the enemy was meant to think that the new weapon was no more than a mobile supply of drinking water. The first British tanks reached the front in September, 1916. They weighed around 26 tonnes, and there were two types, the 'male' and the 'female'. The former was equipped with two cannon and three machine-guns, the latter with five machine-guns. In spite of the considerable impression they initially made on both sides, these tanks proved of limited practical use. Their time had not yet come.

The Battle of the Marne was won by Parisian taxi drivers. ▲

▼ The Mark IV — a masculine type.

An armoured Austin of 1914 which served in the British army. ▼

The world of automobiles.

Surprisingly, the American Doble Steam automobile of 1931 was fitted with a steam engine. The top speed was 140 km/h (94 mph) and the fuel consumption very low.

The nineteen-twenties brought an economic revival after the stagnation of the war years and the automobile industry set off in two different directions. The first was to produce large numbers of cheap, simple, but reliable cars for the general public. There was the Citroën 5CV in France, and the legendary Trojan in England — the cheapest car of all on the British market. In Germany the erstwhile sewing-machine manufacturer Adam Opel put the middle classes on the road with his Laubfrosch (tree-frog), and DKW later followed suit with a two-stroke engine and front-wheel drive.

The more discerning customer still enjoyed a wide choice of vehicles. In 1926 the two leading German firms, Daimler and Benz, joined forces and decided to build fast, powerful thoroughbreds. The Mercedes-Benz K, designed by the famous Ferdinand Porsche, had an amazing 118 kW (160 hp) under its bonnet, giving it a top speed of over 160 km/h (100 mph), though it was not a racing-car.

A pearl among cars at the time was the Rolls-Royce New Phantom, successor to the equally famous Silver Ghost. Many stories about the car's fine qualities are still told to this day, and the price, too, was

fabulous. But what of the French Bugatti Royale, of which it was said that it made the Rolls-Royces, Mercedes and Bentleys look like children's toys?

In the United States the top prestige model was the Duesenberg. Every vehicle had a custom-built interior. Its 6,882 cc eight-cylinder engine developed 192 kW (260 hp). The car was equipped with automatic devices to maintain tyre pressures and warning lights to indicate whether the various parts of the engine were functioning properly. And that was fifty years ago! No wonder such vehicles inspired such a degree of respect that

Among the cheapest and least demanding vehicles were the Hanomag (left) and the Trojan (right) — the cheapest vehicle on the British market.

The American Duesenberg Company
has made some of the most luxurious cars in the world.
This is a 1929 model.

Prince Heinrich. Up till then no one had really needed one, since most cars were not fitted with windscreens. Electric wipers came into use at the end of the twenties. About the same time speedometers were introduced in up-market cars, and before very long the first car radios appeared.

A question which taxed the ingenuity of many designers was the aerodynamics of car bodies — how to reduce the air resistance or 'drag' created by the vehicle's surface, especially at high speeds. German and British designers performed experiments with varying degrees of success, and in the United States an experimental aerodynamic three-wheeler called the Dymaxion was built. In 1934 Hans Ledwinka, chief designer at the Czechoslovak Tatra factory, as the Kopřivnice (Nesselsdorf) works had now become, was the first to employ systematic streamlining in a production car, the Tatra 77.

The spread of motoring increased the demand for safety. Laminated safety glass was introduced, and bumpers were fitted. It took some twenty years for this now standard feature to be appreciated, since the *President* model had left the Kopřiv-

their drivers were often not fined for traffic offences.

On the technical side of things, the cars of the twenties and thirties progressed in reliability, comfort and safety. The first front-wheel brakes were fitted; in 1920 hydraulic brakes were introduced, but it took another twenty years before they substantially replaced the simpler but less effective mechanical type. Hydraulic brakes were the brainchild of designer Walter P. Chrysler, an American whose cars were so successful that they led to the setting up of a huge manufacturing company.

There were rapid advances in the electrical equipment of motor vehicles. Acetylene lighting was replaced by electric lamps, and electric horns made it possible to give a warning that was audible above the noise of the engine. Around the year 1928 direction indicators, at first manual, later electromagnetic, were made compulsory in most countries.

The first windscreen wiper, a mechanically operated one, was patented in 1908 by the Prussian

The Bugatti Royale Victoria (1931), which was considered the rarest vehicle in the world. Only seven were manufactured. The water-cooled, eight-cylinder, 12,760 cc engine develops 221 kW, which is enough to drive the 3,200 kg (3 tons) vehicle at over 200 km/h (125 mph). The consumption is around 6 miles (10 km) to the gallon.

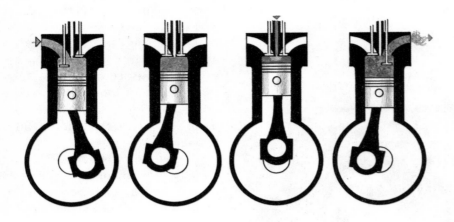

The principle of operation of a diesel engine. From the left: induction, compression, expansion (explosion), exhaust.

The principle of a four-stroke petrol engine. From the left: induction, compression, expansion (explosion), exhaust.

During the 1920s the bus began to look more like those we know today.

nice (Nesselsdorf) factory equipped with the first bumper, albeit only at the front, in 1897.

There was more to the development of the automobile between the wars than a mere increase in safety, technical sophistication and performance. Designers also made an effort to raise aesthetic standards. This was the beginning of the rise to fame of Italian coachbuilders, who managed to elevate their craft to an art form while keeping pace with modern technology.

Following the First World War, the demand for goods vehicles also increased. In the United States the FWD company (Four Wheel Drive) went into mass-production of reliable 4 × 4 vehicles for use both on roads and across country. The best advertisement these vehicles ever received arose from their excellent performance on the battlefields of the Second World War.

Goods vehicles did not really take to the roads of Europe in large numbers until they were fitted with diesel engines. The first diesel lorry was a Benz five-tonner built in 1923. It had a chain-drive, solid rubber tyres, a low box and the engine at the rear. The driver's cab was of modern type. In spite of various

experiments, the diesel engine remains the most suitable power unit for goods vehicles to this day.

The first trailers were used behind lorries in the nineteen-twenties. Heavy vehicles with payloads of up to 20 tonnes were built, incorporating a number of modern features. For instance, mechanical tippers for transporting loose materials came into use in the early twenties, followed a few years later by hydraulically operated systems. Most of these lorries were already equipped with air brakes. Solid rubber tyres disappeared from the roads in 1928.

Bus manufacturers introduced low floors, making it easier to get on and off. The first buses of this type appeared in 1924. Some firms produced models with front-wheel drive. About the same time an effort was made to increase the capacity of public transport vehicles, to meet increased demand. One of the innovations was the transverse seating arrangement generally used today. As with lorries, the most suitable power system for buses proved to be a diesel engine combined with shaft transmission.

One of the notable design achievements between the wars was a 1938 bus produced by the German firm of Büssing-NAG. This giant had two engines and three axles, and was intended for use on motorways. The front engine produced 240 kW (320 hp), the rear one 200 kW (270 hp). This undoubtedly excellent coach did not have much opportunity to prove itself, since the Second World War broke out soon afterwards, and all bus engines had to be converted to burn methane.

Manufacturers' attempts to expand their markets sometimes led to strange experiments. One of these was a bus designed to run, not on the road, but on rails. This first railbus was unable to compete with motorized trains when these were later introduced.

The automobile was conquering the world. By 1930 there were already over 35 million motor vehicles on the road. Most of these were in the United States, where there were around 26.5 million and cars had became a craze. It is interesting to note that Ford, Chrysler, Duesenberg and other automotive giants were still making steam automobiles in the 1930s, but by then there was definitely more than a whiff of petrol in the air.

The Škoda Sentinel lorry was still steam-powered.

The Praga bus of the early 1920s.

The stars of the automobile world.

The pre-1939 period saw not only the unprecedented spread of cars as an ever more general means of transport, but also the era of the great races. The new circuits such as Monza, Monte Carlo, Targa Florio and Nürburgring are still redolent with the smell of burnt oil and victor's laurels to this day.

It was a schoolboy's dream to become a great racing-driver. Men like Rudolf Caracciola, Tazio Nuvolari, Baconin Borzacchini, Giuseppe Campari, Achille Varzi, Hans Stuck, Manfred von Brauchitsch and Bernd Rosemeyer were idols in their day, and their fame lingers on.

The marques that dominated the racetracks of the twenties were Maserati, Bugatti, Alfa-Romeo, Mercedes and Auto-Union. It was usually Bugatti that wore the crown, with Alfa-Romeo challenging hard. The powerful but clumsy German cars found it hard to compete with their more graceful French and Italian rivals. It was not until the thirties that the roaring superchargers of the Mercedes SSK and SSKL took German cars to the head of the field, with the Auto-Union entries not far behind. Between 1927 and 1938, Mercedes chalked up an impressive 191 victories in major races. By that time, average lap speeds had climbed to around 200 km/h (124 mph).

With a single exception, British cars and drivers made little impression on their continental rivals. At the end of the twenties, the Le Mans 24-hour race went through a 'Bentley era'. From 1927 to 1930 Bentleys won this gruelling test of man and machine unchallenged. The 1927 race was the most dramatic one. Three Bentleys were comfortably out in front and looked unassailable, but shortly after nightfall there was a multiple pile-up. Only one of the three Bentleys remained roadworthy, and that only just. Four hours before the end of the race, the surviving Bentley was not only, to everyone's surprise, still going, but was actually in second place, 96 km behind the leading Aries. Walter Bentley decided it was all or nothing, and gave the signal for the damaged car to step up the pace. His gamble paid off — the Aries was forced to follow suit, but broke down, and it was a battered yet jubilant Bentley that took the chequered flag.

The British showed a greater interest in record-breaking than racing, for speed had become the symbol of the age.

The first universally recognized world speed record was set up in a Jeantaud electric car when Count Gaston de Chasseloup-Laubat attained 63.18 km/H (39.26 mph) in 1898. His rivalry with the Belgian 'red devil', Camille Jenatzy, has already been described, and it was Jenatzy who was the first to break the 100 km/h (62 mph) barrier. Then Léon Serpollet came along with a steam-car that did 120 km/h (74.5 mph). The era of the internal-combustion engine had arrived by then, and American millionaire William K. Vanderbilt took a Mors up to 122.49 km/h (76.11 mph). The year was 1902.

The 100 mph (160 km/h) barrier was broken in 1904, and the petrol engine was taking over, though American Fred Marriott managed to get more than 200 km/h (124 mph) out of his Stanley steam-car in 1906. In the fight to be fastest, it was very much a case of many being called but few chosen. Among the chosen

Who will win? The Mercedes and Bugattis vied for leadership in dozens of races between the wars.

were two Britons, Henry Segrave and Malcolm Campbell.

Segrave broke many records. Perhaps the one he was most proud of was the day in 1927 when he became the first man to travel over 200 mph (322 km/h) on land, on the wet sands of Daytona, Florida, in the United States. Segrave set his last record in 1929. In the Irving-Napier 'Golden Arrow' he drove 372.62 km/h (231.54 mph), a feat which earned him a knighthood. A year later he was killed in an attempt on the world water-speed record.

Segrave's greatest rival was Malcolm Campbell. Between 1923 and 1928 alone he broke the land-speed record five times. His car was called 'Bluebird'. In his 1931 'Bluebird', Campbell got very close to the 400 km/h mark, and in 1935 he did 484 km/h (300.75 mph). Six years later he added the world water-speed record of 226.7 km/h (140.87 mph) to his successes.

H. Segrave's record-breaking Sunbeam on Daytona Beach, 1927.

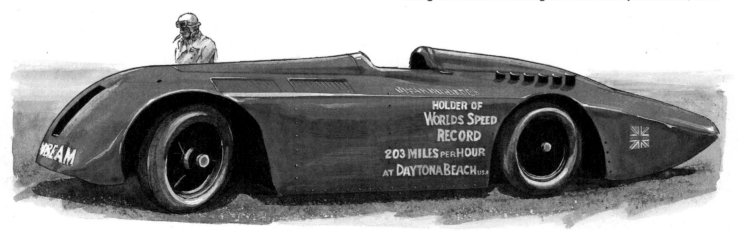

Army Harley-Davidson WLA, adapted from a civil motorcycle.

cle — and that is exactly what it was. It was equally at home in a field or on a road, and it was small, light, simple and yet very powerful. The first jeeps were built specially for the American army in 1941, but after the war they became the prototype for modern field cars in general.

Armoured cars and personnel carriers enjoyed much wider use in the Second World War. They were no longer converted civilian vehicles,

On September 1, 1939 Germany invaded Poland, an event which sparked a conflict that was to prove the greatest test of military technology in history. It was a war that was to see the demise of the military horse and foreshadow the declining importance of the foot-soldier.

At the start of the Second World War, even the most modern armies still used teams of horses as well as motor vehicles. For its Polish campaign of 1939, the Wehrmacht employed draught horses extensively in artillery units, afraid that motor vehicles might find the poor Polish roads too much for them. Yet at the same time the Germans advanced with fourteen motorized and armoured divisions. At this early stage in the war an armoured division had 450 tanks and over 3,000 other motor vehicles. With great courage, but not the least chance of success, the Polish cavalry rode against the panzer units in a gesture that marked the end of an era.

The role of mechanization in the war grew year by year. The mobilization of infantry units and the maintenance of supply lines relied almost exclusively on rail and road transport. The number of goods vehicles at the fronts ran into millions. The most sought-after raw material was crude oil, essential for the manufacture of petrol and diesel fuel.

While motor vehicles had been little more than a curiosity in the First World War, millions of auto-

The Willys Overland Jeep was the unsurpassed vehicle of the Second World War. It was modified many times for a variety of uses.

mobiles and motorcycles became an indispensable part of the war machine between 1939 and 1945. The Harley-Davidson motorcycle was used by the Allies on all fronts. Its strong frame and 750 cc twin-cylinder engine made it an ideal machine for heavy-duty military use.

The real hero of the hour was the jeep. All the armies had lightweight multi-purpose vehicles of this type, such as the German KdF and the Russian GAZ 67, but the one designed by the US company Willys Overland filled the bill so well that its nickname became the general term for small cross-country vehicles. The name 'jeep' was derived from the abbreviation GP, standing for General Purpose vehi-

but were specially designed military hardware. Yet if any vehicle is to be considered the symbol of the Second World War, it must surely be the tank. By then tanks formed part of the equipment of every modern army, and leading automobile manufacturers were closely involved in their development — Fiat in Italy, Renault in France, and Daimler-Benz in Germany.

The German army went to war with many tanks, but the most famous of them was the 55-tonne Tiger, which had 88 mm (3.4 in) cannon and armour plate that was 110 mm (4.3 in) thick in places. The prototypes of proposed German 'supertanks' were, however, largely experimental. The 'Maus', for example, armed with two cannon, 128 mm (5 in) and 75 mm (3 in) in calibre, weighed all of 180 tonnes.

On the Eastern Front in particular, huge tank battles were fought, the like of which had never been seen. At the Battle of Kursk, in July, 1943, there were over 2,000 tanks on each side. The core of the Soviet tank corps was the T34 medium-weight tank, armed with a 76-mm (3 in) (later 85-mm [3.3 in]) cannon and

Bren-carrier,
▲ nicknamed 'maid-of-all-work'.

The 'African version'
of the German Tiger Tank — camouflaged for desert warfare.
▼

two machine-guns. Its V-2 diesel engine developed 368 kW (500 hp), giving it a top speed of around 50 km/h (31 mph). The T34 had a crew of four, and was probably the best tank of the Second World War.

The British army distinguished between infantry tanks, intended to play a supporting role to troops in the field, and battle tanks, designed for mobility and use in separate armoured units. British tanks were notable for their variety and for the fact that they were all inferior in fire-power to those of the enemy. The first British tank that was a match for the German medium-weight 'panzers' was the 28-tonne Cromwell with a 75 mm (3 in) gun, introduced in 1943.

The most numerous tank of all in the Second World War was the American M4, known as the General Sherman. It first saw action in Africa, at the Battle of El Alamein in 1942. The growing esteem in which this type of armament was held is indicated by the fact that in 1940 the American army had a total of only 464 light tanks. In the same year just 300 tanks were produced in the USA. Four years later, American factories were turning out more than 50,000 tanks a year.

The American General Sherman was the most popular tank used in the Second World War and, along with the Soviet middle-weight T34, was one of the Allies' most effective weapons.

Since the Second World War, the development of road transport has taken an immense step forward. Though the overall conception of the road vehicle has remained largely unaltered, individual design features have in many cases undergone a total revolution.

One of the most radical changes affecting the car has been the widespread adoption of the unit construction (monocoque) body. Individual sections of the steel body are pressed on automated production lines at the rate of thousands a day, and these form the basis of the modern mass-produced car.

An important safety feature – disc brakes – began to appear in saloon cars in the first half of the sixties. Disc brakes had been thoroughly tested on racing-cars and sports models, but ever-increasing engine power and improved road-holding made them desirable in mass-produced cars, too.

In 1949 Chrysler introduced a fairly minor modification, but one that has since become a matter of routine for all drivers – operation of the starter from the ignition switch. Another important advance which is now taken for granted arrived in 1950 – the undivided windscreen. In 1954 a Packard was marketed with tubeless tyres, and within six months almost all American manufacturers had taken up the idea.

Many details of interior design also date from the post-war period. Anatomically shaped seating was widely adopted, fan-assisted ventilation was introduced, and Chrysler even started to offer their customers a gramophone built into the dashboard.

Under the bonnet, too, things were changing. These days almost

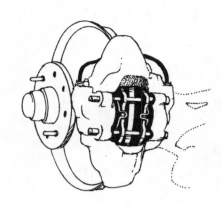

A diagram of disc brakes.

all car engines are of the four-stroke type. The commonest power unit today is the water-cooled four-cylinder engine, though American manufacturers still prefer something bigger, usually an eight-cylinder design. Saloon car petrol engines operate at speeds reaching nearly 6,000 rpm, and those in sports cars may be designed to rev to 8,000 rpm or more. Engine output has risen to between 30 and 40 kW (40–54 hp) per litre capacity.

Electrical equipment has improved enormously, and electronics have arrived on the motoring scene. Transistor or tyristor ignition systems, with impulse-regulated electrical discharges, are commonly used. Dynamos have been replaced by alternators, producing alternat-

The Citroën 2CV was outstanding not only for its affordability but also for its splendid qualities.

On 12th February 1972 the VW broke the production record of the Model T Ford. In all, over 20 million 'beetles' were manufactured.

The principle of operation of the Wankel engine with rotary piston. Induction mixture shown in green, burning mixture in red and exhaust gases in purple.

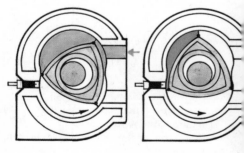

**1965 Citroën DS19 —
perfect suspension,
top speed 150 km/h (93 mph),
consumption 10 litres
for 100 kilometres (27 mpg).**

ing current at a much more efficient rate.

New materials and more precise methods of machining, particularly of moving parts, have now made it possible to mass-produce engines which will run without major repairs, and with a minimum of maintenance, for 120,000 to 150,000 km (75,000 to 93,000 miles). The demands on some engine parts are tremendous. The distributor contacts have to open 440,000 times, the camshaft rotates 110,000 times, the pistons stop and start 220,000 times and the water-pump pumps 5,000 litres (1,100 gal) of coolant — just to drive the average four-cylinder engine 100 km (62 miles)!

In spite of all the improvements which have taken place over the years, the modern car engine remains fundamentally the same type of machine that was being built at the end of the 19th century. Only one significant proposal has ever

been made to replace the inefficient piston-and-crank movement with one which is directly rotary. That was the engine designed by Felix Wankel, which the firm NSU put into production in 1965.

The wide range of vehicles manufactured today includes those with engines at the back and at the front, driving the front wheels or the back, or both, in various combinations. In general, though, what was for decades the accepted design, with a front-mounted engine driving the back wheels, is losing ground today. In the fifties and the sixties it became common, particularly in small cars, to mount the engine at the rear and have it drive the rear wheels. The trend in the seventies and eighties has been towards a more rational approach — to put the engine and gearbox at the front and the drive on the front wheels, too.

The modern car body has to satisfy a number of different demands that are not always easily reconciled. It must be not only serviceable, but also fashionable; it should provide maximum protection in an accident, but should also offer a minimum of wind resistance — i.e. it must be aerodynamic. The trend is therefore towards smoothly sloping back ends, especially with hatchback doors. This type of body gives low drag, roomy interiors, and often a surprising amount of luggage space that is separated from the passenger compartment in many different ways.

At the end of the forties and in the early fifties the main demand in war-worn Europe was for a cheap, economical car. To meet this demand, manufacturers produced not only small 'popular' models, but also various sorts of 'baby' cars

The Fiat 500, the 'hit' of 1957.

Mazda FX7 1985.

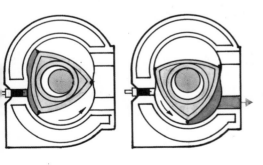

**The Buick Riviera (1985) represents
the classical American concept of the automobile.**

**Lamborghini Countach,
a 12-cylinder car with a top speed
of over 300 km/h (186 mph).**

which could carry two, three or sometimes four people in a modicum of comfort – for short distances, at least. Most of them had air-cooled two-stroke engines with a capacity of up to 400 cc. Three-wheelers, among them memorable 'bubble' cars, were common. Among the best-known were the BMW Isetta and the Glas Gogomobil, which were produced in West Germany from the mid-fifties at the rate of many thousands a year.

Several post-war small cars have earned a place of honour in the history of motoring. The Citroën 2CV of 1948 was a revolutionary design. The original model had a body made of cheap corrugated steel plate, a single headlamp, and an engine that had to be cranked by hand. The four-stroke, two-cylinder, air-cooled engine, with a capacity of 425 cc, had an output of 8.8 kW (12 hp). Though dubbed 'the ugly duckling' and other uncomplimentary nicknames, the 'deux chevaux' became one of the most popular and longest-produced cars in history. A van was also built on the same chassis, and for many years there was also the 'Sahara', an interesting 4 × 4 with two engines – one at the front, the other at the back.

In the second half of the fifties a new small car took to the road, the Fiat 500. Over two million were produced in eight years. The two-cylinder four-stroke engine with a capacity of 479 cc and an output of 9,5 kW (13 hp) was rear-mounted. It gave a top speed of 85 km/h (53 mph), with a consumption of 4.5 l per 100 km (63 mpg). The Fiat 500 incorporated many of the features usually found in larger and more expensive models, such as assisted ventilation and warm-air heating. Part of the roof could be opened.

The greatest success-story ever from the commercial point of view was the Volkswagen 'Beetle'. It was designed by the famous engineer Ferdinand Porsche in the mid-thirties, but the outbreak of war delayed its production. The 'Beetle' was first mass-produced only after the rebuilding of the VW factory in 1948.

1985 model BMW.

The car's body had very advanced aerodynamics. The flat four-cylinder 1,200 cc air-cooled engine was

The Ferrari 308GT with Bertonie bodywork. A 'full-blooded' sports car.

The Vector —
an unusual American design.

rear-mounted. It operated at a low rate of revs, around 3,000, and was both versatile and reliable.

Medium-sized cars such as the Austin A50, the Ford Consul, the Opel Rekord, the Simca 1300 or the Citroën DS19 became popular in the sixties. The DS19 represented a technical departure that set the standard for at least another decade. It differed visibly from the general run of cars in its unusual styling and the wide track of the front wheels. A revolutionary feature was the hydropneumatic suspension, with automatic adjustment of the car's clearance. Pressurized oil was also used to operate the clutch, gear-changing, brakes and steering. The drive was on the front wheels, which were equipped with servo-assisted disc brakes.

In the seventies and eighties a wide choice of cars has been available and innovations have come thick and fast. Most of the major firms offer cars of all types, in order to cover the entire market.

These days Japanese cars have earned a place alongside those of the traditional American and European manufacturers. The three

biggest Japanese firms are Toyota, Honda and Nissan. Their beginnings, however, were very modest indeed. Soichiro Honda, the founder of Honda, began in 1949 by using surplus engines to build primitive mopeds. In a mere eleven years the Honda factory was turning out three quarters of a million motorcycles a year. The first Honda car went on sale in 1964, and within a mere twenty years of starting out the firm was offering strong competition to manufacturers who had been in business for almost a century.

In spite of a trend towards producing smaller cars, American manufacturers continue today much as they have for over fifty years with the production of large vehicles, generally with engines over three litres and a performance to match. Nor are there many striking differences between the models of the different firms.

The situation in Europe is far more complex, and the choice of cars a wider one, in part because of the variety of sports models available.

At this end of the market the Italians are particularly successful, with names like Maserati, Lamborghini and Ferrari, while notable British marques include Jaguar, Lotus and Aston Martin.

The largest firms cannot afford not to offer sports cars, if only for purposes of prestige. Cars which have particularly made a name for themselves include, for example, the Renault Alpine and Gordini, the Fiat-Abarth, and BMW and Porsche models.

The general trend among motor-car manufacturers in the eighties is towards the development of purpose-built models with a high degree of safety, aerodynamic bodies, and high-performance engines that give lower fuel consumption at a time when petrol is increasingly expensive.

One of the greatest problems caused by the spread of motoring has been the harmful effect of exhaust emissions. The first law to control these toxic fumes was passed in California as long ago as 1961. Since then there have been considerable advances in pollution control, but the truly 'clean' engine is still only a designer's dream.

Public transport, too, has changed greatly in the post-war period. Modern buses offer a great deal of passenger comfort. Windows are generous, seats adjustable, and interiors air-conditioned. Long-haul coaches may be equipped not only with a toilet, but even with a kitchen, a bar with refrigerator, and television. Because of its ability to link towns centre-to-centre, the coach can compete in terms of time with aircraft on middle-distance routes.

Luxury long-distance coaches are especially popular in the United States. The famous Greyhound company owns over 6,000 coaches, which criss-cross the continent at motorway speeds of up to 140 km/h (87 mph), often in special lanes. They are noted not only for speed and comfort, but also for safety. According to statistics, the risk of

The modern long-haul coach is particularly designed for comfort.

being killed in a coach is three times less than that of dying in a railway accident and no less than twenty-four times lower than that of being killed in a private car.

In the developed countries at least, the second half of the 20th century has seen the motor-car become something more than just a means of transport. It is not too much of an exaggeration to say that it is with us from the cradle to the grave. Motor vehicles serve all manner of purposes — in commerce, in the health service, in waste disposal; they sweep, sprinkle, put out fires; they transport cranes and mobile platforms, deliver goods to shops — and perform numerous other tasks. Snowploughs and snow-throwers clear blocked roads, and snowmobiles can even drive safely across the Arctic and Antarctic wastes.

Range Rover super-ambulance.

A heavy tractor.

These snowmobiles are a reliable means of transport in the Arctic and the Antarctic.

Heavy goods vehicles have become increasingly large. Today's diesel engines with eight or even twelve cylinders develop up to 300 kW (400 hp), and on a good road can drive even a heavily-laden lorry at a very respectable speed. Heavy vehicles may have either two or three axles, and the rear axle or axles normally have double wheels. The same chassis can usually be fitted with a number of different bodies, according to requirements. Cabs are often of the forward-control type, and can be tilted for access to the engine and gearbox. Many of them are fitted out to a standard not always found in saloon cars.

For short to medium-haul distribution, vans are used. The usual range of payloads is from 1.5 to 3 tonnes. Middleweight lorries carrying 5 to 20 tonnes can exceed speeds of 100 km/h (62 mph).

Today's kings of the road are the heavyweight lorries, nicknamed 'juggernauts', whose bodies are adapted to the type of goods to be carried. The most common system is the articulated lorry with a separate tractor attached to a trailer. 'Artic' tractors have a very short chassis with a beam over the rear axle carrying the revolving joint for the front end of the trailer, which has rear wheels only. Thus a single tractor may tow any number of different trailers. Some of the heavier-duty tractors have four or six-wheel drive.

The biggest lorries of all are giant tippers designed mainly for off-road work, especially on large building-sites and in mining minerals. They have payloads of up to 120 tonnes. The steel box for the load usually has an extension over the driver's cab to protect him from flying stones and the like during loading. These giants may have tyre diameters of up to three and a half metres. The biggest vehicle of this type in the world is the Terex Titan, with a 2,800 kW (3,800 hp) diesel-electric power unit. It has a payload of 350 tonnes, and the driver's cab is five m (16 ft) above the ground.

Exceptionally heavy loads are transported on multi-wheeled low-loaders drawn by tractors. These are capable of carrying items weighing up to about 500 tonnes.

Even heavy lorries can have an exclusive design. This prototype was created by Colani.

The Honda CVX 1000 is one
of today's leading motorcycles.

In the late 20th century, the bicycle and the motorcycle play quite different roles in different parts of the world. In the developing countries they are highly-prized means of transport, while in the industrialized countries they are mainly used for sport and recreation. The humble bicycle in particular is enjoying a comeback in our over-technological, noisy and polluted world.

The velocipede from the turn of the century has in effect come down to us almost unaltered. Thanks to the use of new materials, its weight has fallen to a mere 6 to 8 kg (13 to 17 lb), and modern gear systems give from three to ten gears, thus easing the way on hills and increasing the speed attainable on the flat. Folding cycles have become very popular, being easy to transport by car or public transport to places suitable for cycling.

Among the young in particular, there is a liking for bicycles with an auxiliary engine — mopeds and minimopeds. They are ideal for travelling to school, or going shopping, for example. Most of them can be driven without a licence, and they are simple to operate and maintain.

Touring motorcycles usually have an engine size of between 250 and 500 cc. They mostly have four-stroke engines developing around 22 kW (30 hp), with a consumption of some 4 l per 100 km (70 mpg). Motorcycles in this category are capable of travelling up to 150 km/h (93 mph).

A special type of motorcycle which enjoyed popularity in the fifties and sixties was the motor-scooter. These low-capacity motorcycles were especially suitable for town transport. They had smaller wheels than motorcycles, and a 'floor' to protect the rider from road grime. The motor-scooter had its origins in 1911, in the form of the Scott lady's motorcycle. In the period between the wars, one of those who specialized in scooter

The scooter is ideal for town use.
The illustration shows the Italian Vespa.

The motorcycle is being used more and more as a sporting vehicle as can be seen in these three pictures.

5 sec for 0−100 km/h (0−60 mph). Prices tend to be just as breathtaking.

The seventies and eighties have seen the Japanese reach the top of the league in motorcycle sales, and they now produce around two-thirds of all the world's machines. The four largest Japanese firms alone — Honda, Kawasaki, Suzuki and Yamaha — make over 10 million bikes a year.

The star attraction of the 1980s so far has been the Honda CVX 1000, with a water-cooled six-cylinder engine. It has 24 valves and an output of about 95 kW (127 hp) at 10,000 rpm. The machine also features numerous electronic devices, such as an anti-lock control on the brakes and a multi-purpose dashboard computer.

Motorcycles are often used for racing. There are not only road and track events, but also scrambling, dirt-track and ice racing, steep hill-climbs, and all manner of other events. Motorcycles can go extremely fast, too, as Don Vesco demonstrated in 1974 when, riding a twin-engined Yamaha, he reached a record speed of 450.73 km/h (280 mph).

construction was the Italian designer Trossi, working in association with the famous coachwork designer Pininfarina. They are said to have been inspired by the mini-motorcycles used by British paratroopers.

Recently, very sophisticated motor-bikes have been produced. Cubic capacities have increased from 500 cc to 1,000 cc, giving motorway speeds of up to 230 km/h (140 mph). These machines can weigh as much as 300 kg (660 lb) and have acceleration in the order of

Formula 1 hero, Niki Lauda, at the wheel of a McLaren.

'Races are useful because they speed up technical progress,' said the great Enzo Ferrari, founder of one of the most famous racing marques of all. It is on the racetrack that new ideas are tested, not only engine design but also tyres, brakes and other components, before they are considered for adoption in production models.

After the Second World War all sorts of vehicles took part in motor races. The first post-war race in Europe was held as soon as September 9, 1945, in the Bois de Boulogne in Paris. At first races were held for cars of many different formulae, as decided by the many different organizers. In an attempt to bring some order into the business of racing, in 1950 the Fédération Internationale de l'Automobile laid down the rules for the world championship, allowing only cars with a certain engine capacity to enter races.

In motor racing the greatest glamour attaches to Formula 1. The rules for this class allow engines with a capacity of up to three litres, or, more common nowadays, supercharged engines up to half that size. It was in these superfast racers that the successors to the pre-war racing heroes rose to fame.

In the fifties and sixties the big names were Juan Manuel Fangio, five times world champion, Mike Hawthorn, Stirling Moss, Jack Brabham, Jim Clark, John Surtees and many others. In the seventies and eighties there came Jackie Stewart, Jochen Rindt, Emerson Fittipaldi, Mario Andretti, Jody Scheckter, Nelson Piquet, Gilles Villeneuve, and perhaps the greatest of the present generation, Niki Lauda.

The classic marques of Alfa Romeo, Mercedes and Maserati were replaced by Lotus, Tyrrell, McLaren, Brabham and Williams. Through all the years, however, the most constant star in the galaxy of the fastest cars on earth has been the 'rearing horse', Ferrari.

Though Formula 1 cars are the ones that catch the public eye, they have very little in common with the cars most people drive. Nevertheless, there are numerous competitions in which production cars, in a modified form, compete against each other. On ordinary roads, sometimes through normal traffic — these cars are the successors of those pioneers from the turn of the century which raced in stages from St. Petersburg to Paris, or even from Peking to Paris. The most famous

contest of this kind is the Monte Carlo Rally, which tests cars and crews alike.

Between the wars a new world land-speed record was set by Sir Malcolm Campbell. More than thirty years later, in 1964, his son Donald broke the record with a speed of 648.709 km/h (403.107 mph). Donald Campbell was the last Briton to hold the record. After that speed records became almost exclusively the domain of Americans. The fastest of these, Gary Gabelich, reached the amazing speed of 1,001.670 km/h (622.437 mph) in his rocket-powered 'Blue Flame' in October, 1970. The thousand-kilometre-an-hour barrier had been broken and for thirteen years the record stood.

The British were not idle, however. In 1974, Londoner Richard Noble, then twenty-eight, began making preparations to have a crack at the record. Noble had never raced before. He had had no experience of high speeds, but did not lack courage. His vehicle 'Thrust II', designed by John Ackroyd, was driven by a Rolls-Royce Avon 302 jet-fighter engine. After modification, the consumption of aircraft kerosene was 220 l (48 gal) a minute! The main way of stopping the 'car' was by

A Lancia Stratos
on the Monte Carlo Rally Circuit.

means of parachutes, the brakes being effective only at speeds under 200 km/h (124 mph). In trials on aerodromes at around 400 km/h (248 mph), Noble used Dunlop aircraft tyres. For the actual record attempt on a dry lake bed the vehicle was shod with aluminium alloy, since a blowout at the speeds he was hoping to achieve would have been a disaster.

The first attempts, on the Bonneville salt flats in Utah were foiled by a sudden snowfall, and a year later Noble's attempt was frustrated by rain. It was not until October, 1983, at Black Rocks in the Nevada Desert, that Noble attained a speed of 1,005.5 km/h (624.81 mph) in one direction, and 1,033 km/h (641.9 mph) in the other, to give him an average of 1,019.25 km/h (633.35 mph). He had taken the record.

Eighty-five years had elapsed since Count Gaston de Chasseloup-Laubat had reached the dizzy speed of just over 63 km/h (39 mph) in 1898. And one thing is certain — the contest is not over yet.

▲
A rally car in the Paris-Dakar Rally — one of the most difficult competitions in the world.

One-time world record holder, *Thrust II*.

**Road systems are becoming
increasingly complex.**

In some areas modern roads pass through tunnels. For the most part, tunnels are much more recent than bridges, though there are notable exceptions. Historians claim that around 2170 B.C. the Babylonians made a tunnel over 900 m (2,950 ft) long under the River Euphrates, for both riders and vehicles. The tunnel constructed by the Romans in 36 B.C. to connect Naples and Pozzuoli is said to have been almost 1 km (over half a mile) long.

True road tunnels, however, were first built in connection with motor traffic. The most famous are the tunnels through the Alps of Europe. These allow hundreds of thousands of motorists a year to cross the

On the Autostrada del Sol, Spain.

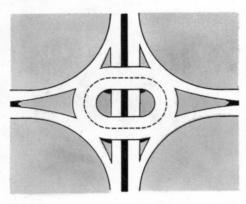

**Different motorway intersections
including the 'cloverleaf' system (bottom).**

The first roads to be built to modern-day standards were made shortly before the First World War in Germany and the United States. The first motorway, in the sense of a road reserved for motor traffic and with split-level intersections, was built in Italy in 1925 and linked the city of Milan with the Alpine lakes. A feature typical of today's motorways, the central barrier or reserve, first appeared on German autobahns, beginning with that from Frankfurt to Darmstadt, completed in 1935. By the outbreak of the Second World War over 2,000 km (1,200 miles) of motorways had been built in Germany, and almost 2,500 km (1,550 miles) more were under construction.

The first few hundred kilometres of American motorway appeared at about the same time, in the nineteen-thirties. The post-war 'expressways' had, in places where traffic was especially heavy, up to fourteen lanes. Fire-services, the police, ambulances and long-distance coaches often have lanes reserved for their exclusive use.

mountains quickly without having to crawl up winding passes which are often difficult to negotiate. They include the longest road tunnels in the world. That which leads through Europe's highest mountain, Mont Blanc, between France and Italy, is 11.6 km (7.2 km) long, while the St. Gotthard tunnel in Switzerland measures all of 16.3 km (10 miles).

The first modern road tunnel beneath water was that dug in 1927 between New York and New Jersey, to relieve traffic congestion on the bridges. The first British road tunnel was the Mersey tunnel, opened in 1934, which was almost three and a half kilometres long. Perhaps the most discussed tunnel of this type is

Some roadsigns. Without these, transport would be chaotic.

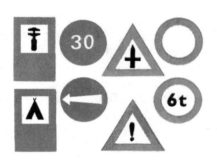

the often-planned, several times started, but as yet theoretical Channel tunnel.

The building of motorways and complex junctions relies on the construction of all manner of flyovers and bridges. The longest steel-arch suspension bridge in the world is Sydney Harbour Bridge in Australia. Though it was built in 1932, its 503 m (1,650 ft) span has never been exceeded. Fifty-two metres above the bay, it carries an eight-lane highway, two railway lines and a footpath.

Among other giant bridges is the Humber Bridge in Britain, whose 1,410 m (4,626 ft) suspension span is the longest in the world. The Bosphorus, too, is easier to cross today than it was for King Darius I in the fifth century B.C. It is spanned by the 1,600 m (5,250 ft) Atatürk Bridge, linking Europe and Asia with a six-lane roadway that carries 20,000 vehicles a day.

The twin mottoes of today's road-builders are speed and safety.

Many large cities now have underpasses and fly-overs.

Motorway intersections are constructed in such a way as to minimize the possibility of collisions, the paths of vehicles never actually crossing each other. The classic design is the 'cloverleaf' junction. Strategic sections of roadway are electrically heated to prevent ice from forming, and intersections and long stretches of road are illuminated.

Other modern main roads also have systems of signs and signals to help the driver. Apart from the usual fixed roadsigns, there are signals to warn of fog and ice, to set recommended or compulsory speed limits according to prevailing conditions, to indicate the closure of lanes and so on. Such signals are either actuated automatically by sensors, or are centrally controlled from switchboards. On major roads in most countries drivers are able to contact the police or emergency services by means of roadside telephones. A driver whose car is equipped with a telephone does not even need to get out of his vehicle. Some sophisticated traffic systems can keep drivers informed about the situation up ahead.

Throughout the development of the car, there have always been some extraordinary models.

The road to technical progress is anything but straight. There are many turnings along it, some of them short cuts, but most of them cul-de-sacs. The desire to come up with something new sometimes leads the inventor astray, gives birth to fantastic devices, weird 'discoveries', and patents relating to the most unlikely contrivances.

From time to time relatively advanced machines have been brushed aside, remaining objects of curiosity simply because they were ahead of their time. Some of these inventions may yet get their chance.

Predicting the future is a tricky business. It is useful to keep in mind the example of a certain physics professor at London University, in 1842, who asserted that the idea of regular steamer services on the high seas was about as fantastic as visiting the Moon. Almost a century and a half later he was, of course, right in principle, though in fact history had proved him wrong on both counts. To avoid the danger of repeating the learned man's error, let us try to predict a mere ten or twenty years ahead, and even then we shall reserve the right to be wrong.

What sort of transport can we expect in the future? Well, for one thing, it seems likely that public transport will take over some of the functions performed by the private car. Public transport is more efficient, it can make much better use of high technology, and it is less detrimental to the environment. Buses often have reserved lanes, which makes them faster than cars. The introduction of automatic drivers is possible, with the required signals being transmitted through underground cables. For urban and suburban transport in particular, buses may soon be powered by electricity or liquid gas.

The motor-car will certainly survive the year 2000, though it will probably get lighter and more streamlined, in order to save fuel. At the turn of the century cars are still likely to have petrol or oil-burning piston engines, but the application of microelectronics to such areas as ignition regulation is likely to reduce fuel consumption, and increase the 'cleanness' of engines.

On-board microprocessors may

Metamorphosis 1: car — submarine.

Metamorphosis 2: car — orange.

A dragster.

well make the life of future drivers a good deal easier. They are capable of creating optimum running conditions for the engine in different situations, automatically operating the lights according to visibility, the air-conditioning according to changes inside the car, or the wipers according to the state of the windscreen, and so on. Such computers can monitor the most important working parts of the car, and warn the driver if anything goes wrong. They may give the driver access to external information systems, thus helping him to avoid dangerous situations. In conjunction with radar, they might, for instance, automatically avoid a collision with the car in front, and given a corres-ponding sophistication of the road network, could even function as an 'automatic pilot', driving the car according to a pre-programmed system of coordinates.

Though it seems that the internal-combustion piston engine is not yet due for retirement, we may soon see the appearance of an improved version of the Wankel engine, and among goods vehicles combustion turbines will certainly find a place.

The problem of air pollution, and the inevitable exhaustion, sooner or later, of petroleum deposits are leading designers to look for new fuels for existing engines, and a new type of engine altogether. The most promising experiments to date have been with modern steam engines,

A vehicle with a huge appetite!

and with modifications of the Stirling engine, originally patented in 1816. So perhaps the future of the motor-car lies in its past...

Amphibian — a flying car or a land aircraft?

Index

numbers in italics refer to captions

Rail TRANSPORT

Before there was any such thing as a steam locomotive or electric power, horses' hooves had started to beat out between the rails the rhythm of the incoming century – the 19th. But not even the simplest of rails came into the world just like that: they were the result of generations of experiment and the handing down of the fruits of human ingenuity.

The first step was the realization that loads are easier to move along on a smooth surface. The Roman historian Pliny described how the Egyptians had stone causeways laid to make it easier for slaves to roll along the boulders used to build the pyramids. The ancient Greeks, too, had a way of improving their transport system. Access to their temples was by means of a network of roads leading along the side of gorges, which had rail-like grooves for the wheels of carts. The 'gauge' of these tracks was standard throughout central Greece, corresponding to the distance between cart wheels. Since trading centres grew up in the vicinity of temples, and traffic became very heavy, 'points' were established at certain places to allow traders to pass each other without having to worry about right of way on these single-lane tracks.

In the Middle Ages, Sebastian Münster wrote an account of what he had 'seen and not just heard of, visited and examined' on his journeys. This included a description of a visit to a mine at Leberthal in Alsace. Among other items of interest he recorded how the miners laid planks down to help them move their tubs of minerals out of the shafts. He was so taken with this system that he even drew a picture of it. Wooden 'rails' became widespread in Germany and England, and before long they were not confined to the mines themselves, similar tracks being laid between mines and docks.

In 1602 a Northumberland carpenter called Beaumont used crossbeams or sleepers to join together

Evidence exists to show that people in ancient times made efforts to use rail transport.

the planks which formed the track. In this way he prevented the planks from sinking into the mud and made them less likely to split. Additionally, of course, sleepers kept the track in place under the heavy wheels of the coal wagons. A similar improved system was used to lay a track between the Walton Hall coal mine and docks on the River Trent.

A medieval mining tub on wooden rails.

Since horses were used there to draw the wagons, this became the first horse railway running between two places.

Wooden rails tended to rot quickly in the damp conditions of mine tunnels, so they were later reinforced with strips of iron. Brittle cast-iron rails were introduced before the end of the 18th century. In

1776 B. Curr used rails with a raised flange along the inside edge, laying them on sleepers.

Up to this point such railways were available for a fee to anyone who had his own horses and suitable wagons. Then Englishman William Jessop replaced the flat L-shaped rail with one having a tall, mushroom-shaped side, designed for use with flanged wheels, which kept the wagons from falling off the track. They were the first railway wheels specially designed to suit the rails, which were laid on a series of stone blocks.

With the replacement of wooden tracks by metal rails, the modern railway line was beginning to take shape, but there were still many refinements to be made. So, for instance, in 1803 an engineer called Nixon was the first to use wrought-iron rails, and in 1820 John Berkinshaw took out a patent on rolled ones. American John Stevens came up with a successful design for the shape of rails, comprising a broad base and a mushroom-shaped head, joined by a narrow web. It was this advance that enabled steam engines to be used for rail traction. It had become clear that rail design had to keep pace with progress in

Wooden rails were replaced by more durable cast-iron ones.

the construction of locomotives. Even the earliest locomotives, which were so light that their wheels tended to skid on the smooth surface of the track, caused cast-iron rails to crack. One of the reasons for George Stephenson's success was that he turned his attention to the subject of tracks as well as of locomotives: he modified the way they were laid on the sleepers, and used rails made exclusively of wrought iron. Stephenson also

introduced the world's most widely used track gauge — 1,435 mm (4 ft 8½ in). He is said to have arrived at this figure by virtue of a regulation which stated that wagons were not to exceed 1,524 mm (5 ft) in width, to ensure that they might pass through the gateways of fortified cities. Stephenson's gauge became statutory in Britain, and thanks to the international success of British locomotives spread to many countries.

Evolution of rails. From left to right:
1776 Curr's rails (a); 1798 Jessop's rails (b);
1830 Dosh and Stephenson's rails (c);
1858 rails used in France (d); rails of today (e, f).

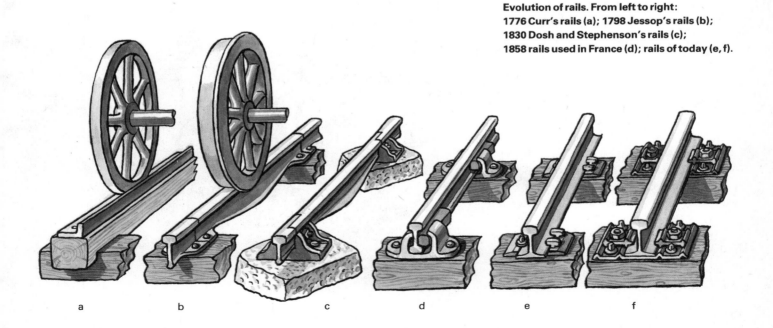

a   b   c   d   e   f

In 1801 the British Parliament granted a concession to operate the first public horse railway, running between the towns of Croydon and Wandsworth. The line was not only used to transport coal: it was available, for a fee, to all who wished to drive their wagons along it. The British example was copied throughout the world. This was hardly surprising, since trials had confirmed that a horse was capable of pulling a load about 10 times greater along rails than it could on a good road surface.

The first major horse railway in Europe was that between Linz in Austria and České Budějovice, now in Czechoslovakia. It was intended to form a link between the Danube and the Vltava (Moldau), a tributary of the Elbe, thus completing an important trade route linking the North Sea with the Black Sea. Originally, the Prague Hydrographic Society had wanted to dig a canal, but influenced by the success attained in Britain with horse railways, Dr. Josef Gerstner proposed a similar alternative. That was in 1808. Twenty years later his son František Antonín, a talented engineer, started work on the scheme.

The story of the line's construction is an interesting one. Before work began, František travelled to England to gain experience. He was particularly anxious to see how natural obstacles were overcome, since the line from Budějovice had, right from the start, to overcome a difference in altitude of 328 m (1,076 ft) over a constant gradient of up to 8.3 : 1000. He was surprised to find that in Britain the wagons were drawn by horses only on level ground. They were unharnessed at the top and bottom of hills, and the wagons were then transported using a special lift. In the case of two-way traffic there was a cable running through a pulley at the top of the hill, and the weight of the descending wagons hauled others up. Where there was uphill traffic only, power was provided either by

The most frequent freight on the České Budějovice—Linz horse-drawn railway was barrels of salt.

a steam engine or by means of a water wheel.

Gerstner was convinced he could do without such aids, and he was right. It was necessary to make higher embankments and deeper cuttings, but he managed to build a track without mechanical aids. Gerstner worked on the principle that 'an iron road must not avoid ravines and depressions, but cross them, if possible in a straight line, and once it has gained height must not lose it again'. It was a principle that proved extremely sound in the building of further railways throughout the world.

While in England, Gerstner learned a great deal about railways using locomotive traction, which he believed to have a great future. He wanted his horse railway to have

Passenger transport on a horse-drawn railway.

a track strong enough to be able to carry steam engines at a later date, but he met opposition from shareholders, who were interested in building as cheaply as possible. When the company got into financial difficulties Gerstner was forced to give way to their demands. The engineer was proved right in the end, however, although only after his death. That part of the track he had built was used for steam traction without modification, while the remainder had to be rebuilt at great expense, but not until 1873. Up until then the sound of horses' hooves continued to echo along the Linz—Budějovice line, long after steam locos had taken over elsewhere.

In an effort to cut costs, the shareholders even tried to replace the horses with oxen — probably the only experiment of its kind ever made. This penny-pinching scheme was quite unsuccessful, as is made clear by the following extract from an 82-page report: 'The ox is naturally unreceptive and slow to learn. Its gait is uncertain, clumsy and impossible to control. It is frequently startled by trivial acts on the part of passers-by, or by umbrellas, and often leaves the track when so startled.'

Work on the České Budějovice—Linz railway was carried out from

The Haselgraben viaduct was one of the great structures of the České Budějovice—Linz horse-drawn railway system.

1825 to 1832, when a regular goods service and a less frequent passenger service got under way. At times there were 6,000 labourers and 1,000 horses working on the line, and its construction was no easy task. Not only did the route lead through mountainous terrain, but the inhabitants of villages along the way hampered the surveyors in their work, and the ranks of the protesters were swelled by postmasters, cabmen, and the landlords of wayside inns on the little-used road. A total of 75 bridges was required, and cuttings and embankments were frequently needed because of the undulating countryside through which the line passed.

The most important freight carried was salt. Passenger trains ran once a day in each direction, except in the winter months. The 1852 timetable shows that trains were scheduled to leave each terminus at 5 a.m. from April 1 to October 31, arriving at their destination between 11 and 12 hours later.

Diagrams to show the difference between the routes of the road *(top)* and the horse-drawn railway *(bottom)* from České Budějovice (in today's Czechoslovakia) to Linz in Austria.

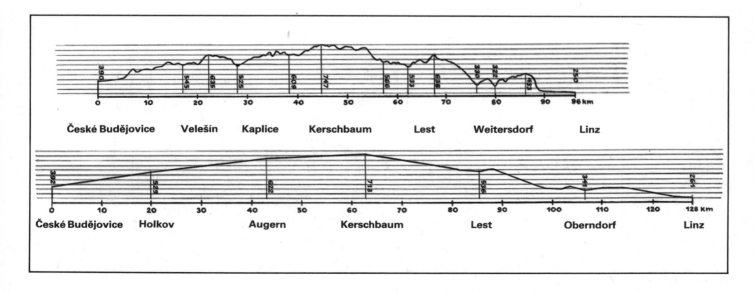

At the start of the 19th century, steam was king. It drove factory machinery and powered ships, and steam vehicles were beginning to appear on roads. It was just a matter of time before it came to the railways.

The historic moment arrived in 1804, when Richard Trevithick's locomotive set off from Pen-y-dar-ran in south Wales pulling five wagons with 10 tonnes of freight and 70 passengers. It covered the 14 km (9 mile) stretch of track in four hours, although in places it reached a speed of 8 km/h (5 mph).

Trevithick's engine − known as a 'tramwagon' − was not a practical success. Although too heavy for the cast-iron rails then current, which cracked beneath its weight, it was too light to provide sufficient traction for hauling heavy loads. So in 1808 the inventor rented a small area of land in London where he laid a loop of rail. His locomotive drove round and round, pulling a small carriage at about 32 km/h (20 mph), and passengers were charged a shilling a ride. A potentially revolutionary invention had degenerated into a fairground amusement. Yet the rails were not even adequate to this relatively light use, and after a number of failed experiments Trevithick died in poverty in 1833. Only a collection organized by friends and workmates saved him from burial in a pauper's grave.

Trevithick, however, showed the way for others. Convinced that locomotives must slip on smooth rails, engineer Matthew Murray and John Blenkinsop, supervisor at a pit in Middleton, devised an engine for use in mines which had a toothed wheel engaged in a toothed rod which ran alongside the rails; but the most curious solution to the problem of traction was that adopted by an inventor called Bruton. He fitted his engine with a system of steam-driven levers which drove it along by thrusting against the ground. His experiment was, however, brought to an untimely

The steam engine *Pen-y-darran*, built by Richard Trevithick in 1804.

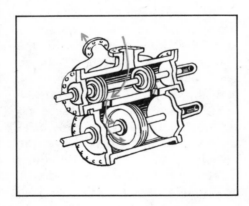

Cross-section of a steam locomotive.

A diagram showing the inside of a steam roller. ▼

end when the locomotive's boiler exploded as it was about to make its first trial run.

It was William Hedley, engineer at the Wylam mine near Newcastle, who was finally successful in

William Hedley's *Puffing Billy*, **built in 1815.**

George Stephenson's locomotive
with chain drive for the Killingworth line.

getting smooth wheels to run along smooth tracks. He built the first really powerful locomotive, which was in service for nearly 50 years before finding a place in the Science Museum in London in 1862. Because of the noisy emissions of steam from its tall chimney, the engine was nicknamed 'Puffing Billy'. It had four axles and eight coupled driving wheels.

As Hedley's engine was taking to the rails, perhaps the most famous figure in the history of rail transport was entering the scene – George Stephenson. His locomotives, which he constantly improved, laid the foundations for the development of railways throughout the world.

Stephenson' father was a stoker at the Wylam coal mine. Instead of going to school, young George helped to earn the family's daily bread. First he worked as a cowherd, later becoming a stoker's mate himself. It is said that he did not learn to read and write until he was 15, but by the age of 17 he had become supervisor of the machinery for which his father stoked the boiler. He soon attracted attention

through ingenious repairs he made to the engines in the pit, and he was subsequently appointed chief mechanic at Killingworth pit.

There, in 1814, he built his first locomotive. Its design was not very different from that of Hedley's 'Puffing Billy'. At first it was named 'Mylord' but was later re-christened 'Blücher', in honour of the famous general and victor over Napoleon at the Battle of Waterloo.

Stephenson went from strength to strength and when, on September 27, 1825 the Stockton and Darlington Railway was opened with great ceremony, his latest engine, 'Locomotion', hauled a train consisting of 12 wagons loaded with coal and flour, an adapted stage-coach named 'Experiment', in which the officials of the railway travelled, and a further 21 goods wagons fitted with benches and carrying 450 passengers. This train, consisting of 33 wagons and a 'carriage', attained speeds of around 19 km/h (12 mph) in places. By this time Stephenson had started his own business in Newcastle and had begun to manufacture his own locomotives.

J. Blenkinsop's toothed wheel
locomotive, built in 1811.

The Rainhill line with locomotives ready to race. From left to right:
Perseverance, Novelty, Sans Pareil **and** *Rocket.*

The steam engine had revolutionized industrial production, and as more and more goods were produced, so the demand grew for the transportation of both raw materials and finished products. It was natural that this growing need should be felt most keenly in the land where the industrial revolution had begun, in England.

The traffic in goods and materials between the port of Liverpool, linking Britain with the outside world, and Manchester, a giant among industrial cities, became so great that traditional forms of transport were unable to cope. When the canals froze over in winter, or a summer drought meant there was not enough water for them to be navigable, road carriers had to be used, but it took them almost as long to get cotton from the Liverpool docks to the factories of Manchester as it took the clippers to ship it from the United States. Steam had

set the mills rolling, and steam was destined to deliver the goods.

When the Stockton and Darlington Railway was opened, it seemed that the nation's transport problems were close to being solved, but the spread of the railways turned out to be more of a social headache than a technical one. Locomotives had to blaze a trail through people's fears and prejudices.

Work on a new railway line between Manchester and Liverpool met with fierce opposition. The farmers across whose lands the tracks were to be laid defended their property with pitchforks and hoes. More than once, clashes with surveyors resulted in damage to expensive surveying instruments. Although the new line had received parliamentary approval, it did not guarantee a smooth run for the builders. Just as the farmers resisted the encroachment of the railway, so the shareholders of the

canal and road transport companies fought tooth and nail to protect their business interests. Bitter protests were voiced in the newspapers, and Stephenson was dubbed a madman for maintaining that rail travel using steam locomotives would achieve 20 times the speed of the fastest coach and horses. Opponents of the new form of transport alleged that the railway would have to cross important roads in several places, that traffic would be disrupted, that steam boilers were a danger to life and limb, liable to explode at any time, that locomotives would frighten horses, that cows would cease to give milk, that smoke would poison the air, birds fall lifeless to the ground and crops wither and die. In the first round of negotiations, the proposal to use locomotives was rejected, but the second time around, after very hard bargaining, the railway builders managed to get approval for their

tonnes at a speed of 21.5 km/h (13.5 mph); then it reached a speed of 46 km/h (29 mph) pulling a wagon with 36 passengers, after which the victorious locomotive set up a new speed record of 56 km/h (35 mph) on its own.

Less than a year later, on 15 September, 1830, just before 11 a.m., eight trains stood in front of the new wooden engine shed waiting for the Liverpool and Manchester Railway to be officially opened. They were all pulled by shiny new Stephenson locomotives.

The guests of honour, chief among them the Duke of Wellington, climbed into their own carriages, loaded on to goods wagons for the occasion, and set off along the technically demanding route, which encompassed 63 bridges, several viaducts and a tunnel 2.4 km (1½ miles) long.

Both the Rainhill races and the ceremonial opening of the Liverpool—Manchester line represented important victories for rail travel. From then on railways spread rapidly in many countries of the world. In 1841 the first international line was opened, linking Strasbourg and Basel, and by the time Stephenson died, on 12 August, 1848, at the age of 67, Britain had more than 9,600 km (6,000 miles) of railway track, which were largely the domain of his locomotives.

scheme, including the introduction of steam traction.

Although George Stephenson was appointed chief engineer for the construction of the new railway, this did not automatically mean that his engines would be chosen for it. First he had to take part in a competition. The competing locomotives assembled on the Liverpool line near Rainhill in October 1829. In addition to Stephenson's *Rocket* there was Braithwaite and Ericsson's *Novelty,* Hackworth's *Sans Pareil,* and Burstall's *Perseverance.* A further entry, a locomotive powered by horses hidden inside it and turning the wheels by running on a continuous belt, was disqualified before the start.

A large crowd gathered to watch the race. Woman spectators sat in grandstands erected at a safe distance, while men were allowed to observe the dangerous machines at close quarters. The first day had

been devoted to an inspection of the locomotives to make sure they met the conditions laid down.

October 8 was the day the actual races were held, with prize money of £500 for the winner. Stephenson's *Rocket* won hands down. First it drew a train weighing 19.4

The most successful of R. Stephenson's locomotives, *Patentee,* was used in many countries.

In the United States, steam was slower in coming to the railways. While the Americans were still making their first rather diffident experiments, reports arrived from across the ocean of the success enjoyed by British locomotives. So in 1828 the Delaware and Hudson Canal Company sent engineer Horatio Allen to England to buy four locomotives and ship them back to the USA. He acquired the first of these, christened 'America', from Stephenson. The other three were purchased from the firm of Foster, Rastrick and company in Stourbridge, which is how one of them came to be named 'The Stourbridge Lion'. American tracks proved inadequate to the demands of steam engines, however. Then in 1830 a domestic invention called 'Tom Thumb' appeared, consisting of a steam engine mounted on a flat wagon. It was a small locomotive with a very small output. Indeed, when it competed with a horse over a 14.5 km (9 mile) stretch of track, it lost.

In 1830 the locomotive 'Best Friend of Charleston' opened a regular service between Charleston and Amboy in South Carolina, but a year later the engine's boiler blew up and an improved version had to be introduced. In 1835 in Baltimore, the locomotive 'Columbus' was unveiled. It had a vertical boiler and pistons. The driver rode on a platform at the front, while the fireman was behind the boiler. Similar engines were built in Germany, but they did not come up to scratch in either country.

In spite of their slow start the Americans soon met with success, and steam engines enjoyed a period of expansion in the New World unmatched by that in the Old. Much of the credit was due to the Baldwin locomotive works in Philadelphia. Matthias William Baldwin began business life as a jeweller and moved on to the manufacture of book-binding tools, but at the end of it all he turned out to have a talent for locomotive design. It took his

The locomotive *Atlantic*. Built in 1832, it was one of the types running in the USA with a vertical boiler.

factory about 30 years to make its first thousand engines, but only seven to produce the next thousand. By the end of the century it was turning out 1,000 a year, and had a workforce of 5,000. Such figures give some indication of the

up to three times the steam pressure of their European counterparts, but the main improvement in design was the placing of pistons. British locomotives had their pistons under the boiler, between the wheels, where access was difficult and a cranked axle was needed to transmit power to the driving wheels. The Americans came up with the idea of putting pistons and connecting rods on the outside of the wheels, a feature which became universal in locomotive design during the 1870s. The idea of providing drivers and firemen with a covered footplate also originated in the United States. The one feature that remained uniquely characteristic of transatlantic 'railroad' engines was the broad 'cowcatcher', which was designed to sweep aside obstacles on the track.

The United States needed railways if anyone did. After all, there were huge areas to be settled and served, and there was not the age-old road network Europeans had grown used to. None the less, rail travel swept through one country after another. In 1832 regular services began on the St. Étienne—Lyons route in France. In 1835 wagons carrying the coaches of the rich rolled into the Belgian capital, Brussels. In August 1837 the Queen of France herself was among the passengers on the first train from Paris to Saint-Germain. Three months later the first Austrian train made the 13 km (8 mile) trip from Florisdorf on the outskirts of Vienna to Wagram. By the following January the line ran as far as central Vienna, and on the day of its inauguration a certain Herr Weissenberger opened Austria's first station restaurant at Wagram. In October the same year the railway came to Russia, with the opening of a line from St. Petersburg (today's Leningrad). The Czar ordered the locomotive to be fitted with a musical device that reproduced the sound of blaring horns and trombones to announce the train's approach.

The locomotive *Lafayette*,
built in 1837 by William Norris
for the Baltimore and Ohio Railroad, USA.

The locomotive *Rhein*, made in Baden in 1847
for the North Swiss Railway.

rate at which rail transport expanded in the United States.

Once it had got off the ground, American steam engine design made a major contribution to world-wide progress. Right from the start Baldwin's locomotives had

A goods train (above) and
a passenger train (opposite)
on the Liverpool—Manchester line.

As locomotive design improved, so rolling stock became better adapted to the purposes it served. The first passengers on the Austrian railways had four classes to choose from. The black and yellow first class carriages were completely enclosed, with glazed windows and upholstered seating for 18. Passengers in the second class sat 24 to each carriage, which had leather curtains instead of window panes. Up to 32 passengers had to squeeze into the wooden benches of the third class, where the carriage roof was supported by poles and the sides were either open or, in bad weather, protected by canvas sheets. Fourth class 'carriages' were entirely open to the elements, and no seating was provided at all. The harsh winter of 1841 drew attention to the inadequacy of such Spartan facilities, and this class was discontinued, although it was reintroduced in an improved form on the North Austrian Railway in 1848.

Early European railway cars had two axles and their interiors retained many of the design features of contemporary road carriages. There was no corridor, compartments being divided by bulkheads, with separate doors at the side. Wooden steps running the length of

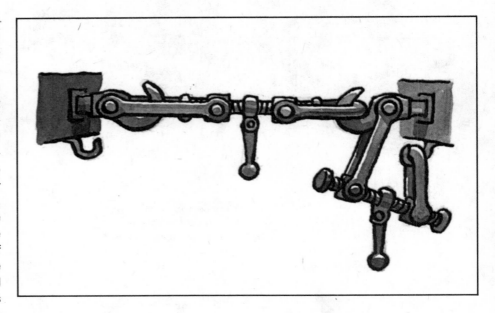

the carriage facilitated the business of getting on and off the train, and were used by conductors for moving from one compartment to the next while the train was in motion. Later the American style of carriage was adopted in Europe, with comfortable seating in all classes, arranged lengthwise along a central aisle.

One of the factors affecting both safety and comfort was the manner of coupling carriages together. Initially, buffers consisted of longitudinal wooden beams padded with

horsehair and covered with leather. Carriages were coupled by means of chains, and the hooks for them were attached to the carriages' end walls. The system did little to improve the smoothness of the ride.

Carriage lighting also has a history of its own. From 1843 first and second class carriages on Austrian railways were illuminated by candles in metal holders. Paraffin lamps were later introduced, but these were prohibited on all but the Austrian and German railways. In Britain gas lighting was gradually

Present-day means of coupling railway wagons: the screw coupling (opposite) and the automatic coupling (below).
▼

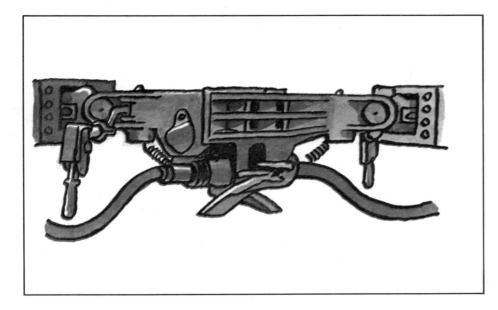

introduced. The gas was contained in rubber bags on the roofs of carriages. In 1867 a man named Pintsch in Berlin invented a device for producing gas from used oil, and carriages with this form of lighting had a series of small chimneys along the roof. Following early failures in the attempt to use electric lighting powered by a central dynamo in the locomotive, a system using batteries and dynamos on the carriage axles was introduced after the turn of the century.

Toilets in railway carriages made

further design changes necessary, requiring a proper corridor. They were introduced on the North Austrian Railway as early as 1869. Heating was another innovation. Early rail passengers had to rely on their clothing to keep them warm. Then five-gallon copper drums filled with hot water or sand were used. Two or three of these were placed in each compartment, and the occupants put their feet on them. Smouldering briquettes were sometimes placed beneath the seats, but this practice was abandoned when it was disco-

vered that they gave off dangerous fumes. Another system was to provide hot water for filling individual bottles from a boiler in each carriage. It was this that later formed the basis of circulatory heating. In 1858 the chief engineer of the Prussian Railways tried out a system of steam central heating which, following various refinements, became generally adopted in 1865.

The inclusion of restaurant cars in trains meant that a safe and sheltered means of passing from one carriage to another had to be provided.

The first goods wagons were short, wooden structures running on two axles. These unsprung, low-sided trucks had no roof, and if necessary the freight was covered with a tarpaulin. Springs were introduced in British goods wagons as early as 1830, since a hard ride tended to damage both wagons and tracks. As time went by special rolling stock was developed for different types of freight. So the story of the progress of rail transport is far from being just that of better locomotives. All the different aspects of railways had to be improved from the point of view of safety, economy, speed and comfort.

Building a bridge has always been a challenge. In ancient times merchants often had to make detours of many kilometres because of the absence of a bridge. Many railway lines could never have existed without bridges. On the Linz—Budějovice horse railway alone, no less than 214 of them were built in the years 1824 to 1827. They were wooden structures with trussed beams. Wooden bridges were also used on transcontinental lines such as those in the United States or Canada, especially in remote areas where timber was the most readily available material. Trusses were made by joining together dozens, even hundreds, of short sections of wood.

Stone bridges have been widely used ever since builders learned to erect arches, a discovery credited to the ancient Etruscans. Because it is strong and durable, stone was also exploited by railway builders. To this day the sheer size of the stone bridge across the valley of the River Göltsch in Saxony, built in 1850, is impressive. At a height of 82 m (270 ft) above the valley floor two 32-m (105 ft) stone arches span the gulf, with four stories of smaller arches on either side. The bridge is about 600 m (850 yards) long, and contains 265 m³ (350 yd³) of hewn sandstone, 87,000 m³ (113,800 yd³) of rubble, and over 20 million bricks.

Cast iron was used in the building of early iron bridges, but after a number of serious accidents it was replaced by steel. One of the most fascinating, and also one of the oldest such steel bridges is the famous Britannia rail bridge across the Menai Strait in Wales. It consists of a huge oblong box, riveted together from sheet metal and solid girders, through which trains pass as if in a tunnel. Openings in the five piers provide ventilation for the long tube in which the trains run. It was built by George Stephenson's son, Robert, between 1846 and 1849. The first cantilever steel bridge spanned the Firth of Forth in

A tunnel on the St. Étienne—Lyons horse-drawn railway in France.

Extensive earthworks for the Liverpool—Manchester line.

The Sankey Valley viaduct on the Liverpool—Manchester line.

Scotland in 1889, but the best way of crossing estuaries and broad rivers is by means of suspension bridges, whose tall towers take the tension of chains or steel hawsers, just as lianas supported the bridges of the ancient Mayas or of Africans. A pioneer of such structures was the American John A. Roebling. In 1855

A wooden bridge on the American transcontinental railway through Dale Creek on the Union Pacific line.

One of the first iron railway bridges, built near Newcastle in England.

he bridged the Niagara Falls, having been successful with his Brooklyn Bridge across New York's East River, which was completed by his son, Washington Roebling, in 1883.

From the very beginning tunnel-building has gone hand in hand with bridge building. Tunnels, too, have proved indispensable in many cases, although at first they caused a good deal of apprehension on the part of travellers.

For early rail passengers, to vanish into the bowels of the earth in a noisy, clanking puffing train must have been somewhat alarming. That this is no exaggeration is made clear by contemporary newspapers. 'It is well known,' wrote one correspondent, 'that engineers and workers employed in tunnels work quite naked because of the heat. Will train passengers be obliged to change their clothes before entering tunnels?' Another wrote: 'Imagine the effect of a change of temperature of eight degrees on the passengers. Travellers will frequently die of heart attacks.' Deaths were also predicted by another writer, who said: 'Should a train have to stop in a tunnel – and how easily that might happen – travellers will be in danger of complete suffocation!' Experience soon showed these fears to be ill-founded.

The heyday of tunnel-building in Europe was the period during which the transalpine railways were constructed. When the first of these, the Simplon, was begun in 1898, the workmen had to use hand drills, the only explosive available was gunpowder, and instead of using pit locomotives, rubble-filled wagons were pulled by horses. The pneumatic drill was used for the first time on the track leading through Mont Cenis on the French-Italian border. Gunpowder was gradually replaced by dynamite, and machinery powered by compressed air was introduced. Tunnellers had to face all manner of dangers inside the mountain. Underground springs flooded the galleries; in places they found clay or sand instead of solid rock, which posed the danger of the tunnel collapsing. Nowadays, modern techniques using tunnelling shields and freezing to keep fluid sections in place make tunnel-digging feasible not only in mountainsides, but also under water.

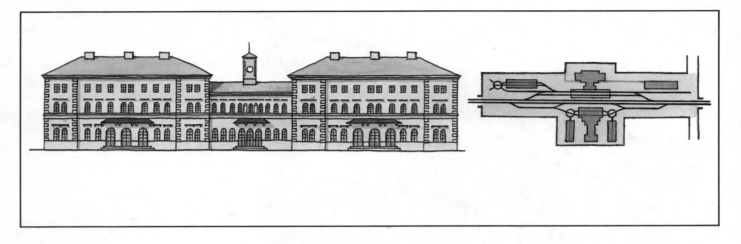

The Empire style, with a sense of symmetry, was even reflected in the design of stations as those in today's Czechoslovakia. Left: the station in Brno in 1849; right, ground-plan of the station in Pardubice.

A railway station can be anything from a simple hut in the middle of a field to shelter passengers from the rain, to a huge complex of modern buildings with a wide range of amenities. In a typical small station, goods traffic is not separated from passenger services; there is usually a waiting-room and a ticket-office, and timetables are displayed showing nationwide services and indicating which trains stop at that particular station. If there is no restaurant, there may well be at least a refreshment kiosk and a news-stand. There might also be a left-luggage office and some sort of parcel service. The facilities available increase in proportion to the size of the town the station serves.

Station buildings developed in parallel with the growth of rail travel. At first they scarcely differed from ordinary houses. The only distinguishing feature of these two to three-storey buildings was a roof of some sort projecting over the platform.

As railways increased in importance, stations moved into town, and with growing numbers of passengers their size increased too. In some cases imposing neo-Gothic or neo-Renaissance buildings with glazed roofs were constructed, and were among the finest examples of architectural design. Surrounding streets reflected the importance of stations and became lined with hotels, restaurants and luxury shops. On the stations themselves services to travellers were extended. These included such things as an enquiry office, a post office, restaurants and various classes of waiting-room; porters bustled to and fro, and refreshment vendors served passengers from the platform. Bookstalls, hairdressers' shops and florists appeared, and taxi-ranks were set up.

Railway stations have their place in record books. The largest in the world is considered to be Grand Central Terminal in New York, built from 1903 to 1913. It covers an area of 19 hectares (47 acres) and has 41 tracks on the upper storey and 26 on the lower. The station can handle 600 trains and 200,000 passengers

The first really functional railway building — King's Cross, London.

York station on the North Western Railway, built in 1877 by Thomas Prosser.

a day. The highest station in the world is at Ticlio in Peru, 4,680 m (15,354 ft) above sea level. A station in Peking has a waiting-room for 14,000 people, and at present the heaviest traffic is handled by Tokyo Central, with 2,500 trains daily, representing two million passengers.

Passenger stations are either of the terminal type, where journeys begin and end, or are simply designed to allow trains to pass through. From the point of view of traffic, some stations handle all types of passenger train such as intercity, local and suburban, although these may be segregated to a greater or lesser extent. Other stations specialize in one type of traffic only. At present the trend is to build stations underground, or to place them on the outskirts of urban areas with good suburban and inner city connections. Modern station buildings have escalators and moving pavements to save travellers' feet. The information system is often automated and computerized, putting passengers in the picture more rapidly and enabling seat and sleeper bookings to be made more smoothly. Announcements and information boards are centrally controlled and operate quickly. Digital clocks are visible from most vantage points. Automatic ticket sales cut down queuing, and luggage lockers are another convenient feature. The traveller's way is further smoothed, particularly at international stations, by big bold signs which help him find his bearings more easily in situations where every minute may count.

A modern railway station.

Originally, trains ran only in the daytime. On the Vienna—Brno line, for instance, there was no night train until 1844. Right from the start, however, it was necessary to be able to communicate between trains, stations and signalmen. Footplate crews used bells or steam acoustic signals from the locomotive or by flags hung on the engine or tender. Trains standing in stations were marked with flags during the day and lights at night. If a train was delayed after dark, it announced its approach by lighting torches. If the driver could not see his way ahead, he stopped his train and got a colleague to walk to the next station and warn it of his approach. If a train was over an hour late, a locomotive would set out from the station to look for it.

Stations had tall flagstaffs where flags or baskets were hung to in-

A trackside signalman with flag.
◄

A bell signal being used.
►

A station signalman
with tall mast and baskets.
▼

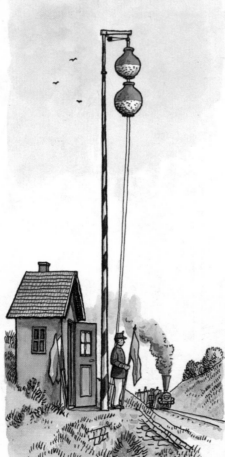

whistles to signal to brakemen, signalmen, stationmasters, conductors and guards. Guards, conductors and brakemen sat on the roofs of carriages where, exposed to smoke, soot and the vagaries of the weather, they kept an eye on the track and on signals from the engine. They used horns, whistles and flags to pass a message on or to signal to the driver.

In the days when trains were few and far between and speeds were low, the safety system was a crude one.

Each company had its own way of doing things. Signalmen were informed of a train's approach by form approaching trains of the situation there. Another safety device was the baton. There was one of these for each section of track, and the engine-driver was not allowed to set off until the stationmaster handed him the baton; he then handed this in at the next station, where he would be given another baton for the next section of track. The first signals were introduced by George Stephenson, who placed along the line rotating boards painted a different colour on each side. At night lanterns with coloured glass were hung on them. Because on some days poor weather made the colours difficult to see, the system was replaced by one where the position of the board carried the message. If it was facing the train, the driver had to stop, whereas if it was sideways on he could proceed. Then moving-arm signals were introduced because it was easier to see them.

In 1841 a conference was held on the use of light signals. It drew up a scale of visibility for lights of different colours which became the basis of the signalling systems of all railway authorities. New types of signals became necessary. In the upper quadrant system a horizontal arm meant 'stop', with a red light showing at night. 'Proceed' was indicated by raising the arm through 45° and a white light. Where a train left the main track, this was indicated by two or three raised arms or a corresponding number of white lights. With increasing train speeds there came the need for additional warning signals before the main signs. These either signalled 'proceed', in accordance with the main signal, or if the latter was at 'stop' they indicated 'slow'. Thus semaphore-type signals gradually replaced baskets and plates situated within sight of individual signalmen. A further safety device was the

sounding of bells to communicate orders and information. The coming of the telegraph and telephone enabled precise information to be passed along the line. For many years the telegraph was preferred, since it provided a written record of the messages that had been sent.

The telegraph and telephone being used by a member of the railway staff.

A manually-operated signal-box.

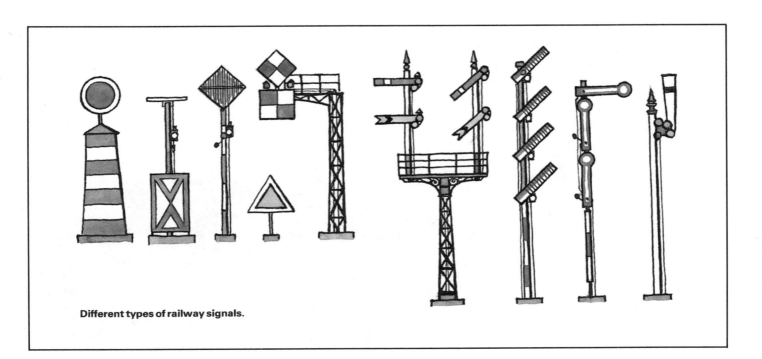

Different types of railway signals.

Though triumphs came thick and fast, the new mode of transport had many 'black' days. From the very first, inventors and spectators were victims of errors in design and operation. When Bruton's 'walking' locomotive exploded in 1813, several people were killed and injured. During the trial run of another unconventional engine in Durham in 1815, a burst boiler claimed some 50 lives, in addition to serious burns and other injuries suffered by numerous people. As designs improved, boiler accidents became something of a rarity, but the large numbers of passengers carried and higher speeds meant that mistakes were liable to cost many lives. To this day, rail disasters attract the attention of the world's press, wherever they occur.

In the early days, level crossings were a constant source of danger. When a train on the Leicester–Swannington line struck a grocer's cart, the railway company was ordered to pay the cost of cart, horse, 22 kg (50 lb) of butter and 960 eggs. It subsequently got Stephenson to devise a steam horn, which was to develop into the familiar warning whistle of later days. Thanks to the introduction of barriers and attendants, such collisions became exceptional, but acoustic warnings

The first major rail disaster was in 1842 in France, on the line between Versailles and Paris.

have stayed with us — and few safety devices can have been acquired so cheaply!

Throughout the history of rail-

The boiler explosion in Bohumín in 1871.

ways, one of the chief causes of accidents has been collisions between trains. One such incident took place during the very first run on the Vienna–Brno line, on 7 July, 1839. Four different trains took part in the ceremonial trip, but the driver of the third, a Briton called Williams, failed to keep the prescribed distance of 4 km (2.4 miles) on the return trip and his train ran into the one in front as it stood at Vranovice station. No one was killed, even though the last two carriages of the stationary train were smashed to pieces. The injured were able to continue their journey after receiving medical treatment, but one of them sued the company, and the case prompted the authorities to introduce a set of safety regulations.

One of the first major disasters, with a worldwide impact, was that which occurred in France in May 1842 on the line between Paris and Versailles. A pair of two-axled locomotives were hauling a long passenger train with the assistance of a third pushing from behind. The leading loco broke an axle, causing the second one to crash into it. The engines caught fire, and the freshly-painted carriages soon went up in flames. Since it was the practice for the guard to lock passengers in their carriages before the train left the

station, there was no escape for the 200 people on board. This catastrophe aroused public opinion throughout the world, and led to an improvement of safety regulations in many countries. In France itself, the minister of public works thenceforth prohibited the locking of carriage doors from outside.

Serious accidents were caused by derailments, whether due to faulty track or to the engine itself. A rather special case of derailment was the Tay Bridge disaster on the Dundee–Edinburgh line, which occurred on 28 December, 1879. In the middle of a gale, the bridge collapsed beneath a passenger train, most of which toppled into the River Tay. Of the eight missing coaches with an estimated 100 passengers aboard, divers found only three, and a small number of bodies. The cause of the accident was faulty bridge design, and it compelled civil engineers to take a new look at safety precautions.

A derailment near Penistone in 1884 led to improved brake design. After an axle failed, 10 carriages filled with passengers broke loose, and as there was no way of braking them, they left the track on a high embankment. The disaster contributed to the replacement of the simple Smith system of vacuum

brakes by the automatic Hardy system. In 1898 a whole series of accidents was blamed on the long hours worked by railway employees, after which shifts were shortened and the 24-hour service was reduced to 16.

On October 22, 1895,
a locomotive ran through a wall
at the Montparnasse Station
in Paris after a brake failure.

On October 20, 1910,
two express trains collided
at Rottemann Station in Austria.

There was a time when it seemed that toothed wheels of some sort would be needed on all railways, since the early locomotives were too light and their driving wheels slipped on the smooth tracks. We have seen how Blenkinsop's first loco had a toothed wheel engaged in a toothed rod. In the United States Colonel John Stevens constructed a similar system in his garden. His vehicle ran on four wheels, again propelled by a fifth, toothed, wheel moving along a toothed rod. As time went on, however, it became apparent that locomotives were in fact capable of moving along smooth rails without assistance. They could even manage considerable gradients that way, the standard becoming 25 : 1,000 for main lines and 40 : 1,000 for branch lines. The rack-and-pinion system still had a role to play, however. In 1847 it was found that a gradient of 60 : 1,000 was unavoidable on one section of the Madison—Indianapolis line, so the tracks were provided with a rack along that stretch. A special locomotive was developed, able to run on normal track or with the aid of a pinion.

In 1866, also in the United States, Sylvester Marsh began work on another mountain railway, which climbed 1,093 m (3,585 ft) in 4.5 km (2.8 miles) to the top of Mount Washington. Up a gradient which averaged 240 : 1,000 and in places was 377 : 1,000, the upright-boiler locomotive hauled a carriage with 50 passengers.

Of the European countries, Switzerland became renowned for its mountain railways. The first of these was the track from Vitznau to the peak of the Rigi. Initially the

▲ A steam locomotive, built for the Vitznau—Rigi line, pushing a carriage for 54 passengers.

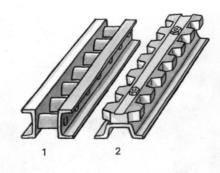

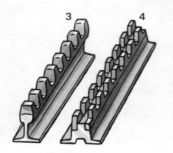

Some types of rack-and-pinion rails:
Riggenbach's at Rigi, Switzerland (1);
Locher's on Pilatus, Switzerland (2);
Strub's on the Jungfraujoch, Switzerland (3);
Abt's system based on Strub's design (4).

The electrified line on Mt. Pilatus, Switzerland.

The Jungfraujoch terminus at a height of 3,454 m (11,332 ft).

Swiss wanted Sylvester Marsh to take on the job. The American declined, but offered to advise the Swiss authorities. Swiss engineer Nikolaus Riggenbach had worked on rack-and-pinion railways with great enthusiasm in the 1860s, and had taken out a patent on his system. He went to see Marsh's railway, and found it to be of similar design to his own. After his return, he and his associates obtained the concession for the new line. It was 7 km (4.3 miles) long and climbed 1,310 m (4,298 ft), with a maximum gradient of 250 : 1,000; there were a total of 69,000 teeth on the rack.

Passengers got their first glimpse from the summit in 1870. Two years later another line was built from the eastern side of the Rigi, setting out from Arth-Goldau. The twin railways made the area a major tourist attraction. Around 40,000 tourists had visited the Rigi annually before the lines were built, but the number doubled almost overnight. They were willing to queue for several hours for the ride, and they were rewarded with a breathtaking view of Alpine glaciers and picturesque valleys from a vantage point few of them could have reached on foot.

The Rigi lines are the oldest in the Alps, but Switzerland also boasts the steepest railway — that which scales Mt. Pilatus, opened in 1889. It climbs from Alpnachstadt to an altitude of 2,000 m (6,562 ft) in 4.5 km (2.8 miles) and in places the gradient is as much as 500 : 1,000. The original steam engines have long since been replaced by electric units. The highest line in the Alps is the Jungfrau railway. It runs from Kleine Scheidegg, at a height of 2,061 m (6,762 ft), through tunnels cut into the Eiger and the Jungfrau to a station 3,454 m (11,332 ft) above sea level called Jungfraujoch, just below the 4,158 m (13,642 ft) peak of the Jungfrau. Along with other mountain railways and funiculars, it opens up the beauties of high mountains to millions of people.

Semmering, Brenner, Mont Cenis, St. Gotthard and Simplon – these had always been the main routes across the Alps, but in the second half of the 19th century the railways came to conquer the mountains that formed a barrier across the continent. The problems were considerable. They were up against harsh Alpine weather conditions, and construction companies had to race against time, since contracts imposed stiff penalties for failure to finish the work on time, and offered bonuses for completion ahead of schedule. Nevertheless, the first task was to overcome a lack of faith in the locomotive itself.

Few experts believed them capable of crossing the Alps on ordinary rails. In Britain, the United States and other countries, trains were hauled up major hills on steep ramps. Little wonder, then, that when the Southern Austrian State Railway planned its line from Vienna to Trieste across the Semmering Pass there were no fewer than 13 suggestions as to how best to cross the mountains. Mathias Schönerer, the engineer who took over the construction of the Linz–Budějovice line from František Gerstner, proposed the use of normal rails. He was convinced that a locomotive could manage an incline of up to 1 : 40 in this way.

In order to win over the sceptics, Schönerer built a special slope at Vienna's Südbahnhof station and demonstrated his theory in practice. Many still mocked his daring plan, however. Had not Robert Stephenson himself, son of the great George, written a report for the Swiss Federal Assembly in 1850, advising that Alpine passes should be negotiated by means of fixed engines rather than locomotives?

The man responsible for deciding the matter was a doctor of mathematics and engineer, Karl von Ghega, who announced his full support for Schönerer's scheme, and after a long struggle he succeeded in having it implemented. In August

The meeting of tunnellers from the two ends was always an occasion for celebration, as here in the St. Gotthard tunnel on 29th February, 1880.

1848 government approval was granted for Ghega's plans, which incorporated Schönerer's proposal. A track leading through ravines, across rock faces and over chasms was built. It was some 42 km (26 miles) long and included 15 tunnels. Valleys and gullies were crossed by means of 118 arched and 11 iron bridges, and there were 16 brick viaducts. The highest tunnel was 1,430 m (4690 ft) long, one of the six longest in the world at that time. Conditions for the workers were extremely poor. Cholera and typhus were rife, and 600 labourers were buried at Semmering in the course of building the line.

Before the line was even completed, a competition was held to find a suitable locomotive for Alpine work. In 1851 four contenders showed their capabilities on a stretch of track near Eichberg.

They were required to climb the section pulling a 140-tonne train at around 14 km/h (9 mph) without the assistance of sand sprinkled on the rails. The German locomotive *Bavaria* was the winner, but even it did not quite come up to requirements and a new engine had to be built. Only then could the first trains run on the first transalpine route, which was opened on July 17, 1854. As soon as railways proved themselves able to attain such heights, more transalpine lines were built.

In August 1867 the first trains crossed the Brenner Pass, forming a link between Italy and Germany via Austria. It had no major tunnel at the top like the Semmering track, but the Brenner route did chalk up a different engineering triumph: it included the first tunnel in the world where the track turns through an angle of 180°.

Lining a tunnel.

A locomotive built after the lessons learned from the Semmering contest.

Four years later, on September 17, 1871, the Mont Cenis line connected France with Italy. The main tunnel was 13 km (8 miles) long and had a curving section at each end. Three and a half million holes were bored to lay the explosive charges, and a million kilogrammes of gunpowder were required to shift the required amount of rock.

After another 11 years Switzerland and Italy were joined by means of the St. Gotthard tunnel, which took 10 years to build. The main tunnel was nearly 15 km (9 miles) long and turned a full 360° in the course of passing through the mountainside. Finally, France was linked with Italy a second time, by a tunnel measuring a little over 19 km (12 miles) — or rather by two tunnels. Simplon I was opened on 1 June 1906 but the second tunnel was not completed until after the First World War.

**Track-laying in the prairies
of the Wild West.**

**A train travelling through
the Rio Grande valley in Arkansas, USA.**

In the Old World, where means of transport changed only gradually over the centuries, the coming of the railways had meant a new way of life, a dynamic new tempo. Planners and builders laid railways across deserts, where workers collapsed in the heat; they laid tracks over high mountains, and through the taiga of the far north, where the ground was frozen solid. Railways crossed jungles, where termites gnawed away sleepers almost as soon as they were laid, and where lush vegetation overgrew the tracks before the first locomotive came along. Rails linked the shores of distant oceans. Railheads marched across all the continents as armies of labourers laid millions of sleepers, leaving along the route thousands of graves dug for those who never saw the line completed.

On 1 July, 1862 President Abraham Lincoln signed his name to the Pacific Railroad Act, heralding the construction of the first transcontinental railway. By linking New York and San Francisco it would also join the shores of the Atlantic and the Pacific. The total distance was 5,319 km (3,305 miles), although since there were existing rail routes at either end, the new section represented a 'mere' 2,800 km (1,740 miles). The route was a daunting one, nevertheless, leading through the prairies of the Wild West, among the towering outcrops of the Sierra Nevada and the Rocky Mountains, and crossing the desert close to Salt Lake.

The task was divided between two companies. The Central Pacific Railroad was to build the section from Sacramento to Ogden, while the Union Pacific's labourers would link Ogden to Omaha. The Union Pacific route for the most part led across the prairies, so that the work was relatively straightforward. Yet there was no ready supply of the basic materials required — wood and stone. The company had therefore to transport these materials an ever-increasing distance as work progressed. The Central Pacific, on the other hand, had difficulty in transporting iron and steel. These had to be shipped to San Francisco around Cape Horn, a journey that took 10 months. There were also the twin barriers of the Rocky Mountains and the Sierra Nevada to overcome.

The workforces of the two companies were also quite different. Because the Central Pacific had to compete with the Californian mines on the labour market, the management decided to recruit a huge number of Chinese immigrants, who offered the additional advantage that they were willing to work for less than half what others would have demanded. The labourers employed by the Union Pacific comprised Irish immigrants for the most part.

The workers of both companies soon found that harsh conditions were not the only difficulty they were obliged to overcome. The building of the railway brought with it a relentless campaign against the Indians, which provided employment for the generals and soldiers from the recently ended Civil War. At first the railroad companies thought that alcohol was the answer to the problem and tried to buy off the Indians with whisky, but many tribes resisted this civilized evil and attacked the slow-moving trains and tried to damage the tracks. Workers who signed up with the railroad companies found they not only had to wield a pick and shovel all day long and drag the heavy rails into place under constant threat of attack — they also had to survive the perils of drunken brawls in the work camps, where conditions were worse than in the back streets of cities.

In spite of these difficulties, the two groups of labourers met at

Typical American locomotive of the 1860s.

Promontory Point, Utah, where, on May 10, 1869, the last sleeper was laid. It was made of the finest wood, and the last nail, a gold one, was driven home by the governor of California using a silver hammer. The telegraph which had been completed simultaneously with the line transmitted the historic moment from coast to coast. With each blow of the hammer it tapped out 'don — don — don', ending with a triumphant 'done'. Each tap of the hammer was marked by the sound of the city-hall bell in San Francisco and

that of a cannon shot in New York. The celebrations reached their climax when the gold nail was slowly approached from either side by the Central Pacific locomotive *Jupiter* and the Union Pacific's locomotive *N 119*.

With the completion of the railway the shores of two great oceans were linked. In between, vast uninhabited areas of the United States were opened up for settlement, and settlers quickly flocked to the new lands where Indians had freely roamed before.

Pullman's express carriage with an observation platform, built for the National Pacific Railway, USA.

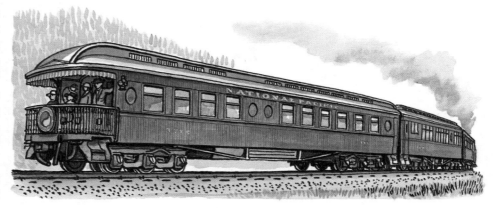

That last gold nail had scarcely been driven home on the trans-American line when plans were made to link Atlantic and Pacific further north, in Canada. The proposed railway from Montreal, close to the east coast, to Vancouver, a port on the Pacific, was to stretch some 4,600 km (2,900 miles). Major railways often have to wait for favourable political conditions and when, in 1871, British Columbia, the westernmost province of Canada, joined the federation, the Canadian parliament was able to give its approval to the project. It took nearly another decade for work to get under way, however. In spite of its size, Canada had less than four million inhabitants and simply could not afford the railway immediately.

Those 10 years were not, however, wasted. The construction companies sent out a series of expeditions to map unexplored territory and find a route for the new line. The chief obstacles were the Gold Range Mountains, the Selkirk Mountains and the Rockies. The eastern part of British Columbia was entirely cut off by mountains.

Canadian cartographers had problems with Indians, too. They were protected by army escorts, so that these surveying trips took on the appearance of a military rather than a scientific venture. In addition some surveyors had to contend with natural hazards. A group of seven died in a huge forest fire, and in a single year a dozen men were drowned in rivers and marshes.

Donald A. Smith putting in the last nail of the Canadian Pacific Railroad at Craigellachie on 7th November, 1885.

If the pathfinders had their problems, the financiers fared little better at first. True, Canada was rich in natural resources such as timber, furs, land and minerals, but until the railway was built they could not be properly exploited. The nation therefore had to fund its great rail-

A water station with a wind pump.

way by other means, so the government sold plots of land along the proposed route to new settlers, who were assured of transport to markets for their products.

Nor was it easy to find a contractor for the building work, although the offer seemed a good enough one. Then the government took the bold step of sponsoring the project itself. This attracted the interest of a consortium of businessmen and financiers from Canada, Britain and the United States, and in 1881 the Canadian Pacific Railway company was set up.

In May of that year work was started on the section between Winnipeg and British Columbia. Again, twin armies of labourers moved towards each other, and thanks to careful preparation and efficient organization the lines met up after a mere four years on 7 November, 1885. The management of the Canadian Pacific chose a much less pretentious completion ceremony than their American colleagues. There were no gold nails or silver hammers, no bells and no gun salutes. The ceremony was dedicated to those who had built the line. On 7 November Governor Donald A. Smith hammered home the last nail, then rode over the spot where the two lines joined, to the cheers of the workmen. The next day he finished the journey when he reached Port Moody on the shores of the Pacific.

Passing as it did through territory where the winter is harsh, the trans-Canadian railway posed its builders many problems. Linemen had to make sure the track was open, and heavy timber roofs had to be built in places as a protection against avalanches. Yet the Canadian Pacific did not stop at the shores of the two great oceans – not as a travel company, anyway. It became the first great international travel broker, buying ocean liners and offering people the chance to travel half way round the world with a single company.

A snow-thrower in harsh Canadian conditions.

The Canadian Pacific made it possible to exploit the rich mineral resources hidden in the until then impenetrable wilderness. Sometimes as many as four steam locomotives had to draw the goods train in order to overcome the natural obstacles.

A type of bridge used on the Trans-Siberian Railway.

The savage wastes of Siberia have been challenged by the track-layers not once, but twice. The first occasion was in 1891, when Czar Alexander II gave orders for a line to be built linking Chelyabinsk with an existing connection to Moscow and then Vladivostok. The work was carried out by 23,000 workmen, of whom 15,000 were Chinese and 2,000 were convicts. Working conditions were atrocious: in summer the temperature rose to 40 °C, while in winter it fell to −50 °C. Over much of the route the ground was permanently frozen, and in winter the rivers froze solid. Summer in the Amur region brought swarms of mosquitos, and there was a lack of food and fresh water throughout. Other perils included bears, tigers and wandering bands of escaped prisoners. Hundreds died along the route, while hundreds more never recovered their health. Nevertheless the world's longest railway was finally completed in 1916; it had taken 25 years to build and measured 8,960 km (5,570 miles). After the October Revolution of 1917 it was decided to build another trans-Siberian line further north, but not until the 1970s was the project begun.

Conditions for workers on the Baykal–Amur link were a great deal better than those their predecessors had worked under earlier in the century. The scheme was renowned for the youth of those involved in building it. A total of 130,000 workers took 10 years to complete the line, and in the final stages about 50,000 men and women under 30 years of age were working on it, half of whom had spent more than eight years in the harsh conditions of the far north. The new Trans-Siberian was completed in 1985, one year ahead of schedule. The 3,400 km (2,100 mile) route from Lake Baykal to the eastern coast crosses 11

Part of the track built in the rocky terrain close to Lake Baykal in USSR, with galleries as a protection against land-slides and avalanches.

major rivers and 7 high mountain ridges. Over 30 km (19 miles) or almost one per cent of the route had to be tunnelled through solid rock — in a region constantly jolted by earthquakes. A total of 3,200 bridges and sluices had to be built, some of the bridges being more than 1,500 m (4,921 ft) long.

The extreme conditions of Siberia presented special problems for the railway builders. During the blasting of the North Muysk tunnel, the longest on the line, they encountered a geological fault, and work on the 14-km (9-mile) tunnel had to be stopped for two years. For the first time in history, space-travel came to a railway's rescue, for it was not until satellite photographs were ex-amined that the true nature of the problem became apparent. It still took a lot of work by dozens of scientists and mining engineers before they came up with a solution, but in the end a route was found which avoided areas susceptible to earthquakes.

When surveyors set out to chart a route for the new Trans-Siberian they found only a few settlements of fur-trappers and lumberjacks along the way. Later on, the construction workers building the line lived in tents and trailers in the midst of the desolate and inhospitable taiga. Yet completion of the line brought new life to the region. Dozens of towns and villages grew up along the route. Factories, schools and cultu-ral institutions sprang to life, including a museum devoted to the project itself. The first trains ran from Tayshent to the port of Sovetskaya Gavan on the shores of the Sea of Japan, and in nearby Kuanda a monument 12 m (39 ft) high was erected to those who built the line. With the completion of the railway other building work began, and it is continuing with the industrialization of Siberia, whose mineral wealth remains largely untapped.

The railway, too, is moving on. The 800 km (500 mile) section of the so-called Minor Baykal—Amur link at present ends at Yakutsk. Plans are under way to extend it to Magadan on the Sea of Okhotsk, and early next century it may reach the Bering Sea.

The Siberian railway network is constantly being extended. The new Baykal—Amur line leads through the uninhabited waste of the Siberian taiga.

The Orient Express.

The kitchen.

▼

In the second half of the 19th century railways spread at a cracking pace. Long-distance tracks not only spanned continents, but joined them one to another. The railway companies of Europe agreed on a scheme to link Europe with Asia and as a result of this decision the most celebrated train of all time, the Orient Express, took to the rails in 1883. It left the Gare de l'Est in Paris for Munich, Vienna, Bucharest and the frontier station at Giurgiu. There the passengers took a ferry across the Danube and continued their journey by train to Varna on the Black Sea, from where a regular steamer service operated to Constantinople, now known as Istanbul. If they preferred, the passengers could travel by fast steamer down the Danube from Giurgiu.

A few years later, on 28 August, 1888, the section of the Orient Express route through Belgrade and Sofia was officially opened. This cut out the complicated journey through Bucharest and along the Black Sea coast, which took a whole week. When the first Simplon tunnel was opened in 1906, the Orient Express began to make the journey to Belgrade through Milan and Trieste. It covered the journey of more than 3,100 km (1,925 miles) in 81 hours 40 minutes. It was the most luxurious train in the world. The interiors of the coaches were fitted out in polished wood and brass, and fine curtains draped the windows. Uniformed waiters served meals in the elegant dining-car. Tickets cost four times as much as those for other trains.

The trip was not always without incident. One of the first trains to travel the route had to cope with floods in Romania, and in winter passengers could be stranded by snowdrifts for days on end in the middle of nowhere. In 1891 the train was attacked by bandits. In 1924 the Turkish reformer Kemal Atatürk used it to transport a consignment of hats which were to replace the traditional fez. When the famous singer Josephine Baker took it, a bomb went off in the locomotive. Once, when it was carrying a Hindu maharajah, the heating failed and the prince paid in gold for warm

Compartment in a sleeper.

The dining-car.

▼

clothing for himself and his attendants. No wonder some 400 books and stories have been written about this train, which has also formed the background for nearly 50 films. Not

for nothing was it called the emperor's, politician's and spy's express.

The glory of the Orient Express faded with the coming of air travel, and on 19 May, 1977 it set off on its last journey, which it completed in 57 hours. It was a truly ceremonial occasion, with memorial medals issued, along with a commemorative certificate, which was stamped on leaving Paris and upon arriving at Istanbul. The Orient Express refused to lie down, however, and the service was revived on its 100th anniversary in all its glory, using original carriages sumptuously refurbished and observing the original traditions.

The Orient Express opened a whole era of luxury express trains. It was soon joined by other famous routes, such as the St. Petersburg—Nice—Monte Carlo run, on which Russian aristocrats and Magyar barons travelled to the gambling centres of the south. Later the Simplon Express from Paris to Venice attracted lovers and honeymoon

couples, not only because of its romantic destination, but for the chance of spending the night in one of its sleeping-cars. In those days the railway was king. It was the fastest and most comfortable means of transport of its age, thanks mainly to the track-layers who had, by the 1880s, joined up most of the world's chief cities.

Another factor in the success of rail travel was the extent to which problems of comfort and hygiene had been solved. This was mainly to the credit of American designers. While European carriages were based more or less on road coaches, the Americans looked for their example to luxurious riverboat cabins, and achieved a standard of comfort which was the envy of the world. The peak of railway carriage design was reached by George Mortimer Pullman, a carpenter by trade, who came up with the idea of sleeping-cars in the middle of the last century, and in 1867 produced the first dining-car, complete with its own kitchen.

Whether out of sheer curiosity or in recognition of the crucial role trains had to play, rulers and aristocrats took an active interest in railways from the start, and it was only natural that they had to be catered for when it came to designing carriages. At first it was considered sufficient to match the comfort of a road carriage, but the size of rail-cars offered much greater possibilities.

In 1842 a royal carriage was made for Queen Victoria which had an interior little short of palatial. A similar style, imitating the salons of the aristocracy, became the rule for early luxury coaches. As longer distances were travelled by train, especially on transcontinental routes, a great deal more comfort became available to less privileged passengers, too.

The man who made the greatest contribution to rail comfort was the American George Mortimer Pullman. He built sleeping-cars from the middle of the 19th century and in 1867 built the first proper dining-car, the President, which had its own kitchen. In the same year he founded the Pullman Palace Car company, which became famous for its sleeping-cars, dining-cars and luxury carriages, all of which set new standards of comfort. It.was several years before the Belgian Georges Nagelmacker took up Pullman's ideas and introduced them in Europe. In 1872 he founded Wagons Lit and four years later the company became international.

When heads of state set out on long rail journeys, whether at home or abroad, a single state-room was no longer sufficient. Whole trains of specially equipped coaches were needed. There would be a car for the baggage, a sleeping-car with marble-lined bathroom, living rooms, a dining-car and kitchen, and coaches for the servants and entourage. In many cases either aristocratic whim or the special nature of a journey demanded special features. As early as 1838, for instance,

State-carriage of the Austrian emperor, built by Ringhoffer in Prague.

the Russian czar's train included accommodation for his dogs and horses. Some trains had observation cars. The pope's train had a balcony from which he could give his blessing to the crowds as he passed. The French empress Eugénie took six coaches full of clothes when she

retired to her château for the summer.

As time went by, carriage interiors took on a more practical appearance. The furnishings were modern and very comfortable. Conference rooms and telecommunications cars were sometimes included, and

State-carriage of the President of Czechoslovakia of 1930, built by Ringhoffer, Prague.

State-carriage of 1906 carrying the Greek Orthodox pope along the Trans-Siberian Railway to places where no churches had yet been built.

many events of international importance have taken place in trains. The fate of one carriage in particular is worth recounting.

CFF conference-car no. 2419 was originally a dining-car belonging to Wagons Lit. It was converted as a conference-car half way through 1918 and put at the disposal of Marshal Foch. It was located at Compiègne, north-west of Paris, and in it the representatives of the defeated German army signed the ceasefire and surrender agreements that formally ended the First World War. Because of its historical significance, Wagons Lit presented the coach to France after the war, and it was later exhibited along with surrendered German weapons in the courtyard of the Invalides Palace in Paris. Because of damage by the elements, it was returned to Compiègne in 1927, and a hall was built for it there.

After the occupation of France in 1940, the Germans had no. 2419 taken back to its original site, where the French leaders were required to sign their surrender as a form of revenge. After that, Hitler gave orders for the carriage to be destroyed, but then had it brought to Berlin, where it was exhibited at the Brandenburg Gate. It was subsequently destroyed during an Allied air raid. After the war the French government bought a similar dining-car from Wagons Lit, and after converting it again put it on show at Compiègne as a memorial.

The adventures of 2419 were exceptional, of course, but state trains have not lost their importance since the end of the Second World War. In 1954 the emperor of Ethiopia visited Britain, France and West Germany by train. The Queen used a train for her tour of Australia in 1954 and during her visit to West Germany in 1965. On the West German trip the train included a special carriage where the royal wardrobe was ironed. The Soviet premier Nikita Khrushchev travelled to France by rail in 1960, and used the same mode of transport on his visit to Austria a year later. For his presidential election campaign General Eisenhower used a train that had no fewer than eight carriages reserved for the use of media representatives.

Specially equipped trains have ceased to be the exclusive domain of heads of state and government officials. Because he was afraid of flying, Elvis Presley went on tour in a train equipped with a swimming-pool, a projection room and, of course, a recording studio.

A modern conference car.

Getting There Fast

At one time train speeds were increasing with almost every trip. The 100 km/h (62 mph) barrier was broken as long ago as 1835. This record was set by a light engine, but four years later it did 80 km/h (50 mph) hauling a train.

The simplest way of increasing the potential speed of a locomotive was to increase the diameter of the driving wheels. Some designers

Express locomotive *Lord of the Isles*, which ran on the Great Western Railway with a wide gauge of 2.134 m (7 ft).

Thomas Crampton's French locomotive.

thought that an increase in track gauge would also help improve the performance of engines, so the British engineer Isambard Kingdom Brunel used a gauge of 2.1 m (7 ft) for the Great Western Railway, and Daniel Gooch designed the locomotive 'Great Western' to run on the line with enormous driving wheels 2.4 m (8 ft) in diameter. It did 96 km/h (60 mph) on the London–Swindon track, hauling a load of 100 tonnes.

Soon express locomotives belonging to many different railways were running at more than 100 km/h (62 mph), although such speeds were not by any means routine, even in Britain. Still, the average of 32–40 km/h (20–25 mph) was very respectable, and was the maximum achieved in most European countries. An exception to this rule was France, where engine speeds almost matched those across the Channel. As we shall see, it is a tradition the French have maintained to this day.

One of the designers who believed in big driving wheels was Englishman Thomas R. Crampton. His express locomotives, which reached speeds of about 120 km/h (75 mph) even in 1846, were popular in many countries. The diameter of their driving wheels was about 2.5 m (8,2 ft), and in order to keep them out of the way of the boiler,

Crampton used one pair of drivers only and positioned them behind the boiler. The boiler could then be given a very low profile, and the resulting drop in the centre of gravity made the engine more stable on bends and at high speeds. The drawback was lack of weight over the driving wheels. Traction was poor, particularly when braking or climbing and in wet weather, when the driving wheels often slipped.

Improvements in the design of steam engines made very large wheels unnecessary, and experience showed that Brunel's broad gauge was not an asset in achieving high speeds. After 1845 locomotives took on new shapes. Long boilers came in, with a greater heat-exchange surface and higher steam pressure. Engine weights also increased, and more driving wheels had to be coupled to produce the necessary traction. Better performances were also achieved by increasing the number of pistons. In addition to the traditional arrangement of one piston on each side of the locomotive, designs appeared with a further one or two pistons inside the chassis. An important improvement came with 'compound' steam expansion. Instead of the pistons being in parallel and giving off steam which was still under pressure, a high and a low-pressure piston were used in tandem so that the steam released

Austrian express drawn
by the successful series-6 locomotive,
built 1894—98.

Austrian 108-class locomotive
designed by Golsdorf and built
between 1901 and 1910.
It attained a speed
of 140 km/h (94 mph).

more useful energy before being expelled.

At the turn of the century Wilhelm Schmidt made another significant innovation by fitting a pre-heater for the steam. From then on most locomotives increased the temperature of their steam, which left the boiler at around 190 °C, to as much as 500 °C. When steam pressures reached 20 to 25 atmospheres some designers experimented with high-pressure locomotives. In 1929 a German locomotive with a working pressure of about 60 atmospheres was tested, and later that year the Schwarzkopf factory produced a locomotive with a steam pressure of 120 atmospheres. Pressures of that order, however,

called for very complex designs, so that high-pressure locomotives failed to make their mark.

Bigger and Better

In the course of 150 years the construction of the steam locomotive underwent many changes. As running speeds increased to more than 100 km/h (62 mph), one of the problems which had to be overcome was air resistance. The German firm of Henschel and Son of Kassel used an aerodynamic shape for their express steam locomotives from 1904.

On 3 July, 1938 the British locomotive 'Mallard Pacific' took to the tracks hauling a measuring wagon in its attempt to break the world

record of 200 km/h (125 mph). The brainchild of Sir Nigel Gresley and built in 1935, the streamlined engine recorded 203 km/h (126 mph). Some say that the fastest steam loco in the world was the American engine 'Atlantic', which is supposed to have done 204 km/h (127 mph) on the Pennsylvania line, but the conditions under which the British engine's speed was measured were much more rigorous.

Steam locomotives were not all of the classical piston type. Considerably improved performances were achieved by steam turbine propulsion, but the systems used were highly complex. The first engines of this type appeared in the first decade of the 20th century, and the

Locomotives Big and Small

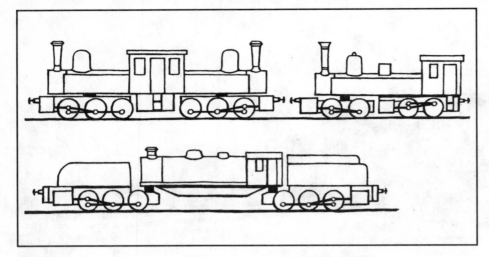

A diagram to show the driving wheels of the Fairlie, Mallet and Garratt system.

Garratt's locomotive on the East-African Railways is the largest steam engine on a one-metre gauge railway.

built across the desert areas of Africa, Australia and Asia, designers came up against the problem of ensuring an adequate water supply. Most locomotives could carry enough water for about 200 km (125 miles) at the most, but that was no longer sufficient. Accordingly, condensation locomotives had to be built which were able to recycle water. The condensation equipment was carried in a separate wagon which was often larger than the engine itself, but locos such as

chief manufacturers were the Milan works in Italy, North British Locomotion and the factory of the Swedish pioneer of turbine power, Birger Ljungström. Krupp and Maffei later produced turbine locos in Germany, but it was the American firm of Baldwin in Philadelphia that made the most powerful ones of all. The giant engines produced there following the Second World War had a turbine power pack producing 4,475 kW (6,000 hp) at 6,000 rpm.

This drove a pair of direct current generators, which in turn powered the electric motors on each of the eight driven axles. The major advantages of steam turbine propulsion were low fuel consumption and smooth running, but the high cost of manufacturing such locomotives and the fact that they operated efficiently only at high speeds was to prevent the system from enjoying more general success.

When railway lines were being

these could cover thousands of kilometres without having to replenish their water supply. Since the condensation equipment was expensive and complex, the system was only used when there really was no alternative.

Designers faced a different task in building powerful locomotives that could cope with the sharp bends of mountain tracks. The first compound locomotive for this purpose was designed in 1878 by Swiss

The British *Royal Scot* **of 1927.**

engineer Anatole Mallet. His loco was divided into two parts, with a separate drive on the front bogie. Mallet's compound locomotives grew extremely popular because of their good performance, and some of them were very big. In 1941 the first of a series of 21 Mallet-type locos called 'Big Boy' took to the rails. It was the heaviest steam engine ever made, with a track weight of 350 tonnes and an overall length of about 45 m (147 ft).

Another type of articulated mountain locomotive was built in 1863 by Herbert William Garratt. Its long boiler, suspended in mid-air, was attached at each end to a pair of independently driven bogies. These powerful engines, mostly used on winding narrow-gauge tracks in South and East Africa, South America and Asia, were also capable of hauling heavy loads up steep inclines. One of Garratt's locos was the biggest and heaviest 1,000 mm gauge engine ever built.

Although representing a high point in technological progress, steam locomotives had their limitations. The chief of these was their uneconomical use of fuel. Furthermore, speeds over 200 km/h (125 mph) were unrealistic because of the unbalanced weight of the piston and crank systems. The time taken to get up steam and the complex nature of the driver's job also contributed to the demise of steam in favour of electric and diesel-powered units.

Goods Locos

Just as special engines were developed for express trains, so the transport of freight called for a particular breed of locomotive. They had to haul heavy loads, and setting a long train of heavy wagons in motion without the driving wheels slipping was no easy task. In addition there were often steep hills to climb along the route. One solution was to use two or more engines on one train. Goods locomotives also became heavier and had increasing numbers of coupled driving wheels. One Soviet loco built in 1935 had seven pairs of drivers, more than any other in the world.

Engine performance depended not only on improvements in the steam engine as such, but also on mechanization of its operation. The limit for manual stoking was about 2.5 tonnes of coal an hour, and by 1855 there was already in use a system that enabled the coal to be transferred direct from bunker to firebox. There were different designs, but the best known was the 'Stoker' patent. Later on the coal was brought from the tender by means of an Archimedean screw and distributed over the grate by a jet of steam. This system was adequate to the needs of even the most demanding locomotive, being capable of delivering more than 10 tonnes of coal an hour.

Steam engines had to carry large supplies of coal and water, unless they were only shunting at a depot. Engines running short distances only were designed as 'tender' locomotives. On these a coal supply was provided alongside the boiler, perhaps, or behind the driver's cab. Some of them also carried a water supply. Long-haul locomotives had a separate tender which they pulled behind them. Before the invention of the screw system of delivery, the tender would be open at the front to allow the fireman to shovel the coal into the firebox.

Although early boilers were liable to explode on occasions, safety devices were soon developed. Every

The streamlined British *Mallard*, which reached a record speed of 203 km/h (127 mph).

boiler had two safety valves which released pressure if the limit was exceeded. The water level had to be kept at least 10 cm (4 in) above the wall of the firebox. Safety plugs were incorporated here, so that if the temperature rose too high they would melt, releasing the water onto the fire and putting it out. At the back of the boiler, in the driver's cab, there was a pressure gauge

with the maximum safe pressure marked on it and two independent water level indicators.

The system supplying water to the boiler first consisted of hand pumps; these were later replaced by mechanical ones, although early models worked only while the engine was in motion. In 1858 the Frenchman Henri Giffard invented an injection system whereby steam

The largest and heaviest steam locomotive in the world, *Big Boy*, built in 1941 in the USA according to the Mallet system.

Goods train of the 1860s
on Ferdinand's North Austrian Railway, drawn by two locomotives.

Camel Type American locomotive. An attempt was made with this to
improve the view of the driver by raising the footplate.

from the boiler was used to drive a supply of water from the tank.

Brakes went through a similar process of evolution. Brakemen originally sat on the roof of wagons; only later did they have cabins. They applied their brakes, which were of the screw type and separate for each wagon, at a command from the footplate. A train required a large crew in those days, and a goods train on a hilly run would have up to 10 brakemen. As speeds grew, braking by hand was no longer sufficient. In 1866 the British engineer Kendall invented a com-

Goods locomotive of the 180-class pulling a test train during air-brake
trials at the end of the 19th century.

pressed air brake. Each wagon had to have its own compressed air reservoir as well as its own compressor, which was driven from the axle by means of a belt. In 1867 George Westinghouse of Pittsburgh brought out an improved version of the air brake. He later invented a system which the driver could operate throughout the train and which also allowed him to apply the brakes of any of the wagons.

Goods traffic was where it all began. The very first trains transported coal in the mines, and later catered for the rapidly growing need to shift raw materials and finished products which resulted from the spread of the industrial revolution. The man in the street was always more impressed by luxurious carriages and express locomotives, but it was the humble freight train that helped to clothe him, feed him and fill his home with the paraphernalia of the modern age.

Small is Beautiful

In the 19th century, railways occupied a privileged position as the first modern means of transportation. They linked big cities, industrial centres, ports and places where

A special locomotive for industry.

raw materials were plentiful, and to a significant extent the railway planners had the power to determine the pattern of settlement. If a town was by-passed by the railway it was condemned to play second fiddle to whichever of its neighbours was nearer the tracks. After the completion of the main lines, there were many minor industrialized towns which needed linking with the main network. So the period towards the end of the 19th century became the era of the branch line.

Branch lines required a new departure in locomotive design. No longer were size and speed the order of the day: it was not record-breakers that were required here, but small engines able to operate economically under particular conditions. The expanding volume of traffic in stations and sidings also called for a new type of locomotive suitable for shunting. Before the advent of motorized shunters in the early 20th century, steam engines had to perform this function as well.

Many tracks served the internal needs of factories, mines and ports, as well as linking them with the national network. The demands on these special trains were frequently considerable, such as in foundries, where molten metal had to be transported. Many countries had forest railways for the transportation of timber. The British army had a small 'portable' railway whose engine and wagons could be carried on the backs of elephants across mountainous tracts of India. Designers were constantly being faced with special requirements.

The needs of the rapidly-growing network of tracks were no less exacting. In 1890 there were around 108,000 km (67,000 miles) of track throughout the world, but by the turn of the century the figure had increased eightfold. Many of the new lines presented special problems. A standard-gauge railway reaching a height of 4,781 m (15,686 ft) was constructed in Peru. The 1,000 mm (39 in) gauge line

across the Andes from the port of Antofagasta in Chile to the Rio Mulatos a Potosí plateau in Bolivia reached a height of 4,880 m (16,010 ft) to become the highest in the world at that time. The mountainous terrain required the inclusion of many sharp bends along the route, a fact which gave added importance to engine design.

The contest between mountain locos at Semmering in 1851 pro-

A station on a narrow-gauge railway in Germany.

A successful innovation on small lines was the combination of the locomotive with a carriage, both for passenger travel, as in the case of this Australian railbus (right) and for shunting, as in the case of the Dutch enclosed locomotive (left).

duced a double engine with the two halves articulated. Robert Stephenson designed a similar dual locomotive for the mountain railway near Genoa in 1847. The advantages of the two were combined by Robert Fairlie, who mounted a long boiler

and firebox on two separate chassis, each of which had its own pistons and three coupled axles. This narrow-gauge engine formed the prototype for later designs of high-performance mountain locomotives.

For urban travel and short runs, designers came up with all sorts of combinations of engines and carriages. One of them stands in Alice Springs as a monument to the beginning of rail travel in Australia. Many local lines were built with highly individual gauges. Among

the narrow gauges there were 600 mm (23 in), 760 mm (29 in) and 1,000 mm (39 in), while broad-gauge railways were constructed with dimensions of 1,524 mm (60 in), 1,670 mm (66 in), and even 2,136 mm (84 in). Different designs and applications led to a great variety of locomotives, and clubs of steam enthusiasts exist throughout the world, preserving veterans of the steam age, keeping them in running order, and from time to time giving public demonstrations of the symbols of a vanished era.

A Siemens train at the Berlin Industrial Exhibition of 1879.

this engine, Werner von Siemens and Johann Georg Halske, did not intend merely to create a fairground amusement, but a locomotive suitable for use in lignite mines. The darling of the Berlin exhibition never saw mine service, but her younger sister, built in 1882, was used for that purpose until 1927.

There had been many attempts to harness electric power for railways before Siemens showed the way. On the Edinburgh–Glasgow line, for instance, an electric loco capable of doing nearly 65 km/h (40 mph) was put to use in the first half of the 19th

Electric locomotives, like Trevithick's pioneer steam engine, started life as a fairground attraction. In 1879 an electric engine first pulled three carriages, with 18 passengers sitting sideways, along a small circuit. The driver sat astride the locomotive, which he controlled by means of a pair of levers — an on-off switch and a hand-brake. This feature of the Berlin Industrial Exhibition seems to have been popular, as almost 90,000 passengers were carried in the four months the exhibition was open. The power supply to the 2.2 kW (3 hp) locomotive was via a raised third rail in the middle of the track. The inventors of

▲
This vehicle achieved a speed of 210 km/h (131 mph) on a test track in 1903.

One of the first electric locomotives on the St. Gotthard line, called the *Schweitzer Krokodil* because of its length.
▼

century. Unfortunately the batteries that provided the power were so heavy that the engine had its work cut out to propel these along, let alone a payload as well. The Frankfurt inventor Wagner, whose electric bell clapper achieved wide use, was commissioned to design an electric locomotive by the German Railway Association, but his engine's power pack was so heavy it could not even move!

It was left to the French inventors Bellet and Reuvre to suggest the possibility of placing the power supply along the track and providing

▲
The French record-breaking locomotive, CC 7107, which achieved a speed of 331 km/h (206 mph) on 28th March, 1955.

The French locomotive, CC 40100, used for four-line systems.
▼

a continuous conductor for feeding power. The idea formed the basis of electric railways as used to this day, although at the time it was put forward it was impracticable.

Thomas Alva Edison also experimented with railway electrification, in 1880, when he tried out a direct current electric locomotive on a 4 km (2½ mile) length of track. But it was Leo Daft who designed, in 1882, the first electric engine to see railway service. He christened it 'Ampère', and it took its supply from a third rail. Soon there was a different task awaiting the electric

locomotive – in the streets of cities, where the horse tram had outlived its usefulness and the steam engine was noisy and ill-suited to the stop-start routine.

The main disadvantage of the early electric traction systems was the very complex manner of supplying the mostly 650 volt direct current. Because of a considerable drop in voltage, long distances could not be served, which is why electrification was initially confined to trams, suburban railways and short mountain runs, where electricity proved superior to steam.

The first breakthrough came in 1903, when trials were begun on a Siemens electric locomotive operating on a three-phase alternating current system. On 26 November of that year the engine, driven by a pair of 200 kW (270 hp) electric motors, achieved a speed of over 210 km/h (130 mph). It was 50 years before this record was broken on rails. However, the need for a system of triple conductors with perfect insulation prevented the Siemens system from being widely adopted.

Around the time that the principle of alternating current was successfully applied, the problems of direct current started to be resolved, and the two systems then developed side by side. As more practical systems and power units were evolved, lines were increasingly electrified. Electricity offers many advantages, such as high performance, economy, cleanness and a low level of noise. The main disadvantage is the initial investment, particularly in difficult terrain. A further obstacle to smooth international travel by electric train is the diversity of traction systems in existence. Even Europe has two a.c. and two d.c. systems, and it is only recently that multipurpose engines capable of using different types of power feed have been introduced.

One of the first Soviet diesel locomotives,
Ee12, built in Germany in 1924.

About the time that the steam engine reached the peak of improved design, the first patents were taken out in Britain and France on internal combustion engines. The idea of doing away with the bulky boiler and introducing an altogether more compact engine and fuel system was an attractive one for inventors. The first four-stroke petrol engine arrived on the scene in 1876 and formed the pattern for later, improved versions. Subsequently, Rudolf Diesel invented a different system of internal combustion.

At first, the new types of engine stood no chance at all of ousting the steam engine from the railways, for manufacturers were able to meet all demands with tried and tested models. The internal combustion engine spent years waiting in the wings. The first loco powered by the new system had a two-stroke engine and a ridiculously small output, just 1.5 kW (2 hp). That was in 1880. It was not until 14 years later that the first petrol-engined loco capable of shunting appeared. The idea then caught on because of the mobility of these units and much-reduced preparation time.

The Swiss firm of Sulzer managed to develop a relatively powerful diesel engine before the First World War, but the coming of war diverted attention from this achievement. Another reason was that oil production was not widespread, whereas coal and water were readily available almost everywhere. Steam engines were producing ever more surprising performances, too.

After the First World War a crisis hit the railways. Roads were by then busy with motor vehicles, and mass transportation by road was expanding fast. Buses were more flexible than trains; they could reach outlying places, and because of their smaller size could offer a more frequent service and still run fuller. Not even an attempt to combine passenger and goods services could make up lost ground for the trains.

The railways decided to fight the buses on their own terms. Buses began to appear on rails, and only the wheels distinguished them from their counterparts on the roads. There were even dual-purpose buses built, having both railway and road wheels. Later on, similar vehi-cles more adapted to rail travel were produced. These were small rail-buses with a petrol or diesel engine developing about 110–190 kW (150–250 hp) which could be made up into trains. The transmission system was practically the same as that used in road vehicles, but it had its limitations and a new system needed to be developed for powerful rail traction units. Hydrostatic, hydrodynamic and electric transmissions were therefore designed.

Motor traction found its main application where large distances or difficult terrain made electrification costs prohibitive. Diesel-electric engines came to be widely used for the transport of freight, offering greater flexibility and single cab control. As many as six locos have been combined in this way to haul extremely large trains. The new type of engine also caught on for long-haul passenger transport. In 1933 the 'Fliegender Hamburger' achieved

Diesel locomotives of this type, built in 1933, reached cruising speeds of 120 km/h (75 mph) on German tracks. Famous names were *Der Fliegende Hamburger* and *Der Fliegende Berliner*.

The Czechoslovak diesel locomotive *Slovenská strela*, **built in 1936**.

160 km/h (100 mph) on the Hamburg–Berlin run. Motorized expresses in the United States were reaching similar speeds. On the Denver–Chicago line the *California Zephyr,* travelling over much less favourable terrain than the German express and over a much longer distance, was able to chalk up an average of 123 km/h (77 mph). The *City of Portland* averaged 147 km/h (92 mph), and had a top speed of 192 km/h (120 mph). By these means diesel engines muscled their way on to the tracks.

It would be difficult to think of an invention that has never been turned to military use, and the railway is no exception. Writing in 1841, an officer by the name of Pönitz in the Austro-Hungarian army greatly underestimated the military significance of rail transport. He saw its importance for troop movement and for maintaining supply lines, but considered that infantry should advance into battle on foot, since long marches were beneficial to discipline and physical fitness. Pönitz considered the transportation of horses by train to be out of the question. He proposed that after several hours' train travel at about 23 km/h (15 mph), soldiers should be given a three-hour break to recover from the arduous experience before continuing the trip until about seven in the evening, when it would be necessary to set up camp for the night.

Even very early experience proved Pönitz wrong. Contemporary newspaper reports suggest that the Austrian army used the railways for a large-scale movement of troops on 31 August, 1841. A second major operation involved the transfer of grenadiers from Brno to Vienna on 14 May, 1842. Since the emperor himself took an interest in

Second World War rail lifter used during a retreat.

the new mode of transport and was waiting at the station in Vienna with his entourage, the event took on considerable significance. Around the station and along the track some 20,000 spectators watched the huge locomotive 'Ajax' arrive, hauling 31 coaches. Two of the coaches contained the infantry regiment's band, three were filled with luggage, and two were occupied by officers. The 324 men of other ranks made the

trip in 24 open carriages, taking turns to sit down.

Various attempts have been made to use trains for military purposes other than troop transportation. Armoured trains were one of these. In fact they were small fortresses on wheels, armed with heavy cannon. The locomotives of armoured trains had to be protected like the rest of the wagons, and steel plate 8 to 20 mm ($\frac{1}{3}$ to $\frac{3}{4}$ in) thick was most often used. Some of these trains had a command post on board, with a watch tower and periscope, but the gun-wagon was the most important piece of rolling stock on armoured trains. The undercarriage was usually a standard one, but the walls were double, filled with sand, and protected by a layer of steel plate 12 to 15 mm (about $\frac{1}{2}$ in) thick. Slits in the sides allowed cannon or machine-guns to fire. Anti-aircraft guns were mounted on similar wagons and were used not only on armoured trains but also to protect other trains from air attack. An armoured train was usually composed of low-loaders out front to serve as protection against mines, a front gun-wagon, a machine-gun wagon, locomotives, a rear gun-wagon, and perhaps two or three tank wagons.

American armoured railcar from the Civil War.

A bridge destroyed by the retreating Polish army at the start of the Second World War.

During the Second World War the chief importance of trains was in moving and supplying troops. The invading German armies, operating a long way from home, were very reliant on rail transport. For this reason a 'battle of the tracks' was fought by resistance fighters in an attempt to put lines out of action. They attacked the most vulnerable spots, usually tunnels and bridges, where repairs would cost the maximum of time and effort. With the help of informants among railway staff, members of the resistance learned of the movement of munitions and other vital supplies, and monitored troop movements. These trains would then be derailed if possible, by damaging or mining the tracks. Allied aircraft also concentrated on rail links. Strategic bombers 'took out' important rail centres, and fighters and fighter-bombers strafed and dive-bombed trains. Hundreds of locomotives were put out of action, helping to paralyse military supply lines. During the war the battle of the tracks often had a direct bearing on events at the front.

A German locomotive of the Second World War pushing a mine-sweeper.

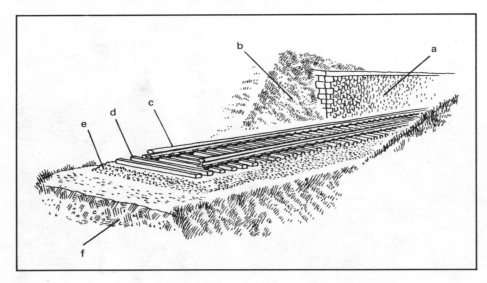

A diagram of a railway line to show screen wall (a), cutting (b), rail (c), sleeper (d), ballast (e), sub-ballast (f).

A well-constructed and properly maintained track is essential to the smooth running of a railway. It has always been so, and with increasing speeds, weights and traffic it has never been more so than today.

Railway tracks comprise a substructure, or roadbed, and a superstructure, or permanent way. The roadbed is basically a modification of the land along the route, with cuttings and embankments where necessary. In places material is added to make up any unevenness of the bed, and ballast is laid along this foundation. Ballast consists of gravel sometimes mixed with clinker, ash, sand or other material, and the thickness of this layer depends on the terrain. The layer of ballast has an important function. It absorbs some of the shocks transmitted by the trains, helps prevent landslips, and keeps the tracks from moving. It must be porous, to prevent the accumulation of water. It is compacted by rolling and tamped under the sleepers to make sure they contact the substructure at all points.

There are usually about 1,500 sleepers per kilometre. Wooden sleepers impregnated with tar or chemicals resist insects and are weatherproof. They have many advantages, since wood is light, flexible, easy to bed down, and rails can be attached quite simply; their durability is also excellent. Attempts have been made to use steel sleepers, which maintain the gauge better, resist sliding and are durable, and even easier to attach rails to. The main disadvantage is cost, but they are also more difficult to bed, and the harder ride means more wear and tear on rolling stock. Accordingly, steel is not generally used. Today, concrete sleepers are widely used, their strength and weather resistance also being good. They are more difficult to manipulate, however, and give a hard ride. In an attempt to improve mechanization, concrete slabs have also come into their own, and these speed up track-laying a great deal. The larger area of contact with the roadbed also means that preparatory work need not be so extensive, and it is only necessary to prepare a flat surface.

Among the important features of the permanent way are rails, points, turntables, buffers and track lights. Rails themselves have passed through a process of evolution, and the material they are made from has not been the only thing to change. The modern rail is designed to give

Modern method of bed renewal.

Manual fixing of sleepers during repairs to a track.

maximum support both at high speed and at rest, to resist stress caused by changes in weather conditions, and to smooth out minor alterations in level in parts of the permanent way. Important changes have taken place in the joining of rails, which are now welded together to form a jointless surface that makes for a more comfortable ride and reduces wear on rolling stock. In recent years some rails have been glued together with a special epoxy resin.

Track maintenance has also been largely mechanized. Among the machines used are defrosters, snow-throwers, snowploughs, and electric rail grinders. New tracks are often laid by a track-layer, which is nothing more or less than a mobile factory. Individual machines are mounted on wagons and driven by diesel engines. These machines first release the old rails from their sleepers, placing them by the side of the track and loading the old sleepers into an open wagon. Then the ballast cleaner comes along, scooping up the ballast in buckets and cleaning the gravel. It is followed by wagons which prepare the bed and lay new sleepers and rails. This 'factory', with 50 or so workers, moves along at the rate of about 400 to 500 m (440 to 550 yards) an hour. Later on a track monitoring vehicle using electronic, ultrasonic and other precise measuring devices will check the track to make sure it is safe for trains to travel on before it is put into use.

Modern methods of changing rails and cleaning ballast.

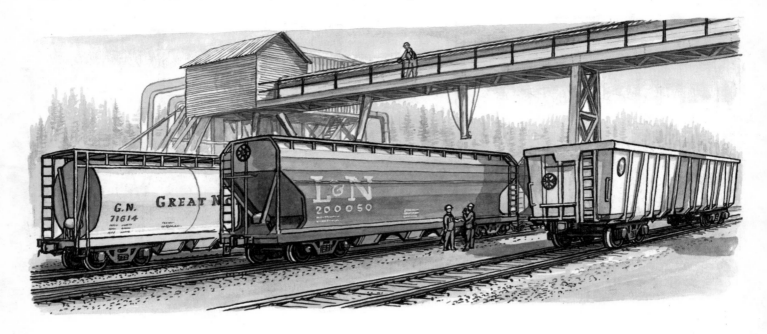

Present-day goods transport requires special types of wagons, such as this tanker (left), covered tipper (centre), tipper (right).

Industrial expansion, with new types of raw materials being used and new products manufactured, called for special types of rolling stock. An example is the box-wagon, with side doors designed to open at loading-ramp level. Many also have sliding roofs so that they can be loaded and unloaded from above, by crane. Cattle trucks are often divided into stalls, while some box-wagons have detachable sides and ends for easy loading. Flat wagons, which have always been useful for transporting timber, piping, rails and boxes, have taken on particular significance with the advent of containerization.

Special wagons with a funnel-shaped bottom and a trap-door can be unloaded directly into underground hoppers. Tank wagons for liquids are a familiar sight, and a special type of wagon is used for the transport of molten metals in foundries. At the other extreme, many cargoes require refrigerated wagons.

A common sight nowadays are car transporters. These were origi-nally used to carry new cars from factories to showrooms but now are also used to relieve people of the need to make long drives. Car trans-porters are usually three-storeyed and have ramps for loading and unloading. In the United States they have even tried loading cars verti-cally in two rows.

From time to time we come across wagons carrying sections of bridges and other huge loads. For such purposes there exists rolling stock having up to 32 axles and capable of transporting loads of as much as 400 tonnes. In many cases the route taken by big loads has to be special-ly planned. Sometimes an escort keeps the trackside clear as they pass.

Methods of loading and unload-ing wagons have also been im-proved. A great time-saver where grain is concerned is the pneumatic conveyor, which can load many tonnes into a wagon in minutes. Containerization is a modern idea that has enjoyed success far beyond the railway lines: the whole point of containers is that they allow car-goes to be moved easily between ships, lorries, trains and aircraft without the need for unpacking. Standardization of container trans-port means that containers can be handled quickly wherever they

Modern method of combined rail and road transport in containers.

Car transporters are often used by holidaymakers who want to take their cars to a certain destination without having to drive a long way.
▼

arrive, provided the right equipment is available of course.

Unified couplings are self-locking and automatically connect the brakes and electricity supply at the same time. International co-operation makes ever-increasing demands on goods traffic. Hundreds of thousands of goods wagons pass along railway lines every day. Since it is difficult to increase the speed of trains further, savings can be made by rapid turn-around and making efficient use of returning wagons. This was the reason the organizations EUROP in western Europe and OPW in eastern Europe were set up. Agreement has been reached on a unified system of markings which can be identified by automatic sensors as trains pass. The data thus obtained is stored and processed in a computer, enabling the movements of individual wagons to be monitored. This means that the recipients of consignments can be informed in advance of their arrival, and rolling stock can be earmarked for freight travelling in the opposite direction.

A modern marshalling yard,
where carriages roll down slopes to their assigned tracks. ▼

lation walking speed, i.e. 1.25 m/s (about 2¾ mph). They are then coupled by automatic couplings. Data on the composition of goods trains is then transmitted back to the computer, which stores details of each wagon's journey.

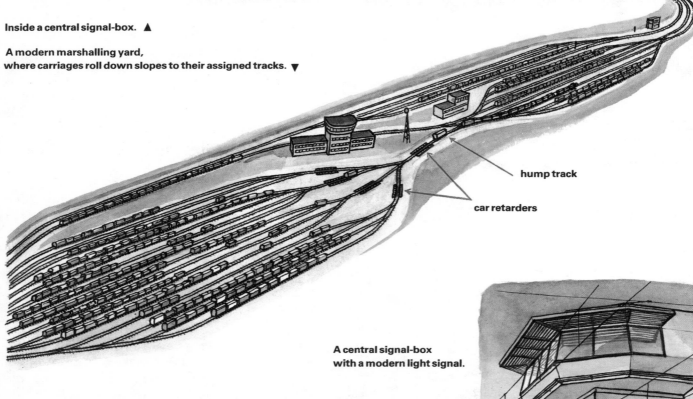

hump track

car retarders

A central signal-box
with a modern light signal.

Today's volume of traffic has made railway stations lively and demanding places to work in. Goods stations, where wagons bound for various destinations have to be made up into trains, occupy a special position. One of the basic principles still used in goods sidings was introduced as long ago as 1846. Wagons are shunted up to the top of a ramp and from there are released and admitted to individual sidings by means of points. These days the system is often highly automated and under the supervision of railwaymen in watchtowers who have a good view of the sidings. Data on the wagons and their destinations may be entered in a computer, which then operates the points automatically. The computer can also regulate the speed of wagons according to a radar sensor, and thus make sure they collide at regu-

Modern technology has brought great improvements in safety on the track. After all, with trains travelling at speeds exceeding 200 km/h (125 mph) a line of signalmen waving flags at each other would scarcely be enough any more, to say nothing of the enormous labour force that would be required. The telegraph and the telephone permitted rapid communication between signal-boxes, but it was not until 1870 that an American called Robinson introduced a principle which made automation possible. It was the electric track circuit: the two rails are isolated from each other electrically, and if a potential is created between them the passage of a metal axle and wheels along a particular section close the circuit. This system can be used to activate signals, level crossing equipment, and so on. Robinson's invention reduced the number of signalmen required by about one per 2 km (1 mile) of track.

Modern systems keep a direct check on drivers, too. Encoded electrical impulses transmit signal information to the engine's cab, and should the driver ignore these or fail to make reciprocal signals of his own to prove he is fully awake, the brakes are automatically applied.

Major lines today have fully automated traffic control systems with two-way communication between train, track and district control centre, where signalmen can monitor the progress of individual trains on a visual display. Since there is a limit to the amount of information which can be carried along the tracks themselves, a system of unshielded cables laid between the rails is used. The train's progress is picked up by these and transmitted to the cab and the control centre. On some railways the signalman in the control centre makes decisions concerning the driving of trains and sends orders to the men on the footplate. On others engine-drivers are autonomous, and signalmen merely monitor the progress of trains in their section, informing them in turn of the situation. Some trains, especially high-speed ones, are fitted with radar, which can warn of obstructions on the track at a distance of several kilometres.

A central processing unit compares train positions and speeds with the timetable, taking into account factors such as inclines and speed limits. Such equipment helps to eliminate human error and also makes traffic management much more efficient, bringing savings all round.

A rail brake, used in conjunction with radar and a computer to regulate the speed of carriages in a marshalling yard.

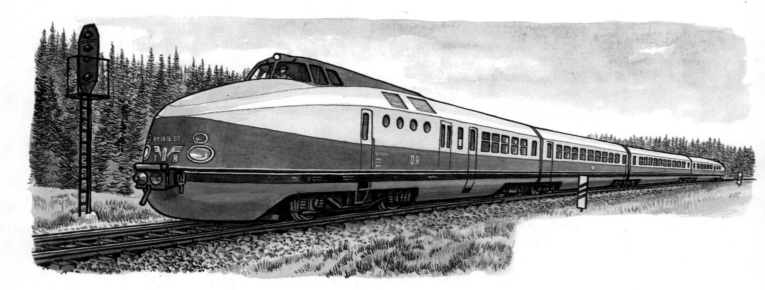

A German diesel express train.

An American express with a steam locomotive.

In the early days the big steam locomotives were the undisputed kings of transport, since there was no other way of getting around so fast, but after the First World War they had road transport and aircraft to compete with. The railways were forced to offer speed with comfort. Many companies aimed at matching the standards of ocean liners, which were very high indeed.

In 1923 the Argentine state railways announced the introduction of special luxury touring trains, and in August of that year the first of these set out on its 12-day 'cruise'. The facilities were admirable. In addition to their own berths, passengers had the use of two dining-cars and an observation-car. One of the Pullman carriages offered dancing to the accompaniment of a piano. In addition, travellers could listen to talks, concerts and drama on the radio. One of the carriages had eight cabins with bathrooms, ladies' and gentlemen's hairdressers, and a manicure salon. A post-office car offered telephone and telegraph services en route.

More recently in the United States the Chicago–Los Angeles express named 'Super Chief' achieved widespread fame. The train covered the 3,600 km (2,250 miles) in 39½ hours. It had observation-cars for those who wished to pass the time admiring the scenery, and a writing room for those with pressing business concerns. Buffets, a bar and a diner offered refreshments and relaxation. The two-tier observation-cars were sufficiently high above the rest of the train to give an all-round view.

Even at the start of the 20th century, the fastest express did more than 100 km/h (62 mph). The coming of motor traction brought with it a new type of express. These trains usually consisted of a number of carriages, dining-cars and sleeping-cars with a motor-powered locomotive at each end. The Americans introduced the aluminium 'flyers' 'Aerotrain' and 'Jet Rocket', partly designed by aircraft engineers. The resulting trains with their aerodynamically shaped locos weighed half as much as existing expresses for the same number of

The Italian express *Settebello*
on the Rome—Florence—Milan—Naples route.

passengers. The air-conditioned 'Aerotrain' carried 400 people at speeds of up to 165 km/h (103 mph) in reclining seats arranged aircraft-fashion, all facing forwards.

As a result of the modernization of European rail services, a network of international expresses was set up. The railways of Belgium, France, Holland, Luxemburg, Italy, West Germany and Switzerland introduced the Trans-Europe Express (TEE). With the age of steam ended and electrification of lines not standardized, diesel-electric locomotives were adopted for the service.

A TEE express usually consists of seven or eight air-conditioned coaches with seating for 120 to 150 passengers in comfortable reclining seats; there is also a dining-room, bar, kitchen and toilets. All the important cities of the member countries are linked by TEE routes, which are now served by all-electric trains as well as diesel-electrics. Many of the TEEs have their own name, usually giving a hint of their destinations. There is the *Rembrandt,* the *Goethe,* and the *Mistral* that runs from Paris to Marseilles and on to Nice. At one time the *Mistral* was the fastest train in Europe and among the 10 fastest in the world.

A modern express buffet carriage.

An express that nowadays commands a great deal of interest is the Spanish *Talgo,* which is built to the pattern of American long-distance trains. The diesel locomotive hauls 16 aluminium coaches each 11 m (36 ft) long, the back ends of which rest on the bogie of the next in line. Stability is impressive, this being an essential quality on the steep inclines and frequent bends of the northern Spanish line. There is no dining-car, however, food being served airline-style in the passengers' seats. The last coach is an observation-car. It is innovations such as these that have allowed rail transport to keep pace with air travel and the private car.

The *Tokaido*,
the first train to reach cruising
speeds of over 200 km/h (124 mph).

The Japanese word 'tokaido' means 'sea journey', but in the history of railways it will always be linked with breaking the 200 km/h (125 mph) barrier in regular rail travel. A standard-gauge track was built from Tokyo to Osaka between 1959 and 1964, alongside the existing narrow-gauge line. The new track was straighter and the bends were as 'open' as possible to allow higher speeds. The route was scarcely ideal, in many places crossing heavily populated areas or mountainous regions. A fifth of the route consists of bridges and embankments, and there are a large number of tunnels.

At the start of regular services 30 trains were running on the new line, each carrying around 1,000 passengers. The journey time from Tokyo to Osaka — about 500 km or 300 miles — was cut from six and a half hours to four. This was later further reduced to three hours ten minutes. Numbers of trains and of passengers have increased steadily since the line was opened in 1964. In order to extend the service to Sapporo, work was begun in 1971 on a tunnel beneath the Tsugaru Strait, separating the islands of Honshu and Hokkaido.

This tunnel is without doubt one of the boldest feats of engineering ever undertaken. Its total length is some 55 km (33 miles), about 22 km (14 miles) of which is 240 m (780 ft)

**The French type TGV train designed for
a cruising speed of 250 km/h (155 mph) or more.**

below the surface of the sea and 10 m (32 ft) under its bed. The structure has to withstand not only immense pressures but also the effects of the earthquakes which frequantly occur in that part of the world. It enables the journey time from Tokyo to Sapporo to be cut from 17 hours, with a ferry journey involved, to a mere six hours.

The high speeds achieved on the Tokaido line place great demands not only on the track but also on the rolling stock. At over 200 km/h (125 mph) a great deal of energy is required just to overcome air resistance, so that the aerodynamics of coach design must be carefully cal-

runs have provided strong motivation. On the world scale, arterial fast rail links include the Washington—New York—Boston run in the United States and the Moscow—Leningrad line in the Soviet Union. In West Germany increases in speed are being sought on the Hamburg—Cologne—Frankfurt—Stuttgart—Munich route. Even Alpine countries are boosting speed. In Italy most attention is being paid to the Naples—Rome—Milan link, while the Swiss are concentrating on the Zurich—Chiasso line. By means of tunnels through the foothills of the Alps, a high-speed north-south connection across Europe will be built.

Advanced Passenger Train made the run from London to Glasgow and has reached a maximum speed of 315 km/h (196 mph) in trial operation.

The pride of French railways is the ETG — Element à Turbine Gaz — which went into service from Paris to Cherbourg in 1970. Two years later there were 16 turbotrains running at speeds of up to 200 km/h (125 mph). In December 1972 a light engine of this type reached a speed of 318 km/h (198 mph). The French superexpress TGV reaching an average speed of 270 km/h (168 mph) was introduced on the Paris—Lyons line in 1981.

culated. This has meant tackling the problem of the spaces between coaches, covers underneath the train, the effect of projections such as handles and the like. Brakes and safety devices also had to meet exacting specifications.

In heavily-populated Europe, divided in addition by the Alps, we can scarcely expect 200 km/h (125 mph) speeds to become general, but there is a constant striving for greater speeds on the main routes. The energy crisis of the 1970s and the hope that trains might take over the function of aircraft on medium-haul

Europe already has its own 200 km/h (125 mph) expresses similar to those on the Tokaido line. The doors open and close electrically, there is double-glazing, air-conditioning and pneumatic suspension. Carriages lean over on bends to prevent passengers from feeling ill. The British Rail version is called the High Speed Train. Seven carriages run between two diesel-electric locomotives developing 1,680 kW (2,250 hp). In 1973 the train set a world speed record for a diesel locomotive of 230 km/h (143 mph). In 1978 the British turbo-powered

The fastest trains on British lines are the High Speed Trains (HST) drawn by diesel-electric locomotives.

With today's top trains doing speeds of over 200 km/h (125 mph) and speeds of around 160 km/h (100 mph) being quite routine on many runs, experts are trying to assess the maximum speeds attainable with the traction provided by conventional tracks, and to come up with a system which would allow these limitations to be overcome.

**An operation trial
for a French Aerotrain,
travelling on an air cushion.**

With train speeds now in excess of 200 km/h (125 mph), designers are looking for new systems to replace the conventional two-rail tracks that have been around so long. Major energy losses take place at high speeds through air resistance and friction at the rail surface. A 200-tonne train requires a power input of around 2,800 kW (3,750 hp) to travel at 200 km/h (125 mph), whereas at 300 km/h (186 mph) this rises to 8,000 kW (10,730 hp), and at 400 km/h (250 mph) to twice that. This means that improved performances call not only for more powerful engines and better aerodynamics, but also for low-friction tracks.

One attempted solution has been the air cushion, which allows trains to travel on a type of rail without making contact with it. The first practical trials of this type were carried out in France, where Jean Bertin's train first ran in 1966. The Aerotrain, as it was called, 'flew'

5 mm (about ⅕ in) above a concrete track of inverted 'T' cross-section and attracted a good deal of attention. It was powered by a Continental aero-engine at the rear by means of a propeller 2 m (6½ ft) long. Although the short test section of rail prevented it from reaching top speed, the train exceeded 130 km/h (80 mph) on its first trial run. The Aerotrain remained in experimental

service for two years, carrying some 5,500 passengers, and in 1967 it reached a speed of 345 km/h (215 mph).

Air-cushion trains were tried in Britain, too, where the Hovercar system used a V-shaped groove instead of a rail. In the United States an attempt was made to develop a hovertrain system to replace internal air links. About 50,000 people a day fly between New York and Washington, which gives some idea of the volume of traffic involved. The introduction of hovertrains, with forecast speeds of some 480 km/h (300 mph) would make connections such as that more economical. However, the various schemes tried soon ran into problems, such as excessive engine noise and the need to expend huge amounts of energy in order to maintain the air cushion.

A further possible means of reducing friction is by the electromagnetic cushion, a field in which German designers have achieved success. In 1976 they broke the 400 km/h (250 mph) barrier with such a train. A new type of motor is naturally required for very high speeds, and some projects using a linear electric motor look

Transrapid is a West German
experimental train driven
by a linear magnetic motor.

Modernization of transport depends
not only on modernization of tracks and
vehicles but also on the use of modern
technology for the administrative work.

forward to speeds of around
500 km/h (310 mph).

Although cushioned-rail systems
are still largely on the drawing-
board, designers are already giving
consideration to a further generation of vehicles, at present beyond
the layman's wildest dreams. These
would be in the form of projectiles,
moving along a tube at speeds
comparable to those with which
a bullet leaves a rifle. Here planners
can find plenty of scope for their
imagination. Some see the possibility of such 'trains' getting up speed
by plunging towards the earth's
core before gradually returning to
the surface, perhaps on another
continent. Or a vacuum might be
created in front of the vehicle, so
that atmospheric pressure would
drive it along the tube like a piston in
a cylinder. Another possibility
would be to pump air from in front
of the vehicle and expel it from
behind... For the present, however,
these are still just dreams.

numbers in italics refer to captions

Water TRANSPORT

Boats have always been more than just a way of getting around. They helped men to trade with each other, and to find and conquer strange lands. Above all they speeded up the progress of civilization. Indeed, there is a saying that Columbus and his caravels sailed not only to the shores of a new world, but to the threshold of a new age.

How did it all begin?

Many thousands of years ago, when bands of prehistoric hunters roamed the banks of rivers and streams, where they had the best

The first genuine water craft were built by sharpening one end of a tree-trunk. Raft building and the construction of the first boats followed.

The basic technique of shaping a trunk was burning and hewing. The technique is still used by some primitive tribes.

Various shapes of paddles.

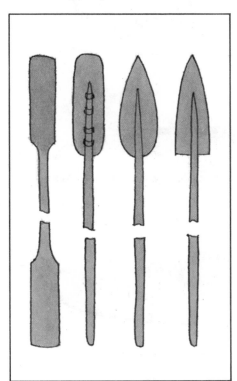

chance of finding game animals, birds and fish, a huntsman discovered that clutching a thick branch or tree-trunk helped him keep afloat. He may have been trying to save himself from floodwaters, as he had seen the animals do, or he may have wanted to cross to the opposite bank. Perhaps it was not a piece of wood, but an ice floe or even a floating carcase that he used. Whatever the case, the world's first boat journey had been made.

As time went by, men realized how much simpler it was to float downstream than to hack their way through the primeval forest, and they began to pay more attention to the tree-trunk. They lopped off its branches and began to ponder over the loads it could carry, its stability, and ways of steering it.

It was then that the first true water craft saw the light of day. One way men improved on the simple tree-trunk was by fastening a number of them together to make a raft. This increased stability a good deal, and what was more it meant that they could carry both cargo and crew; the crew could even steer in a sim-

ple sort of way with the aid of stout branches. The other direction in which the first boat-builders developed their skills was by modifying the individual trunks. They would choose a tree with soft wood, and if possible with one side fairly flat. Then they chiselled and burned a hollow to make a 'dugout', at first quite shallow. There are primitive tribes in South America that use the technique to this day. By and by the bows of such craft, although still rounded, became more shaped than the heavier stern. Then the simple branch used for steering

Different primitive crafts.
Typical Pacific boats are equipped with outriggers.

developed into the paddle, which was not only an effective rudder, but as the first means of propulsion meant that these primitive boatmen were no longer compelled to travel downstream.

Clearly, this reconstruction of the origin of the first boats cannot be uniformly applied to all parts of the prehistoric world. In some places, especially those with a warmer climate, the material used may have been reeds; elsewhere it was bark, or animal hides — whatever happened to be on hand.

Basket-shaped leather boats like this were far from ideally designed and were used for short journeys only.

It is still to some extent an open question when exactly men started to use water craft deliberately, but archaeological finds and other indications give us a rough idea at least. We think it was the end of the first Ice Age at the latest, or around 10,000 years B.C., at a time when the melting ice caused flooding in many areas of Europe, Asia and the Americas, so that men either found something to float on, or drowned.

Leaving aside various ways of carrying or dragging loads, it is clear that the rafts and dugouts of our early ancestors were in fact the very first means of transport man ever had, and the process of improving it has been going on for a very long time. Although it was too long ago for any real evidence of men's early boatbuilding efforts to have been preserved, it is fairly easy to guess what went on by looking at the craft used by primitive tribes today. In many cases such boats exist (or until recently existed) in forms which have changed little over thousands of years.

In some regions the dugout went through a gradual raising of the sides, bow and stern until the piragua came into being. Indian fishermen from the north-west coast of North America were able to make piraguas up to 25 m (82 ft) long from cedar trunks and sailed far out to sea on them, hunting whales with harpoons. The inhabitants of the Pacific islands, on the other hand, used outriggers to stabilize their shallow craft.

Often the material used was not

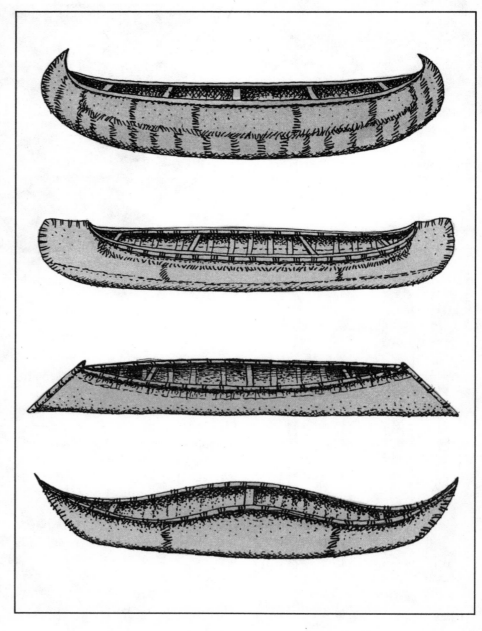

Different sorts of North American Indian canoes. Those with taller bows and stern were used in fast-flowing or rough water.

The Eskimo kayak is still considered one of the best-designed and most manoeuvrable craft in the world.

the trunks of trees. There were many parts of the world where suitable timber did not grow, and leather, for instance, was used instead. At first men just inflated an ordinary leather bag and floated along on that. Then they started to join these bags together. The Assyrians built rafts on such leather floats, which were safe to use even on fast-flowing streams. Another solution was to stretch camel skins over a round, basket-like frame made of wicker or supple branches. Such craft were clumsy, and manageable only in calm, shallow waters, but in the far north of America there was a boat which could be steered perfectly — the Eskimo's kayak, with its frame of whale ribs covered in sealskin. The use of paddles on either side and the slim, purpose-built lines made not only for great manoeuvrability, including the famous 'Eskimo roll', but also for considerable speed in pursuing prey through the Arctic waters.

Apart from kayaks, which were only for the hunters, the Eskimos had a much bigger type of wood and skin boat, the open umiak, which they used for the transport of whole families and their luggage. The umiak was not dissimilar to the currach or coracle of the Irish Celts which were later fitted with sails. There exists substantial evidence that the Celts used such craft to sail to Greenland and America even earlier than the Vikings.

The bark of oak, elm, birch and other trees also served as material for making boats. The most remarkable and most practical of these craft was (and still is) the Indian canoe, constructed of birch bark. It originated in the heavily forested areas of the north-eastern region of North America, criss-crossed with streams and rivers and dotted with numerous lakes. The bark was sewn together in strips and stretched over transverse wooden ribs, and the resulting craft was so light that one man on his own was able to carry it from river to river. There were diffe-

rent canoes for different purposes, as regards both shape and material, and leather was also used for this type of boat.

In the Pacific there were boats (or more often rafts) made of bamboo, or various sorts of rushes. On Lake Titicaca in Peru fishing boats made of strong bundles of rushes may be seen to this day. In ancient Egypt, which records show to have been the cradle of ocean navigation, the papyrus boat marked the start of a process of development that culminated in bold voyages far from land.

At first the Egyptians confined themselves to short trips along the Nile, since their craft made of simple bundles of papyrus with raised bows and sterns were not fit for more adventurous excursions. Yet it was these boats which, according to ancient cave drawings, first used simple rudders in the form of a hanging paddle. In the early days these boats were propelled by paddles, too.

Although we speak of Egypt as the cradle of ocean navigation, it would be more accurate to say that it is there that the greatest number of records has been preserved, ranging from cave paintings, through inscriptions and pottery from the

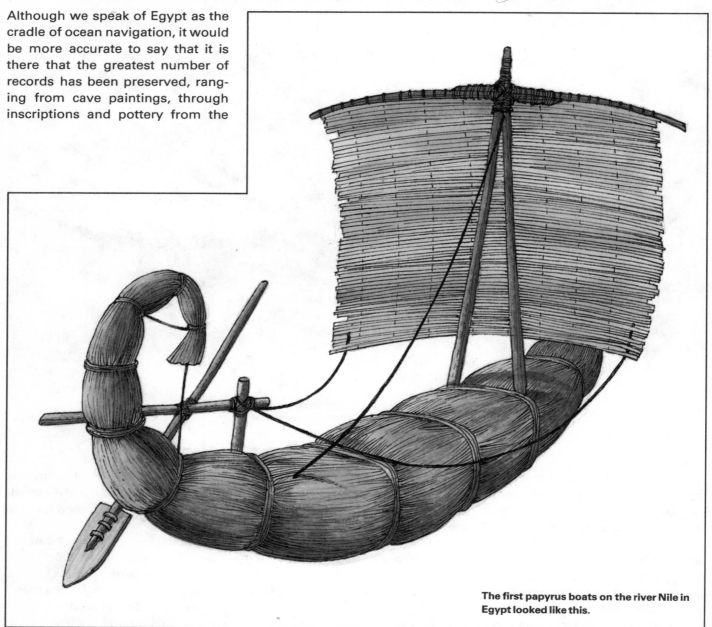

The first papyrus boats on the river Nile in Egypt looked like this.

Nile Valley going back as far as 5000 years B.C., to finds of models or actual craft beneath the pyramids. In fact the whole of the eastern Mediterranean region, including Crete, Syria, Lebanon (Phoenicia) and Greece deserves the honour; these were the same lands where agriculture began, laying the foundations of civilization. In general, however, it can be said that, while the vessels of the Egyptians and Phoenicians were used mainly for trade, those of the Minoans of Crete and later those of the

Romans had a more warlike role to play.

The primitive papyrus boats which were used for transport on the Nile became the starting point for the building of sea-going vessels. As time went by, these acquired a strong, tensioned rope running from stem to stern and held up in between by forked supports, which to some extent did the job of a keel. A simple four-cornered sail appeared, which reduced the oarsmen's exertions, with a following wind at least, and was fastened by

means of two stays to a double folding mast in the bows of the vessel.

Bundles of papyrus soon became inadequate to the shipbuilder's needs. Since there was a lack of suitable wood in Egypt, planks cut from acacia trees were employed, and to some extent also from sycamores, the felling of which had to be approved by the monarch himself. These planks, about 1 m (3 ft 4 in) long, were joined together by wooden nails in such a way that a crescent-shaped hull was gradually built up, which in some places had to be stopped up with bundles of papyrus. It was reinforced not by a keel and ribs, but with transverse hoops and a tensioning rope. The finishing touches were put to the boat's appearance by binding the ends at the bows and stern, often in the shape of a lotus flower. By this time paddles had been replaced by oars.

That, at least, is what the world's oldest preserved ship looks like. It was discovered under the pyramid of Cheops, and is considered to have been the funeral or 'sun' ship of the pharaoh of the same name. Although it was built almost 5000 years ago, the 600 planks that make up its hull have been preserved almost intact in the dry desert air, throughout the whole of the craft's considerable length (40.5 m or 133 ft) and width (7.9 m or 26 ft). In this particular case the builders used rare cedar from Phoenicia.

Naturally, such craft were used more for ocean voyages than for ceremonial purposes. At first this meant trips along the Mediterra-

nean coastline, but later also to Crete and Mycenae, and southwards to the Red Sea. The main reason for these was trade, although ancient records also refer to military expeditions. So, for instance, the pharaoh Snefru, in about 2800 B.C., sent 40 vessels to the Phoenician port of Byblos to buy cedar, while 200 years later another ruler sent eight ships filled with armed men to plunder Phoenicia.

Even around the year 3000 B.C. the lure of rare goods — gold, ivory, ebony, cedar, frankincense, myrrh — exotic animals (such as monkeys) and easily acquired slaves took the Egyptians to the Red Sea region. The most frequent goal was the Land of Punt, probably lying where Somalia is today.

Detailed information on such voyages is provided by the reliefs in the temple of Deir el-Bahri in the Valley

The sailed rowing boats of Queen Hatshepsut of Egypt made a relatively long voyage across the Red Sea to the east coast of Africa.

of Kings. They show that in the first half of the 15th century B.C., Queen Hatshepsut sent an expedition of five barges equipped with sails to Punt. They were around 30 m (98 ft) long and had 30 oarsmen, 15 on each side. The reliefs also show a simple fixed mast amidships, with spars capable of exploiting winds from abeam.

Later improvements in Egyptian vessels are documented by pictures on the walls of the tomb of the last of the great pharaohs, Rameses II, showing his fleet in a victorious battle with marauders from the north around 1200 B.C The sail (without a bottom spar) is controlled by sheets, and at the masthead there is a crow's-nest for a lookout. A ram for destroying enemy ships protrudes from the bow. The sides of the ship are higher than before, offering greater protection for the oarsmen. Since there is no tensioning rope, it must be supposed that these vessels had ribs. This, however, as we shall soon see, was not an invention of the Egyptians, but of their enemies.

For all the advances made in their design, Egyptian sea-going vessels remained little more than glorified Nile barges, and the crews of these frail craft were loath to venture out of sight of land. Soon, however, the first true mariners were to arrive on the scene.

Unfortunately, we still know very little about the craft of the Minoans, the inhabitants of Crete. The vessels used by the Phoenicians are less of a mystery, although most of what we know comes from Egyptian or Assyrian sources, since the Phoenicians themselves guarded their design secrets jealously.

The land of Phoenicia, beneath the Lebanese mountains on the Mediterranean's eastern shore, was settled around the year 3000 B.C. The soil was poorly suited to agriculture, but the coastline offered good anchorages, and cedars, whose wood made ideal shipbuilding material, thrived in the area. It was thus no accident that over the centuries the Phoenicians became renowned both as bold seafarers, with a knowledge of astronomy which guided them on the open sea, and as enterprising traders who founded rich colonies on the Mediterranean shoreline, such as Carthage, where Tunisia lies today. From 1000 B.C. their influence spread steadily. After reaching the shores of Spain, where they founded Cádiz, these dauntless mariners sailed past the Pillars of Hercules out of the Mediterranean, and brought back cargoes of tin from as far away as Britain. At the end of the 7th century B.C. they circumnavigated Africa from the Red Sea, sailing through the Atlantic and back to the Mediterranean, and in the 5th century B.C. the Phoenician admiral Hanno voyaged along the West African coast as far as present-day Cameroun.

The 'sea nomads', as the Phoenicians were sometimes called, had two main types of craft, both already featuring a keel and ribs. The first was a heavy cargo boat, broad

in the beam and with tall sides. It had an oblong sail, a crow's-nest and rope ladders. The second was a much lighter sort of vessel, previously unknown, but later to be called a galley. The Phoenician version, a bireme, was a fast rowing vessel with two banks of oars, a sail, and in particular a huge ram. The fact that the Phoenicians used these craft mainly for raids, piracy and other warlike expeditions is indicated, apart from the ram, by the 'bridge' for warriors that extended down the middle from bow to stern.

The Greeks benefited directly from the naval, trading and colonizing experience of the Phoenicians. From the 8th century B.C. they gradually took over control of the whole of the western Mediterranean, the Black Sea (then known as the Euxine) and the Aegean. Their long voyages were the inspiration for famous legends, such as the *Argosy*, which tells of the voyage of the *Argos* to the fabulous land of Colchis on the Black Sea coast in search of the Golden Fleece, or the *Odyssey*, recounting the Trojan War. Later such voyages were recorded by scholars and historians, such as Pytheas of Massilia, who

A Greek merchant ship.

In contrast to the broad-beamed merchant vessels, Greek warships were slender. The illustration shows a 5th-century B.C. bireme.
▼

describes a voyage to the Atlantic undertaken in 354 B.C. There is also an interesting account of a sea voyage in the story of Alexander the Great's Indian campaign, when part of his army under the leadership of Nearchus sailed from the mouth of the Indus to that of the Tigris and the Euphrates in 324 B.C.

Although Greek cargo ships differed very little from their Phoenician prototypes – the chief innovation being a second, slanting mast at the bows with a sail called an artemon – the design of military biremes had been perfected. Greek biremes were lighter and more manoeuvrable than the Phoenician sort, and apart from the now standard complement of 50 rowers (25 on each side), they carried into battle archers and slingers, standing on a bridge. Before long the Greeks designed a ship which was

probably even more renowned, the trireme. This was usually 35–40 m (115–130 ft) long and 5–6 m (16–20 ft) wide. The number of rowers was increased to 170, sitting in three rows (62 + 54 + 54), although no one knows exactly how. Triremes, like biremes, had two masts which were lowered before joining battle.

The naval prowess of the Greeks is illustrated by the Battle of Salamis in 480 B.C., when 385 of their triremes (200 of them belonging to Athens) were faced with a Persian fleet outnumbering them three to one. The superior tactical skills and better manoeuvrability of the Greeks enabled them to put the enemy ships to flight before the eyes of the Persian King Xerxes himself. They destroyed 200 of the heavier Persian craft for the loss of only 40 triremes.

A Roman merchant ship
of the 3rd century A.D.

An attack bridge,
or raven, on a Roman galley.

The Phoenicians and Greeks had become famous for their boatbuilding and navigating skills, which had brought them victory in battle and taken them to distant lands, but the great naval power of the Mediterranean was to be Rome. For a long time the Romans had no navy. They were poor boat-builders and even poorer sailors. Farmers, soldiers and senators liked to keep their feet planted firmly on dry land, and so the dominion and influence of the Republic was spread exclusively by overland routes. All that changed, however, when they went to war with the Phoenician colony of Carthage over the island of Sicily. The Romans suddenly found that an effective fleet was something no ambitious nation could afford to do without.

To some extent fate played into their hands. In 269 B.C. the Italian coastline was attacked by a Carthaginian naval force, and one quinquireme, a ship with five banks of oars, fell into Roman hands. This gave them an insight into the secrets of shipbuilding that they so badly needed, and soon afterwards the Senate decided that a fleet of 120 warships would be constructed with the help of Greek boat-builders resident in Italy. The resulting vessels were neither particularly graceful, manoeuvrable nor fast, but they were big and strong, which suited Roman naval tactics.

The Romans introduced into sea battles their considerable experience in fighting on land. The most important technical innovation was a drawbridge-like device called a raven used for grappling with and boarding enemy ships; after that the infantry could take over. This new tactic brought the Romans an unexpected victory over the Carthaginians at the Battle of Mylae in the year 260 B.C. and played a major role in their winning the First Punic

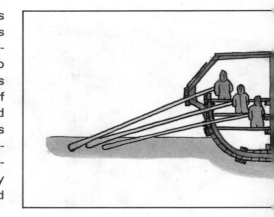

War and taking control of Sicily.

At a later date the Romans added an upper deck to their galleys — the lower deck, below the water-line, housed the oarsmen's benches — which contained catapults and sometimes a wooden superstructure. In 31 B.C., however, when Roman fought Roman at the Battle of Actium — a contest between Anthony and Cleopatra's fleets and that of Octavian — it was lighter,

A diagram to show two possible arrangements of oars and oarsmen in an ancient trireme.

Roman oared warships were designed as fighting platforms for legionaries.

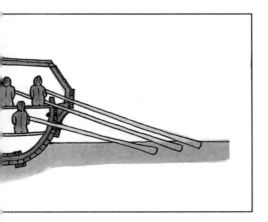

more agile craft that decided the issue as soon as Anthony's ships had taken flight. These were the liburnae, vessels with 25 rowers on each side in a single bank and originally designed to protect merchant ships in the Adriatic.

Roman cargo vessels were also very large — 55 m (180 ft) long on average, almost 14 m (46 ft) in the beam, and 13.5 m (44 ft) deep. As well as the artemon at the bows,

they carried a split triangular sail over the mainsail and more complicated rigging. The oar-type rudder remained virtually unchanged since the days of ancient Egypt.

The early period of sea voyages is naturally associated with the start of navigation. Probably the very first navigational aid came into being back in the days when boats stayed within sight of the shore in the daytime and dropped anchor or were beached at night: this was the lead-line for 'sounding' the depth of water. The Phoenicians later learned to get their bearings by the position of the sun and stars — especially the Pole Star in the constellation Ursa Minor, indicating north. In Homer's days the Greeks already had a wind rose, and had identified the four main wind directions and thus the cardinal points of the compass:

'Boreas' was the north wind, 'Notos' the south wind, 'Euros' the

east wind and 'Zephyros' was the west wind.

Maps were a long time in coming, but various parts of the Mediterranean were described in guides written by those who had sailed there. Around 130 A.D. the first map of the lands and seas then known was produced. It included latitudes and longitudes, and its creator was the astronomer, mathematician and geographer Ptolemy, known as the father of cartography. His maps, which gave a reasonably true representation of the lands from the Canary Islands to China, laid the foundation for the discovery of new continents.

Let us now call to mind one other navigational aid invented in classical times — the lighthouse, the most famous of which stood on the island of Pharos at the entrance to the harbour of Alexandria, and was numbered among the seven wonders of the ancient world.

While the Arabs were taking control of the Mediterranean after the disintegration of the Roman Empire, bringing with them further design innovations such as the rudder and the triangular or lateen sail, it was the members of Germanic tribes, the Norsemen and Vikings, who became the pioneers of seafaring in western and northern Europe.

Ocean-going vessels were used in northern Europe even at the start of the Bronze Age, as shown in cave paintings. By the 4th century A.D. they had reached such a degree of sophistication that Scandinavian tribes could make long voyages in them, especially for the purpose of carrying out their notorious raids, when they plundered and destroyed without mercy. Their courage, discipline, battle skills and defiance of death made them greatly feared. From the 8th century their sudden raids threatened not only the sea coast, but also settlements along the banks of major rivers. These incursions were not the only goal of their voyages, for they also settled and colonized many previously uninhabited areas.

At first the long ships confined their activities to the Baltic and the North Sea, but by the end of the 8th century they became a familiar, if unwelcome sight along the coasts of Britain and Ireland. In the 9th century they appeared on the Rhine, the Loire and the Seine, besieging Paris, and penetrated the Mediterranean as far· as southern Italy and Sicily. The Norsemen ruled much of England and part of the Irish coast. They came from the north-west to take over a large part of what is now Russia; they sailed the Dnieper to the Black Sea and the Volga, and Caspian Sea to Persia.

The same fierce warriors colonized Iceland. In 981 Eric the Red was banished from there for murder, and made landfall in Greenland; soon the Vikings began to colonize its southern coast, though in those days the climate there was somewhat better than it is today.

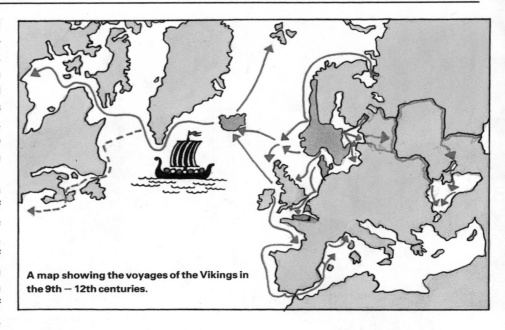

A map showing the voyages of the Vikings in the 9th — 12th centuries.

As well as their voyages of discovery, the Vikings were also known for their conquest and colonization.
▼

The expedition which is considered the climax of Norse seafaring was the voyage to America. In 1001

Eric's son, Leif Ericsson, was the first European to set foot in the New World, and in subsequent years the Norsemen founded three settlements there: Helluland (in Labrador), Markland (Newfoundland) and Vinland (near present-day New York). It is possible that the Vikings had learned of these countries across the ocean in Ireland, back in the 8th century. Celtic legends similar to the *Odyssey* relate the stories of long voyages, such as Maildune's travels or the journey of St. Brendan, who lived in the 6th century.

What were the boats like in which the Vikings undertook such daring journeys? We know the answer from archaeological finds. These northern warriors were so intimately linked with the sea that their chieftains were buried along with their boats, so that Norse vessels have been found in several places,

quite well preserved under layers of mud.

The first such craft were simple affairs hollowed out of oak trees and propelled by paddles; later a keel, ribs, planking, oars and an oar-type rudder appeared. The evolution of the long ships can be traced according to different types named after the places they were found. So the Nydam boat, almost 23 m (75 ft) long and dating from the 4th century, was not suitable for moving under sail. The later Oseberg and Gokstad ships, from the 8th and 9th centuries respectively, had a rectangular sail with a stay, on a short, thick mast.

The Vikings, too, had different ships for transport and for war. The knorr cargo ship was up to 20 m (65 ft) long, with a maximum ratio of length to beam of 4:1. These craft had fewer oarsmen and no deck, the

cargo being carried on the bottom. The slimmer and longer long ships, used for military purposes, were, in the 10th to 13th centuries, about twice as long as the cargo vessels, with a length-beam ratio of up to 7:1. They were propelled by as many as 60 rowers, who also took up arms if required. These vessels, having a tall prow and stern, perfectly planked sides with the planks overlapped like roofing tiles — known as clinker construction — later came to be called drakkars (dragons). In spite of their apparent simplicity, they were capable of long voyages in the Atlantic or through a stormy North Sea. Without doubt the most famous of the Norse ships, celebrated in sagas, was the *Ormrinn Langi* (Long Serpent) of the Norse king and hero Olaf Trygvasson, who died in a naval battle in the year 1000.

In the 12th century, when Viking aggression in the Atlantic and northern Europe was lessening, and the power of the Arabs in the Mediterranean was also on the wane, the golden age of Polynesian discoveries in the Pacific was reaching its climax. These intrepid mariners had made their way from southeast Asia, through Indonesia to what are today called the Society Islands. They then moved on from Tahiti to Hawaii in the 11th century, and in the 13th century reached Easter Island. They are also assumed to have reached the west coast of America and even the edge of the south polar ice-field. These amazing voyages were made in primitive, albeit twin-hulled or outrigged craft — catamarans and proas — steered by means of an oar and powered by a triangular sail in the shape of a crab's claw. The Polynesians used the space between the two hulls as storage or living space, or to transport such cargoes as dogs, pigs or the corms of agricultural plants. These excellent sailors were able to exploit to the full all manner of marine currents and winds, but their chief navigational aid was the stars. They did not rely on a single fixed star, however, but knew by heart the sequence through which certain triangles of stars passed as the heavens 'turned'!

The decline in Arab power in the south-west Mediterranean was accompanied by the growth in importance of a number of coastal towns engaged in commerce, and therefore also in sea travel. Examples were Genoa and later Venice, which reached the height of its power at the end of the 14th century. Of the ports on the Iberian peninsula, Valencia and Barcelona were important on the Mediterranean, Lisbon on the Atlantic coast.

In England and in northern Europe, too, there were ports that rose steadily in influence, especially the German ones, which formed a special league or Hanse to protect

A Mediterranean Crusaders' ship with lateen sails.

their trading interests. This later included not only ports such as Lübeck, Hamburg and Riga, but also inland commercial centres like Magdeburg, Cologne and Cracow.

There was a similar association on the south coast of England called the Cinque Ports, comprising Dover, Hythe, Romney, Hastings and Sandwich. Transportation of goods by sea was cheaper, in view of the various tolls and taxes that were payable along overland routes. It was also safer, since a merchant convoy on the open sea stood a better chance against pirates than a wagon train moving across hilly or wooded countryside on poor

roads did against bands of robbers.

Trade was not the only factor which contributed to progress in seafaring. An important boost was provided by the Crusades, whose participants frequently undertook the uncomfortable voyage in cramped shipboard conditions inspired not only by their Christian faith, but also by a vision of rich booty. The sailing ships used in the north of Europe and in the Atlantic bore for a long time the mark of the old Viking ships, though oars had now disappeared. So, for instance, English vessels still had the typical hull shape, one large rectangular sail, and an oar-type rudder, but

▲
A 13th-century English sailing vessel. These ships began to have a superstructure.

A 14th-century Hanseatic cog.
▼

conspicuous wooden superstructures had appeared at the bows and stern, called castles.

The Hanseatic League ships already had their castles built into the hull, and apart from the single mainmast there was also a bowsprit, later serving for the rigging of jibs. The most significant novelty, however, was the hanging rudder, the oldest depiction of which is known from Winchester cathedral, and dates from around 1180.

The design of Mediterranean vessels underwent changes from the start of the medieval period which were inspired both by the ships of the Northmen and, especially, those of the Arab mariners. There were already two masts on the dromonds, fast warships also powered by oars, and on the Crusaders' ships sailing for the Holy Land. The triangular lateen sail was also widely used.

It was no accident that the 15th century brought a watershed in the history of seafaring. The time seemed to be right for several reasons. The shores of the Mediterranean and the Atlantic were no longer unknown territory where experienced sailors stopped off when they had to; there were now more or less well known ports along the routes taken by merchant vessels or Crusaders' ships, and the unknown, which began to tempt Europeans, lay over the horizon to the west.

The trade which had grown up between the Mediterranean and the Hanseatic ports was still under the control of the Persians and Arabs from the east. Merchants were now anxious to get to India and China directly, to cut out the middleman. Progress in shipbuilding meant that this commercial dream could now become a reality.

At the end of the 14th century the memory of the slender, clinker-built Viking drakkars with their shallow displacement was fading for ever. The development of castles, which were gradually incorporated into the hull, raising the bows and, to an

Mediterranean, square sails were more practical in the frequently storm-tossed Atlantic. When these replaced lateen sails on the mainmast of the caravel, the 'caravel redonda' was born. Square sails were used even more freely on the heaviest ship of the period, the carrack, where only the mizzenmast carried a lateen sail.

Navigation, too, was undergoing a period of rapid improvement.

The hulls of medieval sailing ships grew larger in the 14th century.

A rudder pivoted on the transom (bottom) gradually replaced the oar-type rudder (top).
►

even greater extent, the stern, along with the switch to double afterdecks with cabins, meant that displacements had to increase very substantially. Then, through the combination of the two basic types of sail, the lateen and the square, and an increase in the number of masts to two and later three, the typical design of the late medieval sailing vessel crystallized. It was a ship capable of carrying a large amount of supplies and of staying at sea for long periods.

So the small three-masted fishing vessels with lateen sails gave way in the 15th century to the caravel, capable of carrying twice the cargo. Although the triangular lateen sail on long, slanting stays was excellent for the calm waters of the

Although the magnetic needle had been known in Europe since the 12th century, it was only now that it was put to use in conjunction with a wind rose, divided into 32 points, to form the basis of the modern compass. Ptolemy's maps were brought out again, and the astronomer's astrolabe was adapted to the mariner's requirements. New guides and charts were published, and with the effort to establish latitudes and longitudes the notion of a globe rather than the previously accepted flat Earth surrounded by water began to take root.

All this progress was put into practice in Sagres, where Portugal's Prince Henry the Navigator founded a nautical school, an observatory and a shipyard in 1430. There the Portuguese learned not only to build better boats, but also to draw charts (a subject taught by Catalonian experts), to navigate and, of course, to sail.

Henry also encouraged the first Portuguese attempts to find an eastern passage to India along the West African coast. By the time he died in 1460 his countrymen had got as far as the River Gambia, where at last the coastline turns, as sailors had hoped it would, to the south-east, but it was left to the next generation of mariners to complete the task.

The carrack, *Santa Catalina,* **in which Pedro de Mendoza sailed up the River Plate, Argentina, in 1536.**

Henry of Portugal's successor, Alfonso V, though not himself an enthusiastic sailor, was no less energetic in his support for the drive south along the African seaboard. He was also just as pleased as his predecessor to see how the stone pillars with a cross and a coat-of-arms which marked new Portuguese territory were steadily increasing in number. The sailors themselves, with the prospect of growing rich from gold and slaves, had every reason to press on, and in 1474 they reached present-day Cameroun, in 1482 Angola; and in 1484 Diogo Cão sailed to the mouth of the Congo.

Three years later Bartholomew Dias sailed from Lisbon with two caravels and one cargo ship and, after a stormy trip, reached the southernmost tip of Africa. However, because of a shortage of supplies, and discontent among the crew, he was unable to complete the journey to India, and after 16 months and 17 days he dropped anchor in Lisbon once again. Dias, aptly if somewhat unenthusiastically, named the place he had discovered Stormy Cape, but the king himself later changed this to Cape of Good Hope. Perhaps he wanted to underline that the real goal still lay ahead, or perhaps he thought that any ship that had made it to the Cape had the worst of its voyage behind it.

The Portuguese did their best to keep their discoveries a secret from possible competitors, but before they had the chance to complete the trip to India via the Cape, the whole of Europe was fascinated by news of another voyage of discovery.

The expedition that caused such a stir, and became the most famous voyage of all time, was led by a Genoan called Christopher Columbus. Born in 1451, the son of a weaver, he became a seaman on the Mediterranean and then was a sugar buyer in the Azores and Canary Islands. By the time he was 30 he was a master mariner in the Portuguese merchant service, hav-

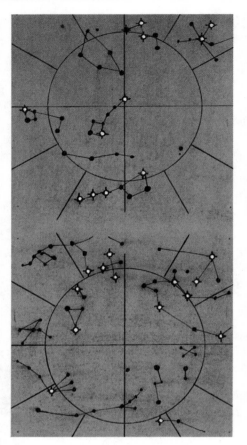

ing studied the science of navigation diligently. When marriage opened doors for him at court, he was able to come forward with a proposal for a completely new sort of maritime expedition to the west, in the course of which he hoped to reach not only India but also Japan and China. After long-drawn-out negotiations he gained the patronage of Ferdinand V and Isabella of Spain, and on 3 August 1492 he set sail from the Spanish port of Palos. His small fleet comprised the caravels *Niña* and *Pinta* and the carrack *Santa Maria,* his flagship, still thought by some to have been a caravel too. After undertaking essential repairs in the Canary Islands and replacing the *Niña's* lateen sails with square ones, Columbus took on the Atlantic Ocean. It was 12

The main constellations of the northern (top) and southern (bottom) sky.

 **Spanish conquistadors.**

October before Rodrigo de Triana on the *Pinta* was able to call out 'Tierra! Tierra!' The coastline he had sighted was that of San Salvador in the Bahamas, although to the end of his days Columbus himself thought it was one of the numerous islands lying to the east of the Asian mainland which Marco Polo had described at the end of the 13th century.

In spite of losing the *Santa Maria*, which was wrecked on the coast of Hispaniola in December, the two remaining vessels visited Cuba and Haiti before setting out homeward on 16 January. In Spain he was fêted and made 'admiral of the ocean sea'.

Columbus made a further three trips westwards, but the first ship to drop anchor on the American mainland, in 1497, was the small carrack *Matthew* of the Italian Giovanni Caboto, known as John Cabot, who

C. Columbus's flotilla — the carrack *Santa Maria* and the caravels *Pinta* and *Niña*.
▼

was in the service of Henry VII. He set a more northerly course, landing in Newfoundland, but icebergs soon forced him to return home. None the less, his voyage was of great significance, although the miserly Henry rewarded him with a mere £10.

Now that the ships of other maritime nations had started to brave the waters of the Atlantic, the Spanish and the Portuguese were quick to ask the Pope to demarcate their spheres of influence. The pontiff complied in full in the Treaty of Tordesillas (1494), which drew a line to the west of the Cape Verde Islands. All discoveries to the west of this were to be Spanish territory, those to the east Portuguese.

The two powers soon took advantage of this. In 1497 Vasco da Gama sailed with a fleet of four vessels round the African coast and towards India. The following year, with the aid of an Arab navigator, he landed in Calcutta.

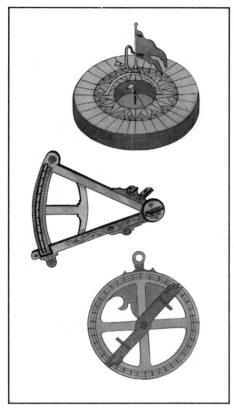

Basic navigation aids: compass (top), sextant used from the 17th century (centre), astrolabe (bottom).

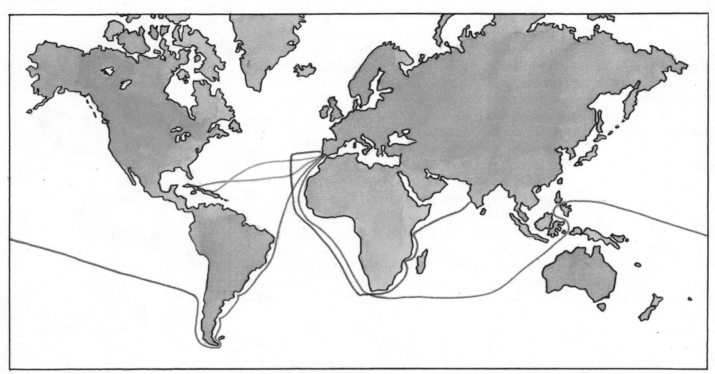

A map of the voyages of three discoverers:
Christopher Columbus (purple),
Vasco da Gama (blue)
and Ferdinand Magellan (red).

Vasco da Gama (1469—1524).

In the early 16th century the great era of medieval discoveries reached its climax with the circumnavigation of the world by the Portuguese Fernão de Magalhães, better known as Ferdinand Magellan. At that time Spain and Portugal, in spite of the Treaty of Tordesillas, were still competing for dominion on the seas.

The design of sailing ships was continually changing, with the emphasis now on long voyages. The caravel redonda and the carrack had proved most suitable for such trips, and their tonnage was steadily increasing. The more complex rigs with three to four masts and the growing demands on navigators meant that both officers and crews required more training than hitherto. The use of gunpowder — on land it had been used since the 13th century — brought with it design changes to accommodate cannon below decks. Coloured sails or pennants were introduced as a means of identification. Ships were mostly

called after saints, but some were given the names of animals. One factor that was crucial to survival at sea was the sort of provisions carried and the manner in which they were stored. No one had yet found a cure for scurvy, but the ship's biscuit had been invented, and fleets undertaking long trips would often take a separate supply vessel along with them.

As Magellan sailed from the mouth of the Guadalquivir with his five caravels on 20 September 1519, charged by the King of Spain with the task of finding a western passage to the Spice Islands (the Moluccas), Hernando Cortez was making ready an expedition to conquer the Aztec capital Tenochtitlán. Six years earlier, another Spanish conquistador, Vasco Núñez de Balboa, had crossed the difficult terrain of the Panamanian mountains in order to catch a glimpse of the South Seas, which Magellan would later name the Pacific Ocean.

Because he had gained royal patronage from Spain, Magellan had to overcome obstacles put in his way by his fellow-countrymen, many of whom regarded him as a 'traitor' to Portugal, before he was able to set sail. Furthermore, he subsequently faced opposition from the Spanish officers in his fleet.

The great Portuguese navigator wanted to find a passage from the Atlantic to the Pacific, so he simply made for Brazil and then turned southwards. He wasted a good deal of time investigating various promising bays, and in March 1520 the coming of autumn to the southern hemisphere found him off inhospitable Patagonia, where his expedition had to sit out the next five months before pressing on south. During that time Magellan was forced to take tough measures to suppress a mutiny on three of his caravels inspired by the Spanish officers, and he abandoned the main offenders on uninhabited shores.

Finally, on 21 October, Magellan found the passage he was looking for, but it took him 38 days to navigate the strait that bears his name and reach the Pacific. During this time the explorer had to contend with storms and more discontent among his sailors, some of whom wanted to turn back.

In contrast, the Mare Pacifico gave Magellan a welcome deserving of its name, but since no one had quite appreciated just how vast it was, it was another three months and 20 days before the sailors tasted fresh provisions. There was nowhere for them to make a landfall, so that Antonio Pigaffeta, who experienced it all personally, writes in his account of the circumnavigation that they no longer had so much as a ship's biscuit, only dust mixed with maggots, cowhide stripped from the mainmast, and foul, stinking water to drink.

At long last, on 6 March 1521, the expedition dropped anchor in the Mariana Islands. But when, on 27 April, Magellan tried to force the inhabitants of the small island of Mactan in the Philippines to submit to the Spanish throne, he and some of his sailors were killed. Only 115 men and the caravels *Trinidad* and *Victoria* continued the journey to Mindanao and on to the Moluccas. There they finally filled their holds with the spices they yearned for, and set sail for home.

The *Trinidad* was wrecked en route but *Victoria,* commanded by Sebastian del Cano, hove to at last in the Spanish port of Sanlucar on 6 September 1522. Just 18 men out of 265 survived the journey of over 73,600 km (46,000 miles). When they stepped ashore in Seville, they celebrated the end not only of the greatest maritime adventure in history, but also of the ancient myth of a flat Earth. It was the first time the size and shape of our planet had been put to a practical test, and the first occasion on which Europeans could testify to the existence and extent of the Pacific Ocean.

Although cargo vessels under sail, such as the caravel or the carrack, also served as warships in the late Middle Ages, the galley remained the typical fighting ship of the Mediterranean region. The design of the medieval galley became fairly standard around the end of the 9th century as the Byzantine type, combining some elements of the oared ships of northern waters with some based on classical galleys. Typical warships of the period were 40—50 m (130—165 ft) long, 4.5—7.5 m (14³/₄—24¹/₂ ft) wide, and were powered by 25 oars on each side, each manned by three to five oarsmen, usually slaves. Lateen sails set on a pair of masts provided an auxiliary means of propulsion. The relatively low and slender hull was finished off at the bows with a ram, although above the water-line; the fore section would also have a bridge used for grappling with enemy ships, later for mounting cannon. Aft of the central section where the rowers sat was the 'tabernacle', a platform for the captain and his officers.

The evolution of naval armament followed an interesting course. Since the days of the Roman Republic, infantrymen had sailed into battle in naval craft and manoeuvrability had been sacrificed for stability, but from the 7th century the first steps were taken towards the use of artillery at sea. Initially this meant 'Greek fire', a mixture of sulphur, oil, coal and other ingredients, which was hurled from the tube of a sort of flame-thrower, setting fire to enemy ships. Incendiary material was also flung from catapults, and sometimes quicklime, or even venomous snakes.

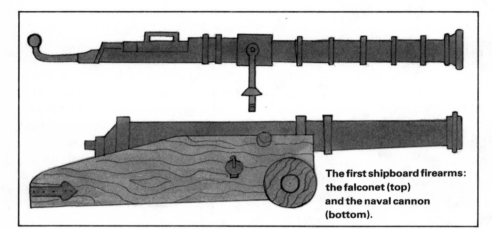

The first shipboard firearms: the falconet (top) and the naval cannon (bottom).

In the 16th century, galleys acquired proper cannon. Originally these were of small calibre and were mostly mounted in the bows, firing forwards. Such weapons soon proved the effectiveness of artillery against galleys still relying on the traditional tactics of hand-to-hand fighting, and early in the 16th century the first three-masted galleasses (galera grossa) appeared. They were 70 m (230 ft) long and 16 m (52 ft) wide, and had upper decks capable of taking several dozen cannon.

Historians are agreed that the greatest naval contest of the Middle Ages was the Battle of Lepanto in 1571, although accounts of how it was fought differ a good deal. It had its origins in the expansion of the Ottoman Empire and the victories of the Turks in the Mediterranean region, which not only meant a loss of influence in the area for the Europeans, but constituted a direct threat. In 1453 Constantinople fell, and the Turks controlled Syria,

The port of Naples in the Middle Ages.

Egypt and Algiers. In 1529 they took Belgrade, and when in 1538 they defeated the Venetians at sea, the going rate for Christians in the slave markets is said to have dropped to one onion. After the fall of Cyprus in 1569, Pope Pius V formed a Holy League with the Venetians and Spain, and they sent out a fleet of 200 galleys and six huge galleasses with 50,000 soldiers aboard to do battle with the infidel.

The Turkish fleet, numbering some 250 galleys with 75,000 soldiers, under the command of Ali Pasha, waited for them in the Gulf of Corinth, off Lepanto, Greece. The Turks' main numerical advantage lay in the number of warriors they had on board; the League's fleet had at its disposal 10 small-calibre cannon on each of its galleys, while the galleasses were armed with up to 50 each, of various bores, some

with a range of over 900 m (2,950 ft). The Christians also had numerous small firearms, which were more effective in battle than the crossbows, bows and scimitars of the Turks.

When the two fleets met, on 7 October 1571, they were each split into several squadrons. The Christian centre, commanded by Don John of Austria, faced a force led by Ali Pasha himself. On the left of the League's battle array was the Venetian Barbarigo, facing the ships of the Turkish second-in-command, Mohammed Sirocco. On Don John's right was the squadron of the Genoan Andrea Doria, sailing to engage that of the Algerian pirate Uluch Ali. The force of the Marquis de Santa Cruz brought up the Christian rear.

The battle began with artillery fire from the galleasses, which sank several Turkish galleys before they

could join battle. Ali Pasha underestimated the Christian firepower and his orders remained unchanged — to surround and destroy the enemy fleet. To the left, his galleys got into shallow water and offered an easy prey, while Don John of Austria broke the Turkish line in the centre by using his reserves at the critical moment. Then Uluch Ali fled to the port of Lepanto with a couple of dozen ships he managed to extricate from the fierce fighting on the right flank. When Ali Pasha himself was killed, the Christian victory was complete. After four hours of warfare nearly 30,000 Turks, 8,000 Christians and numerous galley slaves lay dead; some 12,000 Christians were released from the Turkish galleys. An eyewitness, the Spanish writer Miguel de Cervantes, who was wounded in the shoulder, later described this as the greatest day in history.

The Battle of Lepanto, October 7, 1571, the last great sea battle in which galleys were used.

Although Magellan's expedition of 1519—22 showed that it was possible to reach the Pacific by sailing down the South American coastline, this region remained inaccessible to most maritime powers of the 16th century because of the Treaty of Tordesillas. When Spanish and Portuguese carracks started to arrive back in Europe laden with gold and silver from the New World, spices and rare fabrics from the Far East, and slaves from Africa, the situation began to change, however. France, England and the Netherlands, the last having only recently thrown off the Spanish yoke, began to look beyond the odd pirate raid to spheres of influence of their own, and possible future colonies.

The Dutch concentrated their attention on the East Indies, while in 1534 Jacques Cartier discovered the St. Lawrence Bay and River, where he was later to attempt both to find a north-west passage and to colonize Canada for the French. The English showed an interest in colonizing several parts of the world, from Newfoundland, discovered during John Cabot's none too successful voyage in 1497, when he tried to find a north-west passage even farther north than Cartier, to the long stretch of North American coastline still free between the French in the north and the Spanish in the south.

The Dutch, the French and the English set about building up strong navies; but while the Spanish and Portuguese concentrated on building caravels and carracks with tall poops (up to four decks) and capacities of up to 1,200 tons, which would later make up their Invincible Armada, the ships of the northwestern nations took on a different form.

In the course of the 15th century the Hanseatic cog developed into the hulk, which retained the hull shape of the Viking ships, although the castles were now flush with the gunwhale and there were three

The galleon was responsible for the naval superiority of England over Spain at the end of the 16th century.

Sir Francis Drake (1540—1596).
▼

masts and a bowsprit. Henry VII and Henry VIII of England commissioned huge carracks such as the *Royal Sovereign, Regent* and *Henry Grace à Dieu.* This last was said to be the biggest warship of the early 16th century, and with her 151 heavy cannon, mounted all along her hull, she represented the first step towards the 'ships of the line', although the guns were not as yet on carriages. However, none of these ships were particularly manoeuvrable. Their tall superstructures made them difficult to turn or even keep on course without a following wind, and not even the introduction of a lateen sail on the mizzen-mast made much difference. Nor were they very fast.

It was left to the Elizabethan buccaneer Sir John Hawkins to come up with a revolutionary new design after he had lost the *Jesus of Lübeck* in combat with a Spanish squadron simply because of her clumsiness and lack of speed. He had the

Drake was knighted by the Queen in 1580 and served his country by more than just piracy. Like Hawkins, he devoted his attention to improving the design and armament of medium-sized galleons of around 500 tonnes capacity, and after the outbreak of war with Spain in 1587 became vice-admiral of the fleet. He prepared the way for the defeat of the Armada, and thus the toppling of Spain as ruler of the waves, by his daring attack on Cádiz in 1587, when he destroyed about 30 ships the Spanish were building. But the worst was yet to come for Spain, which lost most of its proud fleet a year later in an attempted invasion of England, either during the engagement in the English Channel or the subsequent flight round the Scottish and Irish coasts.

The galleon *Golden Hind*.

Queen Elizabeth knighted Francis Drake on board the *Golden Hind* when he returned from his voyage round the world in 1580. ▼

forecastle replaced by a much lower, railed structure, lowered the poop and increased the overall length until the length:beam ratio was about 3:1 instead of 2.5:1. This, plus a sharp bow — called a galion, which probably gave the type its name — and a square stern cross-section instead of an oval one, made the new English galleons faster and much more manoeuvrable.

When Francis Drake set out from Plymouth Sound with his *Golden Hind* and four other vessels in December 1577, the Queen's buccaneer could scarcely have guessed that his flagship would become the most famous galleon in the world or that he would be the first Englishman to circumnavigate the globe. The *Golden Hind* not only sailed round Cape Horn for the first time, but in 1580 brought back in her hold half a million pounds' worth of gold won from the Spaniards, the weight of which threatened at times to sink the vessel.

The defeat of the Spanish Armada did not open up the seas to competitors overnight, since the successors of the conquistadors still kept a jealous eye on the coast of the New World, from where riches continued to pour into the royal coffers. But the vast expanses of the Pacific, once a Portuguese monopoly, were no longer guarded, nor could they have been. Portugal had become a vassal of Spain, so that the defeat of the Armada rubbed off on her as well.

Since it was Dutch merchants who had handled Portuguese trade with the Far East, carrying goods first to Lisbon, then on to Antwerp and thence to various European destinations, it was only natural that they should take the greatest interest in taking over the Pacific trade. Dutch trading activity was expanded a great deal after the Netherlands were relieved of Spanish rule in the second half of the 16th century. Whole families of merchants grasped the opportunity with both hands, and the experience of generations of mariners was at their disposal.

At the start of the 17th century the relatively small Dutch nation had a fleet of over 10,000 vessels, although most were quite small coasters of 40 to 50 tonnes. These num-

Dutch fluyt with the typical pear-shaped stern.

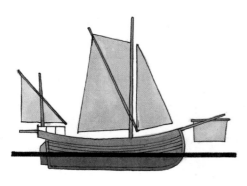

The boyer appeared in the Dutch fleet at the end of the 16th century.

bered among their ranks the boyers and yachts, whose origins can be traced back to the 16th century. They were characterized by lugsails, irregular four-sided sails usually suspended from a yard and often with a boom at the bottom. These gave them a manoeuvrability which stood them in good stead in the shallow waters along the Dutch coastline.

The boyer or boyort had a bulging hull and straight keel, and was about 20 m (65 ft) long by 6 m (20 ft) wide. There were two masts, the after of them being mounted at the very stern. The lugsail on the mainmast was supplemented by a staysail between the mast and the bottom of the bowsprit, and a spinnaker flown from the bowsprit. The yacht, in contrast, had a single mast with lugsails and a square-rigged topsail. The long bowsprit could take up to three rigged sails — a flying jib, jib and staysail. The yacht was first used as a naval reconnaissance vessel, whereas the boyer was a cargo ship.

Dutch expansion into the Pacific was effected by means of much bigger craft, the typical one being the fluyt. The ratio of length to breadth had again increased compared to the galleons, now being 3.5 to 4:1, the length being up to 40 m (131 ft) with a draught of 4 m (13 ft) and a displacement of up to 600 tonnes. The pear-shaped cross-section was conspicuous, with a

A huge merchantman of the East India Company. These ships soon became recognized as independent types of sailing ships.

broad, flat bottom. Fluyts were three-masters, all sails being square-rigged except for a lateen sail on the mizzen-mast. Aft of the pointed bow and bowsprit the forecastle was insignificant, although the poop superstructure remained. The insertion of the tiller in an oval hole in the stern was an interesting feature. The simpler and more easily managed tackle of the fluyt meant that a crew of 10 was sufficient, as opposed to the 30 required on a galleon the same size.

Like the English before them, the Dutch also at first wanted to find a route to the 'kingdoms of Cathay and China north of Norway, Muscovy and Tartary'. The most famous of those who sought a north-east passage was Willem Barents, who had to spend the winter of 1596–97 along with his crew in the Arctic. The idea of a north-east passage

soon became outdated, however, as convoys of Dutch ships began to carry their cargoes from the East Indies by the 'Portuguese route', round the Cape of Good Hope. The Indian Ocean became the domain of the Dutch, though not without competition. There were two East India Companies, the British (founded in 1600) and the Dutch (founded in 1602), and they would vie for superiority for many decades to come. Their huge, well-armed ships, the East Indiamen, were the aristocrats of the seven seas.

The Dutch also made new discoveries in the Pacific when, in 1642–43, Abel Tasman with the yacht *Heemskerck* and the fluyt *Zeehaen* discovered Tasmania and New Zealand and carried out the task he had been set of confirming the existence of a supposed southern continent.

The rivalry between the maritime nations of Europe for monopolies in overseas trade, influence on other continents and the founding of colonies, along with the desire to control sailing routes, led to long-drawn-out wars from the 16th to the 19th centuries. The British gradually became a major sea power, deliberately building up their naval strength from the mid-17th century. At the time a large proportion of world trade was in the hands of the Dutch, who had not only acquired a strong position in the Pacific, but since the foundation of the Dutch West India Company in 1602 had also got a strong foothold in the New World. So the 1651 Navigation Act passed by the British Parliament was mainly directed towards limiting Dutch trading activity. Between 1652 and 1674 there were three Anglo-Dutch wars, mainly fought at sea, where the Royal Navy acquired increasing superiority, due for the most part to the 'ship of the line'.

These vessels were the most powerful of all in tonnage and armaments, playing a decisive role in sea battles right up to the middle of the 19th century. They originated from the frigates, small vessels used by French corsairs, built on a straight keel, with pear-shaped cross-section and gradually less and less superstructure. They were about 40 m (131 ft) long and about 10 m (33 ft) wide, a ratio of 4:1. They had a displacement of around 400 tonnes and their firepower was considerable, consisting of 40 cannon on each gun-deck mounted on carriages and firing from ports. The sails were mostly square-rigged, on three masts and a bowsprit; the mizzen-mast carried a fore-and-aft sail, and later staysails were rigged between masts. There were several sorts of frigate, of which the East Indiamen were a merchant version, in addition to which there were warships of various size, tonnage and armament (such as the frigate, the Blackwall frigate, and the smaller corvette). The biggest of all were not

A Venetian galleass, which was used at the Battle of Lepanto, was the first warship with cannon firing from gun-ports.

called frigates but ships of the line.

The rigging of this type of warship did not differ basically from that of a naval frigate, but instead of a single gun-deck it had three, built into the hull one above the other. Ships of the line of the first class had 100 guns, from 42-pounders (19 kg) to three-pounders (1.4 kg). In addition they carried mortars and carronades, loaded with iron shrapnel.

Ships of the line had double oak sides and were decorated at the prow and stern with rich polychrome carvings. Their manoeuvrability was improved, in addition to the rich complement of sails, by the introduction of the ship's wheel to replace the tiller.

The ships of the line got their name from the battle line which from the mid-17th century became the standard fighting formation in naval encounters. The ships of the

warring fleets would draw up in close line astern and manoeuvre for position in relation to the wind. One of the first interesting battles of this sort was the 'four-day battle' fought from 11 to 14 June 1666 in the Straits of Dover between the English (57 ships under Admiral Monk) and the Dutch (84 ships under Admiral de Ruyter), although the most famous was surely the Battle of Trafalgar on 21 October 1805, when the British admiral of the fleet, Horatio Nelson, was killed, but the French were decisively defeated.

Not all warships took part in such battles of the giants. The ships of the line were those of the first three classes, according to the number of guns (60 to 100). The fourth class (40 to 60 guns) were called cruisers and were used for escort and reconnaissance duties. The fifth and sixth class ships (28 to 40 and under 28 guns respectively) were frigates, used for errands and patrols.

In the course of the 17th and 18th centuries the only changes which took place in ships of the line were an increase in size — from 1,500 up to as much as 3,000 tonnes — and the addition of fourth sails called royals on the mainmast and foremast. Among the most famous of this type were the English *Sovereign of the Seas* (the first real three-decker), Horatio Nelson's flagship *Victory* and the French *Couronne*.

Fire-ships filled with explosives and directed towards enemy formations were also used in battle. Another interesting vessel was the bomb ketch, which was adapted from a small frigate by taking out the foremast and installing instead a huge mortar that was mainly used for bombarding enemy shore positions.

H. Nelson's flagship *Victory*. ▶

A diagram of the battle formation of ships of the line.
▼

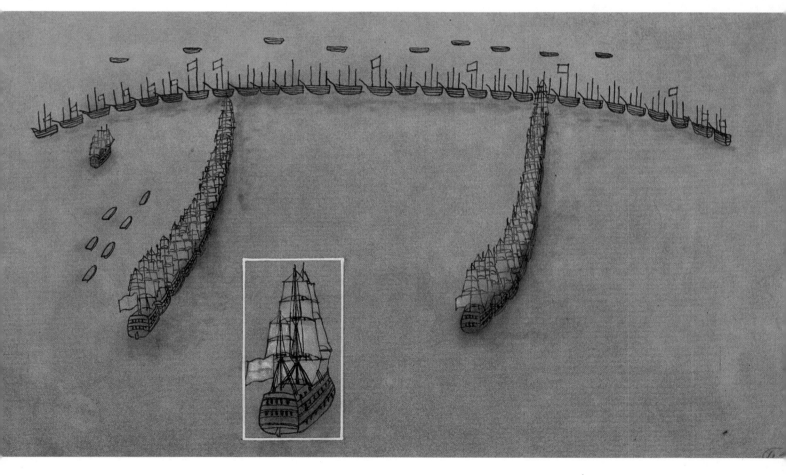

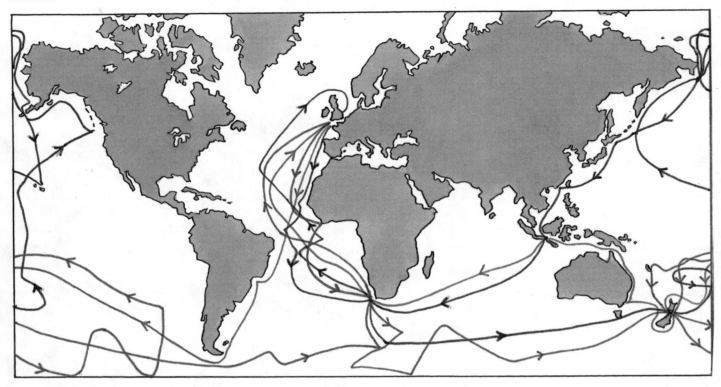

▲
A map of J. Cook's voyages (1st voyage 1768—71 in red, 2nd voyage 1772—75 in blue, 3rd, unfinished voyage, 1776—79 in black, return of Clerk and Gore).

A typical brig from the beginning of the 19th century.
▼

From the end of the 16th century a new scientific approach was brought to bear in maritime matters, as it was elsewhere. An example of this was Gerardus Mercator's successful projection of the curved surface of the globe onto a flat sheet of paper, when he published his famous world atlas in 1594. At the end of the 17th century William Dampier made a major study of wind systems and sea currents, but in the middle of the 18th century one great obstacle remained to successful navigation. Sailors had, since ancient times, known ways of establishing latitude with a fair degree of accuracy, but to do the same for longitude called for an accurate means of telling the time. Britain was one of the nations most likely to benefit from an improvement in the situation, and the British Parliament offered a reward of £20,000 to anyone who could construct a chronometer of the required accuracy.

The task was successfully undertaken by carpenter John Harrison, who in the 1760s designed and made an instrument only slightly larger than a pocket watch and submitted it for the prescribed tests, which it passed with flying colours. None the less, Harrison had to wait eight years to receive his full reward.

Scientific methods of shipbuilding were also adopted. Naval architects studied and tested the optimum shape for a ship's hull, and new methods of construction and materials were also investigated. Thus, although the big warships changed only slowly and in minor ways, many new types of smaller sailing vessels appeared on the scene.

The craft which was most widely used for both naval and trading purposes was the brig. These fast two-masters, having tall, three-sectioned masts, square-rigged, with a mizzen fore-and-aft sail, were up to 50 m (164 ft) long and some 9 m (30 ft) broad, the hull being tapered towards the bows. A variation on the brig was the brigantine, with two-sectioned masts and simpler rigging. In the 19th century schooner brigs appeared, with the mainmast rigged entirely fore-and-aft. At the end of the 18th century the barque also developed from the brig. It always had at least three masts, the mizzen-mast carrying a fore-and-aft sail. The length of barques increased gradually until they were as much as 100 m (328 ft) from stem to stern – although the American *Great Republic* measured 108 (354 ft) – with a displacement of several thousand tonnes. The length-breadth ratio was up to 6:1.

At the other end of the scale, one of the smallest of all sea-going vessels was the sloop. It was used as a small cargo vessel or a fishing or reconnaissance boat, and there was a naval version with cannon on the upper deck. The sloop's sharp bows had a long bowsprit, and a single mast. The hull was usually about 25 m (82 ft) long and some 7 m (23 ft) wide. Variants were the Bermuda sloop (a warship) and the anchor sloop.

An interesting Mediterranean vessel was the shebeka, a three-master with pointed prow and lateen sails which also had two rows of oarsmen. It was armed with cannon at the bows and sides and was especially popular with African pirates.

The increasing pace of progress in ship design and everything associated with seafaring was also reflected in ocean voyages. Although the age when whole new continents were discovered had passed, new expeditions filled in the maps of the seven seas and carried out all sorts of scientific work. In the 18th century there were many important travellers and discoverers, the most celebrated of whom was undoubtedly the Englishman Captain James Cook (1728–79). In his ships *Endeavour, Resolution, Adventure* and *Discovery,* which were rigged as barques and in most cases had previously served as merchantmen, he carried out a series of scientific research programmes. In particular he refuted the persisting theory that there was a further southern continent somewhere in the Pacific, at the same time expressing his opinion that an Antarctic landmass did exist. He discovered many islands, and mapped the east coast of Australia, the whole of New Zealand's coastline and the west coast of North America. He was one of the most outstanding navigators of all time. He was also a pioneer in the field of provisioning, taking along sauerkraut and carrot jam as a means of preventing scurvy.

J. Cook's barque *Endeavour* **which was 30.5 m (100 ft) long.**

One of the first, though unsuccessful, attempts to use steam on water was this boat, built in 1736 by Jonathan Hull.

For thousands of years ships and boats had been propelled by paddles, oars and sails, and sailors had learned to make use of favourable currents and winds, but the dawning of the modern age had shown that speed meant the difference between profit and loss when it came to world trade. The limitations of traditional sources of power had long been recognized in river transport, where sails and oars were inadequate in the face of a strong current, and boats often had to be dragged upstream by men or animals. The method was far from satisfactory, although in some places, such as Czarist Russia, it survived for a long time.

The Romans had known the principle by which a paddle wheel could drive a boat upstream. In the 12th century the Chinese had just such a system, and Leonardo da Vinci did research on the question. The only drawback was that there was no way of driving such a wheel except by human or animal muscle-power, and in that situation oars remained more efficient.

The power of steam had also been known since ancient times, but the idea of putting it to practical use is a modern one. Following some early experimental work in the 16th century, the first real progress was made by the French physician and physicist Denis Papin, who not only invented the pressure cooker but also made a crude steam engine. He is known to have held a demonstration on the Fulda River in 1707, using a boat powered by a steam engine which drove water onto the blades of a paddle wheel. A revolutionary new technology had arrived, although it would be a long time yet before boats could safely be driven this way.

The next important step was taken in 1765 by the Scottish mechanic James Watt, when he designed a double-action steam engine incorporating a separate condensing chamber. Later improvements led to the use of this type of machine as a universal engine, and Watt came to be regarded as its sole inventor.

Soon afterwards, following a number of less than successful efforts, the Saône River in France was the scene of the maiden voyage of the first truly steam-powered vessel. In 1783 the Marquis Claude de Jouffroy d'Abbans sailed his *Pyroscaphe* upstream for a full 15 minutes, the vessel being driven by a pair of paddle wheels on either side of the bows. American John Fitch's boats *Perseverance* and *Experiment* managed to sail along the Delaware River in 1787–88 using some kind of mechanical paddles.

When, in March 1802, a steam boat designed by the Scottish engineer William Symington sailed into the Caledonian Canal, the inten-

The steam-ship *Pyroscaphe* which was demonstrated on the Saône in 1783.

tion was that it should replace the horse-drawn boats then in use. The vessel was named after Symington's daughter, *Charlotte Dundas,* but after a few weeks' service it was withdrawn, since the canal's shareholders were afraid the paddles would damage the banks.

The first successful paddle-boat operator was the American Robert Fulton, some years later. He was present when the *Charlotte Dundas* went into service, and the very same year he demonstrated a boat of his own on the Seine. Unfortunately his steam engine was too heavy, which caused the boat to sink, but he carried on undaunted, and the next year two of his steam boats chugged along on the surface for an hour and a half. He failed to impress the French, however, especially Napoleon Bonaparte, who had considered the fellow a charlatan ever since his first fiasco on the Seine. He found out how wrong he had been while on his way to exile on St. Helena in 1815. The sailing vessel he was on was escorted by a British steamship, and when the defeated general asked who had designed it, he was told that it was Robert Fulton.

By that time Fulton's steamship *Clermont* had been running a successful passenger service for eight years along the Hudson River from New York to Albany (a distance of 195 km or 120 miles), making a full $7 profit on every ticket. Nor could Napoleon have known that another of Fulton's steamships, the *Phoenix,* was operating on the Delaware, and since 1811 his *New Orleans* had been plying the Mississippi.

Europeans were anxious not to be left behind, and in 1812 the Scottish engineer Henry Bell built his *Comet* for the run between Glasgow, Greenock and Helensburgh. It was driven by two four-bladed paddle wheels on either side, one behind the other, and the tall funnel was also used as a mast for the stayed sail. Bell later built other steamships, some for use on the Atlantic

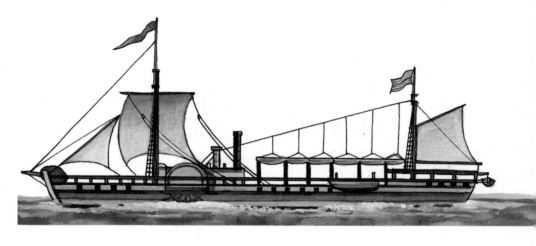

R. Fulton's *Clermont* achieved a speed of 4.5 knots in 1807.

coast of Scotland. The largest, the *James Watt,* was over 43 m (141 ft) long, with 5.5 m (18 ft) paddle wheels.

In 1816 the steamship *Elise* (formerly the *Margery*) crossed the Channel from Brighton to Le Havre. The weather for the crossing was so unfavourable that it had to turn back to the English coast several times, and the trip eventually took 17 hours.

Several other European nations followed the English example, and steamships were built in Sweden and in Russia, where one went into operation on the River Neva between St. Petersburg and Kronstadt in 1815. They were all rather small, and their simple steam engines could only just manage the calm waters of rivers (mostly with the assistance of sails). On the open sea it was still the age of tall ships.

The *Charlotte Dundas* which covered 32 km (20 miles) in six hours.

When the American firm Savannah Steamship Company got into financial trouble, it decided to sell its packet *Savannah* in Europe. This was a sailing vessel fitted additionally with a steam engine of 66 kW (90 hp) driving unshielded paddle wheels on either side of the hull. In inclement weather the paddles could be dismantled and stored on deck. The funnel had a revolving cover to keep sparks and soot off the sails. In 1819 this vessel became the

The *Savannah*, which crossed the Atlantic in 1819, and was still considered a sailing ship.

first steamship to cross the Atlantic when it sailed from Savannah, Georgia, to Liverpool in England in 29 days and 11 hours. As it passed the southern tip of Ireland, the captain of a coastguard cutter took the

The first European steamship which had a speed of 6.5 knots.

smoke issuing from the American ship to be a sign of fire on board, and hurried to her assistance.

The steam frigate aroused much interest in Britain, Scandinavia, the Baltic states and Russia, but failed to find a buyer, so it returned to the United States, this time exclusively under sail, where it was later wrecked off Long Island in 1821.

The importance of the *Savannah's* trip is mainly symbolic, and the time she spent under steam during her first four-week crossing is a matter of some dispute, reports varying from 8 hours to 18 days, although the most widely accepted view is that the vessel spent a mere 85 hours under steam power. A far more important voyage was that made in 1825 by the three-masted lugger *Enterprise* from London to Calcutta. During the 103 day trip of 18,430 km (11,426 miles) she spent a full 64 days under steam power.

By that time the number of steam-sail vessels had grown considerably, yet all had a major drawback: because of the poor efficiency of their steam engines, huge areas of valuable cargo space were taken up by fuel. Not only that, but the paddle-sail combination was an obstacle to proper use of either power source, and frequently even a threat to the ship's safety. This

was the reason ocean voyages under steam were sporadic, and it was not until the 1830s that the first attempt was made to introduce regular transatlantic services.

At the suggestion of Isambard Kingdom Brunel, later to become a famous ship designer, the Great Western Railway Company in England decided to extend its operations by introducing a service from Bristol to New York by ship. So Brunel began work on the *Great Western* (illustration on page 166), a large, luxurious and elegant schooner-rigged four-masted steamship. It was 72 m (236 ft) long with a displacement of 1,340 tonnes, and had two paddles 8.53 m (28 ft) in diameter, giving it a speed of 10 knots.

At the same time as Brunel was building the *Great Western,* a rival company, the British and American Steam Navigation Company, began work on its own ship, the *British Queen.* This project for a giant even bigger than the *Great Western* got behind schedule, so the company decided to use the 700-ton schooner brig *Sirius* instead.

An unofficial 'race' across the Atlantic between these two vessels began on 31 March 1838 when the *Great Western* sailed from Cork harbour. Within two hours, however, it was forced to turn back because of a fire in the boiler room, and did not leave harbour again until 8 April. By that time the *Sirius* had been at sea for four days, and although she got into a storm of such ferocity that the captain had to force the crew to continue at pistol point, and although they later had to burn various fittings because of a lack of coal, she became the first ship to cross the Atlantic entirely under steam, and made the trip in 18 days 10 hours at an average speed of 6.7 knots. The *Great Western* steamed into New York harbour four hours later, having covered the distance in a mere 15 days 5 hours (an average of 8.8 knots) carrying 200 tonnes of coal in special containers. It was

The *Sirius* which, in the course of her victorious voyage, had to have all her wooden fittings burned.

thus proved that steam could halve the journey time across the Atlantic, and from then on there was no doubt about its future.

Apart from the imperfections of the steam engines, which were beginning to be overcome – the *Sirius,* for instance, had a 'surface condenser', which meant that the engine did not have to be stopped to refill the boiler – a major drawback of steamships was propulsion by means of paddle wheels. A real breakthrough came with the introduction of the Archimedean screw. During the first half of the 19th century many inventors in different parts of the world came up with all sorts of marine screw or propeller, situated between the transom and the rudder. The best results were achieved by English farmer Francis Smith and a Swede, John Ericsson, who patented their designs in 1836 and 1838 respectively. After Ericsson's double screws with oblique blades went into service on the *Archimedes,* which from 1839

onwards they drove along the British coast at up to 9 knots, others were quick to follow his example. Among them was Brunel, who used a six-bladed propeller 4.7 m (15 ft 6 in) in diameter to drive what was then the largest commercial ship in the world, the iron-hulled *Great Britain,* launched at Bristol in 1843.

Propellers achieved universal recognition in 1845 as a result of a rather strange tug-of-war. The English roped together the paddle steamer *Alecto* and the propeller-driven *Rattler,* both powered by 147 kW (200 hp) engines. The *Rattler* clearly demonstrated the superiority of screws by pulling her rival along against the thrust of her paddles at a healthy 2.7 knots.

Another innovator who deserves to be mentioned in the history of the ship's propeller is the Czech Josef Ressel. Back in 1812 he had proposed a universal screw for the propulsion of both ships and balloons, but in spite of obtaining the support of the authorities for tests at Trieste in 1827, Ressel was dogged by misfortune and intrigue, and after losing a legal battle to protect his rights he died embittered and unrewarded.

I. K. Brunel's *Great Western.*

When the biggest steamer of the 19th century, the *Great Eastern,* was scrapped in 1892, the skeletons of two riveters who had mysteriously disappeared 50 years earlier while building the ship were discovered in one of the watertight compartments. It was a signal for the press to drag up once more the history of this ill-fated 'Queen of the Seas'.

When she was launched, the *Great Eastern* represented the climax of a period of rapid progress in the evolution of shipbuilding. But she was more than that — she was a symbol and embodiment of the new iron age. For thousands of years ships and boats had been built of materials lighter than water and usually of wood, of which the finest was considered to be English oak.

It was therefore only natural that when the idea of building an iron ship was first aired, it met with more that the usual crop of objections. These ranged from the naïve — iron is heavier than water, therefore the whole suggestion was ridiculous — to the apparently reasonable, such as the possible effects on magnetic compasses, or the fact that iron is less resilient than wood. History was on the side of the innovators, however, and in 1821 the 116-ton steamer *Aaron Manby,* its sides made of 6.5 mm (¼ in) iron plates, crossed from London to Le Havre. The 44 kW (60 hp) engine managed a speed of up to 7 knots. Although she was soon taken off the Channel run and put into service on the Loire, she had proved her point.

More iron-hulled ships followed, though most were still quite small,

The steamship *Great Britain,* **built in 1843. It was not only the first all-metal craft, but had a further new design feature — a six-bladed propeller.**

until in 1837 the 400-ton *Rainbow,* introduced on the London-Antwerp run, proved itself able to carry twice the cargo of a comparable wooden ship. Iron was at sea to stay.

In 1840 the British government offered private contractors the chance to carry the transatlantic mail. With great foresight Canadian entrepreneur Samuel Cunard took on the task forming, along with several fellow-businessmen, what was later to be one of the most celebrated shipping lines of all. Their four paddle steamers *Arcadia, Britannia, Caledonia* and *Columbia* began a service between Liverpool and Boston twice monthly, non-stop, and were so successful that within a few years Cunard was able to build six more ships, each of over 1,800 tonnes. In July 1840 one of the Cunard liners, the *Britannia,* gained the Blue Riband, an award made since the coming of steam to the ship which completed the fastest Atlantic crossing. On that occasion

the time was exactly 10 days, the average speed 10.72 knots.

By that time, however, Brunel was already building his colossal *Great Britain,* a schooner-rigged six-master that was 98 m (321 ft) long and had a capacity of 3,618 tonnes. Its 4.7 m (15 ft 6 in) propeller gave it a top speed of 12.5 knots. Although the ship's performance proved disappointing after its ceremonial launching in the presence of the royal family in 1843 (the first crossing to New York took 15 days), it proved the utility of iron as a ship-building material.

A sadder fate awaited the last and biggest of Brunel's steam-sail vessels, the *Great Eastern.* She measured almost 211 m (692 ft) from stem to stern, and was designed to carry 4,000 passengers and a crew of 418. Her top speed was 15 knots, with the sails assisted by two paddle wheels 17 m (56 ft) in diameter and a four-bladed propeller 7.30 m (24 ft) in diameter. It was not for nothing

that this huge ship was originally called *Leviathan* after the biblical sea monster. The construction itself brought ill-luck and tragedy. The cost exceeded expectations and caused several businesses to go bankrupt. Brunel himself died 10 days before it was completed. The launch in 1857 saw a number of workers killed and injured in an accident, and the sea trials produced a boiler explosion and more casualties. In the end there were only 36 passengers for the maiden voyage.

No wonder the ship was soon withdrawn from passenger service because of its unprofitability. It was used for cable-laying for some time, but eventually was ignominiously scrapped in 1892. Nevertheless, the design of the *Great Eastern* incorporated a number of novel features. There were 10 watertight compartments, a double bottom reaching above the waterline, power-assisted steering, and above all a hydrodynamically shaped hull — not to mention luxurious cabins.

I. K. Brunel's last sailed steamship, the *Great Eastern.*

We have already seen that the evolution of warships took place very slowly, and here, as in other areas of marine engineering, major changes did not come until the 19th century. Although the industrial revolution hastened the appearance of the first steamships soon after the turn of the century, and in 1814 Robert Fulton built the warship *Demologos,* with a steam engine and armed with 20 guns, the last sea battle between sailing ships did not take place until 1827. It was during the Greek struggle for independence, when the British, French, Russian and Greek fleet under the English commander Sir Edward Codrington defeated the Turko-Egyptian fleet at Navarino after a four-hour engagement.

The early unreliability of steam engines, the need to carry supplies of coal, the vulnerability of paddle wheels, and other factors such as a natural conservatism among naval officers, easily outweighed the undoubted attractions of steam, such as increased speed and manoeuvrability and independence of weather conditions, not to mention the increased displacements and better protection offered by iron and steel.

So the first steps towards a new type of warship were not taken until the 1850s, but they were soon to make the ship of the line under sail an antiquated and useless vessel for naval warfare. During the Crimean War there were two innovations which went hand in hand — armour

plating and the explosive shell.

At the Battle of Sinope in 1853, on 11 November, a mere six days after the Russian frigate *Vladimir* and the Turkish warship *Pervas-Barchi* had met in the first ever engagement between steam-sail vessels, six battleships under the Russian Admiral Nachimov defeated a Turkish flotilla of 16 ships, sinking all but one of them without losing a single vessel. This startling setback proved the efficacy of ellipsoid shells, which easily pierced the wooden hulls of the Turkish warships, and the superiority of steam over sail when it came to manoeuvrability. Indeed, the only Turkish ship which managed to escape was the steam frigate *Taif.*

The French also used armour

The first battle between armour-plated warships took place in the American Civil War. On the right *Monitor,* on the left *Merrimac.*

The armour-plated warship *Gloire*.

plate in the Crimean War, in their 'floating batteries', and the British soon followed suit. The first armour-plated warship was made in 1859. The *Gloire,* as this steam-sail vessel was called, was protected below the water-line and at strategic points above it by armour plate up to 125 mm (5 in) thick. It was 77 m (252 ft) long, carried 60 guns, and was capable of doing 13 knots. The next year the British replied with the

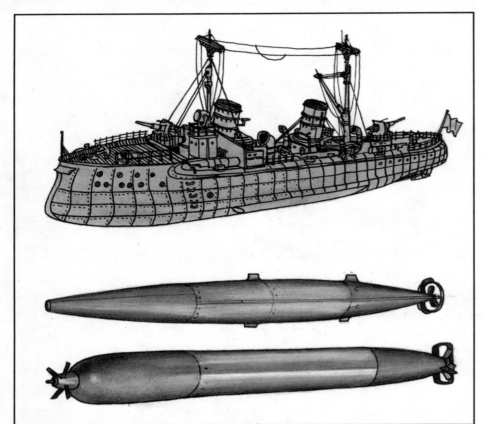

A torpedo boat of the late 19th century.

Locomotive torpedoes from the end of the 19th century.

D. Bushnell's *Turtle*.

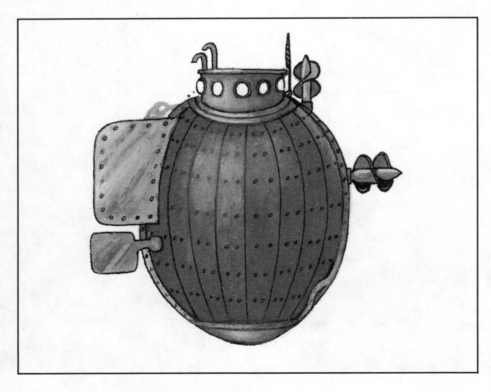

launching of the *Warrior,* the first naval vessel to have a hull made entirely of iron, the *Gloire* having been made of plated wood.

Simultaneously with the introduction of explosive shells, guns loaded from the rear, with rifled barrels, were also adopted. These gave greater accuracy and longer range. The *Gloire* had a displacement of 5,600 tonnes and the *Warrior* 9,210 tonnes, but all maritime powers strove to increase these dimensions still further as the calibre of shells increased, and with it the thickness of armour plating to defend the vessel against them. Then, at the end of the 1870s, steel was introduced, and the displacement of battleships levelled out to around 16,000 tonnes, with a thickness of armour plating at around 300 mm (11¾ in).

Another technical advance was the revolving gun turret, although there is some doubt as to whether its inventor was the English captain Henry Cowper Coles or the Swedish engineer John Ericsson, who since 1848 had been a naturalized American. One thing is certain: it was the

Swede's small ship *Monitor,* with a low profile and a gun turret concealing a pair of 280 mm (11 in) guns, that sailed in 1862 during the American Civil War to meet the Confederate ironside *Merrimac,* which it engaged in Hampton Roads. Though the battle remained undecided, in that neither ship was sunk, the *Monitor* became something of a prototype, especially as regards her turret, for coastal patrol vessels.

The torpedo was invented by Captain Luppis of Austria, and from 1865 was manufactured in Rijeka (Fiume) by the Englishman Robert Whitehead, who himself invented a fully self-propelled torpedo in 1866. By the 1880s it had become a feared weapon on board torpedo boats, and was later used as a defence against them. An attempt to revive the ram (below the waterline) was much less successful, although the Austrians put it to good effect against the Italians at the Battle of Lissa in 1866.

An encyclopaedia dated 1900 describes the submarine as a vessel capable of remaining under water for lengthy periods, that it is used mainly for military purposes but is also used for salvage and engineering work. Clearly the main characteristics of these underwater craft have changed little from the time they first became practical.

Man had long wished to be able to sail under water, and the first attempts to design submarines go back to the Middle Ages. The first recorded success in this field was the boat of the Dutchman Cornelius van Drebbel, whose vessel made the journey from Westminster to Greenwich watched by King James I in 1624. It is unlikely that this was a submarine in the sense we know them today, since Drebbel's earlier experiments at the court of Emperor Rudolf II in Prague smacked very much of charlatanism. Either that, or he was a genius far ahead of his time, since he worked on producing a 'sage's stone', built a clavichord

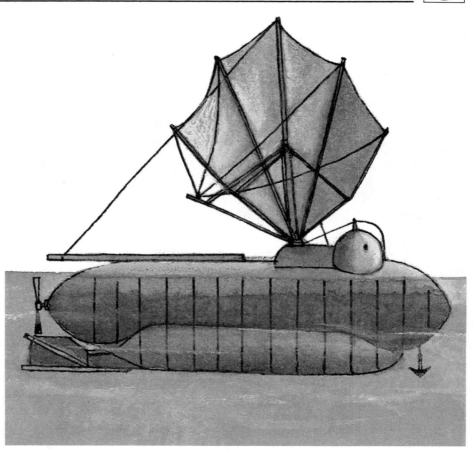

The *Nautilus* was driven on the surface by a sail!

W. Bauer's submersible boat.

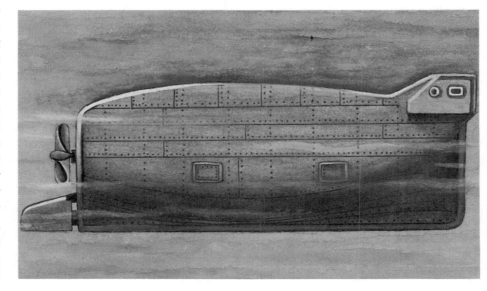

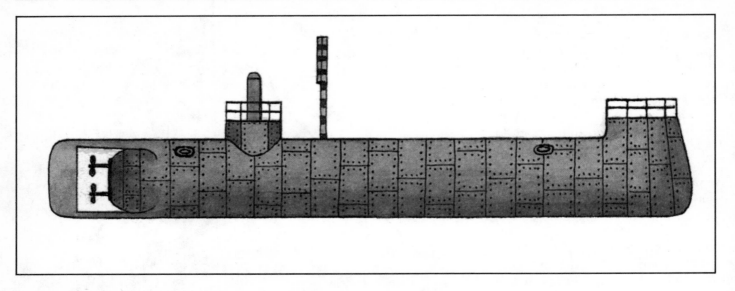

▲
One of the first Russian submarines.

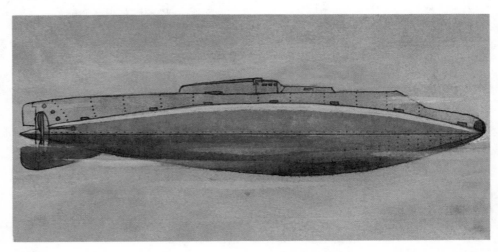

The submarine *Plunger,* **designed in 1896, was a naval vessel.** ▶

which he claimed could be 'played' by solar energy, and 'invented' a lightning machine. His underwater craft was actually a small wooden rowing boat with thick glass window to let light in, and the oxygen supply was probably provided by means of air compressed with bellows.

Drebbel had many successors, but it was David Bushnell who made the first underwater vessel used for military purposes, during the American War of Independence in 1775. It looked like a turtle standing on its hind legs, and was named after that animal. Submerging and surfacing were achieved with the

aid of ballast tanks and pumps, and it was propelled by means of a pair of screws operated manually by the one-man crew. On its back the *Turtle* carried an explosive charge for attachment to the side of an enemy ship after drilling a hole with a special gimlet which also formed part of the equipment, but when Sergeant Ezra Lee tried to fix a charge to the British flagship *Eagle* in New York harbour in 1776, the drill simply bounced off the copper plates attached to the vessel's hull beneath the water-line as a protection against woodworm.

Greater success was enjoyed (in trials at least) by Robert Fulton's

submarine, built early in the 19th century. The *Nautilus,* as it was called, was 6.5 m (21 ft 4 in) long and had a maximum width of 1.28 m (4 ft 2 in). It was designed for a crew of three, who operated a manual propeller when submerged, but used a sail on the surface. The *Nautilus* had vertical and horizontal rudders to achieve stability, and Fulton also used compressed air to replace burnt oxygen. Trials designed to test its ability to dispose of surface craft in a similar manner to the *Turtle* were successfully carried out in France and England, but the naval officers of those traditional sea powers thought the whole thing too underhand, not the sort of thing officers and gentlemen would ever resort to.

The Bavarian Corporal Wilhelm Bauer built a submarine made of iron plates in 1851. It was 8 m (26 ft) long, 3 m (10 ft) tall and 2 m (6 ft 6 in) wide. Three men pedalled a ship's propeller to drive it along. During

submarines. One of these sank the corvette *Housatonic* in 1863. Later torpedoes were self-propelled and were fired from torpedo tubes.

Submarine propulsion also changed. On the surface steam, then paraffin and petrol engines were used. In 1887 Rudolf Diesel invented his new type of engine

the main entrance and the mountings for a periscope, and later for a snorkel. These elements, and the rapid-firing guns which were subsequently mounted on the vessel's deck, were adopted gradually, of course, but by the turn of the century the basic features of this complex piece of military equipment, by

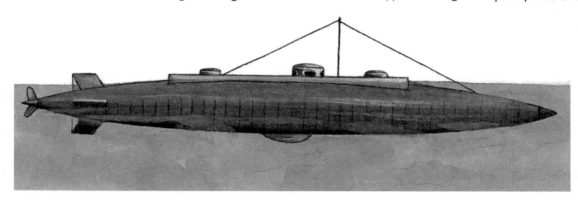

The French submarine
Gymnote.

submersion trials the ballast shifted and the craft sank to a depth of nearly 10 fathoms. The pressure deformed the hull, but when the water got inside, compressed air enabled the crew to open the hatch and save themselves in a water bubble which took them to the surface.

The new conception of shipbuilding, which emerged in the 19th century in connection with the use of new materials, means of propulsion and armaments, was gradually reflected in submarine construction, too. Even during the American Civil War the Confederates used impact torpedoes mounted on the bows of

which, among its other advantages, proved best able to charge the batteries used for underwater travel, and which had been first introduced by the Russian inventor Drzewicki.

Tanks placed between the inner and outer skins of the vessel were later used for submerging and surfacing. The stronger inner shell had to withstand water pressure to a given depth, while the outer skin gave the vessel its hydrodynamic shape. Horizontal and vertical rudders were used to steer the craft, and the water was expelled from the tanks using compressed air when it surfaced. The conning tower housed

now found in all major fleets, had been established for the next 60 years.

Examples were the French *Gymnote,* designed by Dupuy de Lome and Gustav Zede, the American *Plunger,* designed by John P. Holland in 1896, and the notorious German U-boats. This last-named, fearsome craft had a special weakness, however, in that it had to surface while its diesel engines charged the batteries.

A German U-boat — an effective and feared weapon in both World Wars.

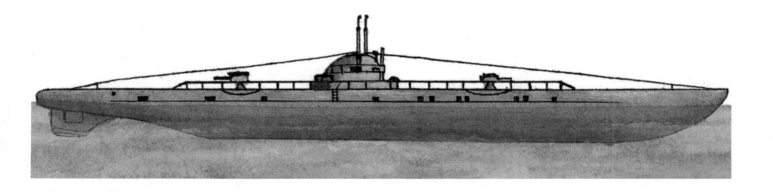

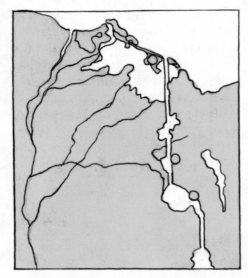

The Suez Canal, 161 km (100 miles) long,
shortened routes as follows:
London—Hong Kong
 5,488 km (3,411 miles), i.e. 26 %
Marseilles—Bombay
10,105 km (6,280 miles), i.e.58 %
Odessa—Bombay
12,680 km (7,883 miles), i.e. 67 %

The growing importance of water transport and the huge amounts of coal required after the advent of steam made the building of canals to save both time and fuel more than just a pipedream. The idea of connecting rivers or seas in this way was by no means a new one. It had existed in ancient times in Egypt, China and Europe, and Roman remains of this kind can be found in Britain. A significant step forward

Suez today.

was made with the introduction of locks, used by the Dutch from the 14th century, and known near Milan in Italy from the 15th. It was then possible to set up gradually an extensive navigation network both in Europe (in France, Belgium, Holland and Russia) and on other continents (Canada and the United States).

The ancient Egyptians had long been attracted by the idea of linking the life-giving Nile to the Red Sea, thus opening up the way to the Far East. In the heyday of the Middle Dynasty, under the pharaoh Sesostris I (1971–1928 B.C.) and his successor, such a canal, called the Ta Tenat, was actually built. The desert sands filled it in, but the idea lived on for centuries.

It was only with the advent of steam that the passage from the Mediterranean to the Red Sea became a matter of some urgency. Suddenly it became clear that the trip round the Cape of Good Hope was an enormous waste of time and fuel. So in 1846 a canal company was formed in Paris, plans were drawn up, and subsequently the French consul in Cairo, Ferdinand de Lesseps, obtained the necessary concession to build the Suez Canal. After numerous international disputes, work was finally begun in 1859. Thousands of fellahin

(Egyptian peasants), mostly from the Sudan, laboured under conditions verging on slavery and with inadequate water supplies, but within 10 years the project linking the Mediterranean and the Red Sea was completed.

The notion of a Panama Canal, whose chief purpose was to provide a short cut between the east and west coasts of North America, was also an old one. Columbus himself sought a way through to Asian shores in the area of the Isthmus of Panama, as did the conquistadors Balboa and Pizarro after him. It was the Californian gold rush of 1848 that gave the greatest impetus to the scheme, however, although the plans went through several versions and the Panamanian railway was built before work began on the canal in 1881. Once more it was de Lesseps who directed operations. Here, too, one of the greatest obstacles was the climate, yellow fever being a constant threat. The canal also had to be protected from the effects of mountain torrents, and cutting through the watershed proved a problem. So in 1889, after the budget had been exceeded and for other reasons, including a bribery scandal, work had to be halted. It was only restarted in 1904, when the United States took over the concession, and on 3 August

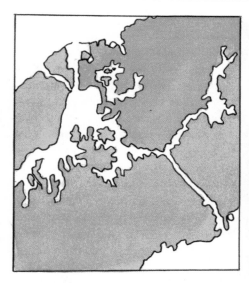

The Panama Canal, 81 km (51 miles) long, meant the following savings:
New York—Panama, around Cape Horn 17,800 km (11,050 miles), through the Panama Canal 3,250 km (2,020 miles).
Hamburg—Acapulco, around Cape Horn 21,368 km (13,280 miles), through the Panama Canal 10,700 km (6,650 miles).
Hamburg—Honolulu, around Cape Horn 22,700 km (14,100 miles), through the Panama Canal 7,000 km (4,300 miles).

1914 the first steamer made its way along the canal.

Of the world's other canals, mention should be made of the Nord-Ostsee Canal in West Germany and the Manchester Ship Canal in England. Canal systems fulfil a broad range of functions: in Holland they help protect the low-lying country from flooding, whereas in the Soviet Union they play an important role in the national economy.

The Nord-Ostsee Canal, which joins the North Sea to the Baltic, is a major route in European commerce. It was constructed between 1887 and 1895 according to Hermann Dahlstrom's plans, and is 98.7 km (61 miles) long. It passes between the cities of Rendsburg and Kiel.

In the pioneer days, when settlers in the New World began to look for a way through to China and the Spice Isles, French fisherman Jacques Cartier discovered the Gulf of St. Lawrence, in 1534. Later he sailed up the river of the same name, and 100 years after that the

French got as far as Lake Michigan. They fancied they could see yellow-skinned people on the opposite bank, so they donned Chinese clothes. The 'Chinese' turned out to be Winnebago Indians, but the colonists discovered long and branching waterways leading through the Canadian lake network. Between 1789 and 1793 the first canal and lock were completed, between Lakes St. Louis and St. Francis, the first such works in North America, and in 1959 the entire route from Duluth on Lake Superior to the Atlantic was opened up, a distance of 3,768 km (2,336 miles).

A no less colossal transcontinental system of waterways is that in the Soviet Union, linking five seas and totalling some 4,000 km (2,480

In building the Panama Canal such technical advances as the railway and the bulldozer were used.

miles) of navigable routes. It began with plans to join the Volga to the Don (101 km or 62 miles) and to the Baltic Sea (368 km or 228 miles). These were first proposed in the time of Peter the Great, but were not implemented until 1952 and 1964 respectively. The Moscow Canal of 128 km (80 miles), connecting the Moscow River with the lower reaches of the Volga, was completed in 1937, and the White Sea—Baltic Sea Canal in 1933. These artificial waterways transformed the natural waters of the European USSR into a single system, linking the main rivers with the surrounding seas.

Through the Panama Canal.

Sailing ships made their exit majestically and in all their glory, for the 19th century, which brought the demise of the tall ships, was also their finest hour. Although the shape of sailing vessels got simpler, as far as hulls were concerned, the complexity of equipment grew, and the number of different types multiplied. New construction techniques and new materials in particular made it possible to build giants over 100 m (328 ft) long, with a ratio of length to beam of up to 7:1. Advances in rigging technology also made possible a great variety of combinations, giving each type of craft a characteristic appearance. The two main types were frigate rigging (predominantly square) and schooner rigging (mainly fore-and-aft).

During the War of Independence (1775–83), the Americans started to build small but very fast ships, of up to 150 tonnes and having slender hulls, sharp bows, an undercut stern, and forward-slanted masts carrying a large amount of square-rigged canvas. While the first clumsy paddle steamers were ploughing their way through the waves, these clippers became queens of the ocean. They were helped in this by the British losing their monopoly of trade with India and China, and by the Californian gold rush, which drew attention to their speed. The first true clipper, launched in 1849, was the 47 m (154 ft) long and 9.55 m (31 ft 4 in) wide *Rainbow.*

A famous shipbuilder of the time was Donald McKay of Boston. Although his boats were made of cheap wood and did not therefore last very long, they were soundly constructed and stood up to the gales encountered when carrying prospectors round the Horn to California. But McKay's reputation was built mainly on the record times achieved by some of these ships, whose length:beam ratio was over 6:1. One of the first, *Flying Cloud,* made the trip from New York to San Francisco (17,597 nautical miles) in 89 days and 21 hours at an average speed of about nine knots. That was in 1851. Later, the clipper *Lightning* covered 438 nautical miles in 24 hours, an average speed of 18 knots, and the *Sovereign of the Seas* even managed a speed of 22 knots during her record crossing from New York to Liverpool in 13 days 14 hours. In the course of the 1850s McKay's ships also proved their mettle during the Australian gold rush. However, the largest of them, the *Great Republic,* was gutted by fire soon after launching.

The successes and also the profits of the American shipbuilders spurred the British on to build their tea clippers. By the time of the American Civil War (1861–65) they had

A diagram of the sails of a barquentine.

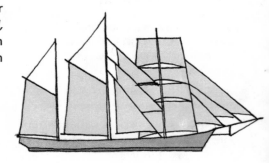

The world's biggest schooner, *Thomas W. Lawson.*

got ahead of their transatlantic rivals again. This was the era of the China to Britain races, of which the most famous took place in 1866, when five clippers left Foochow; the winner, *Taeping*, got home a mere half an hour ahead of its closest rival, *Ariel*. In 1868 the British built the clipper *Thermopylae*, which made the trip from London to Melbourne in 59 days, a record which has never been equalled by a sailing ship.

Undoubtedly the most famous tea clipper of all was the *Cutty Sark*, which cost £16,150, had a length of 85 m (280 ft), a beam of 11 m (36 ft) and a gross tonnage of 963 tonnes. The *Cutty Sark* was intended to be the fastest ship on the tea run from China but she was launched the very year (1869) that the Suez Canal was opened and steamers soon captured the China trade. Nevertheless, she served on the China run from 1870 to 1877 before switching to the wool trade between Australia and England in 1883. The *Cutty Sark* was sold to Portuguese interests in 1895 but later returned to English ownership and has since been fully restored and is now on permanent display at Greenwich.

The clippers were not the only craft which produced excellent performances. Schooners of various sizes were used for all manner of purposes. They were rigged fore-and-aft (mainly with lugsails and Bermuda sails), and also competed for speed. The largest ever schooner was the steel-hulled *Thomas W. Lawson*, which had a length of 132 m (433 ft) and a beam of 16.6 m (54 ft 6 in). Another type of craft with fore-and-aft rigging was the barquentine, although the foremast was square-rigged. The barque *Gatherer* earned notoriety rather than fame, however, and was nicknamed 'bloody'. The officers treated the crew so badly that Captain John Spark was eventually murdered off Cape Horn.

Still around among the larger ships was the frigate, while a popular small sailing vessel was and still is the yacht, which developed from the boyer. Another vessel much used for coastal work was the fishing yawl.

Iron and steel began to find their place in the construction of sailing ships as well as steamers. The three-masted clipper *Sobraon*, launched in Britain in 1866, had a metal frame and wooden planking. She was considered so luxurious a craft that doctors recommended trips on her for those recuperating from illness. She carried her own cows, pigs and hens to supply fresh food, and tonnes of ice to provide fresh water. Of the all-metal sailing ships, famous examples were the iron *Patriarch* (launched in Scotland in 1869) and the five-masted all-steel *Preussen* of 1902, the largest sailing vessel in the world, with a length of 134.5 m (441 ft) and a beam of 16.5 m (54 ft), one of the last of its type in the famous German P series, which also included *Penang*, *Pamir* and *Passat*.

The opening of the Suez and later the Panama Canal meant a decline in the fortunes of sailing ships in favour of steam. Up to the First World War they were still used as cargo vessels on the Australian and South American routes, but after that only as training ships. To this day, however, the sight of a tall ship in full sail is an impressive and almost magical experience, perhaps partly because of our tendency to romanticize the adventure of those voyages of a bygone age.

The American clipper *Lightning*, **which was among the fastest sailing ships of its age.**

Sail Sails On

With the exception of a few training vessels, tall ships no longer ride the waves, but sailing craft are far from being an extinct species. In many parts of the world they are still used by people every day and have continued to develop independently of western ships. On the other hand, small coastal vessels, especially the Dutch ones, gave rise to sporting yachts which also sail the seven seas. Let us take a closer look at these.

In 1660, when the citizens of Amsterdam presented Charles II with the 106-ton yacht *Mary,* they can scarcely have foreseen the fashion they were starting. The Dutch word jacht has connections with chasing and hunting, and that was its original purpose, along with reconnaissance, light cargo work and the transportation of VIPs. It was this last use that eventually made yachting popular with statesmen and other men of means. The small Dutch one-masters had a rounded hull and carried a lugsail and square-rigged topsail, along with a pair of jibs and a staysail. The versions used by the rich for recreation were known as the statenjacht or heernjacht. If we can believe the painting of Willem van de Velde the Younger, the *Mary* was a boat of this type. Over the luxuriously appointed cabin the typical Dutch fore-and-aft sails flew — lugsail, jib, staysail and topsail.

King Charles had a weakness for yachting, and had a fleet numbering 25 craft, the smallest being the 25-ton *Jamie.* Other monarchs followed his lead, and by 1661 the first race took place, between the royal yacht *Catherine* and the Duke of York's *Anne.*

Yachting took the fancy not only of monarchs such as Charles II, Louis XIV and Peter the Great, but also of the aristocracy and the monied classes. Yacht clubs grew up, and the first regattas were held. The most famous club was the British Royal Yacht Club, which organized the Hundred Guinea Cup

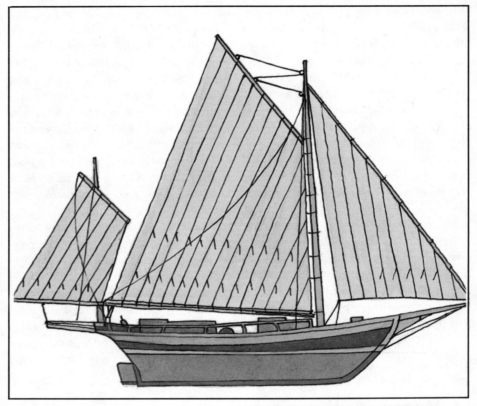

Slocum's sloop, *Spray.* ▲

The *Endeavour II,* **a yacht of 1937. In the same year, she was the challenger of the America's Cup.** ▼

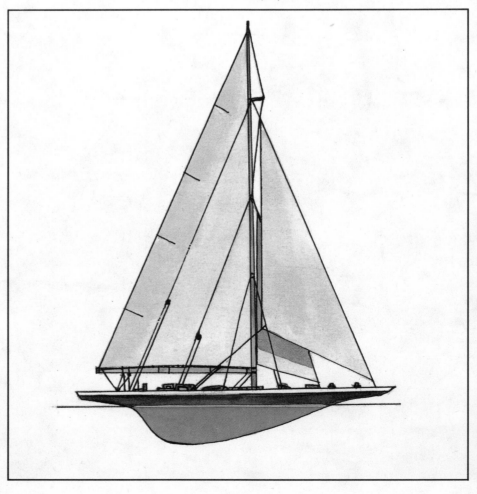

Some types of modern sporting yachts.

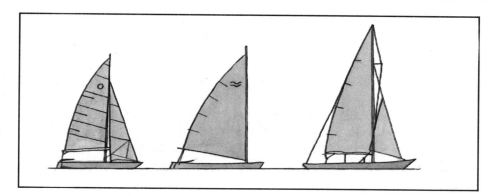

regatta off the Isle of Wight. In 1851 the two-masted schooner *America* belonging to New York yachtsmen took part, and to the surprise of all present won with such ease that she was suspected of being secretly propelled by a screw! Later, with the spread and partial democratization of the sport, although it was for a long time the exclusive domain of the rich, other types of small sailing vessel were included in the regattas; motor yachts, catamarans and trimarans also took part.

Today, yachts are classified for competition purposes according to an internationally recognized system, which takes account of such things as type, size, weight of hull and manner of rigging. Two-masters can be rigged as schooners, ketches or yawls. One-masted yachts are usually cutters or sloops. The most important regattas are in the 12 m (39 ft) group (including the America's Cup), and the Olympic, national and international classes.

A feature of yachting that has always attracted attention has been the feats of lone yachtsmen sailing long distances and even around the world, fighting a solitary battle with wind and wave — a far cry from the well planned courses of regattas. The first was Canadian Joshua Slocum, a sea captain who bought a 100 year-old sloop, rebuilt it, renamed it *Spray,* and on 24 April 1895, at the age of 51, set out to circumnavigate the globe. The 10.6 m (35 ft) *Spray* took him across the Atlantic to Gibraltar, from where he sailed down the coast of South America, passed through the Straits of Magellan, crossed the Pacific to Australia, went on through the

A boat sailing with a spinnaker sail.

Indian Ocean to Africa, and then crossed the Atlantic again to drop anchor in New York on 6 June 1898.

Other lone yachtsmen have included John Voss, who adapted the hull of an Indian piragua for his round-the-world trip, and John Guzzwell, who sailed round the world in the smallest craft, the 6 m (20 ft) long yawl *Trekka,* the voyage taking four years and two days from when he set out on 10 September 1955. Guzzwell, who was later awarded the Slocum Medal, displayed not only exceptional courage but also masterly seamanship.

Although we have so far confined our attention to the western school of boatbuilding, this does not mean to say that boats are no longer constructed elsewhere. Mention has been made of the craft of primitive tribes, and now we shall look at traditional sailing vessels, whose development stagnated at a certain stage compared with the evolution of sailing vessels in Europe, and which, though they have in some cases adopted modern features of one kind or another, remain specific to a particular part of the world.

In the Red Sea and the Arabian Sea, and especially in the many bays found there — the port of Kuwait in the Persian Gulf could be said to be the largest harbour for sailing craft in the world — there are thousands of boats which are generically termed dhows. Their typical feature is the triangular lateen sail, the very sail the Arabs brought to the European part of the Mediterranean in the Middle Ages.

The two-masted baghla and sambuk are reminiscent of the old caravels, having decorative sterns and similarly shaped hulls. The single-masted zaruk and badan, with their pointed bows and stern and the rather peculiar way in which the rudder is handled, are used in shallow waters.

Indian craft with square-rigged sails which carry cargoes along the River Ganges are remarkable for their awnings, often extending the whole length of the boat. Along the coast one can see unconventional craft made out of several large tree-trunks, tapering to a raised prow.

The oldest type of traditional sailing vessel is the Chinese junk. In spite of its clumsy appearance, deriving from its short bows and stern and its flat bottom without a keel, it is very manoeuvrable thanks to its lugger rig (lateen sails with the bottom corner cut off) and is capable of sailing the stormy South China Sea. The good handling qualities of the junk enabled the Chinese to make long journeys in the Middle Ages, going as far as Sumatra, the Persian Gulf and the east coast of Africa.

There are, of course, many types of junk, according to what they are used for, and some can carry up to 400 tonnes. The Japanese version is rather surprising, being heavy and not too stable, with tall superstructures and a foremast rather like that of the ancient artemon.

In Taiwan there are bamboo craft with sails but which are steered and sometimes powered by oars at the side and stabilized by keel fins.

Indonesia has some equally fascinating craft, often with outriggers. The proa or prau varies according to the place it comes from. Those from the island of Madura have two masts and triangular sails, with the mainmast shifted aft and the fore-

A Pacific catamaran.

mast forwards. In contrast to this slim craft, called prau bedang, the prau mayang cargo boat has a rounded shape. These craft are steered by means of an oar-type rudder. Other craft found in Indonesia is the karakor, which is rather like the Viking boats, and outrigged dugouts that have a huge lugsail.

Dug-out and burnt-out canoes made from a single trunk are also typical of the South Pacific. By joining together several canoes by means of a frame and using sails in the shape of a crab's claw, the Polynesians made craft in which they were able to travel extremely long distances. The two-masted lakatoi of New Guinea, consisting of at least three hulls, was just such a craft, as was the Hawaiian double canoe or the Maori tainui, which was up to 20 m (65 ft 6 in) long and was used to transport whole tribes.

Outrigged craft are also used by Malagasy fishermen. Among the most interesting vessels elsewhere are the reed boats of the Peruvian Indians on Lake Titicaca and the dish-shaped sailing rafts used by Brazilian fishermen.

A Chinese junk, the most common craft in the seas of the Far East.

Although sailing ships had by no means disappeared altogether from the world's oceans, in the second half of the 19th century the conditions existed for the rapid expansion of steam propulsion. Briefly, steam engines themselves had been improved, after which steam turbines were invented, high-pressure boilers developed, new materials such as iron and steel used and ship design was advanced. The overall effect was to cut fuel consumption, increase speeds, and allow bigger and better ships to be built.

It was only natural under such circumstances that designs should become more specialized. Apart from liners and combined cargo and passenger ships, a gradual distinction became apparent between craft carrying dry cargoes and those carrying liquid loads. The first tanker, the *Glückauf,* was built in Britain in 1886. There were industrial ships such as fishing and whaling vessels, and technical craft such as tugs and icebreakers. For the moment, however, let us confine our attention to the ocean liner, which enjoyed a truly meteoric rise to glory.

The expansion of passenger travel resulted from two quite contradictory factors. On the one hand millions of poor people from Europe emigrated to North America in search of a better life, while on the other the rich took to sea travel in a big way and were willing to pay

The steamship *Oceanic,* **built in 1871. She anticipated design features of future ocean liners, though she was still equipped with sails.**

Ch. A. Parsons's motor yacht, *Turbinia.*

The *Mauretania.* **She was 240.8 m (790 feet) long, with a beam of 26.8 m (88 feet), and was one of the most successful transatlantic liners.**

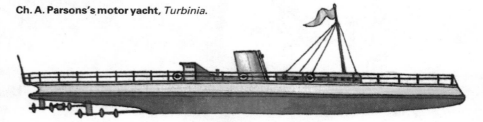

immense sums for stylish shipboard accommodation. These facts were soon appreciated and exploited by the major shipping lines. There were now, in addition to Cunard, the White Star Line, the German Norddeutscher Lloyd and the Hamburg-Amerika Linie, and above all the biggest American company, International Mercantile Marine Company or IMM for short. All these companies began to build huge ocean liners. On board the rich could enjoy the luxuries of well-furnished cabins and other facilities, while the poor travelled in crowded steerage accommodation. The owners of smaller vessels, mostly tramp steamers, also took the opportunity to carry cheap-rate passengers. Conditions on board these vessels, which followed the main passenger routes but stopped off to load and discharge cargoes, were often atrocious, and it was not until after the First World War that things got better.

In 1871 the White Star Line put into service its liner *Oceanic,* which incorporated a number of new features. The best cabins had previously always been at the stern, but now they appeared amidships along with dining rooms, lounges and the bridge. Here they were as far as possible from the vibrations of the

The end of the *Titanic*.

ship's propeller. The captain now had a telegraph at his disposal, and the helmsman's work was made easier by a servo steam engine. The bows of the ship were blunter than those of the clipper type, making for better manoeuvrability.

The *Oceanic,* driven by a single screw powered by two 802 kW (1,075 hp) engines, had a cruising speed of 14 knots. The all-steel liner *City of Paris,* built 18 years later, cruised at 20 knots, had 14,710 kW (20,000 hp) down in the engine-room and two propellers. This not only reduced vibration compared with a one-screw system, but also helped the ship win the Blue Riband in 1889, a tradition which her sister-ship *City of New York* was to maintain.

Building bigger, faster and more luxurious ships became the order of the day. The biggest ship in the world at the time, the *Kaiser Wilhelm der Grosse,* was 209 m (685 ft 6 in) long and over 20 m (65 ft 6 in) wide. She made her maiden voyage in November 1897 and won the first German Blue Riband. The same year saw an even more remarkable event. During a naval ceremony held to celebrate Queen Victoria's Diamond Jubilee, a motor yacht which had no business there suddenly appeared – and none of the other craft were able to catch it. This was the dramatic way in which Charles A. Parsons chose to demonstrate his new invention, the steam turbine. It gave his yacht *Turbinia* an incredible top speed of 34.5 knots and was soon introduced on ocean liners. At the beginning of the 20th century the radio telegraph also became an indispensable piece of marine equipment.

When, in 1906, Cunard launched the sister ships *Mauretania* and *Lusitania,* they set the standard for this type of vessel up to the outbreak of the Second World War. They had a displacement of 40,000 tons, travelled in excess of 25 knots, carried around 2,500 passengers in comfort, and had a crew of about 800 to make sure everything went smoothly. While the *Mauretania* stayed in service till 1935, the less fortunate *Lusitania* was sunk by the German submarine *U-20* off the Irish coast in 1915.

The rival White Star Line was not to be outdone and in 1911 launched the *Olympic* and the *Titanic.* The latter of the two especially, a floating palace 269 m (882 ft) long, 28 m (92 ft) wide, with 11 decks and twice the capacity of the *Mauretania,* was expected to steal passengers from the other lines. However, on her maiden voyage this transatlantic giant hit an iceberg off the Newfoundland coast. It was just before midnight on 14 April 1912, and with a 90 m (295 ft) gash down her side, the 'unsinkable' *Titanic* went down with the loss of 1,513 of the 2,224 people on board. It was not until 2 September 1985 that the wreck was finally discovered, 960 km (600 miles) south of Newfoundland and 4,000 m (13,120 ft) down.

The *Iron Duke*, a British warship, with
a displacement of 25,000 tonnes, a length of
186 m (600 feet), and a speed of 21 knots.

At the turn of the century the largest warships, of steel construction, had displacements of around 17,000 tons and speeds of about 19 knots. Their armament ranged from 305 mm (12 in) guns down to small-calibre weapons, and they were protected by armour plating about 305 mm (12 in) thick.

These figures indicate the progress which had been made in the design of fighting ships, but when in 1903 the Italian marine architect Vittorio Cuniberti proposed the optimum armament for battleships as 12 305 mm (12 in) guns and a speed of 24 knots, the British Admiralty took up the challenge. They were confirmed in their resolve by the most important battle of the Russo-Japanese War, at Tsushima in 1905, where the Japanese victory was attributable to guns of heavy calibre, rapid rate of fire and long range. The need for stronger armour and the usefulness of mines and torpedoes were also underlined.

So it came about that in the incredibly short time between 2 October 1905 and 10 October 1906 Great Britain built a warship with which none of its contemporaries could compare: the *Dreadnought*. It was 160 m (526 ft) long, 25 m (82 ft) across, had a displacement of 17,900 tons and made 21 knots powered by a steam turbine. The main armament was 10 305 mm (12 in) guns mounted on five turrets, 24 76 mm (3 in) guns and five torpedo-tubes below the water-line. The policy to build such ships was mainly decided by the First Lord of the Admiralty, John Arbuthnot Fisher, and was soon adopted by the other naval powers. By the time of the Great War, therefore, the main types of naval vessel which would take part in it had already seen the light of day.

The design of British battleships became fairly standard in 1915 with the Queen Elizabeth class, whose displacement was 33,000 tonnes, speed 25 knots and main firepower

A First World War aircraft-carrier.

was eight 380 mm (15 in) guns mounted on four turrets; she had a length of 197 m (646 ft) and a width of 28.5 m (93 ft 6 in). However, the variety of cruisers which existed at the outbreak of hostilities was maintained throughout the war. In 1907 the *Invincible* had become the first of a new type of warship, the battle-cruiser; it had a displacement of 17,400 tonnes, a speed of 26.4 knots, and eight guns up to 305 mm (12 in) calibre, and the chief feature was heavy guns. The armaments and equipment of other types of warship varied a good deal. Light cruisers, for example, were not very different from destroyers, and used torpedoes as a main weapon.

The destroyer, which went through a period of rapid development during the war, became the universal naval vessel. Apart from being used to destroy torpedo boats and submarines, it carried out convoy escort duties and reconnaissance, was used to mine seaways, sink freighters, and so on. By the end of the war the displacement of destroyers had reached 1,500 tonnes and the gun calibre was 152 mm (6 in).

An important role was also played by fast torpedo boats, whose design was mainly the work of the Italians

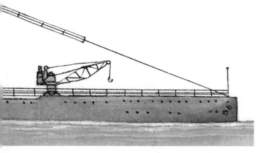

in 1912—14, minesweepers (a total of about 310,000 mines were laid) and above all submarines. German submarines in particular were greatly feared, especially after the declaration of 'total war' on 1 February 1917. At the time they had a range of up to 16,000 km (10,000 miles), a displacement of 850 tonnes, a surface speed of 16.8 knots, and a submerged speed of 8.6 knots. They were armed with 16 torpedoes and two deck cannon (101 mm or 4 in and 76 mm or 3 in). In the course of the war German submarines sank nearly 6,000 Allied ships totalling 13 million tons, while the Allies managed to build only 10 million tonnes of new ships over the same period.

The submarine war, naval blockades and hostilities conducted over ever-widening areas put paid to the still current theory of gaining superiority at sea by dint of a few major battles. The Germans sought a decisive engagement with the British from the start, but after initial success on 1 November 1914, when

they sank two cruisers, they lost the whole of their Pacific squadron at the Battle of the Falklands on 8 December. For a long time after that both sides were reluctant to commit their full strength, until at last they met at the historic Battle of Jutland on 31 May 1916. In all 250 ships with a total of over two million tons were involved. The main aim of the German high seas fleet was to break the Allied blockade. Although Allied casualties were heavier — three battleships, six cruisers and eight destroyers as against one battleship, five cruisers and five destroyers — the Germans failed to break out. As one American reporter put it, they successfully attacked their gaolers, but stayed in gaol.

A major news item at sea was the unsuccessful Allied landing in the Dardanelles in 1915; apart from the warships it involved 108 merchant vessels with 80,000 troops on board. The first attempts to use aircraft at sea were also doomed to failure.

The Battle of Jutland, 1916.

In the wake of the *Titanic* disaster the registration offices of various countries — the oldest of which was Lloyd's Register of Shipping in Britain — undertook measures to improve safety at sea. As far as transatlantic liners were concerned, this meant chiefly the provision of a sufficient number of lifeboats for all those on board (the *Titanic* had had 20 in all, with places for just 1,167 persons out of 2,224), the decision to follow more southerly courses and keep a watch for icebergs, and an attempt to divide the hull into a greater number of watertight compartments.

Besides the flourishing of ocean liners, there were other developments in merchant shipping, 45 per cent of which was British at that time. Boat trains were put in service between Denmark and Germany with vessels of over 3,000 tonnes displacement, and in 1911 the first freighter designed for unit cargoes, the Danish *Seelandia,* was launched. She was powered by a pair of diesel engines, had a capacity of 4,964 tonnes and a speed of 12 knots.

The First World War caused the destruction of huge quantities of merchant shipping which fell victim to German torpedoes, so that after 1918 the losses had to be made up. The spread of motoring called for oil tankers, although their dimensions

The *Bremen,* **which had a crew of 950 and could carry 2,500 passengers.**

were limited by the size of the Suez Canal. Oil was now also used to fuel ships, and heavy diesel engines came into their own. Passenger steamers were still prominent, although the wave of mass emigration had passed. The rich were still keen sailors, and the 1930s were the golden age of the transatlantic giants.

The French company CGT (Compagnie Générale Transatlantique) entered the postwar lists with a strong challenge. It carried about 70,000 passengers a year, and its ship *Île de France* was in 1926 the biggest in the world, having a length of 242 m (794 ft) and a width of 28 m (92 ft). Her four steam turbines

developed a total of 40,448 kW (220 hp), giving her a speed of 23.5 knots. Apart from the luxury of her accommodation, the ship was notable for being able to catapult a mail-carrying seaplane. An even more luxurious French ship, the *Georges Philipar,* had a swimming pool, tennis courts, garages, and cabins with verandas.

The Blue Riband had been held by the *Mauretania* since 1907, and the German lines were anxious to go one up on their competitors by winning it. In 1929 the company Norddeutscher Lloyd put the huge ship *Bremen* into service on the New York route. This vessel had

The *Normandie,* **the largest liner of the period before the Second World War. She was 309 m (930 feet) long and had a speed of 30 knots.**

The *United States,* **which has held the Blue Riband since 1952, cost $72m to build.**

a length of 290 m (951 ft), was 31 m (34 ft) wide and had a capacity of 51,656 tonnes. She took the record on her maiden voyage with an average speed of 28.51 knots, and this was bettered by her sister ship, *Europa,* the following year.

In the 1930s the great liners reached their highest standards of elegance and comfort. Apart from the prestige ships with their extravagant luxury, frequently government-subsidized, tourist class liners also came on the scene. Although considerably cheaper, they also offered a high standard of accommodation. Technical innovations included the multi-blade propeller and welded construction.

When the Italian ship *Rex* was launched in 1932, followed by the *Conte di Savoia,* both of which were intended for the 'sun route' from Genoa to New York, it was hoped that they would capture the Blue Riband for Italy at once. Instead, technical problems meant that the Italians had to wait a whole year before the *Rex* won the award. By that time the French were building the *Normandie,* a further giant which was the biggest ship in the world until 1940 and which took the Blue Riband from the Italians in 1935. The golden age between the wars was brought to a dignified close by the British passenger liners *Queen Mary* and *Queen Elizabeth.* The *Queen Mary,* launched in 1934, managed to take the Blue Riband from the French before the outbreak of war in August 1938, and then served as a troopship. After the Second World War she made 1,000 voyages until 1967, when she was withdrawn from service. She then became a museum and conference centre in California. The *Queen Elizabeth,* launched in 1938, was always described in superlatives. She spent the war as a troopship, and went into passenger service only after the cessation of hostilities. She was destroyed by fire in 1972 in Hong Kong. Other transatlantic liners served similar wartime purposes, and two of them, the *Bremen* and the *Normandie,* were also destroyed by fire.

Throughout the war merchant ships were every bit as important as warships. Because of their length, tankers were converted to aircraft-carriers, and universal freighters of the Liberty class, with a displacement of 10,500 tonnes and a speed of 11 knots, were built from prefabricated sections. In the course of the war the Americans built 2,770 of them for a total tonnage of 29,292,000. They were used for convoy duty, carrying everything from weapons to coal.

The famous *Queen Mary.* **She took the Blue Riband from the** *Normandie* **in August 1938.**

The pocket battleship *Admiral Graf Spee,* **which had a displacement of 12,100 tonnes, a length of 188 m (567 feet), a beam of 20.7 m (62 feet), and made 26 knots with a range of 10,000 nautical miles.**

The Second World War, in which 35 million people from 53 countries were killed, affected almost all the world's seas and oceans. Although the naval weapons of the powers involved were to some extent limited by the 1922 Washington disarmament conference and other conventions, the pace of technical progress between the wars had produced greater destructive potential.

Battleship displacements were around 35,000 tonnes and the largest guns had a calibre of 406 mm (16 in), as laid down by the conference. Nevertheless, some countries chose to ignore this limitation, such as Germany with the *Bismarck* and *Tirpitz,* and Japan with the *Yamato.* Yet these giants were seldom sent into battle for fear of losing them, and most were sunk or damaged in the early years of the war. The leading role was taken over by aircraft-carriers, which were often 300 m (985 ft) long and 35 m (115 ft) wide, with a speed of 35 knots and displacement of up to 55,000 tonnes. They were used most of all in the Pacific theatre, where the Americans and Japanese faced each other at great distances. Elsewhere cruisers became more important than battleships, including 'pocket' battleships, being more flexible and capable of taking on a range of duties from convoy escort to the shelling of coastal targets. Destroyers were also invaluable; thanks to their anti-aircraft firepower and the use of depth charges they were able to serve in either a defensive or an attacking role.

Smaller warships still were the frigates, sloops and corvettes, and other surface craft included minesweepers, torpedo boats and gunboats (operating in coastal waters), and landing craft. The last was a new category designed for the offloading of troops and supplies. There were specialized landing craft for different purposes, such as LCIs (Landing Craft Infantry), LCTs (Landing Craft Tanks), and so on, right up to boats giving cover fire, amphibians and floating docks. Troop carriers were also developed.

Apart from aircraft-carriers, the most important craft of the 1939–45 war were submarines. They now had displacements of 250 to 1,000 tonnes, and apart from their main weapon, the torpedo, they also carried depth charges and small calibre cannon for attacking merchantmen

The aerial and submarine attacks of the Axis powers concentrated on allied convoys.

or for anti-aircraft defence. Near the end of the war the Germans built the XXI-G class submarines which were capable, with the aid of a snorkel, of running their diesel engines without surfacing. But anti-submarine defences also improved tremendously, from Asdic and especially radar to heavier convoy escorts and air support.

The naval strategy of the war began with the attempt by the German navy to cripple the supply lines to the Allies and so limit their fighting strength. In August 1939, even before war had been declared, the pocket battleship *Graf Spee* was steaming into the Atlantic with the job of making the supplying of the British Isles as difficult as possible, and later sinking ships flying the British or French flags. The German marauder was damaged in an engagement with the cruiser *Exeter* at the Battle of the River Plate and ended its career scuttled in Mon-

tevideo harbour on 17 December, but it had claimed nine victims from the merchant fleets, totalling over 50,000 tons. The submarine *U-47* managed to sneak into Scapa Flow on 14 October and sink the battleship *Royal Oak,* killing 833 of her crew.

Similar incidents demonstrated the danger posed by submarines, and subsequent experience was to confirm it. In four months in 1939 the Germans sank 95 freighters for the loss of nine submarines, and by 1942 the figure was 1,570 Allied ships lost at a cost of 86 German submarines. The submarine war was especially significant in the Atlantic, with attacks on convoys by either 'lone wolf' submarines, or 'packs' which coordinated their attacks, often in combination with air support. In this connection it is worth recalling the unfortunate fate of convoy PQ 97, which was sailing with an important military cargo

through the Barents Sea to Arkhangelsk in the Soviet Union. On orders from the British high command the whole group was split up and the escorting warships recalled, so that the Germans were able to sink no less than 24 ships; only 11 of the convoy reached their destination.

By occupying France and Norway the Nazis obtained many new bases for both submarines and surface craft. They therefore decided, somewhat reluctantly, to send even the big battleships into combat, since they still held a sort of fascination for the general public as a symbol of naval superiority. So at the end of May 1941, the huge battleship *Bismarck* of 41,700 tonnes and the heavy cruiser *Prinz Eugen* of 14,800 tonnes sailed out into the Atlantic. After the sinking of the biggest British battleship, the *Hood* (46,300 tonnes), the destruction of the *Bismarck* became a priority — and it took the British three days to do it.

For the German high command this was a body blow, and they did not send other heavy warships into battle again until after Operation Cerberus in 1942, when they successfully transferred the giants *Gneisenau, Prinz Eugen* and *Scharnhorst* (31,800 tonnes) from Brest in occupied France, through the Channel to German coastal waters. At the end of 1943 the battle-cruiser *Scharnhorst* was sent to prowl along the convoy route to Murmansk in the Soviet Union. Along with the *Gneisenau,* this ship had already sunk Allied freighters totalling 116,000 gross tonnes in the course of 1941. Two years later, however, the Allies not only had a clear lead in sea power, but also better radiolocators, so that the *Scharnhorst* was detected soon after sailing and was sunk on 26 November 1943. From then on the large German battleships never left harbour. The last of the giants, the 42,900 tonne *Tirpitz,* was gradually destroyed by miniature submarines and air raids on her anchorage, until finally being sunk by two direct hits inflicted by Lancasters in November 1944.

In the Mediterranean, where the aggressor was Italy, with good naval bases and superiority in numbers of warships, the situation nevertheless developed along similar lines. The Italian navy remained passive and acted in isolation from the air

The Japanese warship *Yamato,* **which was considered unsinkable and carried seven aircraft on its deck.**

force, so that following a British air raid on the port of Taranto in 1940, which put paid to three battleships, two cruisers and two auxiliary vessels, the Axis advantage was lost. Then the Italians were defeated in Sardinia and on 28 March 1941 off Cape Matapan (Tainaron) in Greece, the greatest naval battle of the Mediterranean theatre. Here the Italians lost three heavy cruisers and three destroyers, while no British craft were sunk. This confined furth-

er Italian activity to submarine warfare and air attacks on convoys, but after the Allied landings in North Africa and Sicily naval activity by the Italians ceased altogether.

In the Baltic and Black Seas, where the Germans imposed a blockade and military activity was almost entirely on dry land, submarines and light surface craft none the less carried out a number of operations.

In the huge expanses of the Pacific the naval war was mainly one of carriers and landing craft. The initial strategic aim of the Japanese was to take over the important natural resources of Indonesia. Here the concept of marine warfare differed from that in Europe, with both sides clearly expecting to use air/sea tactics. To begin with the Japanese capability in this field was far superior to that of the Americans. It was not until the spring of 1943 that the carrier-borne Mitsubishi A6M Zero-Sen found itself up against an equal opponent in the Grumman F6F Hellcat, or the Aichi D3A dive-bomber in the Douglas SBD Dauntless. The greatest advantage the Japanese

The naval Battle of Midway in 1942 brought a watershed in the Pacific war.

had lay in the very effective 610 mm (24 in) torpedo called Great Lance. However, the Americans had a much greater industrial capacity, enabling them to make up losses faster, and the Japanese electronics industry was then quite backward, so that the United States was able to take advantage of radar. Add to this the long range US submarines, which preyed on Japanese shipping, and the long-term result of the confrontation was inevitable.

The most dramatic operation of the Pacific war was, of course, the Japanese air attack on Pearl Harbor, Hawaii, on 7 December 1941. This attack on a neutral United States aroused American fury and caused the USA to enter the war on the side of the Allies. The surprise attack on the naval base destroyed four battleships, three destroyers, one minesweeper and 188 aircraft, for the loss of 128 Japanese planes. More than 2,000 people were killed. The only saving grace for the Americans was that none of their carriers was at anchor. Three days later the British lost the battleship *Prince of Wales* and the battle-cruiser

Repulse off the coast of Malaysia, where the Japanese also used air strikes. The Battle of the Coral Sea, between the Solomon Islands and the coast of Australia on 5–8 May 1942, was the first battle fought entirely between naval aircraft, since all the ships taking part stayed out of firing range. The carriers *Shoho* and *Lexington* were sunk, but above all Japanese expansion southwards was halted.

A more crucial battle was that of Midway, on 4 June the same year, when the Americans destroyed four large carriers *(Hiryu, Soryu, Akagi and Kaga)* and prevented the Japanese from landing on the island. After that the Americans took the initiative, and following further bitter encounters in the region of the Solomons (Guadalcanal), won the greatest sea battle of the war, for Leyte Gulf in the Philippines. This engagement began on 23 October 1944 and lasted three days. Enemy losses exceeded by 50 per cent those at the Battle of Jutland.

Similarly to the *Tirpitz,* the Japanese giant battleship Yamato of 72,800 tonnes was sunk near the

end of the war, on 7 April 1945 at Okinawa. Although she was thought to have sufficient armaments to provide her own anti-aircraft defence, she was sunk by aerial bombs and torpedoes.

Other naval actions of great importance were troop landings. The chief of these were the successful German landings in Norway in April 1940, relying on the element of surprise; the bloody Allied defeat at Dieppe in August 1942; and the American landings in North Africa and Sicily in 1943 and, of course, in various parts of the Pacific, culminating in the Okinawa landings in April 1945.

The biggest and most important troop landing in history was that in Normandy on D-Day, 6 June 1944, known as Operation Overlord. A total of 702 warships and 25 flotillas of minesweepers took part. In addition there were 5,000 merchant vessels, 4,000 landing craft, and almost 10,000 aircraft involved. In the course of a week almost 400,000 men and 60,000 vehicles were disembarked, using airborne landings and two artificial docks.

When the echo of the last naval shells, torpedoes, bombs and mines had died away, and the oceans were opened up once more to peaceful traffic, that traffic was busier than ever. The transatlantic and smaller liners came back and the specialization of merchant vessels continued; net losses throughout the war were not all that great, thanks to the Liberty class and later its improved successor, the Victory class.

The *Queen Mary* still held the Blue Riband, but in 1952 it was taken by the US ship *United States,* with an average speed of 35.59 knots. Apart from its widespread use of light alloys this prestigious giant, 302 m (990 ft) long and 31 m (102 ft) wide, was remarkable for the fact that it cost more than $72 million. The *France,* successor to the *Normandie,* was the longest liner in the world at 315.66 m (1,035 ft), while the Italians continued in the tradition of elegant and well-integrated design with the launching of the sister ships *Michelangelo* and *Raffaelo.* Again, however, the Cunard Line had the last word. In 1967, when the 'Old Lady' as the *Queen Mary* was affectionately known, was on her way to retirement, the *Queen Elizabeth 2* — length 293.5 m (962 ft 8 in), width 32 m (105 ft), gross tonnage 67,140 — started her career.

By this time the day of the great liners was past, since they could not compete with rapid developments in air transport and falling air fares. In addition, the price of oil began to rise. This accounts for the fact that liners launched in the late 1960s were both smaller — up to 20,000 gross tonnes — and designed more for cruising. A good example is the Soviet Morpasflot ships, two of which — the *Alexander Pushkin* and the *Michail Lermontov* — were put on the transatlantic route.

Nor were overseas tourism and recreation forgotten in the design of the *QE2,* which regards the passenger as a holiday guest in a hotel. Apart from regular transatlantic

A ferry.

duties the 'Queen' undertakes popular round-the-world trips, cooperating with British airlines and competing successfully with rival companies. Otherwise, liners of her class came to the end of the line in the 1970s.

Other types of ship have enjoyed more business than ever, including ferries carrying not only passengers, but also cars, buses, lorries and trains. In most cases they cross sea straits, and in North America the Great Lakes also. Cars are usually carried on two lower decks, passenger facilities (with only a limited number of cabins) being provided on the upper decks. Typical capacities are up to 1,400 passengers and 300 cars or the equivalent number of other vehicles. The biggest ferry in operation today is the *Finnjet,* operating between Helsinki, the Finnish capital, and Travemünde in West Germany, a distance of 960 km (600 miles). It can carry a total of 1,532 passengers and 350 cars.

Since the density of air is 800 times less than that of water, man has tried to exploit the fact to increase speeds over sea routes. This

A hovercraft. ▼

has produced hydrofoils and hovercraft, used either as ferries or as passenger boats. At present they are small craft that operate over short distances because of the limitations imposed by high fuel consumption. Hydrofoils have wing-like horizontal fins beneath the bows and stern, and at high speeds these lift the craft off the water. The first real development of this old

A hydrofoil. ▲

Ships carrying unit cargoes in packages, cases, sacks etc, in holds fitted with hatches, had a nett tonnage of up to 15,000 tonnes after the war, as did bulk carriers for the transport of ore, grain and coal, some of which are specialized vessels. Today's figure would be more like 250,000 tonnes. The original design, where unit cargo vessels had shipboard cranes and the superstructure was of the typical 'three island' pattern (at the bows, amidships and at the stern), has now given way to vessels with a single superstructure containing all important central facilities.

Containers, which had already been used on the roads and railways for some time, found their way on board ships at the end of the 1950s. They required design modifications, but brought savings in loading and unloading times amounting to several hundred per cent. The advantages were further reinforced by the international standardization of dimensions and the setting up of special container freight terminals equipped with the latest automated machinery and data processing facilities. Although the construction and operation of container ships is relatively expensive, they are also growing in size; the 1981 *Frankfurter Express*, for example, has a net tonnage of 51,540 tonnes. In future they can be expected to take more than 80 per cent of unit freight.

There are other innovations besides containerization, such as the roll-on, roll-off ships with ramps allowing vehicles to drive on and off under their own power. Such ships may also be adapted to vertical loading or 'ro-lo' (roll-on, roll-off and load-on, load-off). In the case of 'maternal' container ships, the cargoes can be floated to a tug, which loads the floating containers on to the mother ship. The first ship of this Seabee type, using floating containers with a net tonnage of 830 tonnes, is the 1972 *Doctor Lykes,* which has a net tonnage of 39,000 tonnes.

cades, was also first implemented in the 1950s. Great Britain especially went in for hovercraft design. Her largest craft of this sort, the SR-N4, 39.6 m (130 ft) long and 23.5 m (77 ft) wide, can take 256 passengers and 30 cars and has a maximum speed of 65 knots. Four gas turbines drive four aircraft propellers, while four 12-bladed centrifuges provide the air cushion. The SR-N4 has operated a regular service between Dover and Boulogne since 1969.

Although with some minor exceptions the size of passenger vessels has decreased since the Second World War, the opposite is the case where freighters are concerned. The world has been opened up to trade as never before, and there has been a sharp rise in the amount of freight transported by sea, so that it now accounts for almost 80 per cent of all goods exchanged. As there has not been a serious challenge from air-transport in this sphere, it was only natural to try to carry more goods on fewer ships.

Freighters fall into two main categories, those carrying dry cargoes, whether in units or in bulk, and those carrying liquid cargoes.

idea was in the Soviet Union in 1956, when hydrofoils were introduced first for river transport and later also on the open sea. The first Soviet type, the Typhoon, carried 105 passengers, and its two internal-combustion turbines with an output of 2,600 kW (3,484 hp) gave it a speed of 50 knots.

The principle of floating on an air cushion, known for several de-

A container ship.

years later the *Seawise Giant* weighed in at an amazing 564,763 tonnes.

The growth in tanker size was due first of all to an increase in oil consumption; then, when the Suez Canal was closed and tankers had to sail right round Africa, they had to be as large as possible to make it worthwhile. So, from 1967, 'super-tankers' began to appear. Over 250,000 tonnes they were called VLCC (Very Large Crude Carriers) and around 400,000 tonnes ULCC (Ultra Large Crude Carriers). The sharp rise in oil prices in the early 1970s, accompanied by a fall in demand and an energetic search for new oil fields in the North Sea, Alaska and Siberia to reduce dependence on the Middle East, and the enlarging of the Suez and Panama Canals to take vessels of up to 100,000 tonnes — all these considerations led to a fall in the mean capacity of oil tankers. Apart from oil, tankers also

The real Goliaths of ocean travel today are the oil tankers. A comparison of tonnages shows what enormous increases in size have taken place. After the war the type T-2 had a net tonnage of 16,600 tonnes, in 1973 the *Globtik Tokyo* raised this to 483,664, and seven

A roll-on, roll-off cargo ship.

A modern oil tanker.

carry chemicals, liquid gas, wine, water and other cargoes, for which they are often specially adapted.

Today's merchant vessels may be specialized, such as refrigerator ships, or multi-purpose, and new applications are constantly being found, although not to the same extent as before the oil crisis of 1973−74. Furthermore, the organization of ships, cargoes and ports is becoming computerized, which points the way to the future.

The great diversity of present-day vessels means that only a few basic types can be mentioned. Let us then move on from cargo vessels, although it would be possible to discuss many more, especially in connection with river transport, and deal with another group of commercial craft, the industrial and the technical.

Typical examples of these are fishing cutters, luggers and

The *Mutsu*, a Japanese nuclear cargo ship.

trawlers, and whaling ships. While the smaller cutters and luggers, up to 150 tonnes, supply the markets with fish from the sea and the coastal waters of the Atlantic, trawlers of about 3,000 tonnes and whalers of about 40,000 tonnes net are deep-sea vessels. Apart

Huge cranes have many uses in water transport.

The type of tug frequently used in river transport.

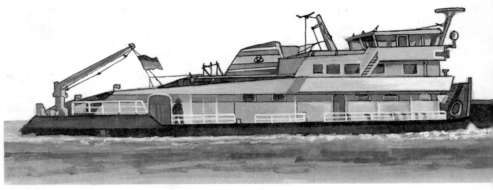

from catching fish and whales, they process them, which is why they are sometimes called factory ships. Unfortunately, since the end of the Second World War such floating factories have all but led to the extinction of some species of whales, so on the basis of international agreements most whaling nations have ceased to catch them and have turned whalers over to other uses.

The various purposes for which ships are built today all present specific design problems. So, for instance, the recovery of oil from sea-bed deposits has made it necessary to design seismological survey ships, drilling machinery, various sorts of drilling rigs and auxiliary platforms (including finding suitable means of anchoring them), pipe-laying equipment and so on, all capable of withstanding the inhospitable North Sea.

A Polish roll-on, roll-off ship from the late 1970s. ▶

◄ **A modern fishing vessel.**

Modern tugs are also remarkable in their own way. In the last century this 'maid-of-all-work' of ports was a very simple craft, but today's tugs are highly specialized, from the largest, ocean-going types with displacements of thousands of tons and lengths of up to 90 m (295 ft), through harbour tugs carrying sophisticated equipment, to the pushing and towing vessels found on inland waterways.

A port tug.
►

Other types of technical craft include dredgers, measuring vessels, lightships, lifeboats and firefighting vessels, each with its own purpose. As a result of harnessing nuclear power the Soviet icebreakers *Lenin, Arktika* and *Sibir* have extended the navigable season along the north coast of the USSR from 90 to 330 days a year.

There are also all manner of special vessels in the fields of sport and research. We have already mentioned yachts and yachting, but there are also motor-boats, canoes, kayaks and rowing boats used for sport on rivers, lakes and reservoirs. Types of competition are many,

A river and coastal container ship.

depending on the number of crew-members and the length and type of course. Canoes and kayaks compete both over normal courses and in slaloms and through rapids, and like yachts are included in the Olympic Games. Water sports are not only competitive, of course, but are used by many as a form of recreation, as illustrated by the craze for wind-surfing.

At the time it was written Jules

The Soviet atomic icebreaker, *Arktika.*

Verne's *Twenty Thousand Leagues Under the Sea* was science fiction, but today that is far from being the case. Oceanographic ships, bathyscaphes and underwater laboratories carry out research on the sea-bed in the ocean deeps and currents for all sorts of reasons, from the search for oil-bearing minerals, through biological and physical observations, to archaeological investigations. In 1929 the American engineer Otis Barton got to a depth of 923 m (3,027 ft) with his bathyscaphe off the Bermuda Islands. In 1948 the FNRS2 of Professor August Piccard reached 1,380 m (4,526 ft) and in 1960 his son Jacques got down as far as 10,900 m (35,752 ft). Among several marine laboratories equipped with highly sophisticated research equipment is the American Sealab, which carries out scientific work on the sea floor.

In 1947, the Norwegian Thor Heyerdahl sought to prove that the Polynesians could originally have been migrants from South America and sailed from Peru across the intervening ocean to Tuamoto on the *Kon-Tiki,* a raft made of balsa wood. It was the first of a number of such voyages made by Heyerdahl himself and others. The Frenchman Eric de Bisschop set off from Tahiti in 1956 on the raft *Tahiti Nui,* heading south, but his vessel sank. Two

The Soviet atomic-powered research vessel, *Vladimir Komarov.*

A river motor-boat.

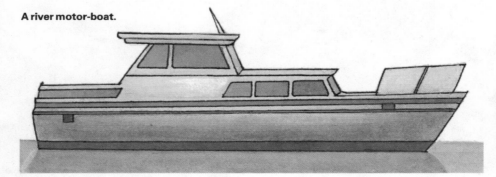

Thor Heyerdahl's raft *Ra II*.

years later Bisschop was drowned when the *Tahiti Nui II* went down off the Cook Islands.

In our atomic, automated and electronic age, the development of warships and their armaments has continued apace. As in other spheres of warfare, the general trend is towards making weapons of mass destruction and devising defences against them. In the postwar

A sporting motor-boat.

J. Piccard's bathyscaphe *Trieste II*.
▼

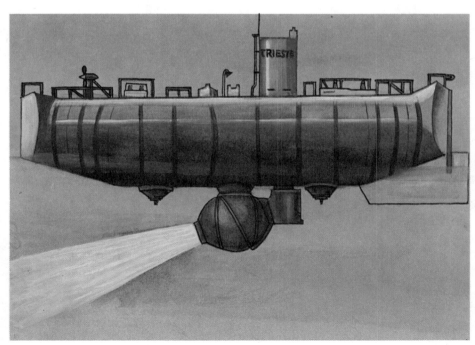

A Soviet Kyev class aircraft-carrier, built in 1975, with a displacement of 38,000 tonnes.

years both the United States and the Soviet Union concentrated on building carriers and submarines, while the numbers of other surface craft were kept down. An example of a modern surface ship was, however, the Soviet atomic rocket cruiser *Kirov,* launched in 1979, which had a displacement of about 30,000 tonnes. The trend among carriers, especially since the use of nuclear power, has been towards greater size. In 1961 the US *Enterprise* had a displacement of 90,000 tonnes, while the next generation, the Nimitz class of 1975, weighed 94,000 tonnes. Submarines with nuclear propulsion gained higher speed and greater range and are bigger than ever. The first American atomic submarine, *Nautilus,* launched in 1954, had a displacement of 4,100 tonnes, but in less than 20 years the Soviet Delta class submarines had a displacement of 10,000 tonnes, and in 1980 the US Ohio class as much as 18,000 tonnes.

Weapon development has been mainly in the area of guided missiles, both defensive and offensive,

The American aircraft-carrier *Enterprise*, **which has a displacement of 90,000 tonnes and carries 100 aircraft.**

A British Resolution class submarine, built in 1964, which carries 16 Polaris missiles. ▼

The Dutch cruiser, *De Zeven Provinzien*.

including ballistic missiles (with nuclear warheads as required) and rocket bombs or rocket depth charges. Today the use of naval forces without air support, unlike in the days of the Second World War, is unthinkable.

An American rocket ship armed with rockets. ▶

A Dutch rocket frigate of the Tromp class. ▼ ▶

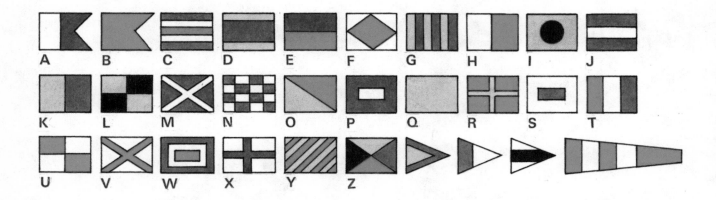

The semaphore alphabet.

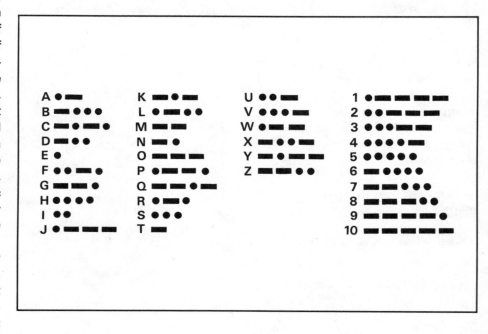

The Morse code.

Just as water craft went through a process of evolution so, too, did means of navigating and signalling. Ways of getting your bearings at sea developed from the observation of familiar coastlines or the release of land-seeking birds, through orientation by the sun and stars, to the use of navigation instruments and aids, which until this century meant the chart, compass, sextant and chronometer. To communicate with each other sailors have used smoke signals, lights, acoustic signals, flags and electrical and telegraphic messages, where Samuel Finley Morse was of great assistance in the 19th century.

After many improvements, nearly all these methods are in use today. So, for instance, the measurement of time has been made more accurate not only by the use of quartz crystals, but also by the building of special time transmitters operating on various frequencies, of which there are now nearly 200 throughout the world. Large ships and aircraft use a radio-sextant, which is not affected by clouds or other obstructions covering up the sun, and they have compasses which are not affected by distorting factors which previously had to be taken into account. Today's lead-line operates ultrasonically, and speeds are logged electrodynamically.

It can be seen from this summary that radio technology and electronics have had a major influence on navigational aids. The principle of radar is as old as that of wireless telegraphy, and relies on the fact that we can calculate the distance and bearing of objects from the speed of radio waves, according to the time interval between sending a signal and receiving its echo. Radar was used on the warships *Repulse* and *Graf Spee* as long ago as 1936, and on the liner *Normandie* a year later. In those days it had a range of just a few miles, and it was only the war and the use of short waves that produced the necessary accuracy, range and sensitivity needed in the fight in particular against submarines. Radar has also become indispensable in peacetime for avoiding collisions at sea and in port, and to prevent ships from running aground.

The most important navigation system, dating from the last war when the invasion of Normandy was being prepared, is 'hyperbolic'

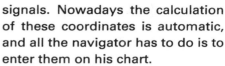

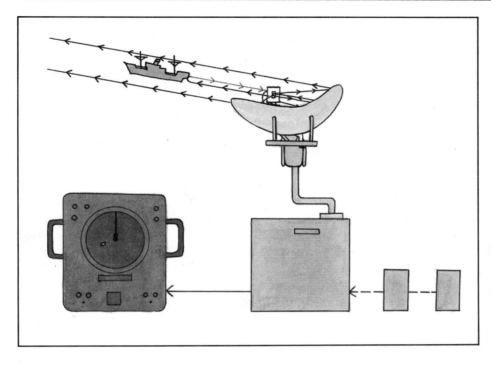

A diagram to show how radar works.

signals. Nowadays the calculation of these coordinates is automatic, and all the navigator has to do is to enter them on his chart.

Since various systems of hyperbolic navigation work on different frequencies, a postwar international agreement determined that four systems should be developed: Consol, Decca Navigator, Loran and Omega. Ten years ago there were 22 Decca Navigator transmitters in Europe, and the system is used for distances up to a few hundred kilometres; it determines positions with a high degree of accuracy and operates on long wave. Loran, however, is used for distances up to 2,000 km (1,240 miles), has a margin of error of up to 5 km (3 miles) and operates on medium and short wavelengths. Satellite navigation systems are already being successfully used by many shipping companies and rapidly penetrate all spheres of ship transport.

The use of computers makes navigation a very accurate, but also very exacting task. Modern navigation is more of a science than the gift it was once considered to be.

Light signalling.

A diagram to show the principles of hyperbolic navigation. ▼

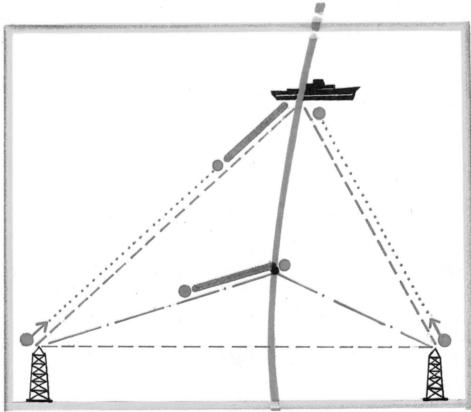

navigation. In practice it means that a radio receiver receives simultaneously transmitted signals from two transmitters at different distances. The interval between receiving the two signals gives the respective distances from the transmitters. In hyperbolic navigation the position of a vessel is determined by hyperbolic coordinates, and the system is based on four shore transmitters, one main one and three subsidiary ones, and the comparison of their

It is to be hoped that the seas of the future will be peaceful places, since one more major armed conflict could make them seas without either ships or people, even seas totally without life, although it was from them that life on Earth originated.

While the history of ships and shipping has never taken a straight line, and there have been many dead ends along the path to progress, the general movement has always been forwards, and never more so than in the last 100 years. Statistics show that sea transport is growing fast even today. In 1960 1,000 million tonnes of goods were transported by sea; within 10 years this had increased to 2,500 million, and in the early 1980s the figure was approaching 4,000 million. By the year 2000 it is expected to be 10,000 million tonnes.

On the threshold of the atomic age, when economic problems seem to be more pressing than technical progress, and indeed affect that progress, the order of the day seems to be the economic use

of the sea and the vessels that ply the waters. Increased speeds are needed, if possible without increasing costs, and distances need to be shortened. One way of doing this would be to open up the Arctic waters and so provide a further connection between the Atlantic and the Pacific — the north-west passage that was sought for so long. The transportation of cargoes under water has certain advantages. Then there is the question of exploiting the resources of the seabed, and coming to grips with the problems presented by working in such an environment.

The most promising development in marine engineering would seem to be the application of nuclear power. It has long been used to power submarines, aircraft-carriers and icebreakers, and steps have already been taken to develop its use in merchant vessels, the American *Savannah* (1959) and the West German *Otto Hahn* (1964) both being nuclear-powered. Although the first was not too successful as a passenger ship and the German ore-carrier has encountered difficulties that caused the power unit to be changed and the ship adapted for containers in 1982, at least the first

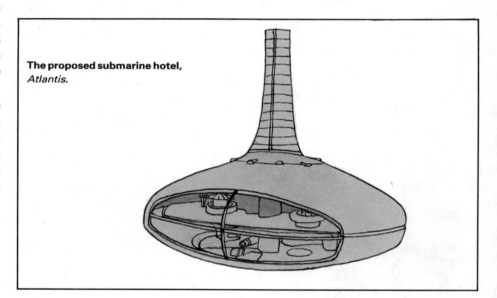

The proposed submarine hotel, *Atlantis*.

Jacques Cousteau's oceanographic submarine which was built in 1959. It was 2 m (6.5 feet) wide and 1.6 m (5.25 feet) high. It had a crew of two and a total weight of 2 tonnes.

steps have been taken towards a new era, when nuclear propulsion will be both safe and economic.

Data processing techniques and automation, which affect everything from loading and off-loading to navigation and crewing, can also be exploited to make fuel savings, as is shown by the 1980 Japanese tanker *Shinaitoku Maru*. This diesel-engined vessel is also equipped with two sets of rectangular sails, which are turned by computer to make optimum use of the wind. As a result this tanker, the first in the world with mechanical sail trimming, saves 10 per cent of its fuel

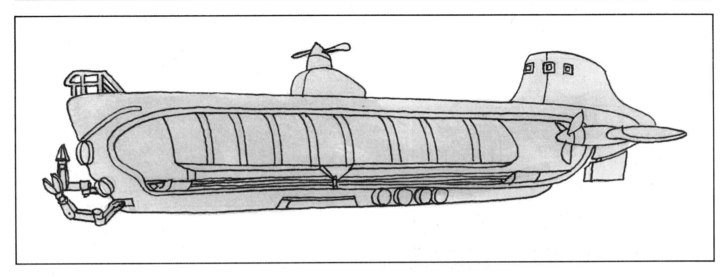

The American bathyscaphe *Aluminaut*, **built in 1965. It could be used up to a depth of 5,000 m (16,400 feet).**

The town of Aquapolis, the greatest attraction of an exhibition on the Japanese island of Okinawa.

consumption at constant speed.

Although laminates are widely used for sporting and other small craft, there is as yet little prospect of their use in hulls of over 30 m (98 ft) in length. Steel is likely to be the preferred material of ocean-going vessels for some time to come.

The prospects for the future are many and varied, including very promising ideas and some that are much less realistic. Certainly the sea will always have an important place in the working of the world, and men will always seek new ways of exploiting it.

Index

206

numbers in italics refer to captions

Air TRANSPORT

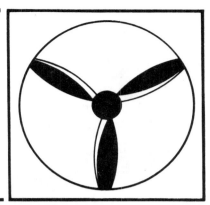

A membrane stretching between their front limbs and their bodies formed their bat-like wings. Pterodactyls became extinct at the end of the Cretaceous, but nature continued to experiment with flight. A sort of intermediate 'design' between pterodactyls and birds was *Archaeopteryx lithographica,* which

Balloons, airships, aeroplanes, rocket-planes — man has used them all to conquer the skies, to satisfy an ancient longing to emulate the birds. None of them was invented overnight. All of them evolved along the protracted and often tortuous path which aviation has been forced to follow.

The first conquerors of the air were the prehistoric pterodactyls. Fossilized skeletal remains of these, the largest flying creatures of all time, have been found in the American state of Kansas. The pteranodon had a wingspan of up to 16 m (52 ft) and lived in the Cretaceous period, i. e. some 136 million years ago.

was about the size of a pigeon. Its wings were underdeveloped and it probably had to take off from treetops after climbing up. Not until the Tertiary period, some 26 million years ago, did the first birds fly by flapping their wings.

Let us leave prehistoric times behind and move on to the relatively recent past, to the age of the advanced societies of Egypt and Mesopotamia. The ability to fly was deemed a privilege of the gods. Ancient Assyrian reliefs depict gods with human faces and birds' wings. The Egyptian sun god Osiris and the Greek goddess of victory, Nike, both had wings.

The first human flight ever reported was that of a kingly ruler of the city of Kish, whose adventures are related in legend. On the wings of a huge eagle the king rose to the heights of heaven in search of a miraculous herb. The most famous legend about flying, however, comes from ancient Greece.

King Minos of Crete commissioned the brilliant Greek sculptor, painter and builder Daedalus to create the huge Labyrinth in the city

In the legend, Icarus flew on wings of wax and feathers. He flew near the Sun so the wax melted and he fell to his death.

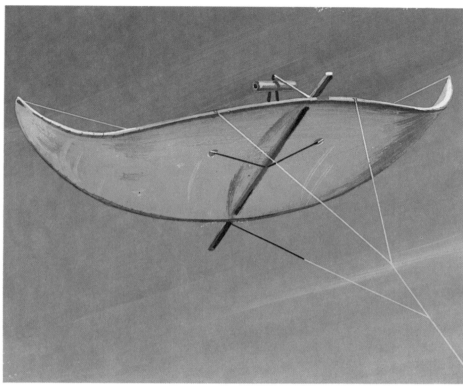

A Chinese kite.
These solved the problem of stability.
Their wings, made of thin sheets of wood,
were joined together with strings.
Kites are the oldest form of aircraft.

musical kite, carrying a bamboo whistle which gave out a protracted note audible at a considerable distance. Chinese kites came in weird shapes, symbolizing human figures, animals or fabulous monsters. There were military kites large enough to lift an observer and allow him to carry out aerial reconnaissance of enemy troops.

At a much later date, in the 1880s and 1890s, kites were worked upon by the Australian inventor Lawrence Hargrave. He designed a box-kite, the principle of which was adopted by many aircraft designers in the First World War. For almost 30 years similar kites were used to collect meteorological data at great heights. Weather stations were equipped with kites capable of flying to an altitude of almost 15 km (9 miles). Kites had also been used at the end of the 18th century by American scientist Benjamin Franklin to carry out electrical experiments.

of Knossos. It was a work of unmatched splendour, and the king resolved to keep Daedalus in captivity so as to prevent him from creating anything that might rival it. The only possible escape from his island prison was by air. So Daedalus made two pairs of wings from feathers held together by wax — one for himself, and the other for his son Icarus. For Icarus the flight proved to be a fateful one. In spite of his father's warning, he flew up close to the Sun, the heat of which melted the wax, causing Icarus to fall to his death. This legend — one might almost say fairy tale — has remained with us as a symbolic expression of man's ambition to fly.

Today, kites are a familiar toy, but they were really the first heavier-than-air flying device constructed by man. The Chinese used kites several centuries before Christ; in 196 B. C., for instance, General Han Hsin employed them in battle. Kites were far from being only a weapon of war. An essential ingredient of favourite Chinese games was the

**Leonardo da Vinci's drawing
of a helicopter, based on
an Archimedean screw. The brilliant Italian
was offering a solution
to the problem of gaining height.**

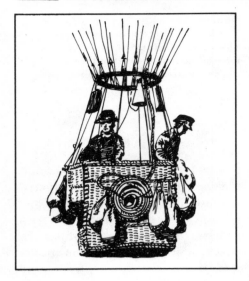

The balloon's basket was usually made of wicker, and, apart from the crew, it also carried sacks of sand, a rope and an anchor.

The Montgolfier brothers' paper balloons were filled with hot air. The source of heat was a fire on the ground, and the balloon lost height rapidly after the air inside it cooled. The use of a fire on the balloon itself increased flight time.

The balloon has earned a special place of honour in history, since it was in a balloon that man first conquered the air. This lighter-than-air device ruled the skies of Europe in the 19th century.

The first records of balloons can be traced to China. At the beginning of the 14th century a hot-air balloon is said to have been released at the coronation of the emperor Fo-Kien. The Chinese were therefore aware of the lifting force of hot air before Leonardo da Vinci and another learned Italian, Evangelista Torricelli. The flight of a hot-air balloon was demonstrated at the court of King Juan V of Portugal by Bartolomeu de Gusmão, a Brazilian nobleman, in 1709.

Three-quarters of a century later, the Montgolfier brothers, Jacques Étienne and Joseph Michel, finally presented their invention in public. They were paper manufacturers, and it was waxed paper that they chose as the material for their balloon. They began by experimenting with small balloons filled with hot air over the hearth. On 4 June 1783 they gave a public demonstration in the square at Annonay, near Lyons. King Louis XVI wished to have a demonstration for himself, and invited the brothers to Paris. There, on 19 September 1783, they released a new, larger balloon with a cock, a sheep and a duck riding in a basket underneath. After eight minutes this 'crew' landed safely about 3 km (2 miles) from Versailles.

The time had now come for the first manned flight to be attempted, and the Montgolfiers created a craft worthy of this momentous occasion. Their blue-and-gold ornamented balloon was 15 m (50 ft) in diameter. In a gallery around the air-hole stood the 26-year-old Marquis François Pilâtre de Rozier. The historic flight took place on 15 October 1783 and lasted 4½ minutes. The same de Rozier shared with the Marquis d'Arlandes the honour of being the first to go up in a balloon in free flight. On 21 November 1783 they took off from the Bois de Boulogne and in 25 minutes flew about 8.5 km (5 miles). At the same time as the Montgolfiers were building their balloons, Professor Jacques Charles was constructing one of his own, but using hydrogen

The night take-off of a balloon
from the besieged city of Paris,
during the Franco-Prussian War.
In 1870, aeronaut Nadar
organized air communication
with unoccupied territory,
which meant over 100 people
were able to leave Paris.

accident when, on 15 June 1785, Frenchmen Jules Romain and François de Rozier died in an attempt to make the crossing. In fact the Channel had already been crossed in a balloon by Jean-Pierre Blanchard and the American scientist, Dr. John Jeffries. In the course of their dramatic flight on 7 January 1785, these intrepid airmen had been compelled to jettison everything they could — including some of their clothing.

In the 19th century an attempt was made to turn the balloon to scientific use. At last it was possible for observations to be made at altitudes which had previously been unattainable. By 1803 the Belgians Robertson and Lhöest reached a height of 7 km (23,000 ft). A year later the famous French physicist Joseph Louis Gay-Lussac and a companion took measurements of temperature, atmospheric pressure and the Earth's magnetism at an altitude of 6,400 m (21,000 ft). More than a century later Professor Auguste Piccard of Switzerland made a number of ascents during which he obtained important data on the upper layers of the atmosphere. Not until the advent of rocket probes did high-altitude balloon flights diminish in significance.

To this day, however, ballooning remains a popular sport. One of the most famous races is the Gordon Bennett Cup, first held in 1905. At present there is a revival of interest in the hot-air balloon with the British firm of Cameron the best-known manufacturer of craft in the Montgolfier tradition. Today this type of balloon has a synthetic fibre envelope and propane-butane burners. There are many competitions in Europe and the United States, such as the Alpine Balloon Week at Mürren in Switzerland. In 1981 a four-man crew took the balloon Double Eagle across the Pacific from Japan to California. The world height record of 34,668 m (113,740 ft) has been held since 4 May 1961 by the Americans Malcolm D. Ross and Victor A. Prother, who made their ascent from the deck of the US *Antietam*.

The Swede S. A. Andre's
indirigible balloon which took
off on July 11th 1897 from the Spitsbergen,
heading for the North Pole.
It had no means of being steered.
The debris of the *Eagle*
was discovered 33 years later
by a Norwegian expedition.

instead of hot air. He improved the construction of the envelope by using rubberized silk.

The first balloons were already lifting off in other countries, too, notably Britain and Holland. Even at this very early stage of aviation the Channel had an important role to play. It was the scene of the first air

Man had taken off, but he was still more the plaything of the air than its master. Balloons were obliged to fly where, and as far as, the wind took them. This may have suited sporting balloonists and even scientists, but it severely limited the practical applications of the new means of transport. The dirigible or steerable airship was an important step forwards, being the first aircraft capable of following a predetermined route.

France was the cradle of aeronautics, and it was there that the idea of a dirigible first saw the light of day. As early as 1785, Lieutenant Meusnier of the French army drew up plans containing all the important features of such a system, but it was several decades before the idea came to fruition.

It was not until the autumn of 1852 that French engineer Henri Giffard actually took off from the Paris racecourse L'Hippodrome in a steam-powered airship. His was in fact the first aircraft engine ever to see service. A three-bladed propeller just over 3 m (10 ft) across was

The first dirigible airship, built in 1852 by the Frenchman, Henri Giffard. The heavy, and not very powerful, steam engine drove a 3-bladed propeller. The steering of the balloon depended a great deal on a favourable wind.

able to drive the airship along at an average of 0.75 km/h (1/2 mph) with a following wind. Further experiments showed the steam engine to be too heavy and not powerful enough for the job, so trials with electric motors followed, and this form of propulsion was first used by

One of the German Zeppelin airships which proved themselves before the First World War, when the company DELAG used them for sight-seeing flights. During the war, improved models were used to carry out raids on Britain. The armament, crew and engines were carried in gondolas under the fuselage.

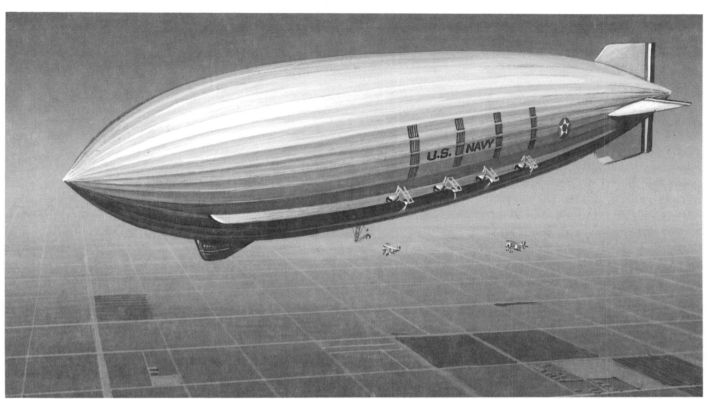

The giant airship *Macon*, built in USA in 1933. It was defended by Sparrowhawk fighters carried in its hold. These took off and landed using a sort of retractable platform. In 1935 *Macon* crashed.

the Tissandier brothers in 1883. A year later, on 9 August 1884, French aeronauts Charles Renard and A. C. Krebs completed an 8 km (5 mile) circuit in their craft La France.

The characteristically spindle-shaped airships were appearing in the skies of France more and more often. Flying attracted such adventurers as Alberto Santos-Dumont, a Brazilian living in Paris. In 1901 he gained popular acclaim by circling the Eiffel Tower, a feat underwritten by a rich patron of aviation and member of the French air club, Deutsch de la Meurthe, to the tune of a 100,000 francs. Santos-Dumont owed his success largely to a light-weight internal-combustion motor-cycle engine.

The 20th century brought another innovation, the frame-construction airship. It was on 2 June 1900 that the 130 m-long (426 ft-long) cigar of Count Ferdinand von Zeppelin first took to the air over Lake Constance. The reinforced structure employed aluminium struts, and the envelope

was divided into sections filled with hydrogen. Its two Daimler engines were inadequate for propelling this giant of the air, so Zeppelin had to carry out further improvements. From 1909, however, the first commercial air company, DELAG, was operating regular sight-seeing trips over Germany.

After the outbreak of the First World War, German Zeppelins raided Great Britain. For the first time in history civilians hundreds of kilometres behind the battle lines were subjected to the terror of enemy bombing. The first duel between a zeppelin and an aeroplane took place on 7 June 1915 when Second-Lieutenant Reginald Warnerford managed to drop six bombs on an airship, which went down in flames near Ghent. In the latter half of the war Zeppelins were able to operate only at night, when they

had at least a measure of protection from British fighters.

The Royal Navy successfully introduced the Sea Scout airship, nicknamed 'blimp', to protect convoys and help in the fight against submarines. They incorporated the somewhat bizarre idea of suspending the fuselage of a reconnaissance aircraft beneath the envelope of an airship. They were able to stay up for more than 24 hours at a time, which was ideal for naval support duties.

The period following the First World War saw the climax of attempts to make the airship a reliable means of air transport. The British R34 chalked up a memorable first by crossing the North Atlantic in June 1919. The trip took 108 hours. In May 1926 the Norwegian explorer Roald Amundsen flew over the North Pole in the airship Norge.

'Your Lordship hired me to drive, not to fly,' was the bitter complaint of Sir George Cayley's coachman when, in 1853, he was required to pilot the glider it had taken his master years to build. The unfortunate fellow was doubtless oblivious to the fact that he was about to go down in history as the first flier to control a glider featuring all the basic characteristics of the modern aeroplane. Cayley designed his glider with the right sort of wing shape and cross-section and the correct arrangement of tailfin and tailplanes. He even came up with the idea of a triplane. He justified individual design features by means of calculations before trying them out on models. Cayley's approach was rigorously scientific and he is often called 'the father of the aeroplane'.

Placed alongside Cayley's work, the steam aeroplane Ariel, designed by his fellow-countryman William Henson, gives the impression of being a rather unlikely creation. A drawing of it, published in 1843, includes a number of progressive ideas, however, such as a three-wheel undercarriage and a closed cockpit slung under the rectangular wing. The means of propulsion was, of course, chosen with a view to the technical achievements of the day.

Frenchman Alphonse Penaud took over where Cayley's experiments left off. *Planophore,* his elegantly shaped monoplane, had a means of propulsion that model enthusiasts were to rediscover in the 20th century. It was driven by a twisted bundle of elastic filaments – in effect, a giant rubber band!

The protracted experiments of the Frenchman Clément Ader came to fruition on 9 October 1890 when his aircraft Eole, with its bizarre-shaped

The idea of a steam airship,
as suggested by Sir William Henson, in 1843. The design was the first to include wings, rudders and an undercarriage.

'bat's wings', took off for a few seconds. Although powered by an exceptionally efficient steam engine, this fragile and almost uncontrollable construction represented the utmost that could be achieved by such a combination. Most aeronautical inventors were still convinced that the road to success lay in imitating bird flight. Among them was L. P. Mouillard, who stubbornly defended this misconception in his work *L'Empire de l'Air,* published in 1881.

Samuel P. Langley, the secretary

of the American scientific organization, the Smithsonian Institution, was convinced that heavier-than-air craft had a great future. He tested his ideas on a series of model gliders called Aerodrome. Success with these led him to build a full-scale aircraft which was supposed to take off from the roof of a houseboat moored on the Potomac River, but in repeated attempts in October and December 1903, his invention landed ignominiously in the river.

The most important contribution

Otto Lilienthal made hundreds of successful flights using gliders he made himself. He had an artificial hill built near Berlin to assist his take-offs.

to the practical realization of gliding flight was that made by the German pioneer Otto Lilienthal. He, too, began with the study of bird flight and was sure that only perfect imitation of the structure of a bird's body could achieve the desired goal. His aim was to construct an operational ornithopter, i. e. an aircraft propelled by the flapping of its wings. During the last five years of his life he made some 2,000 attempts with 18 different gliders he had built himself. At first he took off from a hill near Berlin, later from the roof

of a newly-built hangar. In the end he had an artificial hill about 15 m (50 ft) high built, from which he took off in various directions according to which way the wind was blowing.

Lilienthal built his first glider in 1891. It weighed a mere 20 kg (44 lb) and was made of osiers stiffened with flax. The pilot was suspended by his armpits, and steered by moving his body to change the centre of gravity. It was this manner of controlling his gliders that spelt Lilienthal's doom. During a flight on 9 August 1896 he suddenly lost height, and the ensuing fall broke his spine. Two years later the Austrian Igo Etrich bought the wreckage of the glider to study its construction. By combining it with the properties of the airborne seeds of the plant *Zanonia macrocarpa,* he was able to build a glider with considerable stability. By that time, however, the first proper powered flight was just around the corner.

The Frenchman Clément Ader's *Avion,* **which was clearly inspired by the shape of a bat's wings.**

This clumsy craft never actually flew.

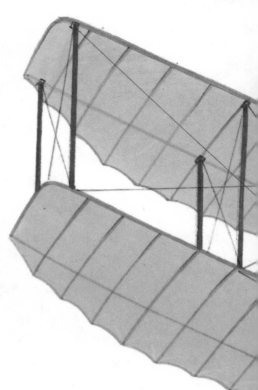

In 1900 the bicycle-makers Wilbur and Orville Wright approached Octave Chanute for assistance. This 68-year-old scientist was an expert, not on bicycles, but on gliders, and the correspondence between the Wright brothers and Chanute grew into close and cordial cooperation. Chanute offered the brothers, who had been interested in the problem of powered flight for some time, his latest glider design, and he did so without thought of profit. The Wrights had mixed success in their flying experiments and their early achievements were more by way of extended hops into the air. Nevertheless, Chanute's good advice, and above all the strongly reinforced glider with its double wings, enabled them to make rapid progress.

By the autumn of 1900 the brothers were successfully testing a new type of glider among the sand dunes of Kitty Hawk in North Carolina. This solitary stretch of sands had been recommended by the US Navy's weather service as offering the most constant strong winds, and it was there that the Wrights set up a wooden hut and two large canvas tents as a base for their activities. The location was ideal, not only from the point of view of wind conditions, but in offering almost complete secrecy.

After a series of modifications, the two men arrived at the design of a glider which was completely navigable with the aid of a rudder and curved wingtips. In September 1902 the Wright brothers' third glider, the immediate predecessor of the first powered aeroplane, took off.

They soon built an engine with a satisfactory power-to-weight ratio, along with a gearbox and propeller, and on the morning of 14 December 1903 the lot fell on Wilbur to take the controls of the world's first powered heavier-than-air flying machine. *Flyer,* as the aircraft was called, was powered by a water-cooled four-stroke petrol engine developing 9.7 kW (13 hp). At 10.35 there was a roar from the engine, driving a pair of propellers by means of chains, and the aeroplane set off along its guide track. Momentarily *Flyer* was in the air, but then it tilted up sharply and Wilbur, overreacting, crash-landed in the sand. It was very frustrating, but the pilot was unhurt and the plane was repaired within 48 hours.

On 17 December the weather was cold and stormy. The puddles were frozen over and the spectators from the nearby meteorological station, whom the Wright brothers had the foresight to invite, stamped their feet to keep warm. A camera stood on a tripod, ready to film the event. Again at 10.35 the engine came to life and *Flyer* took off, this time staying up for 12 seconds and covering a distance of 37 m (121 ft). Further flights followed, ending only when the flaps became damaged.

After that the Wright brothers continued to experiment eagerly. They took off several times a day, and now described circles and figures of eight in the air, proving they could navigate their craft. By the end of 1904 they were able to stay in the air more than five minutes. Twice that year the brothers invited reporters, but each time engine failure grounded them.

The Wright brothers' efforts might well have remained little known for much longer were it not for ever-increasing reports of the feverish activity of European inventors and aviators. Information and

The design of *Flyer* **was the original work of the Wright brothers. The most revolutionary innovation turned out to be the complete manoeuvrability of the aircraft, and its light but powerful petrol engine.**

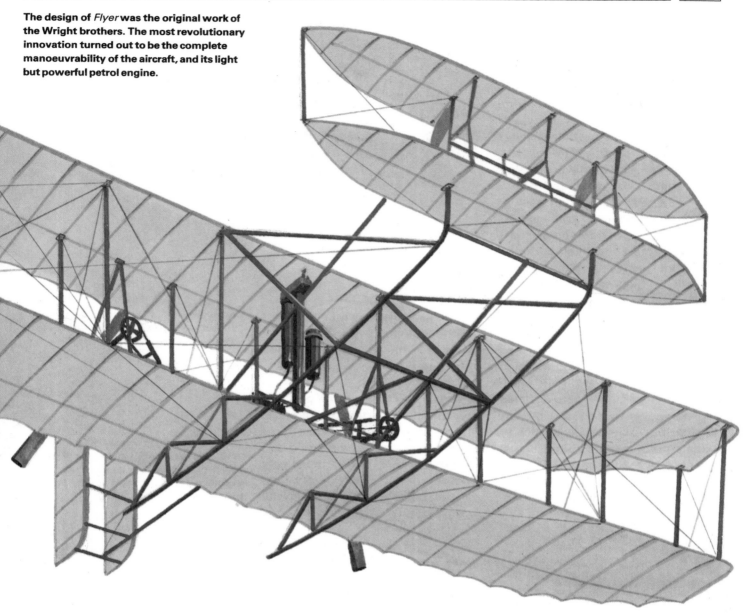

photographs were released to the press, and the full implications of the brothers' achievements were demonstrated for all to see when, in 1908, *Flyer 4* was taken to Europe and successfully flown.

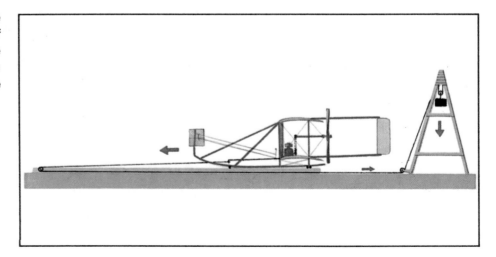

Take-off was achieved with the help of a trolley moving on rails, the direct forerunner of the catapult.

Man had learned to fly in a craft heavier than air, but what sort of flying was it? His new toy was a fragile structure consisting of wooden or bamboo struts and spars covered with canvas and held together by numerous rods and wires. The weak engines and large wing areas made flying a fair-weather pastime. The light craft were unable to fly against the wind, and would float like a tethered balloon.

At the beginning of this century there were no such things as comfortable seats and closed cockpits. The pilot sat on a simple seat, entirely at the mercy of the elements, and was often sprayed by oil leaking from the makeshift engine. The undercarriage was usually a cross between wheels and skis, to absorb the sudden bumps which occurred when taking off and landing on the parade-grounds, fields and meadows that passed muster as airstrips. Any sizeable stretch of flattish ground would do; the actual business of taking off and landing did not occupy all that much space, but gaining height was a problem.

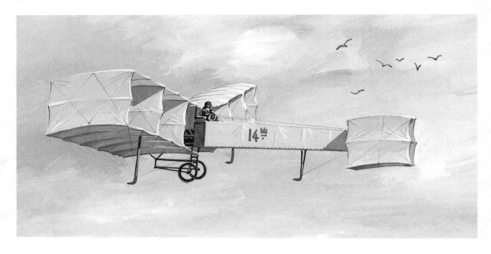

The planes of the day mostly flew at heights of up to 20 m (65 ft).

At this time aviation in Europe lagged behind the United States. While the Wright brothers systematically eliminated one problem after another in their gliders, in Europe the view seemed to be that if enough new patents were tried out, someone would hit on the magic formula sooner or later. Very little was actually known about the

On November 12, 1906, the Brazilian Alberto Santos-Dumont was the first European to fly a heavier-than-air craft.

Louis Blériot's flight across the Channel took 37 minutes. He is said to have completed it only thanks to sudden rain cooling his overheated engine. This in no way detracts from his achievement.

underlying principles of aeroplane construction. The design of flying machines was left, literally, to the imagination, and there seemed to be enough of that.

One man who emerged from this theatrical scene with honour was the Brazilian-born Alberto Santos-Dumont. In July 1906 he finished building his aircraft, which had

New pilots and designers constantly appeared. In the autumn of 1907 the painter, sportsman and later famous designer, Henri Farman, first took to the air. Gabriel and Charles Voisin flew aeroplanes inspired by the box-kite, and in 1908 they set up the first aeroplane factory at Billancourt. They introduced the use of metal structures. Sculptor

Levavasseur's Antoinette of 1909, powered by a 37 kW (50 hp) eight-cylinder engine, would have set you back 25,000 francs.

Frenchman Louis Blériot really hit the headlines when, on 25 July 1909, he became the first man to fly an aeroplane across the Channel. It brought him a prize of £1,000 offered by the London *Daily Mail* and

The first seaplane, *Hydravion,* is reminiscent of a fragile dragonfly. Henri Fabre took off in it from the port of La Mede near Marseilles, France, on March 28, 1910.

'wings' shaped like Hargrave's box-kites. The 17.9 kW (24 hp) Antoinette engine was mounted at the rear. The pilot stood in the fuselage ahead of the wings for better visibility. To enthusiastic ovations from the spectators gathered in a meadow at Bagatelle, near Paris, on 12 November 1906, Dumont made several flights, the longest of which measured 220 m (720 ft). He thus became the first man in Europe to make a powered flight in a heavier-than-air plane.

Others followed suit before long. A popular venue for such attempts at flying was the Issy-les-Moulineaux training-ground, and there were many others in the vicinity of Paris. In those early days France was very active in aviation.

Léon Delagrange undertook daring flights in Voisin aircraft, sometimes taking a spectator along for the ride.

Rapid progress was made in the shape and performace of aircraft. This was evident in the elegant monoplane Antoinette, designed by Léon Levavasseur, in which his fellow Frenchman Hubert Latham made an attempt on the Channel less than a week before Louis Blériot. He had to make a forced landing in the sea because of engine failure. The list of names and 'firsts' is a long one. Almost every week brought something new. Everyone wanted to fly; it was a sort of aviation fever. It was no problem to have your own aircraft — so long as you had the money to pay for it.

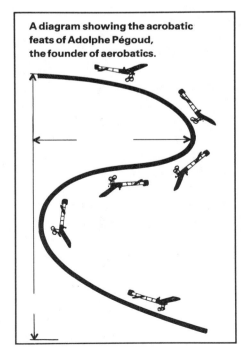

A diagram showing the acrobatic feats of Adolphe Pégoud, the founder of aerobatics.

made him the darling of an admiring public.

The spirit of competition inspired pilots, designers and spectators alike. The urge to fly further, higher and faster spurred aviators on to many great sporting performances.

The first major sporting event in the history of aviation was the air week held near Rheims from 22 to 29 August 1909. A total of 38 aircraft was entered, but 15 of these had to be withdrawn. Among the starters were seven planes from the Voisin factory. The race saw a number of new records set. Latham reached a height of 155 m (508 ft) in his Antoinette, while the fastest flier was American Glenn Curtiss with 77 km/h (47 mph). True to his name, Henri Farman took the distance record, covering 180 km (112 miles) in 3 hours 5 minutes. Like Blériot's feat, the meeting in Rheims helped popularize aviation.

The following year, races, rallies and contests were held by the dozen. On 27 March, for instance, a London-to-Manchester air race was held. The distance involved was almost 300 km (186 miles). There were only two entrants, and the winner was the French pilot Louis Paulhan, who only three weeks before had taken the world's first aerial photographs. The way he acquired his plane was interesting. In 1908 he had gained first prize in a modelling contest and won a Voisin biplane, minus the engine. Paulhan had to wait another year for that.

Better performance and improved control set the scene for aerobatics. Adolphe Pégoud looped the loop and flew upside down in a Blériot monoplane. It had been specially reinforced, and the pilot was strapped into his seat. Pégoud gradually expanded his repertoire, performing rolls, spins and other feats.

In the period just before the outbreak of the First World War, air races had become gruelling long-distance events flown in stages. There was the European circuit, the

Michelin Grand Prix, the Deutsch de la Meurthe race, and many others. The renowned Gordon Bennett race in 1912–13 featured an exciting tussle between fellow-Frenchmen Védrines and Prévost, in the course

A makeshift wooden platform was all the American E. Ely required to make the first take-off from a ship. It was from the deck of the warship *Birmingham* in November, 1910.

small part to the smooth lines of his monoplane, *Deperdussin*, designed by Louis Bécherau. Its 119 kW (160 hp) Gnome rotary engine was enclosed in a carefully-designed cowling. *Deperdussin* showed the world that the aeroplane could be a fast and reliable means of transport.

Perhaps the greatest achievement of those pioneer days was the crossing of the Mediterranean in September 1913, when Frenchman Roland Garros covered the 729 km (451 miles) from France to Tunisia in eight hours.

In 1913 the Russian designer Igor Sikorsky made the first practical multiple-engined aeroplane, having four wing-mounted engines. It had a roomy and comfortable passenger cabin with electric heating and lighting which was quite spectacular in its day, and paved the way for the modern airliner.

By 1913, in the space of a mere 10 years, aviation had made huge strides. From being the dangerous pastime of a handful of adventurers, regarded as eccentrics by most people, it had become a reliable means of transport and a popular sport. Unfortunately, it was also soon to prove a formidable weapon of war, and many who had helped fulfil man's dream of flying would shortly learn how much destruction it could cause.

The first air show was held in late August, 1909 near Rheims, France. A total of 38 craft were entered, though 15 of these were prevented from taking part by engine failure.

The first race between an aeroplane and a motor-car took place in the USA in 1910. The result was clear. The car won hands down.

of which the world speed record was broken no fewer than 10 times. The final victor was Maurice Prévost, who on 29 September 1913 reached a speed of 203 km/h (125 mph). His success was due in no

The Gnome rotary engine. Made in 1908, it brought a major increase in aircraft performance and reliability. The first engine of this type had five cylinders and developed 50 horse power.

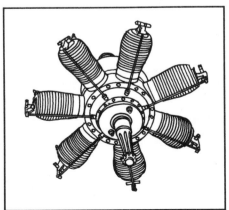

The air combats of the First World War were nicknamed dogfights, an apt enough description of the way they were conducted.

At the outbreak of the First World War in 1914, the warring nations had a few hundred aircraft each, for the most part unarmed. The generals had little notion of what they might be good for, considering them (if anything) as a possible substitute for observation balloons. The idea of the warplane — the fighter, the bomber — was something which only emerged as the conflict progressed.

The first aerial 'combat' was a somewhat farcical affair. Three weeks after the start of the war, the crews of a trio of British planes, brandishing revolvers, forced down an Albatross of the German observer corps, but they failed to capture the enemy airmen, who made their escape into a nearby wood. At that stage the view was still prevalent that the role of the air corps was to observe, not to fight. Aircraft did not seek to do battle, but gathered information regarding the position, strength and movements of enemy forces. Consequently, most of them were unarmed, carrying a crew of two. The observer studied, photographed, drew and estimated the situation on the battlefield below. Spotter aircraft directed artillery fire using a predetermined system of signals. In this early period, the airmen of opposing sides saw little of each other, and if they did they were more likely to exchange waves than gunfire.

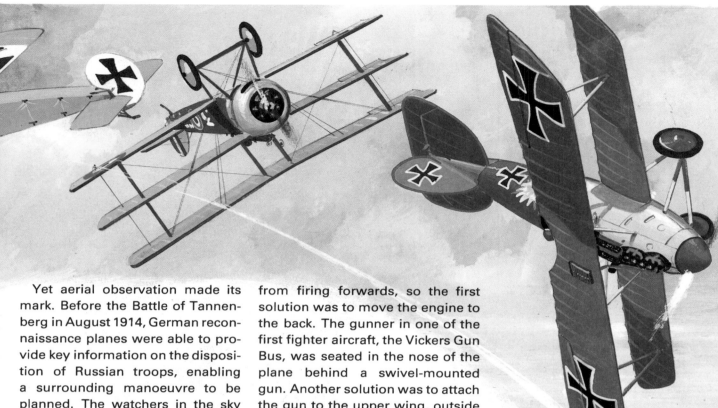

Yet aerial observation made its mark. Before the Battle of Tannenberg in August 1914, German reconnaissance planes were able to provide key information on the disposition of Russian troops, enabling a surrounding manoeuvre to be planned. The watchers in the sky proved similarly useful as preparations were being made for the landing of the British Expeditionary Force in France.

It became clear that things must be made more difficult for the enemy's 'spies in the sky'. That meant the introduction of armed aircraft; the rifle and the revolver were no longer adequate. An idea first tried out by Charles Chandler in 1912 was reintroduced: the mounting of a machine-gun. The main problem was that the propeller prevented a fuselage-mounted gun

from firing forwards, so the first solution was to move the engine to the back. The gunner in one of the first fighter aircraft, the Vickers Gun Bus, was seated in the nose of the plane behind a swivel-mounted gun. Another solution was to attach the gun to the upper wing, outside the radius of the propeller, although this arrangement required the gunner to stand. It was not until 1916 that the Englishman F. W. Scarff suggested mounting a machine-gun on a ring round the gunner's cockpit, enabling it to be fired in all directions.

The problem of firing through the radius of the propeller was somewhat alleviated by a French pilot called Gilbert, who simply had the endangered section of the propeller steelplated. The Germans responded with a much better idea

— the synchronized machine-gun invented by Anthony Fokker. He used it in the E. III monoplane, where a special device interrupted the firing of the gun each time one of the propeller blades passed the mouth of the barrel. This gave the Fokkers a decisive advantage in aerial combat for many months.

So began the contest for air superiority, later to be fought with more powerful engines, heavier armament and all sorts of other technical innovations. Flexibility, manoeuvrability and climbing speed were all important in the air duels which soon became a familiar sight. Examples of the effort made to improve the handling of aircraft included the triplanes, such as the British Sopwith Triplane and the German Fokker Dr. I. One important feature of the dogfights, as they came to be called, was that the fliers had no chance of escaping from a crippled plane. The first parachutes were not devised until the end of the war.

At the time when bombs were mainly dropped by hand, the Russian air force introduced this heavy four-engine bomber *Ilya Muromets.*

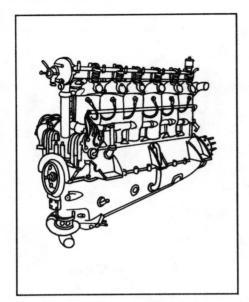

A diagram of the Mercedes 180 HP aircraft engine of 1917.

Repeated victors in air combats became known as aces. One of the best-known was the German Red Baron, Manfred von Richthofen.

The possibility of aerial bombardment opened up a new theatre of war — cities and towns far behind the enemy lines. One of the pioneers of aviation in the USA, Glenn Curtiss, had even in 1910 given a display to military experts of what might be called the principle of attack from the air. From a height of around 100 m (330 ft) he dropped large tin cans onto an area of water marked out with buoys. Four years later a German aircraft appeared over Paris. It was the first time a city had been threatened from the air. True, the three grenades dropped from the plane did little harm and were more of an aggressive gesture than anything else, but they heralded the coming of aerial bombardment.

At the start of the First World War aeroplanes were no match for airships in either the loads they could carry or the range they could travel. The German zeppelins proved a dangerous weapon, and only three days after the start of hostilities they made their first raid on Lutych. During 1915 the airships turned their attention to Britain. On the night of 20 January the hum of their engines, closely followed by the roar of exploding bombs, was heard over Norfolk, where they bombed a fortification. Four months later these ominous 'aerial cigars' appeared over London. The tonne of high explosive they dropped from the sky killed seven people, all civilians.

The design and tactical use of airships were continually improved. They were soon capable of staying up 36 hours, travelling at over 80 km/h (50 mph), and carrying, in addition to 10 machine-guns for their own protection, around 4 tonnes of bombs. The average crew numbered about 20. Attacks were made mostly at night, which meant that defence against them was difficult.

Anti-aircraft techniques were also constantly improving. In addition to anti-aircraft batteries and searchlight teams, there were now fighter planes in action, able to ignite the hydrogen-filled giants with incendiary bullets.

The soaring casualty rate forced the zeppelins to be gradually withdrawn from service. They were replaced by the multiple-engined Staaken and Gotha bombers. These

A British fighter attacking a highly inflammable hydrogen-filled German observation balloon. The average life of a balloon at the front was two weeks. Fighter planes attacked enemy observation balloons and shot them down; before long reconnaissance aircraft were required. The crews made contact with the ground by telephone, and were equipped with parachutes.

The cockpit of a fighter. This was very simply equipped. An altimeter, a revolution counter, a fuel gauge, an oil temperature gauge and an oil pressure gauge were the only instruments. Instead of radio contact the pilots signalled by waving their wings.

were much faster, with a top speed of 140 km/h (87 mph), had a range of 840 km (520 miles), and could fly in all weather. The air raids on London and other cities gave a bitter foretaste of the new age of total air war, bringing suffering and casualties to the civilian population.

The year 1917 brought an innovation which had far-reaching effects on naval warfare. The first take-off and landing ramps were installed on the British warship HMS *Furious*, allowing fighters with wheeled undercarriages to operate from shipboard. Although most of the early trials ended in accidents, eventually the first aircraft-carrier sailed into action with great success. Sopwith

Camels took off from her deck to bomb a German airship base at Tondern.

At the end of the war both sides were using armour-plated aircraft, and flying-boats and other seaplanes were widely used. In essence all the different types of warplane had come into existence, and the rapid expansion of this new branch of warfare is shown by statistics. At the start of the First World War in 1914 the opposing armies had around 2,300 aircraft at their disposal, while at the end of 1918 the figure exceeded tens of thousands. By then the speed of a fighter plane had almost doubled since 1914, and was over 200 km/h (124 mph).

The sensational spectacles displayed by flying circuses won pilots public interest and essential finances.

fanciful name Carrier Pigeon. Gradually, passengers were admitted on the mail planes, especially after Charles Lindbergh's successful transatlantic flight of 1927, which won over American public opinion to the virtues of air transport.

The Dayton-Wright, with its modern conception, including retractable undercarriage, took part in the Gordon Bennett Cup speed trials in 1920.

Hundreds of thousands of stunned Parisians came to greet the conqueror of the Atlantic, Charles Lindbergh, and his aircraft, *Spirit of St. Louis,* on May 21, 1927 (see page 228).

The First World War was over. There were thousands of aircraft lying around that had been built for the forces. There were also hundreds of experienced young fliers trying to find a job where they could make use of their experience, but only a few were lucky enough to be able to go on flying. Perhaps the French air force veterans were best off, since their government provided funds for the setting up of an extensive network of air routes, which in the early 1920s already extended beyond the borders of France and into its African colonies.

In Britain and the United States aviation had a bumpier ride. One exception to this general rule was the US post office, which began an air mail service in May 1918. An important role was played by the transcontinental route from Washington D. C. through Chicago and Salt Lake City to San Francisco. The limited range of the aircraft meant that 'staging posts' had to be set up — a series of 18 airfields where the mail was transferred to a 'fresh' plane, just as teams were changed in the days of the stagecoach. None the less, the system worked, and in March 1924 night flying was introduced.

One of the first aircraft designed especially for postal duties had the

At the beginning of the 1920s groups of pilots started to put on shows. Acrobats would perform on a trapeze suspended from the plane, or stand and walk on the wings. The airmen simulated crashes and dogfights, and film companies made movies showing aircraft carrying pianos or beds. These companies of fliers were known as circuses, and the pilots were called barnstormers. The whole business of 'crazy flying' was very American, predictably dangerous and highly undignified, but it helped a good many pilots to make a living at a time when interest in flight had reached its nadir in the United States.

An important step towards regular air services was the operation by the RAF of a London-Paris run, started in 1919. The first passengers were members of the British government taking part in the Paris peace conference. The aircraft used were warplanes, modified only to the extent that their guns had been removed. The passenger sat in the gunner's seat, his head exposed to the elements. He was protected only by a flying-hood, goggles and a leather coat. Some passengers offered plenty of scope, and the Atlantic was the greatest goal of all. It was first crossed in stages by the American Albert C. Read in 1919. Read flew a Curtiss seaplane. Through having to land in the Azores to refuel he could not claim the £10,000 prize offered for a non-stop crossing. This feat was first accomplished on 14–15 June the same year by British air force officers John William Alcock and Arthur Whitten Brown in a modified Vickers Vimy bomber. In spite of un-favourable weather conditions they made the trip from Newfoundland to Ireland in just over 16 hours. The first flight around the world (in stages) was made by four Douglas World Cruisers between 6 April and 28 September 1924. The scene was set for two decades of tremendous expansion, leading up to the outbreak of the Second World War.

The first man to fly over both poles was R. E. Byrd. He crossed the untamed Arctic wastes in a three-engine Fokker F VII called *Josephine Ford*.

found a hip-flask the best way to keep warm. Andrew Bonar Law, an MP, had the clever idea of adding a glass cover to the passenger cockpit.

Pilots welcomed a challenge, and the aircraft manufacturers were anxious to demonstrate the quality of their products. The unconquered expanses of seas and oceans

The four-engined biplane Handley-Page HP-42 offered great comfort. The company, Imperial Airways, used these aircraft on flights to every corner of the British Empire.

The long-distance record breaker ANT-25, flown by V. P. Tchkalov. It made a non-stop flight from Moscow to the United States across the North Pole in 1937.

A Shrinking Earth

Shortly before 8 a.m. on 20 May 1927, a single-engined aircraft with the inscription 'Spirit of St. Louis' on its nose began to move sluggishly across New York's Long Island airport. Under the weight of a heavy load of fuel, the plane's wheels sank into the waterlogged ground, and an escort of fire-tenders followed close behind. Fortunately, however, the small plane lifted off safely.

A pair of Short-Mayo flying boats was one possible answer to the question of extending the range of mail aircraft.

The pilot was 25-year-old Charles Lindbergh, who was hoping to make the 5,810 km (3,602 mile) trip to Le Bourget airport near Paris. He had filled virtually all the available space inside his Ryan NYP *Spirit of St. Louis* with extra fuel tanks. After 33 hours and 39 minutes he touched down on French soil, with some difficulty, since the huge crowds of spectators left him little room for the manoeuvre. The French, though still smarting from the tragic failure of Charles Nungesser and François Coli, two of their countrymen who had made the same attempt, gave Lindbergh a hero's welcome. The first man to complete a solo crossing of the Atlantic was hailed on both sides of the ocean; not only that, but aviation got just the fillip it needed.

Air travel went from strength to strength, following a whole series of 'firsts' like that of Lindbergh. British pilots sought the most convenient routes to the Middle East, India and Australia. The light, reliable and relatively cheap biplanes made by the British firm of de Havilland became especially popular. It was in a de Havilland Gipsy Moth that Amy Johnson made a solo flight from England to Australia in 1930.

The vast expanse of the Pacific proved a difficult nut to crack. The first aircraft to cross it was a three-engined Fokker FVII flown by an Australian crew under Charles Smith. They followed a daunting route nearly 12,000 km (7,440 miles) long from Oakland, California, to Brisbane, via Honolulu and Fiji.

The French concentrated on routes to west Africa and South America. In October 1927 Dieu-donné Costes and Le Brix crossed the South Atlantic from Senegal to Brazil, a distance of 3,420 km (2,120 miles) in a Breguet XIX.

The generous support of the French government helped to found many airlines, one of the first of which was Latécoère, which made an experimental mail run from Toulouse to Barcelona as early as December 1918. In the mid-1920s the British airline Imperial Airways,

one of the pioneers of civil aviation, was formed. The company's routes linked the main cities of the British Empire; one of the most formidable, and to a degree typical, routes was Delhi-London, for which the airline commissioned a four-engined airliner HP-42 from Handley-Page. The long fuselage of this impressive machine seated 38 passengers and offered a good deal of comfort, including hot meals. Soon there were airlines sporting names which have become familiar today, such as Lufthansa in Germany, Sabena in Belgium, Swissair and KLM, the Dutch national airline.

The rapid progress in air transport which came about in Europe during the 1920s would have been impossible without two eminent designers. The first was Professor Hugo Junkers, who designed the first all-metal commercial aircraft, the F-13. The wings and fuselage were covered with corrugated metal sheets and the airframe was made of duralumin — a light but strong alloy of aluminium, copper and magnesium that was to play a vital role in aircraft construction. The second great designer was Dutchman Anthony Fokker, who introduced the cantilever wing — i. e. without the struts and stays typical of biplanes. The three-engined Fokker FVII in particu-

lar broke many distance records.

The Great Races

Naturally enough, aviation lent itself to the spirit of competition and the desire among men to see just how far things could be stretched. Long-distance flights were mostly undertaken by courageous individuals flying solo, but right from the start, speed records were a different matter. In a way they were a social affair; it was a question of teamwork between pilots and designers, making their machines demonstrate the progress that aviation had made.

The first aeronautical contest, held near Rheims in 1909, has already been mentioned, but it was

Norwegian explorer Roald Amundsen tried to reach the North Pole with two Dornier Wal seaplanes in 1925. They were forced to land 245 km (152 miles) from their goal.

not until the First World War was over that air races really came into their own. Gradually, the initial contests of speed, distance and endurance were extended, taking in competitions in navigation, obstacle courses, aerobatics, and so on. In Europe, cross country navigation contests, circuits and stage races between towns were particularly popular. Pilots vied with each other

Boeing 314 Atlantic Clippers made regular transatlantic flights from 1939. The name was taken from the famous 19th-century sailing ships.

keenly, often pulling off amazing feats of skill, and there was almost as great a struggle between newspapermen to put in the most dramatic report. At last, aviation was in the limelight.

European and American competitions took rather different views of these aerial contests. European contests emphasized the practical qualities of the aircraft, such as economy, low weight or high performance of engines, take-off and landing distances, the view the pilot had, and so on — in other words, matters of importance in the spread of the sport. The renowned Challenge Internationale des Avions de Tourisme was entered by the cream of European pilots, and the results of the race had an impact on the sport as a whole.

Races, such as the National Air Races or the Schneider Trophy, put a premium on speed, thus encouraging purpose-built planes. The speed race founded in 1912 by French industrialist Jacques Schneider was a special one for seaplanes and acquired a following throughout the world. The first race, in 1913, was won by a French pilot, M. Prévost, flying a Deperdussin aircraft with a 120 kW (160 hp) engine. The last Schneider Trophy race was held in 1931. This time the winning Supermarine S6B was powered by an engine developing 1,753 kW (2,350 hp). Though the aircraft taking part in the races were

more or less experimental machines with a short engine life, and tended to be not very manoeuvrable, the Schneider Trophy produced many technical innovations. World speed records were regularly broken. The sleek, aerodynamic shapes of the British and Italian aircraft built for the race were unmistakably products of their era, but the experience gained on them was later put to use in the Second World War. The elegant seaplanes built by Supermarine and the powerful Rolls-Royce engines were the immediate forerunners of the Spitfire and the Merlin engine.

There is a long tradition in the USA of 'round-the-pylons' races. Mid-way through the 1920s a number of races were combined in the National Air Races, including such famous contests as the Pulitzer Trophy, the Thompson Trophy and the Bendix Trophy. These were organized in several categories, of which the most popular was the 'free-for-all'. In the period 1920–30 most victories were scored by Boeing and Curtiss production fighters. In the 1930s, however, they were supplanted by aircraft specially built for speed by small firms or by amateurs, such as Wedell-Williams, Laird-Solution, and the famous Gee-Bee Super Sportster. It was in a Gee-Bee, which caused the death of many a pilot, that James Doolittle won in 1931 and 1932. After the war the competition was dominated by

The fast, comfortable and safe Douglas DC-3, which carried 21 passengers at a speed of 320 km/h (200 mph). The aircraft chalked up one success after another after their introduction in 1936.

World War II fighters and their successors.

Douglas Rules the Air

Lunch in New York, breakfast in Los Angeles: such might have been the proud boast of the American airline Transcontinental Western Air, better known by its initials TWA, in August 1934. It had come up with a startling offer: coast-to-coast in 18 hours at 320 km/h (200 mph) in the comfort of a luxury airliner. Passengers embarked at New York's Newark airport at four in the after-

The contest of speed called the Schneider Trophy was dominated in its last three years by the Supermarine seaplanes.

noon and stepped out onto the tarmac in Los Angeles at seven the next morning, ready to do a full day's business. The public interest aroused by the scheme exceeded all expectations, and the company gained an impressive lead over its competitors.

The technology behind TWA's commercial coup was the new Douglas DC-2 (DC stands for Douglas Commercial), the brainchild of the noted designer John K. Northrop. At the request of American Airlines, Douglas continued with its development programme, and

under the title DST (Douglas Sleeper Transport) produced a roomy and comfortably equipped machine which offered up to 14 passengers a standard of luxury to rival that of a Pullman sleeping-car. The bunks were divided from the aisle by curtains, and there was even a 'honeymoon suite'.

In addition to a new standard of comfort and speed, the aircraft had two major aeronautical innovations: automatic adjustment of propeller pitch and provision for the removal of ice from the forward edges of the wings and tail. This marked a great improvement in air safety, for many lives had been lost in attempts to cross the Atlantic due to icing.

Douglas had the edge on its rivals for many years, thanks to its twin-engined machines. This supremacy reached its peak with the DC-3, which literally took over world air transport. Dakotas, as they came to be called, are still in service in many corners of the globe.

An interesting chapter in the history of aviation was the era of the flying-boats, large seaplanes with boat-shape fuselages (hulls) which enabled them to take off, land and float on water — despite their size. The German Lufthansa company began a regular postal service from

The rather warlike Gee-Bee Super Sportster, nicknamed the Flying Barrel, which easily won the Thompson Trophy in 1931.

Europe to South America via Africa in 1934. The first stages of the trip were made in aircraft with wheeled undercarriages, but for the long Atlantic hop the all-metal flying-boat Dornier Wal was used. The reason was simple: the aircraft of the day were unable to make such a long crossing without refuelling. So a suitably equipped ship waited approximately half way between the two continents; the mail plane would land on the sea, tank up and make any repairs it might need, and continue its flight. The service cut the delivery time for mail from 15 days to five. A similar system was used to speed up the delivery of mail from ocean liners: at a given distance from shore an aircraft would take the ship's cargo of mail on to the other side. This method was first used during the voyage of the German steamer *Bremen* to New York, on 22 July 1929.

'Forty tons of flying beauty' was what someone called the huge flying-boat built for Pan American Airways by the Boeing company. The 10-man crew had their own bedroom, while the passengers enjoyed hotel comfort in four luxury cabins. The giant Yankee Clipper began a regular transatlantic run on 20 May 1939, making the trip from New York to Lisbon in around 24 hours. One of the reasons for the popularity of flying-boats among the airlines was the safety aspect. In an emergency they could land in the sea and wait for rescuers to arrive.

In the 1930s oceans were not the only major obstacles that long-haul airliners had to overcome. High mountain ranges such as those running from north to south across much of North America also presented considerable problems, requiring aircraft to fly at heights where the air is rarified. The Boeing company got over the difficulty by introducing the first airliner with a pressurized cabin. This aircraft was known as the Stratocruiser, clean air being forced in under pressure.

War in the Air

It was the foggy morning of 1 September 1939. On a German airfield near the Polish border the engines of a trio of Junkers Ju-87 Stuka dive-bombers roared into life. Shortly after 4.30 the blood-curdling wail of their sirens announced to Poland and the world that the Second World War had begun, and its first bombs exploded on the road across the River Visla.

Supported by the formidable Luftwaffe, German panzer units cut a swathe through the defending Polish forces, and in April 1940 they rolled into Denmark and Norway. In the Scandinavian campaign, the Wehrmacht first used airborne troops. Transport planes dropped parachutists behind the enemy lines to occupy key positions. In May 1940 the German army coolly circumvented the Maginot Line, a chain of fortifications that was intended to protect France from invasion. The rapid subjugation of France was a triumph for the German strategy of blitzkrieg (lightning war), whose two components were the armoured divisions and the Luftwaffe.

The key to the Germans' success in their push to the south and west was their capture of an important Belgian fortress. In the course of that operation they employed military gliders towed behind Junkers Ju-52 transport aircraft. When they reached the vicinity of the landing area, the gliders were unhooked and continued their flight alone. A necessary precondition for such operations was superiority in the air, which the Luftwaffe achieved with its fast and well-armed Messerschmitt Bf-109 fighters. These also opened up the skies for the bombers, for which the long columns of fleeing civilians and retreating soldiers were sitting targets. Even more feared were the terrible Stukas, swooping on victims like rapacious birds. After the capitulation of France, Hitler de-

▲ Frequent rivals in the dogfights over England were the German Heinkel He-IIIs and the British Hawker Hurricanes.

Aerials of radiolocation stations on the English coast. On the left the transmitter, on the right the receiver.

British fighters put V-1 flying bombs out of action by means of a risky manoeuvre in which they 'flipped' one of the bomb's wings to turn it over.
▼

cided to bring Britain to her knees.

The hammer that was to beat the island empire into submission was the Luftwaffe. The German High Command wanted to implement the views of Italian general Giulio Douhet, who claimed that a war could be won simply by acquiring air superiority and then 'taking out' the enemy's industrial and administrative centres.

From August 1940 huge numbers of bombers raided the British Isles. An average of 400 planes a day took off to attack ports, airfields, docks, power stations and factories. The Germans did not content themselves with destroying strategic targets. By bombing London and other cities they did their best to break the will of the British people. On the night of 14/15 November 1940, a total of 437 German aircraft approached along three flightpaths to rain destruction on the city of Coventry. The last bombs dropped in the raid were of a special type called Jericho; they were fitted with sirens, whose wail was supposed to signal the annihilation of the city. The name Coventry went down in history as a symbol of aerial terror

directed against the civilian population. In a mere two months of the Battle of Britain, 13,000 people died in London alone.

But Fighter Command hit back. Updated versions of the Supermarine Spitfire and Hawker Hurricane, with more powerful engines and armed with cannon, entered the fray. Fighter squadrons were divided into four regional commands, and their movements were directed from operations rooms where all available information was assembled. A dense network of coastal observation posts and radar stations announced the approach of the German bombers well in advance. Luftwaffe losses steadily rose. Not even the use of long-range, twin-engined Messerschmitt Bf-110 fighters as escorts was able to change that.

The RAF gained the extra minutes it needed. Thanks to efficient organization it was possible to base the fighter squadrons on a large number of small airfields. The early warning given by radar enabled the 'few' to seem many. Not even a two-to-one numerical advantage could prevent victory slipping from

the Luftwaffe's grasp. It had suffered its first major defeat.

Aircraft versus Ships

'The Flying Tank' was one of many nicknames acquired by the renowned Soviet fighter-bomber Ilyushin Il-2, the Stormovik. In just one attack on German panzer columns during the Battle of Kursk in July–August 1943, these planes destroyed no less than 70 tanks in 20 minutes. The low-flying Stormoviks would suddenly appear above the enemy, cannon blazing and bombs and rockets flying, and they inflicted heavy damage on rail and road transport, fortified positions and airfields. The cockpit and engine were armour-plated against anti-aircraft fire. To reduce the risk of fire should the fuel tank be hit, the airspace above the fuel was filled with cooled exhaust gases. There were four tracks under each wing for launching RS-82 rockets. During the Battle of Stalingrad in 1942–43 a tactic was developed whereby observers on the ground watched enemy movements and radioed exact attack instructions to the Stormoviks.

These planes startled the German command when the Soviet Union was first invaded in 1941 and remained a very effective weapon throughout the war.

March 1943 saw the first action on the Eastern Front by the French Normandie-Niemen fighter unit, whose pilots flew the excellent Yakovlev Yak-3 aircraft. These planes, which brought the French fliers many successes, represented the peak achievement of Soviet design with the emphasis on simple manufacture and operation combined with lightweight and heavy armament.

In the Pacific theatre the importance of military aircraft was underlined right from the start when, on 7 December 1941 Japanese planes crippled the US Navy's 6th Fleet at anchor in Pearl Harbor. A typical feature of the war in the Pacific was the use of carrier-based aircraft. The main strike aircraft were dive-bombers and torpedo planes. Airborne attacks were able to decide the outcome of naval battles before the battleships could fire their first shots. The British noted this to their cost in 1941, when Japanese aircraft sank the warships HMS *Prince of Wales* and the *Repulse,* and the

On April 18, 1942, sixteen B-25 Mitchells took off from the carrier *Hornet* to make the first air-raid on Tokyo. The partial removal of their armaments increased the aircrafts' range.

Carrier-based American Grumman Hellcat fighters excelled themselves in the battle of the Philippine Sea. They swept the Japanese fleet air arm from the skies.

overriding importance of air power at sea was confirmed throughout the Pacific war. The first duel between aircraft-carriers, fought at a distance, took place in the Coral Sea in 1942.

In the early stages the war in the Pacific was dominated by the Japanese A6M Zero, whose armament, speed and range gave it clear superiority over its American rivals. The introduction of carrier-based Grumman F6F Hellcats in January 1943 turned the tide, however. Hellcats had three 12.7 mm machine-guns in each wing, armour-plated cockpits, and fuel tanks surrounded by a self-sealing envelope that prevented fuel from escaping in the event of a hit. Like other types of carrier planes, they also had folding wings, allowing them to be raised in lifts to the flight-deck from hangars

in the bowels of the carrier. Hellcats, and later also F4U Corsairs, shot down enemy Zeros by the dozen. During a battle in the Philippines on 19 June 1944, Admiral Ozawa sent 328 planes into action from a distance of 500 km (310 miles) away and two-thirds of them failed to return. In a single day the core of the Japanese fleet air arm had been destroyed.

As American marines gradually won control of the islands of the Pacific, the time came for the huge four-engined B-29s, the Superfortresses, to begin their raids on Japan.

With the end in sight, the Empire of the Rising Sun attempted to stave off defeat by using rocket-powered Ohka flying bombs. In these,

kamikaze suicide pilots dived on American ships in the belief that their sacrifice could alter the course of the war. Over 5,000 Japanese pilots threw away their lives in this manner.

Bombs Away

The Royal Air Force mounted bomber raids on Germany from the outbreak of the Second World War. The first attacks, using twin-engined Vickers Wellington bombers, were made at the expense of heavy casualties, which caused the RAF to switch to night raids. These were made more effective with the arrival of the four-engined Short Stirling bomber, and in 1942 Bomber Command took delivery of its Avro Lan-

casters and Handley-Page Halifaxes. With their considerable range, the British heavy bombers were able to reach the whole of Germany and a large part of occupied Europe. A landmark in the course of the air offensive was the raid on Cologne on the night of 30/31 May 1942, the first to involve over 1,000 aircraft. They attacked their target in a series of several waves.

Night raids were usually started by selected aircraft known as pathfinders. Their task was to illuminate the target using parachute flares. The lightweight bombers de Havilland Mosquitoes proved valuable in this role. A command plane would circle the target area, from which the mission commander directed the raid by radio.

With the aid of searchlights, German night-fighters and 'ack-ack' guns counter-attacked the raiders. From the second half of 1943 the German air defences had their own radar to help locate attackers, and passed on information to the fighters. An ingenious way of confusing German radar, codenamed Window, involved having decoy aircraft drop strips of aluminium foil.

From January 1943, RAF planes operating against Germany were reinforced by bombers of the US 8th Air Force, flying from bases in Britain. The mainstay of the enormous US strike-power was its four-engined B-17 Flying Fortresses and B-24 Liberators, which flew one mission after another against key industrial centres, shipyards, munitions factories, chemical works, power stations and other vital components of the German war effort.

The heavy armament of the American bombers allowed them to set up a mutual defence screen of crossfire. The planes were divided into groups called combat boxes. A box consisted of 18 aircraft, each 'toting' no less than 10 machine-guns. Different boxes flew at different heights to give each other cover from marauding enemy interceptors.

The raid on a ball-bearing factory at Schweinfurt in August 1943, when the Americans suffered heavy casualties, showed that daylight raids were not a practical proposition without fighter cover. At the end of 1943 this was provided by adding extra fuel tanks under the wings of fighters to improve their range. The P-51 Mustang was especially successful in this role, but the P-47 Thunderbolt and P-38 Lightning also performed bomber escort duties. These were not confined to protecting the bombers, but included attacks on trains, stations, anti-aircraft positions, airfields and the like. It was thanks to these planes that the Allied air forces gained superiority in the skies over Germany.

The air offensive against Germany hotted up after the introduction of the four-engined heavy bombers, Avro Lancasters. The sky above the cities of Germany was, however, criss-crossed with the light of searchlights, the fire of anti-aircraft guns, and swarms of night fighters.

Some of the most difficult missions flown by Bomber Command were undertaken by 617 Squadron, which was equipped with specially adapted Avro Lancasters whose bomb-bays had been enlarged. In March 1945 they destroyed a railway viaduct near Bielefeld with a 10-tonne Grand Slam bomb. It was the same squadron that had carried out the famous 'dam-buster' raid on a trio of dams in the German Ruhr valley which supplied an important industrial area with electricity. The raid, which took place in March 1943, employed a special bouncing bomb designed by Sir Barnes Wallis. These round bombs were released as the Lancasters flew low over the water, and bounced across the surface until they struck the dam wall. They were timed to go off after sinking to the bottom of the dam.

The massive air offensive against the Third Reich was maintained right up to the end of the war and helped bring about Germany's defeat. Success was, however, bought dearly, costing the lives of many civilians as well as airmen, not to mention huge material losses. In a last desperate attempt to regain the initiative, the German High Command came up with several 'miraculous' new weapons – jet aircraft, V-1 flying bombs, V-2 rockets, and others. But by then not even the most advanced technology of destruction could stop the advance of the victorious Allied armies.

An effective weapon against German tank columns was the Soviet fighter-bomber Il-2 *Stormovik*, nicknamed The Flying Tank. Apart from cannons it was equipped with special bombs and rockets.

On August 27, 1939, the world's first jet aircraft, the Heinkel He-178, made its first short flight a few metres above the ground.

The Gloster E28/39, which showed the first really practical application of the jet engine to aircraft. The results of intensive research were applied to the design of the Meteor, used in action at the end of the war.

The rapid development and improvement of aircraft during the Second World War brought with it the realization that propeller-driven planes were reaching the limit of their potential. Evidence of this fact was provided by the air-speed record set up in 1939 in a Messerschmitt Me-209 by a German pilot, F. Wendel. His 755 km/h (468 mph) was not beaten by a piston-driven aeroplane for 30 years. It was clear that if aviation was to make any further substantial progress a new form of propulsion must be found.

Reactive propulsion entered the scene, based on Newton's third law of motion, which states that to every action there is an equal and opposite reaction. Simple, isn't it? But how long aviation had to wait before this principle was exploited!

Although these were experiments by the ancient Chinese, the first real theoretical studies on jet propulsion occurred at the end of the 1920s. Research reached an advanced stage in Britain and Germany in particular, where the first practicable jet engines were developed. In the space of a single month, quite independently, Sir Frank Whittle in England and Pabst von Ohain in Germany completed the first jet power units. With the financial and technical support of Ernst Heinkel, the world's first jet-powered aircraft was built in Germany, and first flew on 27 August 1937. The He-178 remained no more than a prototype, however.

Thanks to energetic research the Germans took the lead in this new field. In June 1938 they used the first viable jet engine, the HeS3B, slung underneath a propeller aircraft. In May 1941 the first British jet plane, the Gloster E28/39 Squirt, took to the air. The advantages of the new propulsion were immediately apparent, since the Squirt reached the top speeds of contemporary fighters at half throttle.

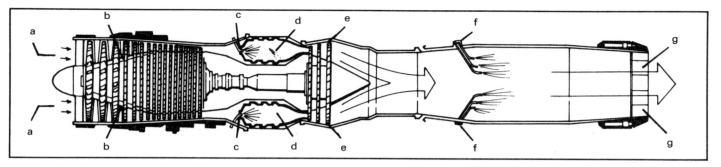

Cross-section of a jet engine:
a) air intake
b) compressor
c) fuel injection

d) combustion chambers
e) turbine
f) afterburner jets
g) adjustable propulsion jet

The first American jet aircraft, the Bell XP-59 Airacomet, took off from the Muroc Base on October 11, 1942. Its performance, however, was no better than that of contemporary propeller aircraft. ▼

Within the framework of allied cooperation Whittle's jet engine was made available for study in the USA, where General Electric soon updated the new invention and made it possible to build the first American jet plane, the Bell XP-59. Much less successful experiments took place in Italy where, though the Caproni-Campini N1 first flew in 1940, it reached a speed of only about 200 km/h (124 mph). The Japanese, too, tested a jet called the Nakajima J8NI Kikka towards the end of the war.

At the end of the war the Allies used the British Gloster Meteor, which was successful in hunting down V-1s, themselves powered by a form of jet engine. In its death throes the Luftwaffe tried out several designs powered by jet or rocket engines, especially the jet fighters Me-262 and He-162, and the jet bomber Arado 234.

Reactive propulsion brought so many far-reaching changes in the construction and performance of aircraft that it amounted to a revolution. Increasing performances called for new structural designs, and new materials capable of withstanding higher temperatures and greater stresses. Adapted versions of conventional aircraft could only be considered a stop-gap measure. For

instance, it was necessary for the new aircraft to be able to fly over a much greater range of speeds. Low-profile wings and tails and arrow shapes came into use, facilitating the transition between subsonic and supersonic speeds. Swept-back wings required increasingly complex systems for controlling the aircraft's flight. It was also necessary to find a new way for pilots to escape from their plane in an emergency, leading to the development of the ejector seat, which eventually became effective enough to work even during take-off.

In the post-war period jet aircraft continued to develop rapidly in Great Britain, the United States and the Soviet Union. It soon became apparent that, in order to deal with the quite new problems associated with flight at speeds approaching that of sound, experimental designs would be needed, such as those of the American Bell X-1 and Douglas Skyrocket rocket-planes. There were also intensive tests going on in the Soviet Union, where one after another the prototypes of the jet-fighters Yak-15, MiG-9 and later, in 1947, the famous MiG-15, took off.

In the autumn of 1947 Captain Charles Yeager of the US Air Force became the first man to cross what had once been considered the ultimate boundary, when he flew an experimental Bell X-1 at 1,078 km/h (668 mph) in level flight — i. e. Mach 1.015. For the first time the familiar sonic boom which accompanies the breaking of the sound barrier was heard.

Mach numbers are named after the Austrian scientist Ernst Mach, who studied the behaviour of sound waves. Among other things he found that the speed of sound in air varies with altitude. The instrument in an aircraft which measures its speed relative to the local speed of sound is called a machmeter, Mach 1 being the speed of sound.

Though progress in aerodynamics put Britain ahead of other countries in the development of jet planes, the British had more difficulty than the Americans or Russians in breaking the sound barrier. The first to succeed was an outstanding test pilot called John Derry, who on 2 September 1948 managed to exceed the speed of sound in a nose dive in a de Havilland Swallow.

Progress in aviation has always been made at a price. Wing vibrations around the speed of sound led to the destruction of the DH-108 Swallow and the death of its pilot, Geoffrey de Havilland. His aircraft was torn to pieces in mid-air by a phenomenon called flutter.

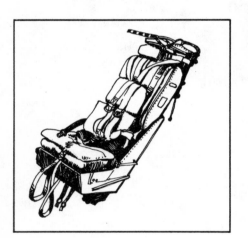

◄

The Martin-Baker ejector seat. It allows the pilot to leave his aircraft even at high speed by means of rocket propulsion. The cockpit cover is first discarded.

The Soviet jet fighter MiG-15 was robust, fast and well-armed, and clearly demonstrated the advantages of swept-back wings.

The speed of sound was attained by Charles
E. Yeager on October 14, 1947 in the
rocket-propelled test aircraft Bell X-1, which
was carried to its take-off height by
a bomber. Captain Yeager was the first man
to cross the sound barrier in level flight. He
flew at Mach 1.015 over Muroc Base in
California.

Increasing speeds revealed previously unknown phenomena, which sometimes claimed the lives of test pilots. Among them was the skilled and popular Geoffrey de Havilland, son of the founder of the well-known aircraft manufacturing company, who was killed on 27 September 1947. His experimental tailless DH-108 Swallow literally fell to pieces in the middle of a dive.

The cause was something which had already been observed by the pilots of fast fighter planes at the end of the war; the most serious consequence was loss of control, and pilots spoke of the threshold of death. They described a sort of layer of thickened air on the wings. To see this shock wave, as we call it today,

was usually to look death in the face.

What caused this phenomenon? Every aircraft, no matter what its speed, is subject to air resistance, but at higher speeds this resistance increases. Below the speed of sound it does not present a particular problem, but at speeds approaching 1,000 km/h (620 mph), i. e. around Mach 1, a new type of resistance appears, something which was quite unknown in the 1940s.

The phenomenon may be com-

pared to the ripples produced when a stone is dropped in still water. An aircraft flying through air produces similar 'ripples', or shock waves. At around the speed of sound it catches up with its own shock wave, and this constitutes a physical 'barrier' to the aircraft's passage. It was this that threatened the early jet planes at around Mach 1. Pilots lost control; the rudder would refuse to respond, and sometimes the needles of the instruments would actually break off. An unseen force tried to tear the aircraft apart, and in many cases it succeeded. Aerodynamics had to come to the rescue with such innovations as swept-back wings, reinforced structures and more powerful engines.

'The propeller won't lie down' might have been the phrase to sum up the situation in civil aviation at the end of the 1940s. Air transport had undergone considerable expansion during the Second World War, building on the successes of the 1930s. Allied air forces made good use of the legendary Dakota, the Douglas DC-3.

Commercial airlines began to think of re-opening and extending routes in advance of the end of the war, and so leading manufacturers like Lockheed, Douglas and Boeing started work on new types of civil aircraft. It was clear that the requirements of post-war civil aviation would call for the use of four-engined airliners, exploiting experience gained on the big bombers.

The new generation of airliners started to appear even before the cessation of hostilities, and in October 1945 the Douglas DC-4 was introduced on the transatlantic route, which became the main battle-ground in the competition between leading airlines and manufacturers.

For their North Atlantic services, TWA and Pan American used the Lockheed Constellation, which had been born in the war years but had been adapted and greatly improved since then. Its cruising speed was

The four-engined Lockheed Constellation ▲ airliner of the late 1940s had a characteristically elegant appearance.

The first turbo-prop in passenger service was the Vickers Viscount, introduced on the London — Paris route in 1950. ▶

around 480 km/h (297 mph). Constellations, with their pressurized cabin and underslung freight compartment, called a speed-pack (for almost 4 tonnes of cargo), enabled the American airlines to set up a dense network of intercontinental routes. With the expansion of air traffic went a rethinking of airport construction. Alongside the American giants stood Britain's BOAC and, from 1 August 1946, also BEA, British European Airways.

The success of the Lockheed Constellation acted as an inspiration to the Douglas Corporation, whose DC-7 in its Seven Seas version represented the finest achievement in propeller airliners. Both Douglas and Boeing were constantly modifying their basic designs, the tendency being to extend the fuselage in order to increase the passenger-carrying capacity, or in some cases to make room for extra fuel tanks and thus increase the aircraft's range. The Boeing 377 Stratocruiser was a particularly well-appointed long-haul craft, its 'double-decker'

layout being popular with passengers since it allowed them to take a stroll and visit the bar or smoking-room. With the option of fitting out as a sleeper, it presented a standard of comfort not matched until jumbo jets came along many years later.

The average propeller-driven airliner of the day carried 70 to 80 passengers, flew around 500 km/h (310 mph), and had a range of about 5,000 km (3,100 miles). Yet rapid developments in aeronautics, especially the introduction of jet and turbo-prop engines to power military aircraft, were signalling the

▲
A fully-loaded Tu-114 turbo-prop aircraft weighs 175 tonnes, and can carry up to 220 passengers. It flew the Moscow — Montreal route non-stop.

end of the era of piston power.

Great Britain made use of its lead in aero-engine design to chalk up two 'firsts'. In 1948 the world's first turbo-prop aircraft, the prototype Vickers Viscount, took off. It entered service, and with success, on the London-Paris route. The main advantages of the new engine were a shortening of flying times, less

The Douglas DC-7 Seven Seas was introduced to the transatlantic route by Pan Am in 1956 as the latest, and in fact the last, piston-propelled aircraft. ▼

noise inside the cabin, and a reduction in vibration. The Viscount clearly proved the case for turbo-props.

The use of jets in civil aircraft turned out to be more of a problem. On 2 May 1952 the very first jet airliner, the de Havilland Comet 1, inaugurated a regular service from London to Johannesburg. The extent of the revolution brought to air transport by the jet engine is demonstrated by the fact that the Comet cut the journey time on the London-Singapore route from two and a half days to 25 hours. However, a year after the introduction of the Comet there were three successive accidents which set back the use of jet airliners for several years.

The beginnings of the large jet airliners were much more complicated than was the case with turbo-props. The Vickers Viscount demonstrated convincingly the advantages of the latter system of propulsion, but airline operators held strong prejudices against jet travel; the opposition of the American Big Four companies was especially strong. Their doubts were not in any way alleviated when three Comets crashed, but a number of manufacturers put considerable effort into research into jet propulsion, and their foresight was soon to be rewarded.

On 15 July 1954 the first test flight of a Boeing 707 took place. Even a casual glance showed this to be the first really modern jet airliner, with its wings swept back 35° and its engines mounted on 'stalks' under the wings. The performance figures were also most impressive, for the 707, which derived from experience gained in building jet bombers, could carry 179 passengers almost 5,000 km (3,100 miles) at 917 km/h (568 mph). It thus had all the

prerequisites for a successful trans-atlantic airliner.

On 26 October 1958, a Pan Am 707 christened 'Maria' flew the first New York-London service non-stop. The flight time was cut to six and a half hours. Compared with its piston-driven contemporaries the DC-7 or the Constellation, the improved Boeing 707-320 performed impressively, covering the same number of passenger-kilometres in half the time. The 707 put Boeing at the forefront of the new jet era.

In the mid-1950s the Soviet Union was also preparing to step into the new age. The Tupolev design studio drew up the plans for the Tu-104 airliner, the prototype of which flew on 17 June 1955 with the first production models going into service the following autumn. The placing of its twin jet engines next to the fuselage was unusual at that time. The undercarriage retracted into spindle-shaped housings which gave the wings, with their sharp sweepback, a characteristic shape.

For the next 20 years the Soviet Tu-104 was one of the most

favoured jet airliners in service.

Another novelty came out of the Tupolev workshops, too. It was the giant turbo-prop Tu-114, powered by four engines and with a laden weight of 175 t, which for almost

The French jet airliner Sud-Aviation Caravelle brought a design innovation — engines at the rear of the fuselage. The idea was that of P. Satre.

For many years, the Boeing 707 dominated the fleets of many of the leading airlines and enjoyed a privileged position.

The British de Havilland Comet 1 was the first jet airliner in regular service on its introduction in May 1952. It was withdrawn after a number of disasters, returning six years later.

a decade made it the biggest aircraft in service in civil aviation.

The French Caravelle — named after the ships that plied the Mediterranean in medieval times — cruised the skies over five continents. The novel position of the engines at the rear of the fuselage kept the noise level in the passenger cabins very low, and the wings had excellent aerodynamic characteristics. The plane's safety margin was demonstrated by a number of flights on one engine. In August 1956 a Caravelle flew from Casablanca to Paris and back twice over with one engine out of action. Another factor contributing to the Caravelle's popularity was the manner of boarding and disembarking — the rear of the fuselage let down to form a sort of gangway.

Air France first used Caravelles on the Paris-Rome-Istanbul route in May 1959. The aircraft carried up to 80 passengers on short and medium runs, and its popularity went from strength to strength. Other western European companies followed the example of Air France, and in 1961 the Caravelle succeeded in breaking into the American market, where it flew successfully in the livery of United Airlines.

In spite of the success of jet engines, it was obvious that they could be made more economical by improving the power-plant. Around 1960 the double-flow ('turbofan') jet engine was introduced; its fuel consumption is similar to that of a piston engine, although the output is several times higher.

About the time the jet engine began to dominate civil aviation, in the late 1950s and early 1960s, the idea was voiced in several countries simultaneously of using supersonic aircraft for airline service. The technology required was investigated by leading manufacturers in the United States, the Soviet Union, Britain and France. The last two countries joined forces to work on a project symbolically named Concorde. Though it was clear from the start that the programme was not going to be a simple one, few can have expected the number of technical problems that arose. Still fewer people might have supposed that this technical miracle, symbol of the 'supersonic century', whose prototype first taxied out on 3 March 1969, would lead to the production of a mere 16 planes. Potential customers apart from the British and French cancelled their orders because of the high operating costs.

Almost at the same time as Concorde, the Soviet supersonic Tupolev Tu-144, carrying 117 to 140 passengers, was developed. It first flew on 31 December 1968, thus becoming the first supersonic airliner. Though the Concorde and the Tupolev look practically identical, their designs are quite different.

Because of its electronic complexity, the Concorde is flown by a crew of only three, with a staff of six stewardesses to look after its 108 to 144 passengers. Four sophisticated and powerful Rolls-Royce/SNECMA Olympus engines give the Concorde a top speed of around Mach 2, or 2,143 km/h (1,328 mph). In the development stages the Olympus engines and the undercarriage were tried out under Avro Vulcan bombers, and the wings on the experimental aircraft BAC-221. The Soviet designers of the Tupolev adapted a similar approach.

One of the main problems with supersonic flight is the enormous stress exerted on the structural materials by the heat which is produced at high speeds. This necessitates the use of special alloys of steel and titanium, and composite materials. The wide range of speeds at which the aircraft has to fly meant that the delta wing shape was most suitable — in the case of Concorde with the characteristic 'Gothic' inflection of the leading edge. Another technical problem was the fuel system. Some of the fuel tanks are used as ballast tanks, and as the tanks empty, the aircraft's balance is maintained by means of a system of pumps which redistribute the fuel. The pilot's view was also a problem. This was solved by the use of a tilting nose, which points downwards during take-off and landing to give the pilot maximum visibility. Brake-parachutes are used to cut the landing distance.

Though the Concorde and the Tu-144 represent major technical achievements, they have enjoyed

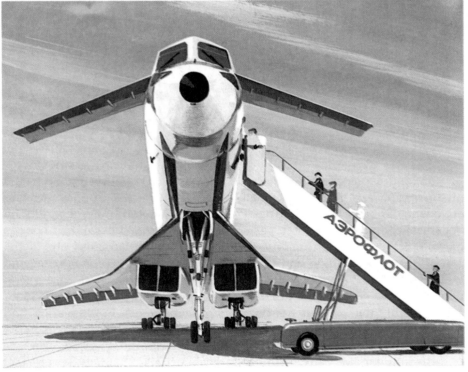

▲
The Concorde supersonic airliner is the result of long cooperation between Britain and France. It carried its first passengers on January 21, 1976. The fuel consumption is three times that of conventional airliners.

▶
A diagram to show how, by pumping fuel from one tank to another, the Concorde maintains its equilibrium when crossing the sound barrier.

The Soviet supersonic airliner Tu-144. ▼

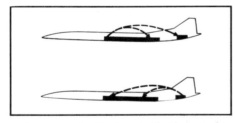

only very limited practical use, for a number of reasons. One of these is the high running costs due to high fuel consumption and the relatively small number of passengers carried. In addition, there has not been the amount of interest in supersonic flight that was imagined earlier. The limited space in Concorde's cabin means it can scarcely compete for comfort with the big airbuses. Environmental factors have also played a role in the opposition to supersonic aircraft, in particular the question of engine noise. A decisive influence was the withdrawal of American manufacturers from the supersonic programme and the difficulties encountered by Air France and British Airways in obtaining landing rights for Concorde at New York's Kennedy Airport.

A diagram of Kennedy International Airport in New York.
1 – control tower, 2 – landing and take-off runway, 3 – airline offices, 4 – taxiing runway, 5 – fuel stores, 6 – car parks.
New York air traffic represents a complex system, including three large airports, the most important of which is Kennedy Airport, linked with the city centre by a helicopter service run by New York Airways. Kennedy Airport handles around 20 million passengers a year. The original architecture of this huge air crossroads is the work of the Finnish architect Eero Saarinen.
The control tower is the nerve-centre of traffic both at the airport and in the air. The airspace is divided into individual sectors which are controlled by air traffic controllers. They are in constant radio contact and keep a check on plane movements along predetermined routes using a call sign, and

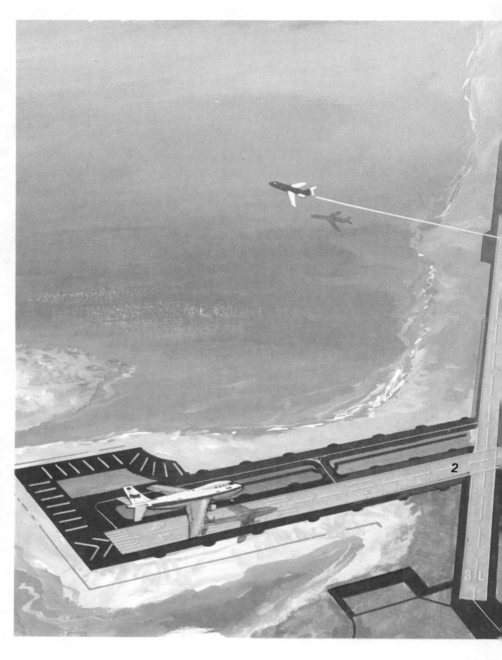

In the beginning there were flat tracts of meadow where those magnificent men lifted off and touched down their flying machines. The concept of an airfield did not develop until some time later, with the gradual appearance of hangars, runways, runway lighting and other equipment. In time the first modest buildings for the use of passengers were added. The familiar red and white windsock gave an indication of wind direction and strength, and later a man with a red flag signalled permission to take off. At the end of the 1920s radio communication was introduced.

As aircraft design went through changes that led to an increase in weight, grassy fields ceased to be suitable places for taking off and landing. In 1928 the first New York airport opened, with the world's first concrete runways. In the 1930s passenger services were added to the technical equipment of airports; these included banks, hotels, restaurants, car parks, and transport systems running a shuttle-service between airport and city. Today it is no exaggeration to say that large airports themselves have all the characteristics of cities.

There are many different systems of organizing a big airport, but all are based either on centralization or decentralization. In the first case, passengers and luggage are processed in a central building and make their way to the aircraft independently. In the second case, the passengers and their luggage are both handled in the immediate vicinity of the aircraft. This method makes use of projecting loading bays, forming a system of satellites joined to the main building through moving walkways, often underground. The use of these and escalators speeds up passenger handling and helps travellers get from plane to road and rail connections, and vice-versa. Telescopic gangways link the loading bays directly to the planes, and passengers are thus totally isolated from the weather outside. The system of satellite loading bays, in fact

a radar code for the type of aircraft and its speed, place of take-off and landing and time of arrival at various points along the route. The take-off and landing runways are interconnected and supplemented by taxiing runways which form the network of traffic at the airport itself, which is also controlled from the control-tower. Vehicles with the well-known sign, Follow Me, drive across the runways to lead the aircraft to their respective aprons.

The handling of passengers takes place quickly and smoothly at satellite bays. There are various ways of organizing the boarding of passengers. One of the most interesting, technologically, is the system of fingers which are telescopically extended from the terminal itself. New methods of passenger handling have been made essential by the introduction of giant aircraft of the jumbo jet and Airbus types.

a series of small airports, has been successfully applied in many of the world's leading airports, such as Charles de Gaulle Airport in Paris, Los Angeles International Airport and New York's Kennedy International Airport. Another possibility is to use coaches to ferry passengers to their planes, which, given the size of today's jumbo jets, means maintaining a sizable fleet of vehicles.

The number of passengers using airports is constantly on the increase. In 1938, for instance, Tempelhof Airport in Berlin had an annual capacity of 300,000 passengers, while today London's Heathrow Airport handles over 20 million passengers a year. These figures indicate the importance of having an efficient means of transporting passengers between airports and the cities they serve. Apart from motorways and rail links, helicopters are also used at some airports, since these are able to take off and land from the roofs of, for instance, New York skyscrapers. A study is also being made of the feasibility of employing VTOL (vertical take-off and landing) aircraft.

One of the key roles of an airport is to ensure the safety of air traffic. The International Civil Aviation Organization (ICAO) lays down rules and guidelines for this. The airport control tower gives information and instructions to arriving and departing aircraft, including data on their own and other planes' positions, weather conditions, and so forth. The tower not only controls aircraft in flight, but also taxiing on the ground and the movement of emergency vehicles in case of an accident. Individual air traffic controllers constantly observe aircraft on radar screens and maintain radio contact with the crews. It is no simple matter to guide an aircraft onto a strip of concrete little wider than the span of its wings, and to do so in all weather conditions, but modern air traffic control systems comprise complex arrays of equipment using the latest computer technology.

As we have already seen, the tendency in the development of passenger aircraft was for the manufacturer to cater for the varying demands of airlines by adapting, and if necessary, 'stretching', their basic models. By extending the fuselage they could increase the payload or make room for extra fuel without the lengthy and expensive process of designing a new aircraft.

The dramatic increase in air traffic in the 1960s called for a wholly different approach. In cooperation with Pan Am, the Boeing Corporation came up with a design for a new, wide-bodied airliner. Commercially, the venture paid big dividends for the partners. The huge Boeing 747 jumbo jet was born.

With more than twice the space available on board compared with the famous 707, the jumbo was able to offer almost every conceivable comfort of modern air transport. The broad fuselage meant that pas-

The Airbus has managed to break the monopoly of the big aeronautical firms, which manufacture around 90 per cent of all long and medium-haul jets.
The Airbus A 310 is the successor to the A 300. The development and manufacture of the huge Airbus 310 was carried out by a consortium of firms from West Germany, Holland, France, Spain and Great Britain. ▼

The Boeing 747 jumbo jet brought a new dimension to air transport.

The Ilyushin Il-86 is the Soviet answer to airbus design. The prototype first flew on 22 December 1976 and required a surprisingly short take-off run. It can carry up to 350 passengers. The large area beneath the cabin floor is used for freight and baggage, but is also a sort of entrance hall where passengers can leave their overcoats and hand luggage. They then climb a spiral staircase leading from the 'ground floor' to the cabin above. Since there are four doors on each side of the fuselage, embarkation and disembarkation can be completed very quickly.

landing wheels instead of the usual eight. The engines have a low fuel consumption, high performance and low noise level. There have been other changes too with the coming of the jumbo jet, relating to airport procedures. In particular, the decentralized handling of passengers and their luggage has proved to be most efficient. The 747's excellent flight characteristics were demonstrated when one carried a space shuttle on its back across the Atlantic to appear at the Paris Air Show.

In the early 1970s new jumbos began to appear. The McDonnell Douglas DC-10 and the Lockheed L1011 Tristar are both distinguished by the same rather unusual engine arrangement — two on pillars under the wings, and one in the tail section of the fuselage.

As a result of cooperation between France, Britain, West Germany, Holland and Spain, the A300 European Airbus, carrying 220 to 300 passengers, made its maiden flight on 28 October 1972 and two years later was operating a regular Air France service between London and Paris. Various modifications are again available to suit the individual needs of customers. The main requirement continues to be to minimize running costs. The idea of an aerobus, first proposed in 1930 by an American designer named Bellanca, has caught on at last.

sengers could be seated 10 abreast instead of the usual six. The plane's three decks provide 12 toilets, a restaurant/lounge, a bar and a cinema. Along with the crew of three (two pilots and a flight engineer) and 15 stewardesses, the huge passenger-carrying capacity means that more than 500 people can be carried. Several variants are available, such as 66 first class seats plus 308 economy class, or 490 economy class only. It is this latter version that has enabled companies to offer low-price seasonal fares between Europe and the USA. In this way jumbos have opened up air travel to a wider section of the public.

The enormous weight of wide-bodied aircraft has meant that runways have had to be reinforced. The huge dimensions of these planes also mean that new design features have been necessary, such as 16

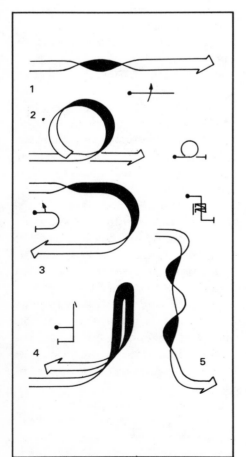

Basic elements of aerobatics:
1 — slow roll
2 — somersault
3 — half roll
4 — half roll and loop
5 — corkscrew

The Zlin series of aerobatic aircraft were among the best immediately following the Second World War. In a Zlin Z-50 L, the Czechoslovak pilot Petr Jirmus won the title World Champion (in 1984).

The flying bug bit more and more people all the time. There were flying clubs in existence even before the First World War, but the real heyday of the sport came in the 1920s and 1930s, especially in Britain and the United States. In a sense, though, it had always been a sporting urge that led to progress in the early days of aviation — the drive to go further or faster or higher than anyone else.

The first aerobatic stunts were performed in 1913 by two famous pilots, the Frenchman Adolphe Pégoud and the Russian Captain P. I. Nesterov. Even in those days Pégoud was publicly performing such manoeuvres as looping-the-loop, side-slipping, corkscrews, upside-down flying and other feats of aerial wizardry. Pégoud's party pieces were immensely important to aerobatics, demonstrating just how manoeuvrable a plane could be.

Today, aerobatics is an independent, highly specialized branch of flying, controlled by the Fédération Aeronautique Internationale and governed by a set of rules. After the Second World War there was a regular competition called the Lockheed Trophy, held in England and considered to be the unofficial world championship for aerobatics. Another well-known event is the Léon Biancott Cup, held regularly in

France to commemorate a fine pilot who was killed during the first ever aerobatics world championship, held in Czechoslovakia in 1960.

Czechoslovakia has given the world a long series of famous aerobatics aircraft under the name Zlin. The present-day Z-50 follows on from the successful tradition of the Trenér type. Planes for aerobatics are specially reinforced to take the extra strains exerted on them. Most of the more difficult aerobatic feats are included in the Aresti system, named after the Spanish pilot who created it. Aresti's method allows the elements of a performance to be expressed in simple graphic form on paper; by comparing the actual performance with these pictures, a more or less objective assessment can be made of the quality of the flight.

Modern high-performance gliders employ the most advanced aerodynamics. Streamlined aircraft are built largely of fibreglass. They have very long narrow wings and tailplanes which are easily removed when transporting the craft on a trailer.

The most commonly used elements in aerobatics are the somersault, backwards somersault, half roll, half roll and loop, spin, Immelmann turn, corkscrew and slow roll. There are also many refinements and combinations, where the flight-path and precision of the performance are judged. One of the most difficult and most rarely performed pieces is the 'lomcovák', a speciality of Czechoslovak pilots, in which the plane rotates simultaneously around all its axes.

In connection with unpowered flight we may come across two different terms, gliding and soaring, which most laymen would be unable to distinguish. In fact a glider is said to be gliding in the true sense of the word when it flies through still air, losing height. If it makes use of air currents to stay at the same height, or even climb, then it is said to be soaring.

In spite of modern technology, gliding has retained its magical attraction. We have already mentioned the very first man-made gliders and their precursors in nature. The modern glider is an aerodynamic, highly efficient construction which exploits plastics, laminates and other lightweight materials. These days there are also 'powered gliders', which have a small engine to help them reach the thermals in which they can then soar without power. Most gliders are either launched by being towed behind a powered aircraft, or from the ground by car or winch. After release the pilot may glide down again, or make use of thermals to rise to a possible height of several thousand metres, which allows him to fly distances of several hundred kilometres under favourable conditions. Chilean glider pilot Alejo Williamson flew across the Andes in 1964 in an all-metal Czechoslovak L-13 Blaník glider.

The hang-glider, or rogallo, has become a popular form of flight.

The Gossamer *Albatross,* driven by human muscle power, conquered the Channel in two hours 49 minutes (in June, 1979).

An interesting development in the history of aviation is the current trend back to ultra-light aircraft which are in many respects very reminiscent of the devices on which man first taught himself to fly. Take the Santos-Dumont Demoiselle of 1909, for instance: then, as now, the ideal was of flying as a sport for everyman, simple and cheap.

American designer Paul McCready earned himself a proud place in the annals of flight when, on 12 June 1979, his super-light Gossamer *Albatross* crossed the English Channel — the only source of power for the 23 kg (50 lb) plane being the muscles of its pilot, Bryan Allen. The *Albatross,* covered in transparent plastic film and with a transparent, pedal-driven propeller, might have indeed been made of gossamer as it skimmed across the waves on its flight lasting almost three hours. History repeats itself: then Blériot, now Allen.

McCready has since produced another ultra-light aircraft, this time the *Solar Challenger,* powered by the sun. The electric motor was driven by no less than 2,800 solar cells, and the plane covered the distance from Paris to Kent in 5 hours 23 minutes. G. Rochelt's Solair 1 uses the same power source, and is in fact a power glider.

Micro-lights are attracting an ever-widening circle of enthusiasts, though they are still far from being a form of sporting aviation for the general public.

Hang-gliding is by no means a new idea. With only slight exaggeration we might trace its origins back to the ancient Chinese kites. The idea received new attention at the end of the 1950s in connection with the NASA space programme when Francis Rogallo proposed a simple folding wing consisting of three spars joined together with a sheet of dacron, beneath which a space capsule could float to Earth. Hang-gliders were never actually used this way; instead, it was men who appeared on trapezes slung beneath the multicoloured wings. This new kind of sport has much in common with bird-flight, which man had dreamed about for so long. The butterfly kite has captured the imagination of thousands, and spread from sunny California to the whole world.

The romance of the early days of flying seems to have a special appeal to today's enthusiasts, apparently sickened by a surfeit of modern technology, where man is merely a part of the system — and one that can often be replaced by an automatic pilot or an on-board computer. There is a return to the hot-air balloon, a revival of Montgolfierism, but these days the envelope is nylon and the source of heat a propane burner. Only the hanging basket has remained virtually the same as it was 200 years ago. The only instrument on board, apart from a pocket compass, is a variometer; the only controlled manoeuvre is movement up and down. For seekers of peace and quiet there is nothing else they need.

Modern Montgolfier balloons, filled with hot air, are popular in Europe and the United States. A well-known manufacturer of brightly decorated advertising balloons is the company Cameron.

Ultralights give everyone the opportunity to fly. This old dream was revived half way through the 1970s by an American, J. Moody. There are about 35,000 ultralights in use in the United States, alone. ▼

Another sport involving aviation is parachuting. The first successful jump was made from the gondola of a balloon in 1797, by the Frenchman Jacques Garnerin. The parachute became an essential part of the flier's equipment at the end of the Second World War. Many international contests are held, and parachute design is constantly being improved. Instead of the classical umbrella-shape, wing-shaped designs are now in use that can be steered down onto a target a mere 10 cm (4 in) across.

A fast and well-equipped Falcon aircraft, one of the business jets.

General aviation takes in all manner of aircraft, from business planes through those used in agriculture to the family's weekend pleasure trips in their private aeroplane. In fact, it means virtually everything except the big airliners and transports and military craft. This branch of aviation is biggest in the United States, where there are around 150,000 planes in this category. Apart from transporting people and freight, they spray crops, fight fires, take photographs and measure the ground beneath them, to name but a few special applications.

Aircraft with special designs may be powered by jets, turbo-props or piston engines. General aviation is the most rapidly expanding area of flying, a fact that is connected with a change in the business strategy of the big airlines. The huge fleets of aircraft which were maintained in the days of the Dakota are now almost a thing of the past, and most airlines run a limited number of large airliners on a small number of routes. Thus there is immense scope, in the USA especially, for charter flights. Only a handful of the 13,000 airfields in the United States are linked by regular flights operated by the big companies. The rest are the domain of the small-time operators.

An important factor in the use of air transport is the immense distances sometimes involved, and the fact that some places are not easily accessible by road or rail. Such is the situation, for instance, in Australia and Canada. For farmers in remote parts of the Australian outback or for Canadian lumberjacks, aircraft represent the only source of provisons, supplies and medical aid. They also offer rapid relief in the event of natural disasters such as earthquakes and heavy snowfalls, where aircraft may be the only means of supplying or evacuating the local population.

The Australian Royal Flying

The Cessna light aircraft dominate the general aviation category.

Doctor Service, operating since 1927, is a fascinating rural institution. It solved two problems in one – the huge distances between holdings, and the lack of a telephone network. Farmers can get in touch with their local centre by radio, asking for medical assistance or transportation to hospital.

Aircraft are extremely useful for locating and fighting major forest fires. Regular fire-watching flights were first introduced in the United States in 1919, and aircraft were gradually introduced for this purpose in a number of other countries. An experienced observer can spot a fire in its early stages, when rapid intervention can prevent it from becoming a major conflagration.

The technology of aerial fire-fighting has changed a good deal over the years. Just after the Second World War specially trained parachutists ('smoke jumpers') were dropped; later on, 'water bombers', first used in the Canadian province of Ontario in the 1920s, became widespread. Former air force Catalina flying boats were used for the purpose. Many countries nowadays use the special amphibian Canadair CL-215 aircraft, which is fitted with a pair of tanks holding up to 5.5 tonnes of water. The plane can pick up a full load in 20 seconds by skimming across the surface of a lake and taking in water through openings under its fuselage.

Today, aircraft are indispensable in agriculture. Over the huge areas of modern farms they spray insecticides quickly and according to a precise timetable, deliver liquid or powdered fertiliser, and even sow seeds. In North America, aerial sowing is the rule rather than the exception. Aircraft also spray pest control agents over large areas of forest.

An important sphere of general aviation is the training aircraft that are used to teach civil and military pilots to fly. Basic training is mostly done in single-engined two-seaters, where pupil and instructor sit side by side with dual controls. Apart from the air forces and airlines, air clubs also teach many trainee pilots to fly.

The water bomber Canadair CL-215 allows the rapid containment of fires in large forests. The tanks hold over 5 tonnes of water.

The present generation of military aircraft incorporates a breathtaking array of high technology. The latest jet engines have revolutionized performances, especially with regard to speed. Armaments, too, have undergone a transformation since the Second World War with the introduction of self-targeting air-to-air and air-to-ground missiles. Electronics have also come on board the warplane in a big way, many functions being performed automatically by an in-flight computer. Radiolocators find and identify targets while other instruments help fly the aircraft and are capable, for instance, of 'copying' the shape of the ground in low flight to avoid radar detection. Interceptors frequently fly at speeds of Mach 2. These speeds place immense stress on the aircraft and produce high temperatures on its surface, which means that special materials such as carbon and titanium alloys have to be used.

Every military aircraft is a complex technical system relying on many different branches of science, and its design requires a large team of experts and advanced data processing techniques. In addition, 'design philosophy' has undergone a transformation. Fighter planes, as well as ensuring air superiority, must now be capable of reconnaissance and of offering support to ground forces.

Dassault Etendard taking off from the deck of an aircraft-carrier using a steam catapult. Its armament consists of air-to-sea Exocet missiles.

AWACS — early-warning aircraft. The large ellipsoidal cover over the fuselage contains the rotating radar aerial.

Bombers have made a comeback following a period when their role was considered obsolescent in view of the development of long and medium-range missiles, and of their vulnerability to ground-to-air defence systems. Variable-geometry bombers can manoeuvre at a wide range of speeds and are capable of launching cruise missiles against distant targets, making effective anti-aircraft defence virtually impossible. At the same time their own 'hedge-hopping' capability helps them avoid enemy ground radar and interceptors.

One of the latest innovations in aerial warfare is the introduction of aeroplanes designed to fight on the radioelectronic front, being equipped to 'jam' the enemy's radio communications and homing devices. These aircraft would accompany attack formations and make it possible to 'blind' hostile equipment and penetrate enemy airspace. AWACS advanced warning aircraft constantly gather and process huge quantities of intelligence information. Their computers evaluate data on

the movement of both hostile and friendly air and ground forces, their strength, composition, and so on. Highly sensitive electronic equipment receives signals from hundreds of kilometres inside enemy territory. At the same time strategic reconnaissance aircraft keep a constant watch on enemy installations from a great height, the data again being processed by computer.

Naval air forces are both carrier and land-based. Atomic-powered aircraft-carriers can remain at sea for months on end without having to refuel. There are special patrol planes for detecting enemy submarines and destroying them with rockets, torpedoes or depth-charges. Even quite small warships may be used as a base for VTOL planes.

Some army air forces now have their own jumbo transports, capable of carrying hundreds of fully-equipped soldiers thousands of kilometres. Mid-air refuelling, which increases the range of fighters and bombers, is nowadays a matter of routine.

▲
The Harrier vertical take-off and landing aircraft, needs no more than a small woodland clearing or a platform on a ship, to take off or land.

The French Dassault Mirage 2000 fighter is well-equipped electronically, has a top speed of Mach 2.2 and carries six tonnes of armaments.

▲
The Sikorsky S-61 helps build and supply drilling rigs at sea.

The Soviet Mi-12 can carry over 40 tonnes of cargo. It has broken a number of world records and won the Helicopter Association of America Award.

▼

The helicopter is a special type of aeroplane equipped with a multiple rotating wing (a rotor), whose blades perform basically the same function as the fixed wings of other planes. As with so many other technical discoveries, the principle of the helicopter was known to the ancient Chinese. When and how the idea reached Europe is not known, but Leonardo da Vinci's notes indicate that he was able not only to understand and explain the theory but also, on the basis of his own calculations and observations, to suggest various ways of using an Archimedean screw to make practical use of it.

Sir George Cayley's Helici-Aeroplane, which combined the advantages of the helicopter and the fixed-wing aeroplane, was far ahead of its time. The use of both vertical and horizontal rotors was to have given vertical take-off and landing together with considerable forward speed, but in the 19th century there simply did not exist a suitable power unit.

The year 1907 saw the first take-off of Frenchman Paul Cornu's helicopter. Though the flight lasted less than a minute and the aircraft remained less than a metre off the ground, Cornu was still the first man to fly a rotary-wing craft. Nor was that his only 'first'. He designed and tested a mechanism to change the angle of attack of the rotor blades, which is a basic principle of the control of helicopter flight.

▲
An Alouette III of the Alpine Rescue Service. Helicopters are used almost daily in the Alps for mountain rescue work, and they also keep high-altitude chalets supplied with food and water. Regular patrols mean that help is always at hand. In 1955, a helicopter saved the life of climber W. Bonatti.

The Russian Igor Sikorsky, whose early work was done before 1910, later designed and built the first usable helicopter, the VS-300. He was to devote his entire life to helicopters, founding the famous firm that bears his name and achieving outstanding results. The American firm Bell Helicopters holds an unusual record, their Bell 47 having been produced in various versions for more than 30 years.

The idea of the autogiro is associated with the Spanish pioneer Juan de la Cierva, whose work received much-needed support in Britain. The autogiro, with its rotor blades for the first time attached by means of swivel joints, remains a milestone in the history of helicopters. Several hundred of them were built in the 1930s for use not only in air clubs but also for military purposes.

The reason helicopters caught on and autogiros did not is because of a fundamental difference in design. Autogiros have to keep moving forwards, since their rotors are not powered and perform the function of wings only, turning of their own accord. Such aircraft cannot take off and land vertically, nor can they hover. It is just these advantages that make the helicopter so useful.

These days helicopters are widely used in all manner of circumstances. They transport travellers from city-centre heliports to large airports, situated well out of town. A classic example is the New York shuttle service. At one time the system was also used by the Sabena airline in Brussels.

Especially heavy or bulky loads can be moved by special helicopters known as flying cranes. They transport electricity pylons, sections of pipelines, large tanks, and so on. Helicopters are very useful in air-sea rescue work. They have also proved their worth in tropical and polar regions for ambulance and supply services to remote areas. Specially adapted helicopters are also used for crop spraying, and their military uses are manifold, including anti-submarine warfare.

Clearly, the evolution of such a complex branch of technology as aviation could not be expected to take a single direction. Every problem demanded a new approach, and novel designs emerged to replace conventional ones, which always have their shortcomings. It is difficult to think of another area of knowledge which has, in so short a time, undergone such rapid

sign with the Convair XF2Y-1 Sea Dart. This was the first seaplane with delta wings, and it took off and landed by means of retractable water skis. Although it was the first seaplane to break the sound barrier, it never reached the production stage.

Since the moment the Wright brothers' Flyer first left the ground, there have been many attempts to

accidents by crashing during a demonstration flight over California in 1966. 'Ducks' have become very popular in sporting aviation. The designer Burt Rutan came up with a machine he called the VariEze, which marked a real revolution in both the use of new materials — glassfibre and polyurethane foam — and the application of new design principles. 'Duck'-type sports

▲
The flying wing designed by J. Northrop was equipped with elevons instead of tailplanes.

The monstrous dimensions of the Super Guppy allow it to carry Saturn rockets.
▶

development. We have already mentioned some of the milestones along the way, such as the coming of the jet engine. Now let us take a look at some unusual ideas, which partly showed designers which way not to go, but may also have had some useful elements. Progress in science and technology enables designers to take a new look at the ideas of the past, and they often find that there really was something in them.

There was a time when the idea of a monoplane, and one with self-supporting low wings at that, seemed fantastic. Today we take it for granted. In 1952 an attempt was made to revolutionize seaplane de-

return to the 'duck' principle of design with the engine at the back. It has reappeared in Britain, the United States, Germany and the Soviet Union. At the end of the Second World War the Japanese built an interesting fighter called the Kyushu Shinden (Lightning), whose handling qualities were good. It was driven by the six-bladed propeller of a rear-mounted engine. This, too, was destined to remain an experiment. At present, however, the design is again in vogue among military and sporting aircraft, mainly because of the good handling it offers. A 'duck'-type plane, the XB-70 Valkyrie bomber, earned a place in the sad history of flying

The Focke Wulf A 19 Ente had a horizontal
rudder at the nose. ▶

**The Focke Wulf A 19 Ente had a horizontal
rudder at the nose.** ▶

aircraft all have engines at the
rear of the fuselage and are pushed
along by their propellers.

For many years an American called Burnelli put forward an aircraft
design in which a broad fuselage
doubled as the wings. The large
capacity available for passengers or
cargo was inviting, but other features failed to convince the airlines,
and so Burnelli's idea led up a blind
alley.

An interesting suggestion was the
flying wing, enthusiastically proposed by the American John Northrop and the German designer Walter Lippisch, but Northrop's planes
never got off the drawing board.
Neither did Charles Zimmermann's
proposal of round wings. His bizarre
fighter F 58 Skimmer was nicknamed the 'flying pancake'. The
Super Guppy transport, designed
by J. Conroy, has a strangely wide
fuselage that is intended to carry
huge Saturn rockets or the bodies of
Airbus A-310 jumbo jets.

The Rotabuggy flying jeep was actually ▶
a combination of helicopter and car.

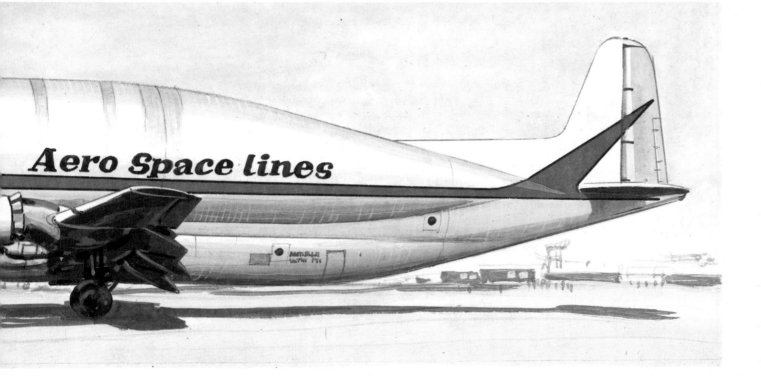

Aircraft designers have long been interested in creating planes that would not be reliant on the long runways of major airfields. This was something that particularly preoccupied the military mind, but was not without interest to civil aviation companies, obliged as they were to operate between the crowded airports of big cities. Additionally, of course, anyone flying in the mountainous regions of Switzerland, in the Australian outback or the northern provinces of Canada, to take but a few examples, would welcome an aircraft which combined the flexibility of a helicopter with the speed and range of a fixed-wing plane. It was the problem of difficult terrain that brought together the Swiss firm Pilatus and de Havilland of Canada to cooperate on the question of short landing and take-off.

There is a difference between short take-off and landing, STOL, and vertical take-off and landing, VTOL. The first aircraft in the former category were used by both sides in the Second World War. Widely used designs were the German single-engined high-wing aircraft Fieseler Fi-156 Storch, capable of operating from grassy airstrips and uneven surfaces, and the British Westland Lysander, successfully used to create diversions to the rear of the enemy.

Present-day STOL aircraft are characterized by good handling at low speeds, achieved by means of various devices to alter the aerodynamics of the wings. These planes have become popular where natural conditions preclude the building of concrete airstrips and for 'suburban' services using short runways. The most successful manufacturer, de Havilland of Canada, has been working on this type of aeroplane since 1945. In the types DHC-5 Buffalo and the four-engined DHC-7 Dash, the firm makes use of a specially-developed system called the augmentor wing, combining the effects of the moving parts of the wings and directed exhaust gases. This modifies the air flow over the wings to such an extent that it is possible to take off and land in a distance of around 300 m (985 ft).

▲
The French Coléoptère **C-450 took off vertically. The ring-shaped wings gave the aircraft an unusual appearance.**

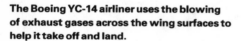

The Boeing YC-14 airliner uses the blowing of exhaust gases across the wing surfaces to help it take off and land.

▽

This short take-off and landing aircraft, de Havilland of Canada's Dash 7, has a low noise level, allowing it to operate from city-centre airports.

In the context of short take-offs, let us recall a device which has been used since the time of the Wright brothers, the catapult. The first proper catapult was that of the American Captain W.I. Chambers, in 1912. The aircraft taking off was placed on a trolley, propelled by compressed air, on rails. This gave the aircraft a speed which it would not otherwise achieve without a long run-up. Today's catapults are steam powered and are a normal piece of equipment on aircraft-carriers. Similarly, landing distances are shortened by means of a nylon rope which catches a retractable hook, and sometimes by means of a net or parachutes.

Vertical take-off planes are gradually leaving the experimental stage and becoming established. The first design to be produced on a large scale was the British Harrier. In the near future we can probably expect the first passenger aircraft of this type if research on the American Bell XV-15 is fruitful.

Several methods of achieving VTOL have been developed. Among them is the use of swivel engines at the wing-tips, giving vertical thrust for take-off and then horizontal thrust for normal flight. Swivel wings offer another solution, successfully employed in the American transport Ling Temco Vought XC-142. Another possibility is changing the attitude of the whole aircraft so that it takes off pointing upwards and levels out to fly, something like the space shuttle.

The Bell XV-15 combines the advantage of aeroplane and helicopter, using swivel engines.

Since the Second World War aviation has advanced very rapidly to become a very complex subject, quickly making use of the results of progress in individual branches of science. The romantic picture of the bold aviator flying a plane he has designed and built himself survives only in the field of sporting aviation. Today's plane-builders are highly specialized, work in large teams, and have at their disposal vast resources of data-processing and test equipment.

The whole approach to design has changed, too. Gone are the days of trial and error, and rushing out to try the next idea. New materials, engines, aerodynamic computations and hypotheses, electronic equipment, safety equipment and other types of innovation are first tried and tested in the laboratory to the most rigorous standards. In the end, even a modern plane has to make its maiden flight at a test centre, with a test-pilot at the controls. Every aircraft has its experimental stage, its prototypes; some even are built solely to try out a new idea, to find out more about a problem, perhaps as a scaled-down version of the projected final design.

Experimental aircraft usually come up with something entirely new, like the first jets, the first supersonic planes, or VTOL. They are often used to test designs for large and expensive projects. So, for instance, Concorde's 'Gothic' wings were tried out on the BAC-221. Similarly, the MiG-21 was in some ways a scaled-down version of the Tu-144. Test aircraft were also used to try out variable-geometry wings, which give supersonic planes the required characteristics at maximum and minimum speeds, and they enable scientists, engineers and designers to study in practice the effectiveness of new materials. This applies to new alloys, carbon composites and even ceramic materials designed to resist high temperatures and still retain the required properties. Much

valuable information was obtained on the heat properties of materials from the experimental rocket plane North American X-15, which was used to investigate the 'heat barrier'.

The Bristol T-188 was built to test a cooling system to protect the pilot's cabin.

·New engines are sometimes tried out using modified versions of existing aircraft. An example of this is the mounting of the engine for the Boeing 747 on the already successful 707. The Olympus engine for Concorde was tested on a Vulcan bomber.

In the building of the SR-71 Blackbird test aircraft, high-temperature-resistant titanium was widely used.

An important part of the test equipment used in aircraft design is the wind tunnel, where the aerodynamics of new shapes are studied using models. Fuselage and wing structures are subjected to fracture tests to learn how strong and resilient they are, or how long they can last before metal fatigue begins. Engines are bench-tested using a so-called exhaust brake to determine the interval between overhauls. Such tests are especially strict for airliner engines, where a very high safety level is required. There are also special tests on undercarriages, and so the list might go on, for designing even the simplest of aircraft involves finding the best solution to countless problems.

The rocket plane X-15 achieved up to seven times the speed of sound and withstood a surface temperature of 650 °C (1200° F).

Men have for centuries been fascinated by what lies beyond planet Earth, but for most of this time the mysteries of space surpassed human understanding. At first only mythology and astrology fed man's imagination, and in its infancy even astronomy failed to get much nearer the truth. The first great breakthrough came with Copernicus's model of the Solar System, and the discovery that the Earth is not the centre of the Universe. There were numerous fantastic ideas as to how mortals might reach dizzy heights, including the use of a team of eagles. The hero in Jules Verne's From the Earth to the Moon was shot from a huge gun. In fact, the real expedition which took place many decades later was not all that different.

The first requirement for space travel is a means of propulsion sufficiently powerful to enable a vehicle to overcome the force of the Earth's gravity. The means we have is a rocket, using reaction thrust. Leaving aside the rockets of the ancient Chinese and their medieval successors, the first successful rocket designer was Colonel William Congreve, a British officer whose rockets were used against Napoleon's army at the Battle of Waterloo in 1815.

The men who really put the design of rockets and rocket motors on a scientific footing were the Russian Konstantin E. Tsiolkovsky and the American Robert H. Goddard. Quite independently they both demonstrated mathematically the need to use rocket motors employing liquid fuel. In 1903 Tsiolkovsky published the results of years of research and at the same time laid down principles of rocket design, including methods of controlling and steering rockets, cooling their motors, etc. Unlike Tsiolkovsky, Goddard was able to test his theories on a number of experimental rockets. Further improvements were made in rocket technology by the Germans during World War II on the basis of the ideas of Hermann Oberth.

On April 12, 1961, the voice of the first man in space, Major Yuri Gagarin, was heard from on board the craft Vostok 1.
▼

A diagram to show the first artificial Earth satellite, the Soviet Sputnik 1, which sent its radio signals on October 4, 1957.
►

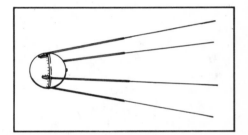

▲
The American space probe *Viking* made a soft landing on Mars in 1975 and transmitted much data to Earth.

Meteorological satellites continuously photograph the cloud systems and snow and ice, and can detect the beginnings of hurricanes.

and in the Soviet Union. The famous American launching-site was first used in 1950, while its Soviet counterpart, Baykonur, followed in 1957 with the Sputnik launch. Today's launching-sites are equipped with assembly shops, test facilities for rocket motors, assembly towers, fuel stores, computerized control centres and airfields, but their beginnings were altogether more humble.

The first living creature in space was the dog Laika on board Sputnik 2 in November 1957. Dozens of American and Soviet satellites were to follow, bringing new information on the weather, the Earth's mineral resources, and many other subjects, deepening man's knowledge, not only of space itself, but of his own blue planet.

The rapid progress made in rocket propulsion since the war owes much to competition between the Soviet Union and the USA. By the mid-1950s technology was able to offer all the requirements for the conquest of space. During International Geophysical Year in 1955 both superpowers announced their intention to put up the first artificial satellite. Months of tense expectancy came to an exciting climax on 4 October 1957 when the transmitter aboard Sputnik 1 put out its first beeps from space while orbiting the Earth. Four months later the first American satellite, Explorer 1, went up. After that new space events followed thick and fast. On 1 October 1958 NASA, the National Aeronautics and Space Administration, opened for business with the task of coordinating American space research. The new vocabulary of space travel quickly filtered through to the public, eagerly following events at Cape Canaveral

Major Yuri Gagarin's flight in Vostok 1 in 1961 marked the start of a new era: man had finally entered space. On 20 July 1969, Verne's prediction came true when the first earthling stepped out onto the surface of the Moon. It was Neil Armstrong, one of the crew of Apollo 11. A few moments later he was joined by his companion, Edwin Aldrin.

The Moon expedition was a tremendously complex and expensive project which formed the climax of

operation thanks to the Lunar Rover moon jeep. Instruments were left on the Moon's surface, some of which are still operational. The huge amount of information acquired during the Apollo programme took several years to analyse. It has been of immense benefit not only to astronautics, but also to other branches of science.

In the first half of the 1970s cooperation between the USA and the Soviet Union in space

superpowers was reached on 17 July 1975 when cosmonauts Leonov and Kubasov met astronauts Slayton and Stafford after a docking operation. They flew together for nearly two days, during which time they carried out a number of experiments.

Space research is concentrating at present on making best use of the information obtained by orbiting space stations such as the American Skylab or the Soviet Salyut-Soyuz.

The first man on the Moon was Neil Armstrong.
He spent almost 22 hours there, in the area of the Sea of Tranquility,
with Edwin ('Buzz') Aldrin.

a desire, announced by President Kennedy in 1961, to land a man on the Moon before the end of the decade. This triumph of human achievement was watched live on television by hundreds of millions of people around the world. There followed five further expeditions to various parts of the Moon, from which samples of 'moon rock' were brought back to Earth for investigation. The Apollo 15, 16 and 17 crews were able to extend their scope of

research grew closer. A joint space flight was planned, with crews from the two countries training together and designers collaborating to produce a docking module which would allow a link-up between the Soyuz and Apollo spacecraft. The docking manoeuvre was a complicated affair, requiring the two vehicles to be brought into a common orbit at a height of 223 km (138 miles). A milestone in post-war scientific cooperation between the

The spaciousness of these stations allows spacemen to stay in orbit for long periods and to perform numerous experiments and scientific observations. These include medical and biological investigations, astronomical observations, tests on various materials in weightless conditions, and research into making new alloys, artificial crystals, and many other things. Alloys obtained under the conditions of a space laboratory have properties which

The shuttle's cargo bay is capable of carrying almost 30 tonnes of space freight. This opens up the possibility of taking up parts of huge orbital complexes — 'flying factories'. These could then supply the Earth with materials otherwise inaccessible.

In spite of the great emphasis now laid on the practical application of space research, investigations will continue into individual planets of the Solar System. It is believed that interplanetary probes will be launched from shuttles before long. In May 1986 the probes *Galileo* and *Ulysses* of the International Solar Polar Mission set out for Jupiter. On their way, they will make further investigations of Mars and Venus. They are to reach their destination in 1988.

cannot be produced on Earth. In this way orbiting space stations mean another step towards practical results from space research.

Space flights have always been a very expensive business. An attempt to bring about a radical reduction in costs led to the design of the space shuttle, a reusable form of space transport. Shuttles can be sent into space many times over, perhaps as many as 100 times. They can be used both to launch satellites or to repair them, either in space or after bringing them back to Earth.

▲
In July 1975, the Soviet-American combined space project Soyuz-Apollo reached its climax. The crews worked together for two days.

A diagram of a rocket engine: fuel (a), oxygenator (b), combustion chamber (c), reactive jet (d). ▶

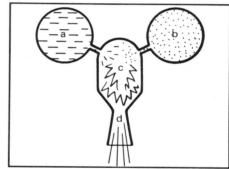

The space shuttle takes off vertically from an astrodrome using rocket engines and lands like an ordinary aircraft. ▼

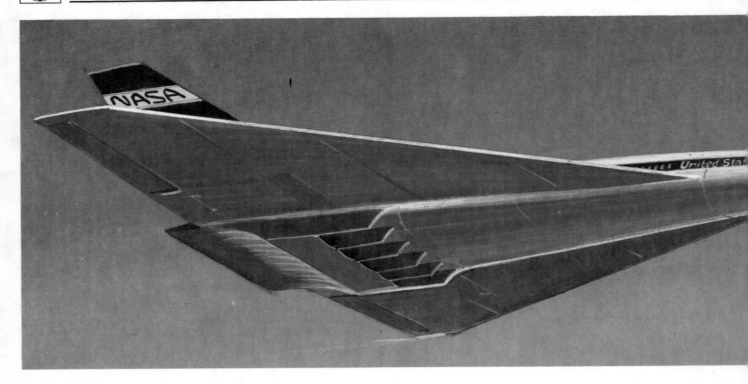

One of the possible shapes of the supersonic airliner of the 21st century, suggested by the Lockheed company. The engines are to burn liquid hydrogen.

Using titanium and special steels, the aircraft would attain a speed of 6,500 km/h (4,030 mph).

In recent decades the direction that the rapid advances in aeronautics have taken has mainly been towards greater speed, longer range and higher capacities. Shorter take-off and landing distances, the use of new plastic and composite materials, and new designs and techniques of construction also give a hint of what we can expect as the 21st century approaches. But it requires a good deal of boldness to make predictions. At times technological progress has outstripped man's wildest dreams, while there have been periods of consolidation where we have simply made steady progress by improving existing ideas. Today's aeroplanes result from complex team-work between experts from many different branches.

In civil aviation the aircraft of the early 21st century may be expected to fall into the same main categories as those we know today, i. e. short, medium and long-haul. Attempts

will continue to improve passenger comfort, reduce noise levels and increase efficiency, especially by saving fuel and keeping down prices. We should see even wider application of STOL and VTOL. The technical problems of vertical take-off and landing have been solved; what remains to be done is to find the optimal designs from the point of view of economic operation. Environmental considerations are also coming to the fore, requiring limitation of harmful exhaust and noise levels. A new generation of jet engines which will satisfy most of these requirements is already being designed.

The experience gained from Concorde and the Tu-144 will probably be put to use in the further development of supersonic transport. Although at present this type of travel is not really economic, further progress will probably allow designers to return to the question with fresh hope. The success of the Space

It is supposed that at the end of the 20th century short take-off and landing aircraft, carrying up to 100 passengers will be introduced on short-haul runs. Their VTOL capability will enable them to

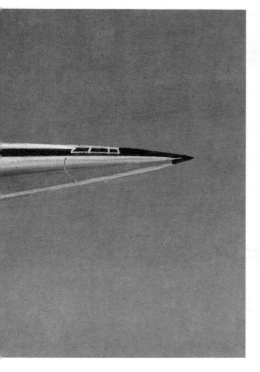

The airship Cyclo Crane filled with helium. One of the possibilities for future use of airships is that offered by the company Aerolift, whose helium-filled craft turns about its horizontal axis. Auxiliary engines and wings are mounted on its perimeter. Compared with a helicopter of similar carrying capacity, the Cyclo Crane is 75 per cent more economical. Plans have also been put forward for a passenger version capable of carrying 530 people. Consideration is being given to the possibility of transporting whole factories, dwelling houses or oil drilling equipment. The price of air tickets could be cut to a quarter of present levels.

operate between city centres. The Bell company has been working on this idea for decades, and successful tests with the XV-15 indicate that the research is bearing fruit.

Shuttle shows how air transport may take on quite new forms in the future, though the accident involving *Challenger* in January 1986 put this programme back considerably.

In military aviation, some people believe that within a decade the aircraft we know today will have ceased to exist, that they will have been replaced by 'trans-atmospheric vehicles' routinely flying in space. Boeing has made plans for a twin-engined craft quite similar to the space shuttle. Even more advanced ideas are being developed, such as liquid hydrogen motors.

Designers' thoughts are constantly returning to the airship. Goodyear in America is preparing a hybrid airship with features of a helicopter. Its payload is expected to be around 74 tonnes. A project has been put forward in the Soviet Union for using groups of airships to move loads of up to 200 tonnes, allowing large building sections to be carried, or minerals, timber and the like to be transported from remote and inaccessible areas. There are also plans for nuclear-powered airships, although many problems remain to be solved, especially the protection of the reactor against accident. Nor can we exclude the possibility that new power sources altogether will be discovered, thus cutting the cost of air transport.

Revolutionary discoveries and inventions are constantly extending the scope of human achievement. Throughout its history the aeroplane has stood at the forefront of man's ingenuity, and often moved ahead of his dreams. The Icarus urge has taken us to the threshold of almost limitless potential — provided, of course, we are able to turn it to our advantage.

Index

numbers in italics refer to captions

Municipal
TRANSPORT

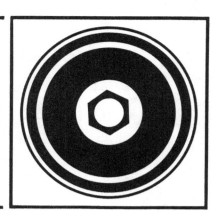

The shape of the ferry remained almost unchanged for centuries, with only the bows becoming shorter and the planks becoming thinner.

In the early Middle Ages there was really no such thing as municipal transport. Towns were small, mostly less than a kilometre across, and although populous suburbs grew up around their walls, distances were easily covered on foot. Anyone who was in a hurry, or was too lazy to walk, could go around on horseback, while old people liked to ride donkeys or mules. In any case most people, serfs in particular, had neither the need nor the opportunity to leave their homes, which usually meant their birthplaces.

Only the requirements of trade called for people to travel and to transport loads. This usually meant taking goods to market. There were, of course, exceptions. Most towns grew up from groups of clusters of mercantile communities, villages and hamlets occupying convenient sites in the vicinity of some administrative centre — in most cases a feudal landlord's home.

The choice of the main site was influenced by a natural feature, such as a ford across a river, high ground, or a protective combination of water and sloping terrain, which afforded some strategic or commercial advantage.

The maintenance of river crossings of a permanent nature was a major technical problem in those days. At first carters and riders had to rely on finding and, if possible, improving fords; their usefulness, however, depended largely on the level of water in the river, which varied according to the time of year. In spring and autumn fords were frequently impassable, which meant a regular breakdown of trade, supply lines, administrative communications and military movements. It was clear that a system of boat crossings was required, i.e. permanent ferries in more or less regular operation.

It was much easier and cheaper to set up ferries than to build bridges, taking into account the constant maintenance bridges also required. In those days a river in flood would frequently destroy bridges altogether, and was sure to cause considerable damage to their flimsy structures. Ferries, by contrast, were usable even when rivers were swollen — depending on the experi-

One of the steamers which were part of municipal transport on the Thames in London.

A beach tram in Brighton. A similar means of transport was used on the French coast at Saint-Malo.

ence and skill of the ferryman — and thus could operate almost all the time the water was not frozen. The capacity of the ferry depended on the size of vessel used, although there are no records of any large enough to carry a cart and horses in the early days. The most widespread type of ferry-boat was the scow, a broad, flat-bottomed craft made of pine planks. Though dugouts made from tree-trunks are known from prehistoric times, there is no evidence of their having been used for such purposes.

The ferryman propelled his boat by means of a long pole which he thrust against the riverbed, whose lay-out he knew extremely well. Only in the case of very broad rivers with muddy bottoms were oars used to row ferries. Where the crossing was a short one, the passengers remained standing, placing their baskets and bundles on the bottom of the boat. The ferry took some three to five minutes to get across, according to the width of the river, the strength of the current, and the skill of the ferryman, who

A water bus in modern Venice.

could make use of the river's flow by turning his boat accordingly.

The ferryman's calling was not numbered among the medieval trades and there are no records of the profession. They were recruited from the ranks of fishermen and oarsmen; ferrying was originally not their main means of support. They had to have the permission of the owner of the land on either side of the river before they could make crossings.

In towns that extended along both banks of a river, or were built on a shallow bay like Venice, water transport was not confined to ferries. As they grew in size, regular transport came to be provided by barquees and gondoliers. In the 19th century, with a steep increase in the populations of towns, larger forms of transport were called for and manpower was no longer sufficient as a means of propulsion. The age of steam was dawning, and the advantages of the marine propeller, invented by Josef Ressel in 1826, soon became apparent.

Paddle steamers had proved too cumbersome and poorly manoeuvrable for narrow canals or river channels, and the 1870s lightweight screw-driven steamers with very shallow draughts could be seen plying the Seine in Paris, the Danube in Budapest and Vienna, the canals of Venice or the River Vltava in Prague. They had various names: bateau à mouches on the Seine, vaporetto in Venice, and propeller on the Danube. They were driven by means of a small horizontal boiler and a vertical two-cylinder steam engine. Later models were fitted with a vertical boiler and a fast-turning steam engine placed amidships. These riverboats usually had a covered lower deck and an open upper deck protected by an awning or a metal roof. They looked like large double-decker buses. There were some amphibious vehicles which moved along rails laid under water, of which the beach trams of Brighton were typical examples.

As towns grew larger and economic activity increased, with tradesmen becoming more and more specialized, it became necessary to provide for the ready and fast transport of people from one place to another. For centuries, however, such traffic was not on a large scale and the need was met by carriers and cabmen. For short distances, various sorts of sedan chair were in use from the Middle Ages. In essence, such conveyances consisted of a narrow cabin with a seat, a door, or sometimes just leather curtains,

at the side, and pairs of poles at the back and front to carry them with. The bearers eased their task by means of straps slung across their shoulders. Sedan chairs had to be of very light construction, usually only an ash or alder frame covered with cloth. The relative anonymity offered by this means of transport made it very popular. In addition to the aristocracy it came to be used by the richer merchant classes, especially bankers and financiers.

It was only a short step to the introduction of sedan chairs for hire and the start of another occupation in the transport business. For the most part, bearers would stand at key points along the road or in front of the better-class inns; in Paris they were to be found at certain street corners and worked for entrepreneurs who held a concession for this form of transport. The situation was similar in other European cities, especially in the 17th and 18th centuries. Court sedan chairs were still in use in Dresden at the end of the 19th century, although of course they were never in a position to

compete with forms of mass transportation.

The means of public transport in the true sense of the word, the omnibus, developed in a very erratic manner. Its real father and patron was the famous French mathematician and philosopher, Blaise Pascal. This is not as strange as it might seem.

As a scientist, Pascal was far from being well-to-do, yet he often had to use the services of cabmen. It did not take the mathematician long to work out how much cheaper it would be to use a form of conveyance to carry greater numbers of passengers. He had the idea of replacing the hire coaches of Paris with larger vehicles running along the most frequented routes.

Pascal's vehicles were called five-sou coaches because of the fare charged; it was the first time a flat-rate fare had been used. In 1662 these coaches went into service on five regular routes and enjoyed great success, but they were soon crippled by a blow from an unexpected quarter. A government order

A sedan chair of the turn of the 17th and 18th centuries.

The fiacre was a large carriage, usually for four to six people, with a convertible roof.

Typical two-wheeled London cabs, and a horse omnibus.

was issued prohibiting 'the common people' from using the new form of transport for fear of giving offence to those higher up the social scale. The five-sou coaches went out of business in 1675, in effect because they had introduced too much democracy to the transport system.

The omnibus was not to return to city streets until the 19th century, but the use of hackney carriages, known throughout much of continental Europe as fiacres, expanded rapidly. They got their name from the building in Paris where their main station was located and which was called after St. Fiacre.

Hackney carriages were basically four-seater carriages with two seats facing each other, a fixed or folding (leather) roof, and a driver's box at the front. It took a pair of horses to pull them. The cabriolet or 'cab' which was typical of London streets was a lighter vehicle, drawn by a single horse harnessed between shafts. Passengers entered from the rear and communicated with the driver through a small window at the front, or simply by banging on the roof with a cane. Cabs were only big enough for two passengers. They provided fast and above all relatively cheap transport, but they never caught on in continental Europe.

However, the demand for a light conveyance drawn by a single horse grew, even on the Continent, and in the first half of the 19th century such a vehicle did indeed appear. It was the droshky, which first became widely used in Vienna, although its name is Russian. The droshky grew in popularity because of the railways; apart from the omnibus, it was the most common means of transport to and from railway stations. Their drivers were supposed to be dressed alike, and had to carry a watch so that they could time their arrival to connect with the trains. Droshkies, like fiacres, had to be registered and numbered, but they were much cheaper than omnibuses, costing at most just half the price.

The oriental equivalent of the droshky and the cab was the rickshaw, with the difference that the driver pulled his vehicle himself. It was not until the middle of the present century that the rickshaws of Asian cities were modernized by using bicycles.

▲
Rickshaws were widespread, not only in Chinese and Japanese towns, but also in most of the cities of the Far East.

Droshkies were originally a shortened version of the closed carriage.

The basic principle of the horse-drawn tram was first used in the United States in 1832, when a rail link was set up along the Hudson River valley to connect the rapidly expanding towns of New York and Harlem. Because of the wooden buildings which lined the route, the city council was not willing to allow steam locomotives to be used. They suggested using horses to pull the trains, but the animals proved unable to draw the heavy railway wagons.

Vehicle designer John Stephenson found a solution. He built special lightweight cars, similar to the omnibuses of the day but adapted to the needs of the railway. They had a driver's seat and shafts at both ends, so that they did not have to be turned round, large-diameter wheels to minimize the effort required of the horses, and a lever-operated handbrake. Stephenson made getting on and off easier by lowering the floor almost to the level of the axles and having the upper parts of the wheels run underneath the seats. All those who used the service were impressed by the quiet ride and the relative reliability of the system, and the idea was soon copied by many other towns along the east coast.

An enterprising Frenchman named Alphonse Loubat started to develop Stephenson's design, improving the layout of the cars and the boarding platforms, and introducing a type of rail suitable for cobbled streets. In 1853 he applied for a concession to build an 'American railway' in Paris. In England the horse tram was introduced to Liverpool by W. J. Curtis in 1859 and to Birkenhead and London by G. F. Train in 1860-61. Horse trams using the 'American system' were subsequently used in many European cities: Geneva in 1862, Copenhagen in 1863, The Hague in 1864, Berlin, Warsaw and Vienna in 1865, Budapest and Hamburg in 1866, Brussels and Brno in 1869.

Some European cities were loath to give up the omnibus, although the advantages of the horse tram were clear. Various hybrid systems appeared, such as that of Keuffler, where the omnibus moved along rails but its wheels were unflanged.

A horse-railway vehicle from Dresden, Germany.

Horse railways in American towns were often run by several companies, whose carriages differed in appearance and design.

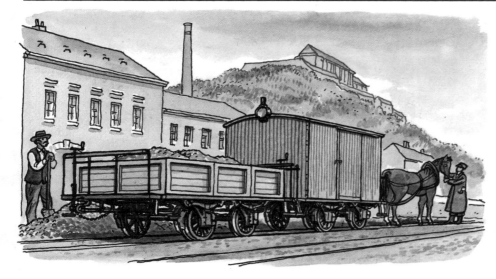

A horse-drawn sled in Winnipeg, Canada.
The replacement of wheels with runners
in the winter was probably easier
than removing snow from the rails.

the edge of the roof. For the most part windows were fixed. A subsequent novelty was the 'convertible' car, where the windows could be removed. The average capacity was 16 sitting and 12 standing passengers, a load which a single horse was able to pull.

The first double-decker trams appeared in England, the design later being adopted in Europe and called the 'imperial'. For a long time the trams of Paris faced in one direction only, with the entrance at the back, and they had to be turned round at the terminus. Another peculiarity in Paris was vehicles with a dual undercarriage, allowing them to run either on or off the rails. This was a similar compromise to the Keuffler system. In Winnipeg in Canada a dual system was used in which the bodies of the trams were put on sledges during the winter, this being found more convenient than shifting the snow off the rails.

The expansion of horse trams was rapid, but it brought problems, too. For instance, after 45 to 60 minutes' work the horse had to be unharnessed and allowed to rest for a considerable period, which meant having a good number of animals in reserve. In some cities there were several thousand of them. Mass stabling brought the spread of epidemics, one of which, in the 1870s, put the trams of several American cities out of action. Other difficulties arose with the clearing of dung and the provision of fodder and water. Veterinarians had to be on hand to look after the animals, and the number of ancillary staff kept growing. There was an attempt to find a way of doing without the conducter, although his job included such important duties as seeing that the tram was not overloaded, making sure the weight was evenly distributed (to avoid derailments), and, of course, signalling for the vehicle to start and stop.

The vehicle was kept on the rails by a fifth wheel on the right-hand side of the driver. When the omnibus left the rails for part of its route, this wheel was raised and fastened.

A number of design features of horse trams were intended to improve passenger comfort. From the start there were winter cars with roofs and summer cars with an awning on poles. Closed vehicles were usually divided into smoking compartments and ladies' compartments. Cars which were not divided were called saloons. Seats were wicker or were made of leather or waxed canvas with a horsehair filling. It was only later that seats with wooden slats were introduced. At first, lighting was by means of candles placed in glass cases on the front wall, but these were later replaced by oil lamps. This primitive form of illumination required small metal chimneys through the roof for ventilation. There were large boards on the front of the tram to show the destination. They were replaced at night by large lanterns with coloured glass which were hung from

The drawbacks of the intensive use of horse trams grew more and more apparent. In cities where traffic was very heavy — in New York, for instance, the interval between trams was just three minutes — it was a very difficult problem just to clear away the dung. More and more people complained of the smell, which was particularly obnoxious in summer. Municipal health officers tried to limit the use of trams, which was, of course, far from being in the interests of city life. So a great effort was made to find a 'clean' means of propulsion.

It was not long before the idea was put forward of using cables propelled from stationary engines along the track. It was not a new notion, having first appeared in Britain before the use of steam locomotives and then been applied on coal railways in places with steep slopes. It had, however, been unable to compete with the locomotive for normal use over long distances. The fact that the idea was revived in the United States can be attributed to the grid pattern of American street plans and to the hills of San Francisco in particular.

The successful inventor of the cable car was Andrew S. Hallidie, a Londoner by birth. His father left him a steel cable factory producing cables for the funiculars of the Sierra Nevada silver mines. Hallidie saw the problems caused by the horse trams, and he noted that they were unable to run up the steep slopes of some quarters of San Francisco. He came up with a relatively simple solution.

Hallidie proposed that an endless steel cable be laid in a narrow groove between the tramlines and driven at a constant speed by a central steam engine. Streetcars (the American name for trams) could be attached to or detached from the cable by means of special pincers dropped into the cable groove, which would act as a friction coupling. Hallidie lost no time in progressing from actions to words, and

A vehicle of the San Francisco cable railway of 1875. The traction unit was called a dummy.

founded a cable car company at once. He applied for a concession from the San Francisco authorities, and built his first line in Clay Street, which had an inclination of up to 12 per cent. Despite early difficulties, the Clay Street line proved effective and safe, and in 1877 Hallidie built another line. Three years later San Francisco already had 180 km (112 miles) of cable tramways run by different companies.

Other cities were quick to follow suit. The advantages of cable cars were self-evident: they were clean,

Combined cable railway vehicle in Portland, USA. The open platform enabled the crew to have a good view, which was essential.

they were quiet, and they moved at twice the speed of the horse trams. It was possible to attach various numbers of cars to the cable as required. The major disadvantage was their cost — $ 100,000 a mile. In 1894 there were about 5,000 cable cars in use in the United States, with over 1,000 km (620 miles) of track. The cable was about 3 ½ cm (1 ½ in)

Paris was the only city in Europe where cable railways were used.
▼

▲

A cable railway in Cincinnati, USA, which allows trams to go up steep slopes.

pest, built in 1869 with a gradient of 62 per cent, and the Lausanne-Ouchy line, completed in 1877.

Towards the turn of the century cable railways began to appear in the hilly cities of Europe at a tremendous rate. They were constructed in Vienna, Salzburg and Prague, to name but a few. In Nizhni Novgorod in Russia two cable railways formed part of the municipal tram network, while in Cincinnati in the USA funiculars raised whole tramcars so that the passengers did not have to change vehicles.

The first moving pavement was demonstrated at the Paris exhibition in 1889.

in diameter, with each of its six plies consisting of 16 to 19 steel wires. It had a core made of hemp to improve its flexibility and was lubricated with linseed oil.

In their original form, American cable cars appeared in Europe in London and Paris only, but as funicular railways introduced to overcome steep slopes, they were widely used. Among the oldest were the Croix Rousse funicular in Lyons, built in 1867 with a gradient of 16 per cent, the castle lift in Buda-

▲
A Merryweather traction-engine,
tested in 1876 in Vienna.

It was a fairly obvious step to re-place the slow-moving draught horses with steam locomotives. However, the locomotives in use on the railways were quite unsuitable: they were too large and too heavy, built for greater speeds and heavier loads, and their starting and stop-ping distances were much too great. It was necessary to come up with a much lighter version suitable for the start-stop operation of trams and capable of negotiating safely the sharp bends of narrow city streets. It was also of great impor-tance that neither the engine nor the other moving parts should scare draught horses, and that passers-by should not be inconvenienced or wooden structures endangered by smoke and sparks.

The first successful design, which more or less served to popularize the new form of traction, was the tram locomotive of Henry Merry-weather. The design was quite ingenious. The small upright boiler and two-cylinder steam engine

A steam tram in Geneva,
Switzerland, in 1892.

were enclosed in the vehicle's body, and the entire undercarriage was also covered up. A narrow chimney took the exhaust vapour through the roof, where condensation pipes changed it to warm water, which was then returned to the boiler. Provided anthracite or coke was used as fuel, the locomotive hardly smoked at all. The miniature, toy-like locomotive had a cylinder bore of 17 cm (6 ½ in), weighed 5 or 6 tonnes laden with fuel and water, and had an output of around 15 kW (20 hp). Because it could be coupled

to existing horse tramcars, the con-version was relatively inexpensive. The system was thus of great inter-est to all the large cities of Europe where horse trams were in use.

Merryweather locomotives be-came most widespread in Britain, Holland and Belgium. In Holland the firm Backer and Rueb began to build a successful copy of them, using it not only in town, but also along

▲
A Rowan steam vehicle,
used in Berlin in 1885.

A steam vehicle of the Komarek type
used in the Vítkovice foundries
in Czechoslovakia.

a dense network of narrow-gauge country lines. These were easier and cheaper to build than roads.

The Krauss locomotive works in Munich followed the fortunes of Merryweather engines closely, and developed its own design for a simple, robust and powerful tram locomotive. The firm produced a series of two and three-axle engines of differing performance and for various track gauges. They had a horizontal boiler and semi-enclosed body, with the undercarriage remaining covered. The company built and operated suburban lines in Vienna. Where freight carriage was not undertaken as well, the powerful Krauss locomotives were not fully exploited.

Locomotives had to be moved to the other end of the tram at every terminus and required regular replenishment of fuel and water, which made the maintenance of a satisfactorily short interval between trams impossible, especially in the rush-hour. Outside peak periods, on the other hand, steam locomotives were uneconomical, and in many cities mixed traction was used for a long time — steam in the rush-hour and horses off-peak! A search went on for some way of cheapening steam trams and cutting out some of the dead weight.

The improvement which emerged consisted of an idea first used on the railways of Britain in the first half of the 18th century. Each carriage was fitted with a vertical boiler fired by coke. A small two-cylinder steam engine mounted in the chassis drove one axle. Various designs emerged, such as the Rowan system, used in the streets of Paris and Berlin. The roomy tramcar was constructed like an articulated lorry — a two-axle traction unit with a single-axle trailer resting on it by means of a swivel joint. These vehicles were able to take sharp corners, and were light. The use of coke to fire the boiler meant that one man could operate the tram.

The desire to come up with a cleaner form of city transport led to a number of other inventions besides the cable car. They relied on scientific principles which were already known. One idea was to design a traction engine that was capable of running along the horse tram lines, without being expensive to operate or requiring complex auxiliary equipment. The first practical solution of this kind was the compressed-air tram. The principle of the expansion of compressed gases was an attractive proposition for vehicle propulsion simply because it permitted the use of a piston such as that found in steam engines. A Polish-born Frenchman called Mekarski managed, in 1882, to come up with a reliable form of air engine. He got over the twin problems of unwanted condensation in the cylinders and excessive cooling caused by the expansion of compressed air by mixing steam heated to 165 °C with the air.

Another design employed air heated in a small boiler fuelled by charcoal, located in the vehicle itself. This also lowered the consumption of air, since heating increases the pressure of a constant volume of gas. Mekarski's trams had a main air tank containing 1,300 litres (285 gallons) and a reserve tank for 700 litres (153 gallons). They were replenished at terminuses by means of a compressor. The vehicles were quiet and smokeless, producing only a quiet hiss, and passengers liked to travel in them. Since they were not heavy, they were able to run along the existing tram lines without expensive reconstruction being needed. Air trams were most used in Paris, where over 200 operated. In Switzerland they were introduced to Berne and Neuchâtel.

Unfired steam locomotives worked on a slightly different principle. They had a large boiler filled partly with hot water and partly with pressurized steam. This created

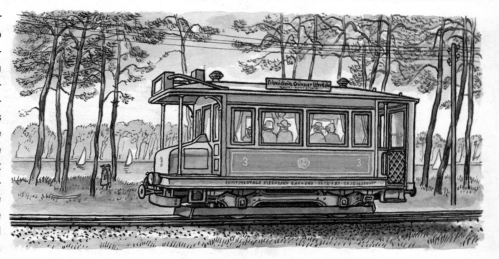

▲
A tram with an internal combustion engine used in the Berlin suburb of Schmöckwitz from 1914.

◄ Steam accumulator locomotive made in 1870
at the Baldwin works in Philadelphia, USA.
One way these engines were used was to 'motorize' the horse trams.

A heat accumulation steam tramway in Minneapolis.
The engine was constructed by the Baldwin locomotive works in Philadelphia, USA, in 1886.
▼

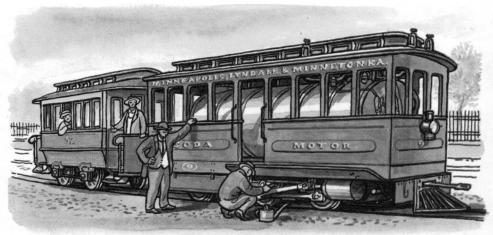

A tram driven by coal gas in Dessau, Germany, in 1896.

a sort of 'pressure-cooker', where the boiling point of water was much higher than 100 °C. When the locomotive set off and started to use up the steam, the pressure in the boiler fell, causing the water to boil and produce more steam. This process went on until the pressure and the water temperature fell to such an extent that no more steam was produced. The boiler then had to be refilled with hot water and steam. The system was developed by the engineers Henri Lamme and Léon

A compressed-air tram in Berne, Switzerland.

Francque, and was used by a number of cities in the USA and also in Paris.

A variant of the accumulation steam engine was patented by the German engineer Moritz Honigmann. His source of accumulated heat was a caustic soda solution. This was poured into a special 'boiler' — in fact a heat exchanger — which then heated water. The trick was that a caustic soda solution can be heated to a much higher temperature than the boiling point of water, which ensured a supply of pressurized steam over a long period. Exhaust steam was led into the solution, which produced more spontaneous heat, which in turn produced more steam. The engine went on working until the soda concentration was diluted beyond

the point where it would produce further heat.

The soda locomotive was used in Aachen in 1885, and was tried out in the streets of Leipzig. Honigmann managed to sell a licence for his patent to the American firm of Baldwin, which manufactured such engines under the name 'soda motor'. The idea did not catch on, however, mainly because the hot soda solution attacked the copper boilers and the life of the apparatus was short.

The ammonia engine worked on a principle similar to that of the soda engine. It exploited the compressibility of ammonia gas and its solubility in water. The engine had a reservoir of compressed ammonia, from which the gas was led to a small piston-operated power unit. When its work was done, the ammonia was dissolved in tanks filled with water. This was heated to give off ammonia gas again. A prototype was put into operation in 1886 by a New Orleans company, but the noxious smell and low power output prevented ammonia trams from being viable.

Gas railways were actually powered by a type of internal combustion engine. The German engineer Nikolaus Otto invented a four-stroke gas engine in 1876, but it was not until 1892 that this cumbersome piece of machinery was developed by others to the stage where it was usable for rail transport. The first gas tram on this principle went into service the same year in Dessau, and it was also tried out in Dresden. A similar device in America used kerosene vapour instead of gas. A special earth was soaked in kerosene in a container warmed by exhaust gases from the engine. Evaporating carbohydrates were ignited in the cylinder by a spark from a small dynamo. This form of propulsion was tried out on the overhead railway in Brooklyn and in the town of Elizabeth in 1890 and 1891, but the engine's rough running and excessive exhaust emission made it unsuitable for municipal transport.

The beginnings of electrical propulsion were tedious and fraught with problems. Experiments with electric motors were long considered to be interesting (but not especially useful) games suitable for the physics class at school. In those days the only source of current was the galvanic cell. Nonetheless, a number of technicians and scientists succeeded in putting together electrically driven wheeled vehicles, whether as working models or as actual prototypes. Davidson, Farmer, Page, Rouvre and Bellet all proved that simple electric motors could drive a wheeled vehicle along rails, and they did so in the 1840s. The difficulty was that the energy source was soon exhausted. It was only when Werner von Siemens designed a dynamo capable of producing a considerable voltage and current that the pioneer efforts seemed to have been vindicated.

In 1879 Siemens was already able to demonstrate a reliable electric locomotive at an industrial exhibition in Berlin. For most people it was still no more than a clever novelty,

but there were many who saw what a great future it might have. Thus the 1880s brought a rush of inventions. Besides Siemens, Thomas A. Edison and S. D. Field both took out patents on electric rail transport.

A successful rival in the United States was Leo Daft, who was already working on the idea of electrifying trams by means of independent engines which he himself called tractors. Daft's tractors were relatively powerful, with an output of about 6 kW (8 hp) and capable of drawing several cars of the horse tramway at the dizzy speed of 15 km/h (9 mph). Daft also experimented with overhead power supply in the form of thin gas pipes attached to wooden booms. Along the pipes ran a four-wheeled trolley which was pulled behind the tractor by means of the supply cable. This primitive design was far from satisfactory, however.

Another pioneer of the electric tram was joiner and amateur electrician Charles J. van Depoele. As early as 1882 he built a trial section of track in Chicago.

Meanwhile in Europe, Siemens was enjoying great acclaim. In 1883, following the success of a trial section in Berlin, he built the first electric railway in Austria from the Viennese suburb of Mödling to the resort of Hinterbrühl. Power take-up was achieved by means of brass shuttles which ran in a pair of parallel hanging tubes slit along the bottom. It worked quite well, since the shuttles did not fall out and the system was not vulnerable to icing, as was the case with trolley systems. On the other hand the overhead conducters required a very complicated system of points. A year later Siemens used the same design for an electric railway between Frankfurt and Offenbach. Both these lines were narrow-gauge, with a distance of 1 m (3 ¼ ft) between the rails, but they operated satisfactorily until the turn of the century, when they were rebuilt.

Nevertheless, these early electric transport systems were far from being reliable and simple to run. Motors were lacking in power, transmission was by dint of ropes or

An electric motor vehicle of Siemens' experimental tram in Berlin's Lichterfelde, 1881.

The traction unit of the first Austrian electric railway in Mödling, near Vienna. So-called shuttle collectors ran in a longitudinally-split iron pipe, shown in the detail.

chains, there was no way of regulating the speed of motors, and the power take-up system was complex and prone to faults.

As it is so often the case, it was time for the intervention of someone who had not only enthusiasm and technical competence, but also practical design experience. That someone was marine engineer Frank Julian Sprague. In 1883 he left the navy and became Edison's assistant. When he saw that the great man was not interested in electric railways, he quickly branched out on his own.

His first practical experience was with the electrification of the overhead railway in New York. In 1885 he set about tackling the problem of mounting an electric motor on the chassis and ensuring efficient power transmission. As an experienced mechanic, he knew that the most

effective means of transmission was via toothed wheels, as used in the engine-room of a ship. The problem with applying such a system to trams was this: since the unevenness of tracks required axles to be sprung, geared transmission from a rigidly mounted motor would lead to the gear-wheels becoming disengaged or jammed as the axle moved. Sprague saw that the obvious way round this was to

suspend the motor as well. So he allowed one end of the motor unit to pivot on a beam of the chassis, while attaching the other directly to the axle by means of special bearings. In this way the motor moved with the axle and the gear-wheels remained engaged. Sprague also improved the trolley system of power take-up, and thus removed the last major obstacle to the widespread use of the electric tram.

A tram named *Evangeline*
built by Charles van Depoele
for the municipal transport system
in Wheeling, USA, in 1887.

Sprague's electric trams in Richmond, USA, in 1887. They were the first to use a trolley-arm
system for power transmission.

The rapid growth of industrial towns reached its peak just before the turn of the century with a fashion for pretentious public buildings, broad thoroughfares, and whole new suburbs. Clearly, existing forms of municipal transport were not able to cope. The establishment of a system of electric trams was more than just a measure of the prestige and modern outlook of city fathers: it was a step of great practical importance, especially since it usually meant the building of a power station.

So it was that in many of the cities of Europe it was the new trams that brought electricity to town. For electrical firms the contracts for municipal transport systems were extremely lucrative, and competition was fierce. Many companies contracted to operate as well as to build the tram networks. It was in their interests to have satisfied customers, and they paid considerable attention to the comfort of passengers. Thus vehicle design was steadily improved in the early decades of this century.

The first motorized trams were no more than converted horse trams, but it soon became apparent that the adoption of electricity as the power source, the fitting of effective brakes and the power suspension of the tram body required a special type of chassis. The originally wooden undercarriage reinforced with sheet metal at the sides was replaced by steel beams, either cast or pressed, joined together by cross-members which also served to support the engine and brakes. The wooden body rested on the chassis using either leaf or coil springs, or a combination of the two. Because of the sharp bends on the first city tracks to be laid, the wheelbase was never longer than 1.5 to 1.8 m (5 to 6 ft). The first chassis were of American design and were built according to the McGuire, Brill, Peckam and St. Louis Car Co systems.

For a long time car interiors

A Berlin tram of the years just before the First World War.

A circuit diagram of a tram:
a) take-up arm with trolley
b) main switch
c) controllers
d) motors
e) resistors
f) heating elements
g) lights

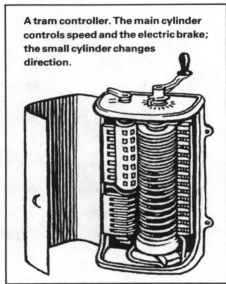

A tram controller. The main cylinder controls speed and the electric brake; the small cylinder changes direction.

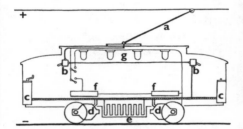

remained much as they had always been, with longitudinally arranged seating, sliding windows and long skylights which ensured relatively good ventilation. As trams developed, the traditional small car ceased to meet the needs of the day. First of all the driver's platform was enclosed — this had always been open to ensure a good view — and then the passenger cabin was enlarged and its suspension improved.

The 'imperial' design was revived, with its open seats on the roof, and this was used mainly in Britain and France, while in Germany, Austria and the USA designers tried out long cars running on a pair of two-axle bogies. Soon electric heating and lighting were also introduced. Increasingly powerful motors

made it possible to use trailers.

Since the original design of the two-axle bogie employed only one motor, it actually exploited only 50 per cent of the adhesion provided by the vehicle's weight. An improvement here was the 'maximum traction' system, using a driven axle whose wheels had a larger diameter, and a secondary axle with smaller wheels. The fulcrum of the bogie was placed asymmetrically, closer to the driving wheels, which meant that up to two-thirds of the weight of the vehicle could be utilized for traction. However, this type of undercarriage was of significance only when motors were very large; as the ratio of size to output decreased, it was possible to use two motors. Another solution was the use of motors with their rotors placed di-

A gritter (above) and a snow plough (above right) of the tram service in Prague.

A driver's platform in a classical tram. Beside the braking wheel is a conspicuous funnel used for dropping sand on the rails.

The undercarriage of a maximum traction tram. It made it possible to use all the motors and to concentrate the weight of the tram on the driving axle, ensuring smooth running around tight corners.

rectly on the axle, but because of their complexity and difficult maintenance they were never widely used.

On the electrical side, too, progress was rapid. Tram motors were made in series connection for a d.c. supply at 500 to 750 V. A motor connected in series means that the windings of the stator (magnets) and the rotor (armature) are in series. It has the advantage of producing high torque at low revolutions, while the torque falls off of its own accord as the revolutions increase. This meant that the characteristic was right for both moving off from stationary and smooth running at speed. As motors improved, they even tolerated overloading, and in addition permitted electrical braking, a condition where the

motor is used as a generator. The resulting current was fed into resistors until the vehicle stopped.

The first motors were open to the elements, which led to frequent breakdowns caused by water and dust. Soon they were enclosed in cast-iron covers. These were mostly of a type where the bottom could be opened over an inspection pit and various parts of the motor removed. Regulation of the motor's speed of revolution was at first achieved by means of a very primitive system which was actually no more than flat rheostats whose dimensions allowed just a few different resistances to be used. With the weak motors and low speeds used in the early days, this was sufficient. The rheostats were placed under the vehicle and operated from the driv-

er's platform by means of a handle and a control cable. With so few contacts trams moved off jerkily, and the rheostats were worn away by sparking. It was essential to increase the range of resistances available, replace wire resistors with cast-iron ones, and arrange the contacts in such a way as to minimize sparking when they were switched over. In American designs, cylindrical controllers were introduced with a greater number of acceleration and breaking degrees. Sparking was reduced by creating a strong magnetic field using 'extinguishing coils', and later each contact had its own spark extinction chamber. Bronze spring contacts were replaced by carbon ones, and subsequently by cam switches. Where pairs of electric motors were used, it was possible to switch between serial and parallel connection of the motors, which was more economical than using resistors.

The advantages of electric traction and the growing length of track available made the idea of using tram systems for the transport of freight an attractive one. Special vehicles for carrying goods or postal packages appeared. The needs of track and cable maintenance gave rise to the building of special vehicles used as snow ploughs, salting cars, sprinklers and maintenance platforms for the overhead conductors.

During the First World War the lack of other suitable vehicles in many of the cities of Europe led to the tram becoming the universal means of transport. It was used to distribute coal and basic foodstuffs, to supply markets, and to ferry wounded soldiers to hospital and dead ones to the cemetery from railway stations. Such use for funerals lingered in the United States and Mexico long after the war, and the transport of civilian dead formed a normal part of the tram service. In the 1920s increasing urban populations and greater mobility enabled trams to go from strength to strength.

Tramcars and their equipment developed impressively. The continuing effort to increase the capacity of passenger cabins made it necessary to increase the wheelbase of two-axle models, which were simpler and cheaper to produce than bogie designs, to as much as 3.8 m (12½ ft). In the end this led to the use of a new type of chassis made of pressed steel plate, or to a return to the free-axle system, where the axle guides were attached directly to the reinforced floor of the body, and the axles were sprung by a system of leaf springs similar to those used on railways. Some designs employed swinging or pivoting axles. The former meant that the car ran on Adams-type axles, where the axle guide stays could move with a sliding motion, while the latter comprised a pair of single-axle bogies. The limited movement offered by these mechanisms usually caused uneven wear on flanges and rails, and a tendency to derailment, so that the design was soon abandoned. A much more attractive system was the use of three axles with the middle one transversely adjustable; this system was still used in some types of vehicle at the end of the 1960s in Munich.

Electrical equipment was also getting better. Apart from motors, braking systems were improving, and electromagnetic rail brakes were widely introduced. Some trams, especially in towns with steep hills, had Knorr pneumatic brakes, trailers being equipped with the usual solenoid-type electric brakes. By this time brake discs and drums were beginning to appear alongside the traditional blocks. The requirement for a smooth start brought attempts to use indirect control and semi-automatic systems. Indirect control meant in essence the removal of the clumsy controller from the driver's platform and its replacement by a simple selector where the driver could engage forwards, cruising (where motors were connected in parallel), reverse and braking. The actual control device was placed under the vehicle and was operated by a servomotor in an auxiliary circuit.

An inter-city tram used in Holland in the 1920s.

A goods tram and a mail tram used in the Jablonec municipal transport system in Bohemia in 1905.

Increasing competition from automobile transport, and in particular the spread of bus services, which were cheaper for operators to run, meant that the tram companies had to work hard to stay in business. The first designs of large articulated vehicles with transverse seating, of double-deckers, trams with low floors to make embarkation easier, and so on, were soon introduced, but a genuine revolution in tram design came with the PCC vehicle, first made in the USA in 1933. It resulted from the combined efforts of the tram companies to meet the challenge of the buses, and they concentrated on passenger comfort.

The vehicle was commissioned by the heads of leading transport companies, hence PCC, standing for Presidents Committee Car. It incorporated a number of truly novel features including a large passenger compartment and a brand-new electrical system that gave rapid yet smooth acceleration and efficient braking. The chief innovation was a controller with 99 steps for accelerating or decelerating, operated by a servomotor and directly connected to the resistances — i. e. something like the original rheostats. An important feature of the system was that it could be switched from any stage of travel to instant braking. The vehicle had three different sorts of brakes. The transmission was also revolutionary: the powerful motors were placed longitudinally and drove the

A prototype of an articulated tram tested in Berlin in 1932.

axles by means of jointed propeller shafts and hypoid gears. Suspension returned from the use of springs to rubber blocks; light alloys were widely used, the wheels were solid and disc brakes were fitted. The PCC led to widespread rationalization of tram design, and soon had its effect in Europe also. It formed the basis for the post-war development of the modern generation of trams.

A prototype of the d.c. tram, type PCC, in America in 1933.

The steep increase in car traffic which followed the Second World War soon led to a clash of interests between cars and trams in city streets. Trams, confined as they were to their rails, were at a disadvantage compared with both private vehicles and buses. In addition, the investment required to renew rolling stock and rails after the neglect they had suffered in the war years led many cities to abandon rail transport and replace it with cheaper buses. This often turned out to be ill-conceived, since no account was taken of the difference in capacity between the two forms of transport. It was soon shown that under the right conditions — in cities with over 100,000 inhabitants, for example — it was difficult to provide an adequate service without trams, not to mention the fact that they were much cleaner.

The main problem, that of competition for space between trams and cars in narrow city streets, was tackled in two ways. In some cases pedestrian precincts were established where trams were retained. This was particularly suitable in the older quarters of cities — and worked on the same principle as the American system of 'park and ride', with drivers leaving their cars on the outskirts and continuing their journey by public transport. In the other system, tramlines were segregated from other traffic. This involved confining trams to special lanes or streets and constructing separate fast routes for them, especially in outer-city areas. A certain compromise was sometimes made by taking tram routes underground at key points where traffic was always heavy. Such a system has been adopted in Vienna. Since the difference in cost between this compromise and the construction of an underground as such is small, and since underground sections of tramlines only partly relieve the problem, this idea has not caught on.

The transition to a system of fast tram connections has meant updat-

PCC vehicles became widespread in Europe after the Second World War. These ones are in The Hague.

The accelerator, allowing continuous acceleration and deceleration, replaced the original cranked controller. It is pedal-operated, with a servomotor.

The driver's cab of a modern tram, type Tatra T 5.

ing both vehicles and tracks. At high speeds it is no longer possible to rely only on the driver's view ahead of him, and safety devices have had to be introduced.

The progressive design of the PCC trams means they have come into their own at last, especially their quick acceleration and higher speed (60 km/h or 37 mph). For the most part articulated units are used, with a large passenger-carrying capacity and either an unidirectional or a re-

vived bidirectional seating arrangement, which makes for more flexibility, eliminates the need for track loops, and allows trams to reverse along short sections of track in cases of breakdown.

Energy conservation is also an important feature of modern tram design. A novelty here has been the use of tyristor converters or pulse control. This serves to simplify the tram's equipment, eliminating the accelerator and to a large extent

▲
An articulated Czechoslovak tram
in the USSR.

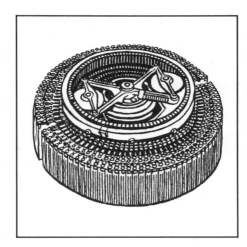

A modern articulated tram in Brussels.

also the resistance method of control, with its considerable energy losses. Tyristors allow the regulation of the current fed to the motor over a broad range, with little energy loss. A further advantage is that when the motor is converted to a generator for the purposes of braking, the resulting current can be fed back into the supply instead of being dissipated. This brings about a saving of up to 30 per cent. The use of tyristor regulation also permits

the application of an entirely new system of controlling the starting and stopping of motors. Pulse 'dosing' allows the exploitation of the entire nominal rating of a traction motor.

In both Europe and America manufacturers are striving to apply these new techniques to the full in their design for city transport. The tendency in Europe is towards the use of articulated vehicles, while the Boeing Corporation in the USA

adopts a rather different approach. The Boeing supertram is a single high-speed car designed to run at short intervals in town centres, and in outer-city areas to link up in groups with longer intervals between trams. In the opposite direction the situation is reversed. The system seeks to cater for the differing needs of suburban and city-centre transport and to simplify the links between the city centre and dormitory suburbs.

Rails and overhead wires, although now an essential part of tram transport, went through a complex process of development. The idea of laying rails across an uneven road surface to ease the turning of vehicle's wheels was copied from central European mining technology of the 15th century. Ore was brought to the surface in wooden tubs, whose small wheels often got bogged down in the mud of the narrow mine passages. So the miners laid thick planks and beams to form a smooth surface for the tubs to run on. To stop them falling off, the tubs had a short peg protruding from the bottom which ran between the two beams. In the course of the 16th century these trolleys spread not only in Europe, but to many of the mines of Britain. That is where the expression tramway originated. English miners, half corrupted, half translated the German expression 'thram-weg', meaning a 'beam' way, as tramway, a word used until the 19th century to describe mine tracks. These were improved by fixing iron strips to transverse beams, a system which was adopted by the horse tramways, for whose light vehicles these simple and cheap rails sufficed. Because it was necessary to guard against derailment, A. Loubat invented a grooved type of rail to take a wheel

Diagrams to show the development of tram rails, from a flat rail, on wooden sleepers or sunk into stone blocks, to the modern type of rail.

A trolley maintenance vehicle in Prague, in 1910.

flange, and it was this type which became typical of town transport. Because they wore quickly, and replacement was laborious (the sleepers often had to be changed as well), many systems developed renewable rail heads.

An increase in the weight of trams, especially with the coming of steam, necessitated stronger, and therefore heavier, rails. Many types, differing in size, were developed. The largest and heaviest were the grooved rails which allowed railway rolling stock to be used. These were laid in cities which used freight trams. The latest type of tram rail is the BKV design from Budapest, which consists of compact concrete slabs in which a special steel strip with a groove is laid and sealed with rubber. The renewal of rails is a simple matter, and a large quantity of steel is saved this way.

The other important side of tram transport is the electricity supply. Tram wires also went through many stages before the modern pantograph system was developed. The first system used by Siemens was a central live rail, but it was soon evident that even though a low voltage was used this presented a danger to other road-users, and in future only overhead conductors were used. Daft's trolley pick-up was unreliable (it used to fall off

during frosts), and the shuttle system was complex and expensive. Siemens therefore adopted Reichl's loop collector system, called the 'lyre', while all other manufacturers used Sprague's system of a pole and pulley.

Then a new obstacle reared its head — public opposition to the multiplicity of wires. This caused many cities to construct expensive and impractical electricity supplies hidden in a special channel in the street. In Vienna, Budapest and Berlin they used the Siemens-Halske system, where one of the rails was split, and a collector ran along the

gap, reaching into a channel which carried both poles of the direct current. In Britain the Hollroyd-Smith system was adopted, where the positive conductor was laid along a channel between the rails, while the rails themselves were

Basic designs for the electricity take-up of trams: trolley and arm (left), the arched system known as a lyre (centre), pantograph (right).

used as the negative. In Paris they tried out systems of contacts such as the Pollack-Biswanger design, where the moving tram closed contacts between the rails. Since these systems all brought problems, a return was made to the pole system of power take-up, where the pulley was later replaced by a sliding carbon shoe, or the yoke system, which was replaced by the pantograph, ensuring constant and even pressure on the wire. The design of pantographs was subsequently simplified until it took the form of today's type of two-armed structure with a crosspiece.

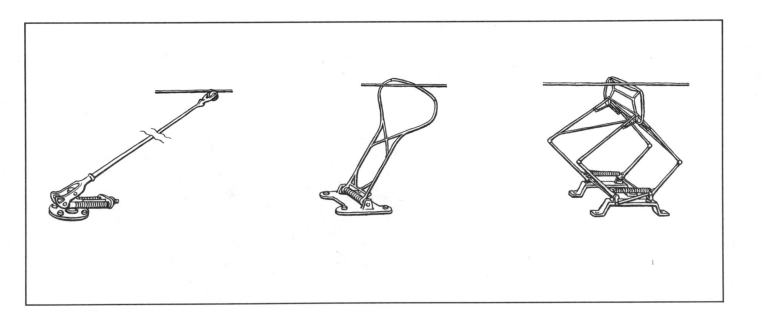

In parallel with the evolution of the tram, attempts were made to use electrical power in railless transport, too. The first road vehicle driven by electricity was demonstrated by Werner von Siemens in Berlin in 1882. It had a trolley system of power take-up, which Siemens had adopted after Leo Daft. The idea was further developed in Germany by M. Schiemann, who in 1901 built the first regular route, in Königstein in Saxony.

The Viennese engineer Ludwig Stoll was more successful. In cooperation with the design departments of the Daimler and Mercedes factories he came up with a practicable and reliable vehicle with electric motors developing around 15 kW (20 hp) in the hubs of the front and rear axles. The frame was riveted together from steel profiles, with a wooden body very similar to that of contemporary buses, the driver's platform being open. The power take-up was by means of a trolley which ran on a pair of overhead wires 30 cm (12 in) apart and was pulled along about 3 m (10ft) behind the vehicle on a disconnectable cable. The cable was some 6 m (20ft) long and gave the vehicle useful manoeuvrability, even allowing it to turn round. However, the wooden-rimmed wheels were still fitted with solid tyres.

Stoll founded branches of his company in Britain and France. From 1903 to 1910 he built trolleybus lines in eight towns in Austria alone, with another three in England (in London, Leeds and Bradford) and two in France (in Marseilles and Vincennes). The Siemens company built trolleybus lines in Germany, and in 1902 in northern Italy. The coming of the First World War interrupted progress, however.

The first trolleybus service to be opened between the wars was in Birmingham, in 1921. In 1923 a long-distance track was built between Modane and Lanslebourg in France, and in 1927 Vicenza in Italy acquired the newly popular form of transport. The first track in the USA was that opened in 1928 in Salt Lake City.

The 1930s saw the spread of the trolleybus almost throughout the world. Vehicle design improved tremendously. Large capacity buses were constructed, and in Italy there was even an articulated design. Powerful electric motors of 45 to 75 kW (60 to 100 hp) were used, either placed directly on the rear axle or using the classical automobile arrangement of motor-propeller shaft-gearbox-differential. For simplicity's sake, trolleybuses to this day use 550 V d.c. current, like trams. The braking system is usually a triple one: electrical recuperation brake, resistance brake and air brakes, not counting the hand-brake and a possible emergency air brake. The driver has either two or three pedals. Control is either by means of contactors, which may be pneumatically operated or worked by an auxiliary circuit, or in the most modern systems by means of tyristors. Modern trolleybuses are manufactured and developed in many countries, including Czechoslovakia, Yugoslavia, Italy, Switzerland and Canada.

The trolleybus relies on a network of wires, which may give rise to complications at points and crossings. One of the fascinating ways in which designers have tried to get round this difficulty is the gyrobus. It was first tried out in Italy, but the first practical use of the system was in the small town of Yverdon in Switzerland. Gyrobuses were developed and manufactured by the firm of Oerlikon in Zurich, and they worked on a simple principle. Energy was accumulated by means of a large flywheel weighing 1.5 tonnes and mounted underneath the floor in a special casing filled with pressurized hydrogen to reduce friction and air resistance to a minimum. The flywheel was connected to an electric motor which in the course of 'charging' set it spinning at 3,000 rpm. When this had been accomplished (it took about three minutes), the motor was switched to the generating mode and, driven by the flywheel, produced a current which was fed to the traction motors. The vehicle could travel up to 6 km (3 ¾ miles) on the flat before running out of power. It was 'charged' by means of folding pole collectors which were con-

Daimler-Stoll trolleybus in České Budějovice, 1909.

Modern articulated Škoda-Sanos trolleybuses.

nected to a charging pylon at certain stops and drew on the ordinary three-phase mains voltage of 380 V. In fact the gyrobus was not a practical success, however, because its precision bearings became damaged by the rough roads and hilly terrain. After a few years' trial, the line was reconverted for use by normal trolleybuses.

That was not the end of the line for the free-running trolleybus. In 1974 the companies Daimler-Benz, Dornier and Bosch in Germany began working on a new version, called the Duo-bus, based on a rather different principle. It looks like an ordinary articulated trolleybus, but in addi- tion to its trolley it is equipped with batteries and an auxiliary diesel engine. While running beneath trolley lines, the vehicle collects enough current to run and to charge its batteries. At any point it can leave the lines — it has a retractable trolley — and if necessary charge its battery by means of its diesel engine.

Siemens experimental trolleybus in Berlin. The motor drove the front wheels.

A gyrobus in Yverdon in Switzerland. The vehicle is taking on 3-phase current at a stop in order to turn its flywheel.

▲
The most common type of London bus
in the first decade of this century.

Paris buses kept ▶
the traditional 'omnibus' entry at the back.

The first bus services were probably those run by Hancock's steam omnibuses in the suburbs of London in the first half of the 19th century. They failed to become established because the poor roads and insufficiently powerful steam engines meant they were unable to compete with railed transport. It was only after the invention of the internal combustion engine, or rather after its improvement by Benz and Daimler in 1886, that the way was opened to this type of vehicle, but it was a long road from the early omnibuses, on four tall wheels and driven by a coughing and spluttering motor which had to be kept going by a heavy cast-iron flywheel, to the prototype of today's familiar buses. Although Benz designed and built a motor omnibus in the 1890s, the time was not ripe for them to be used regularly for passenger services. It was still too unreliable for such duties.

The first proper municipal bus service was operated in 1904 from Peckham to Oxford Circus in London by Thomas Tilling. His buses were fitted with 30 kW (40 hp) Daimler engines made under licence in England, and the first bus bodies were designed and made by the Milne works. Gradually a standard 34-seater double-decker with an open roof was developed. This type, later called Type B, was the most widely sold omnibus. By 1914,

A Berlin double-decker of the post-war years.

A West German articulated bus, Neoplan, in its municipal transport form.

2,900 had been manufactured, and a number of other firms simply copied the design. The less than perfect reliability of the Daimler petrol engines is indicated by the fact that many steam-propelled vehicles were also in service, such as De Dion-Boutons, Darracqs, Serpollets and others. The English Clarkson system lasted longest, and there were still 184 of these steam buses in service in London in 1919.

By 1908 London had over 1,000 omnibuses. Paris took up this type of municipal transport in 1905, with great success. By the following year several routes of the horse trams had been taken over by buses, and the new vehicles gradually edged out the old. The promising development of buses was interrupted by the First World War. In London the army commandeered 1,300 buses to send to the French front, and it is true to say that municipal transport vehicles helped the Allies win the war.

When the war was over, the omnibus continued to develop in the sphere of improved engines, the evolution of which had been stimulated by the war effort. Many firms such as Leyland started to specialize in large goods and passenger vehicles. With the coming of the Second World War in 1939 new obstacles were placed in the path of municipal transport vehicles. This time they were not requisitioned, but there was a serious lack of fuel.

A feverish effort was made throughout Europe to find a solution to the problem. The simplest way was to use coal gas. Buses carried gas containers on their roofs or drew them along behind on a trailer. The carburettor was replaced by a mixing valve. In Germany a liquid propane-butane mixture was used. This gave better engine performance and did not require such large containers. The most widely used fuel was generator gas, which was safest and cheapest. Vehicles were equipped with a cylindrical generator which was filled with logs of wood, beech being the best to use. These were allowed to smoulder slowly, which produced methane; the gas was then mixed with air and sucked into the engine. This had to be started with petrol. The operation of generators was not entirely straightforward, and services were frequently interrupted for lack of gas.

The second golden age of buses began in the 1950s. In the United States they even put the railways out of business for a time. The means of increasing the size of buses previously used, such as double-deckers and trailers, were not entirely satisfactory, so new designs were introduced for jointed or articulated buses. At present there is a trend towards superbuses or maxibuses, with capacities comparable to trams. The future is likely to see an attempt to introduce a cleaner method of propulsion — perhaps electrical, using fuel cells.

A steam locomotive from the London Underground in the 1870s. The condensation equipment, which prevented the tunnels filling with steam, can clearly be seen.

Even in the 19th century the narrow streets of ancient city-centres began to be inadequate to the needs of ever-intensifying traffic. The creation of large suburbs called for fast radical connections which neither the omnibuses nor the horse tram were able to provide. The only answer was either to travel above street level or to go underground.

In 1863 the first line of a dual-track underground railway was opened in London, running from Paddington station to the outskirts of the City. Trains were hauled by steam engines, equipped with condensation devices to keep the vapour in the tunnels to a minimum. At the end of the decade Alfred Ely Beach tried to build a pneumatic underground railway (also known as a subway) in New York, but the experimental section beneath Broadway, 150 m (500 ft) long, was to remain the only one. Fears of the high cost and the ability of America's wide and straight city streets to carry traffic in volume put paid to Beach's farsighted idea.

The construction of overhead railways was cheaper and simpler. Their steel frames were easily assembled, and there was no difficulty in using steam traction. Still the disadvantages were clear and inventors tried hard to find another feasible form of propulsion, from the cable tow used on Brooklyn bridge to compressed air. In the end, steam triumphed over its rival because of low running costs. An-

thracite was used as a fuel because it produced low amounts of smoke and ash and had a high calorific value. Forney-type locomotives were manufactured by the dozen in the Baldwin loco works in the USA. They were short, simple and robust locomotives with tenders, capable of hauling quite a heavy train consisting of five eight-wheeled carriages at up to 50 km/h (30 mph). They could reach full speed over a distance of a mere 130 m (425 ft).

American developments in the field of fast urban railways were

watched eagerly in Europe, but the situation there was different. The ancient cities of the Old World, many still retaining their medieval street plans, were wholly unsuitable for the construction of overhead railways. Only on the outskirts was it possible to cut broad swathes through existing built-up areas or to make use of places where buildings were thinner on the ground. Steel structures were not generally used, the only exception being the Wuppertal monorail in Germany. This consists of a series of gantry

Part of the New York overground railway in the 1890s.

structures supporting a rail, from which hang cars that travel along the River Wupper. It was built in 1901 and was influenced by American overhead railways. In recent years it has been modernized and continues to run to this day.

For the most part, however, European overhead railways were built on solid stone or brick viaducts, which divided cities like the Great Wall of China. In Berlin and Vienna these lines were considered part of the general railway network and connected with main-line stations.

An attempt was made to allow long distance trains to run right into the centre of town and city-centre trains to ply back and forth between the inner city and very distant suburbs, using the ordinary railway lines. Here too, at quite a late stage, large steam locomotives were used, but successes with electricity on underground railways encouraged new experiments with it. Once again Sprague won the day, using a tram motor built into the chassis and a lateral third-rail power take-up. After the turn of the century all

overhead railways were gradually electrified.

The overground systems of rapid city transport failed to come up to expectations, however. They were unable to solve the problem of congestion where it was at its worst, in the very centre of the city. Voices began to be raised in favour of London's answer to the problem – the underground. A leading campaigner for a Berlin underground was Siemens himself. It was only when London's 'Tube' was successfully electrified in the 1890s that the underground idea proved technically satisfactory. The one major difficulty that still remained was the huge cost of such systems.

The first city to start building an underground after London was Paris, with its famous Metropolitaine, or Metro, which made use of the city's favourable geological situation. It was intended to go into service before the end of the century. The Parisians were beaten to it, however, by the city of Budapest, whose underground progressed very rapidly in the city's broad avenues and was opened in 1896. Because the 'tunnels' had to be very low, the carriages were constructed on the 'gondola' principle, with the body slung between the bogies. The Paris underground was opened in 1900, and the cities of Berlin, New York and Hamburg followed suit in 1902, 1904 and 1912 respectively. The underground railway had come to stay.

An underground carriage in Budapest,
Hungary, in 1899.

fast and cheap means of building was successfully developed using 'Milanese walls'. This is really a modification of the 'cut-and-cover' method used in Budapest, whereby narrow trenches are 'dug' by a series of bores and then filled with concrete to form the side walls of the tunnel. Concrete roof panels are then laid on these, at which stage the tunnelling is begun, followed by the drainage and flooring of the

A Paris Metro train on inflated tyres.

A diagram showing a vertical cross-section of the Paris Metro. ▼

The underground solution to city transport problems was adopted by large cities in the period between the wars, and again after 1950. A number of ways have been found of improving on the earlier systems, such as the introduction in the Paris Metro of Michelin tyres running on concrete strips, which cut down the noise a great deal. Although the ride is soft as well as quiet, the disadvantage is a greater consumption of energy, since rubber tyres present more resistance than metal wheels. For increased safety steel flanges and guide rails are also used. The undergrounds in Mexico City and Montreal, built in the 1960s, were similarly conceived. The Moscow underground, begun in the 1930s, is notable for its architecturally impressive stations and for the design of the track network, with radial lines, joined by circular routes. Since the war, work has begun in the Soviet Union on undergrounds for Leningrad, Tbilisi, Kiev and other cities.

Italy, too, built undergrounds, in Rome and Milan. In Milan a new,

A station on the first line of the Moscow Underground.

route. This method is the quickest where the ground is poorly consolidated and the layout of buildings permits it to be used.

For traditional tunnelling operations the driving shield had proved very satisfactory. Its prototype was designed by Isambard Kingdom Brunel for the tunnel he and his father dug under the Thames in the mid-19th century. Behind the slow-moving shield, the tunnel walls are lined with steel plates by means of a hydraulic arm, the individual

frequency of trains (the interval may be as little as 90 seconds), an automatic block system is used, and the whole equipment is checked by a back-up device. Train crews and the central control staff communicate by means of radio telephone.

Underground tracks usually have the normal railway gauge of 1,435 mm (exactly 56 in), with 1,520 mm (59 1/4 in) in the USSR, and 1,581 mm (61 2/3 in) in the city of Philadelphia alone. Most now operate automatically, using computers, and experiments are being made with driverless trains. This is not exactly a new idea, since a similar system has been in use for many years on special types of underground railway, such as the freight subway in Chicago and the underground postal line in London.

London still leads the world's undergrounds with regard to length, having 383 km (237 miles) of track, just ahead of New York with 375 km (232 miles). Paris is in third place with 184 km (114 miles), Moscow in fourth with 160 km (100 miles), and Washington holds fifth place with 122 km (75 miles). The fastest-growing underground is that in Tokyo, with up to 25 km (15 miles) of new track laid each year, under very difficult conditions, as the tracks must be earthquake-proof. Since 1950 Stockholm has also had its own underground (called the T-bana), where the tunnels are bored in hard granite, and can therefore be very spacious. In parts of the stations concrete lining is not required. The Stockholm stations reflect modern architecture and are appropriately decorated. They are the only ones in the world that are heated. At present almost 60 cities in the world have working underground railways, and they are also being built in Vienna, Prague, Warsaw, Sofia and Bucharest.

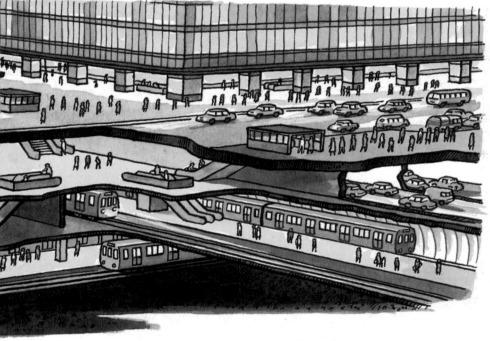

segments being joined by bolts. The space behind is filled with concrete under pressure. This technique was first used in London in 1866, when the tunnels beneath the Thames were built to carry the Tube, which was literally what these tunnels were – huge steel tubes, adapted to the shape of the carriages. Nowadays specially prefabricated concrete cladding is also used.

The rolling stock of all underground railways is built according to the same basic principle. The carriages are four-axled bogie cars, with separate cabins for the driver. There are three to four doors on each side of the carriage to ensure a rapid turnover of passengers. The power feed is by means of a side-rail along which a carbon-lined shoe travels. The voltage is between 550 and 650 V, and the current is d.c. The traction motors, which are located in the chassis, are regulated by means of either indirect resistances or tyristors, which are more economical. Because of the high

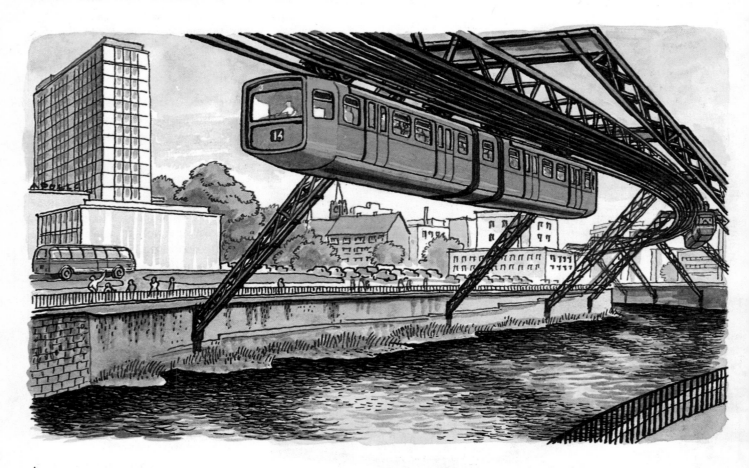

▲
**The Wuppertal overhead railway in West
Germany.**

Along with the continuing process
of improving the city transport systems of the present, a good deal of
research has gone on in recent
years into unconventional methods
of travel. The vision is of a fully
automatic transport system providing a dense network of independent
lines operating on a level other than
that of the street. Most such ideas
are based on the principle of suspended railways, but the latest concept foresees a greater number of
more mobile and smaller vehicles
than in the past, i.e. a small cabin
system. Various forms of propulsion and motion have been put
forward, from air cushions to tyres
and from magnetism to a revival of
the cable tram, using electricity.
High speed is not required, the main
aim being ready availability and
continuity. The cabins could travel

individually along 'branch' lines,
and in trains along main routes.
A computer control system would
operate in such a way that the
traveller would enter details of his
destination and the cabin would
then be routed automatically.
Where the passenger wished to go
to several different places, the system would take them in order, like

**An experimental train of the automatic
PAAC system in Pittsburgh, USA.**

a contemporary automatic lift.
The French city of Lille already has
in trial operation the VAL system
with carriages for 52 passengers,
moving along a concrete track at
a speed of about 50 km/h (30 mph)

concrete viaducts or, in the case of the American OTIS system, hover along concrete troughs. For the time being all these designs are more complicated to build and operate than normal rail links. For this reason there has been a revival of the idea of having moving pavements at road level, which are not difficult to construct and for which suitable power can be provided. The only remaining problem is how to get safely on and off them if they are to move faster than walking pace. Such systems might be used in extensive but traffic-free city-centre zones. Another idea, put forward by the American firm of Goodyear, visualizes a sort of personal container transport, where 'vehicles' would automatically move on and off a conveyor belt.

The chief feature the transport systems of the future have in common is that they require cities of the future in which to operate. Travel in today's city-centres will probably continue to consist of several different types of transport, for the most part using the existing road system. Here one is tempted to think in terms of some sort of electric bus, perhaps supplied with current and controlled from underground, and possibly with semiautomatic, programmable operation. In combination with an underground railway, or possibly other forms of ground-level transport, these buses might function as high-capacity links concentrated in key locations. They might work as an independent transport system in towns with up to 100,000 inhabitants. Totally automated rail travel systems such as driverless Tube trains or the BART fast railway in San Francisco form a sort of transitional stage. These seem to be the city transport systems of the present and the immediate future.

Small and large cabins of the CAT (Cabinentaxi) system in trial operation in Hagen, West Germany.

by means of an electric motor. The carriages can be made up into trains or disconnected automatically as required. Similar systems are on trial in many American cities, although only between airports and air terminals as, for example, in Dallas and Pittsburgh. In Hagen in West Germany the CAT (Cabinentaxi) is being tried out, where the

cabins are of various sizes. The system is interesting. In one direction the cars move on a viaduct-type track, while in the other way they run below it, which saves on track-building. The cars move at about 35 km (22 mph) and set themselves in motion. The electric motors which drive them are very economical, with an output of 5 kW (7 hp) and a top speed of 2.5 m/sec (5 ½ mph). When the system is completed there will be up to 8,000 cabins.

Trains run by linear motors are also being tried. They travel on

Index

numbers in italics refer to captions

Special

FORMS
OF
TRANSPORT

Wherever natural or artificial obstacles have to be overcome, especially steep slopes, funiculars come into their own. They allow even the least agile (or laziest) of tourists to climb high mountains, and are a popular attraction in city parks. They can also be used for transporting material from mines to power stations or railways, for instance.

Funiculars can be divided into lifts and railways. Most lifts are of the two cable type, where vehicles are drawn along a thicker cable by means of a thinner one. Some funiculars have only one cable, along which the vehicles travel either using their own engines or with the aid of gravity. Gravity funiculars are mainly small, frequently portable 'lifts' employed by

The modern cable railway at Grouse mountain near Vancouver, Canada. The cabins can carry 100 passengers and rise 818 m (0.5 miles) along the track, 1,611 m (1 miles) long.

▲

The only form of transport which can go up and down very high mountains is the cable railway. Shown here is one of the first goods lifts in the Andes.

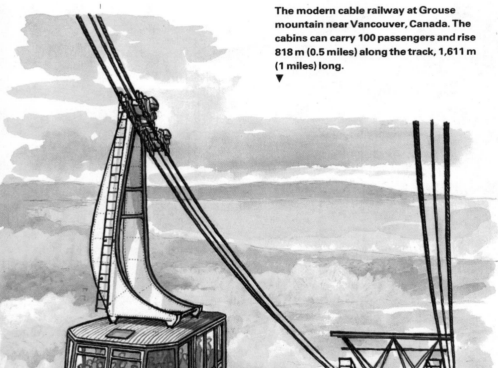

▼

lumberjacks or used on mountain farms. Monocable systems where the cable is used to haul vehicles along a suspended rail are often used in industry, especially in mines. They are sometimes known as aerial tramways.

Lifts used for transporting people are usually either chairlifts or cabin-lifts. Most chairlifts work on a continuous system, while cabin-lifts nearly all operate a shuttle service. A special type of lift is the ski-lift, or ski-tow, by which skiers are hauled uphill with the aid of individual cables or bars attached to a main cable.

The first short funiculars began to appear in Europe in the 15th century, and were mainly used for transporting cannon and building material during the construction of fortifications.

One of the most remarkable goods lifts was that built from Chilecito railway station in Argentina to the snow-capped peaks of the Andes. It started at a height above sea level of 1,080 m (3,542 ft) and climbed to 4,590 m (15,060 ft), and was designed to carry ore from the rich mines above to the valley below. The rocky, inaccessible slopes of the Andes presented the engineers with a problem of unusual magnitude. The route was divided into eight sections, each with its own steam engine. The distance between supports was 800 m (2,625 ft). The lift ran from the tropical climate of the base station to altitudes where temperatures never rose above freezing. Until the first stages of the lift were operational, all building material had to be taken up the mountainside by hand. The static cables, weighing more than two tonnes, had at times to be hauled by hundreds of men.

In spite of these difficulties, the building work was completed in less than 15 months. On 1 January 1905 the first cars set off up the mountainside to the realm of the condors, where man had rarely ventured.

Passenger lifts were first used early this century. One of the first was in Hong Kong, where it daily transported railway navvies from their mountain dormitories to where the tracks crossed the yellow-fever-infested swamps.

Funiculars, too, are often impressive. The longest span between supports can be found on the line which climbs the San Jacinto mountain range in California — 4,114 m (13,500 ft). The longest funicular in the world is the Teleriférico Mérida in Venezuela, the total length of its four sections being 125 km (77 miles). It also holds the altitude record, the terminus being at a height of 4,764 m (15,640 ft).

Among the largest cableway cabins are those of the funicular on the banks of the American Indians' fairytale Lake Tahoe, on the Californian Nevada border, where one cabin can carry 125 people. It was here that one of the worst accidents in the history of funiculars occurred, in 1978, when one of the static cables broke away from a pillar in

One of the first cabin cable railways in the Alps, which began operation in 1912. It went from Bolzano 295 m (970 ft) above sea level, to Bauernkoglern, 1,129 m (3,646 ft) above sea level. The cables carried cabins for 15 passengers along the 1,650 m-long (5,414 ft) route.

the middle of a storm and fell on a passing cabin carrying 55 people, slicing it in two. Four people were killed and 22 injured.

At one time it was popular to build cable railways to vantage points in cities. They operated on a shuttle system and sometimes employed unusual means of propulsion. At the top station, tanks in the car would be filled with water until it was heavy enough to pull the other car up. At the bottom the water would be let out, and the whole process would be repeated.

An even more interesting system was proposed for a railway in Salzburg, Austria. The cabin was to be raised with the aid of a balloon, before taking on water to assist its downward trip. This design, however, was never implemented.

Cable railways were popular in England in the 1820s and 1830s. It was the designer's answer to the problem of slopes too steep for normal railways to cope with. Sometimes the wagons (usually carrying coal) were hauled by a stationary steam engine, while elsewhere the locomotive would

climb a steep gradient on its own and then pull the rest of the train up by cable after anchoring itself securely.

One of the earliest passenger cable railways is that which went up Mt. Vesuvius in Ital (see picture on page 309). It was built in 1880, and although only 820 m (2,700 ft) long, it offered its passengers an unforgettable view of Naples and the clear blue Mediterranean.

A primitive open car, with only a light roof to keep off the scorching sun, carried a maximum of 30 passengers up a single rail. Balance was maintained by means of a pair of wheeled guides which slid along flat iron strips on the sides of the longitudinal sleeper. Surprisingly, however, this railway was not a commercial success. Within seven years it went bankrupt, and in another 13 it had been reduced to ashes by the lava of a new eruption from the volcano.

The Vesuvius railway was steam powered, but only five years later, in 1885, the first electric cable railway climbed the Leopoldsberg hill near Vienna.

Today most modern cable railways are to be found in the Alps.

They include the biggest in the world, Kaprun 2, on the Kitzsteinhorn. Its train, the Glacier Dragon, can carry up to 180 passengers from a height above sea level of 911 m (2,988 ft) to 1535 m (5,035 ft) over a track measuring 3.9 km (almost 2 ½ miles), of which 3.3 km (2 miles) is tunnel, at a speed of 36 km/h (22 mph). All these specifications represent world records.

There is a peculiar cable railway near Marseilles. Tourists who take a ride in its cabin can spend an interesting half hour studying the fascinating life of the sea-bed at a depth of 10 m (32 ft) below the surface.

The submarine funicular is just that proverbial exception which 'proves' the rule. Cableways were invented to take us up slopes by the shortest possible route. The vertical lift is merely an extension of the same principle.

The lift, or elevator, is a much older piece of equipment than one might at first suppose. The first lift mentioned in historical sources goes back to 236 B.C. The cabin was hung on a hemp rope and raised by means of a manual winch. The design is attributed to Archimedes. Another lift is said to have been used by the Roman Emperor Nero. It had a large, inflatable leather cushion underneath to soften the emperor's landing in case the cabin broke loose.

At a much later stage a papal lift was installed in the Vatican. This had a winch propelled by a large treadwheel. The French 'Sun King', Louis XIV, also had an aversion to stairs, so the royal engineer built him a lift which even incorporated a counterweight. It was known as the 'flying chair' and is said to have been luxuriously appointed.

All the lifts mentioned so far belong more in the category of historical curiosities than serious forms of transport. The modern lift is really the invention of miners. The original manual winch developed into a geared windlass, often driven by animal power.

The water-wheel also came into use. Agricola the writer describes a 'reversible' water-wheel, having two sets of blades pitched opposite ways. The operator changed the direction of rotation by directing the flow of water onto one set of blades or the other, according to whether the rope was required to go up or down.

The great turning point in the evolution of hoists came with the invention of the steam engine. The

The modern cable railway Kaprun 2 takes passengers to Alpine peaks in search of snow and sun.

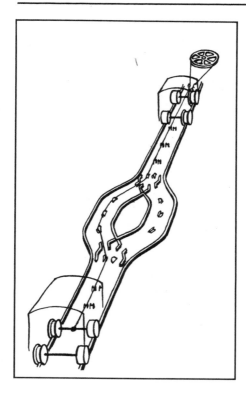

The cabins of funiculars with a shuttle system of operation pass each other in the middle.

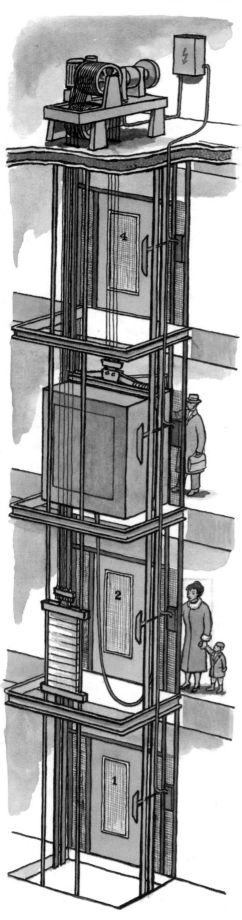

new means of propulsion permitted heavier loads to be raised at greater speeds. The original hemp ropes no longer sufficed, and the first steel cables appeared. The now familiar headframes with their huge hoisting drums were first built at mineheads. In 1894 the first electric hoist was constructed in Germany, and this means of propulsion was gradually to take over as the way of raising loads from mines.

The first lift used in a dwelling house was installed in Jena around 1670 by Erhard Weigel. Little is known of the system of propulsion used, but a counterweight seems to have been involved. It was not until the 19th century that lifts became widespread. They were either steam-powered or hydraulic. In 1854 the American Elisha Graves Otis invented a lift running along guide-rails and having a safety device, thus becoming the father of the modern lift. His first passenger lift was installed in the Haugwont department store in New York. It served five floors and travelled at around 0.7 km/h (a little under half a mile an hour).

Electric power was applied to lifts by the well-known German electrical engineer Werner von Siemens. He exhibited his design at the Mannheim trade fair in 1880.

Today's lifts achieve considerable speeds — up to 10 m/s, which is the equivalent of 36 km/h or 22 mph. The most modern lifts are controlled by systems which programme their movements with maximum efficiency.

Even miners in the Middle Ages used lifts, with animals instead of engines.

Modern tall buildings would be difficult to imagine without a lift.

The Roman aqueducts were among the first forms of mass continuous transport. They carried water.

In transport by pipeline, unlike all other systems, the means of transport stays put, and only the cargo moves along. The idea is by no means a modern one, of course. Many centuries before Christ the Chinese used bamboo pipes to transport water and even piped natural gas over long distances. Roman water systems with their lofty and monumental aqueducts still bear witness in many places to the skill and ingenuity of their builders.

The modern symbol of pipeline transport is the long-distance movement of oil and gas. In the pioneer days crude oil was moved from well to refinery in leather bags or wooden barrels, but as early as 1865, shortly after petroleum was discovered in Pennsylvania, the first pipeline appeared. It was made of 5 cm (2 in) iron pipes and was only 9 km (6 miles) long, but it saved its owner 300 workers and a great many barrels, even if people treated it as a joke. The total saving was $25,000 a week. That was enough to convince engineer Benson, and he drew up plans for an oil pipeline 160 km (100 miles) long across the

Allegheny Mountains. He, too, was thought crazy until he successfully implemented his project. The 15 cm (6 in) pipe led through mountain passes and over natural obstacles with a good deal more ease than road or railway. The oil was propelled along by a series of steam pumps along the length of the pipe.

Today the total length of oil pipelines throughout the world exceeds 500,00 km (310,700 miles) and the amount of oil pumped through them annually is more than 500,000 tonnes. Placed end to end these pipelines would circle the Equator 12 times. The minimal internal diameter of modern oil pipelines is 30 cm (12 in), while the steel pipes intended for long-distance transport are often more than 1 m (39 in) in diameter. The pipes are either sunk into the ground or simply lie on the surface. Pumping stations are installed at intervals along the pipeline to help the oil on its way, especially where it has to go uphill; the speed at which the oil moves varies between about 1 and 3 m/s (that is between 2 and 7 mph).

The world's longest oil pipeline is the Družba pipeline, leading from

the Kuybyšev region of the Soviet Union to Poland, Czechoslovakia, Hungary and East Germany. The total length of all its branches is over 5,500 km (3,420 miles). Among the world's other giants are the Big Inch pipeline in the United States, covering 2,190 km (1,360 miles) from Texas to Pennsylvania, the Canadian Interprovinciall measuring 2,057 km (1,278 miles) and the 1,700 km (1,055 miles) Trans Arabian pipeline, running from the Persian Gulf to the shores of the Mediterranean through the deserts of the Arabian peninsula.

Though not the longest, perhaps the most famous pipeline of all is the Alaskan. In 1968, when petroleum deposits amounting to over 1,500 million tonnes were discovered in Alaska, the main problem which presented itself was how to get the oil to a refinery. The sea route was cut off for most of the year by pack ice which not even tankers doubling as ice-breakers were able to get through. The only conceivable overland transport was by pipeline, and the way south from Prudhoe Bay to the all-year port of Valdez is 1,262 km (784 miles) long.

The pipeline's builders had to contend not only with the ravages of the local climate, but also with the demands of conservation for the route of the pipeline, almost half of which is on the surface, crossed the migration route of huge herds of caribou. It was necessary to construct bridges and underpasses for the animals, and it was not until it had been shown that the pipeline did not have a detrimental effect on the caribou that the government gave permission for its construction.

There are 12 pumping stations along the route, and in winter the crude has to be warmed, since there are frequently frosts of -40 °C in Alaska. The pipeline also has to withstand the occasional earthquake and is built to tolerate lateral movement of up to 0.5 m (20 in) without rupturing. The oil flows at the rate of 12 km/h (7 mph) and the total capacity is up to 300 million litres (66 million gallons) a day.

Oil and water are not the only substances which can be piped to good effect. Solids such as coal or ash are also transported in this manner, but with the aid of water, so that the method is known as hydraulic transport. Such systems can be used to move all manner of loose or granular material over distances varying from a few dozen metres to hundreds of kilometres. The diameter of pipe used may be anything from about 10 cm to 1 m (4 to 39 in). The material moves either by gravity or by means of pumping stations. This method of transport is very effective, cheap, and virtually harmless to the environment. The only disadvantage is the high consumption of water, which is becoming a precious raw material in the world.

Apart, however, from water, oil, gas or ash, pipes can also be used to deliver letters. In fact, at the beginning of the century the pneumatic delivery of telegrams and letters was very fashionable in the cities of Europe and America.

Post offices and other institutions were linked by the tube post. Smooth steel pipes about 8 cm (3 in) in diameter joined the sending to the receiving apparatus. Messages were placed in metal cylinders, which were then propelled along the pipes by compressed air. American cities had tubes measuring up to 35 cm (14 in) in diameter, so that quite large packets could be sent along them. The tube post often comprised a complex network of pipes linking dozens of places throughout the city. In such cases there was a central clearing house where the dispatch was directed to the addressee either manually or by means of electrically operated 'points'. Because of its ready accessibility and speed over short distances, tube post is still used in many places to this day, although it now seems somewhat old-fashioned.

One of the forms of transport of the future is said to be the movement of containers along oil and gas pipelines. Various deposits form on the walls of oil pipelines, reducing their efficiency. In order to clear these, devices called 'hedgehogs' are sent along the pipes from time to time. It was probably this that led to the idea of sending containers with useful cargo along such pipelines. Transport 'downstream' offers few problems, but how are the containers to be dispatched back to where they came from?

The herds of caribou have become quite accustomed to the Alaskan oil pipeline.

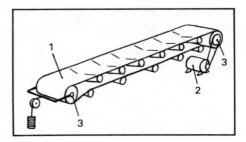

A simplified diagram of a small conveyor belt showing the continuous belt (1), electrical drive (2), and drum (3).

Research into this question is proceeding with the idea of exploiting the principle of a vessel sailing close to the wind. In this case the sails are replaced by a rotating ring with vanes on it, and wheels that run along the wall of the pipeline. The faster the flow of oil or gas, the faster the vaned ring turns, driving the 'sailing boat' upstream. There is even a proposal to use a 'train' of several containers driven by a single 'tractor'. Calculations indicate that such container trains might cover some 260 km (160 miles) a day, transporting millions of tonnes of freight annually.

The main advantages of pipeline transport are smoothness and continuity, but these are virtues shared by conveyor belts. The basic feature of these is an endless belt supported on rollers. At one end there is normally a drive, at the other a drum which serves to reverse the belt and send it back. Conveyor belts are most frequently used in mining minerals. The broad reinforced rubber belt usually measures between about 80 cm and 2 m (31 and 80 in) across, and the working length of the conveyor is up to about 500 m (550 yards).

In open-cast mining, where a huge amount of earth has to be removed before the coal can be 'mined' by huge excavators, large quantities of material must continuously be taken away, and conveyor belts have proved ideal for transporting earth to spoil heaps or coal to preparation plants. This led to the construction of a series of belts often several kilometres long which frequently run on gantries. For long distances and large capacities, transporters operating on the 'cable-belt' system are used.

In spite of its rather antiquated appearance, this pneumatic postal machine is still used in some places.

Index

Index

Biographical Names

numbers in italics refer to captions

Geographical Names

numbers in italics refer to captions